MAKING FOREIGN PEOPLE PAY

Teyzeme, anneme ve babama

An interdisciplinary book series from Ashgate/Dartmouth on European and international legal and political issues.

Studies in Modern Law and Policy

Series Editor: Dr. Ralf Rogowski LL.M, School of Law, University of Warwick, United Kingdom.

About the Series

The series provides a forum for the discussion of new fields and new theoretical analyses of law. It seeks to publish research which is located at the interface of law and policy. It is devoted to the contextual analysis of law. Context is understood as meaning both the political and social context as well as the international context of law. Accordingly the series comprises international and comparative as well as interdisciplinary approaches to the study of law. A special emphasis lies on socio-legal studies of international legal trends.

About the Series Editor

Ralf Rogowski is Senior Lecturer in Law at the University of Warwick. He was trained as a German lawyer and is a graduate of the European University Institute in Florence, the Free University of Berlin, and the University of Wisconsin-Madison. His main areas of interest are European and global legal and political developments. He is author or editor of a number of theoretical, empirical and comparative studies, including Civil Law, Reflexive Labour Law, Labour Market Efficiency in the European Union, and Challenges to European Legal Scholarship. He has a special interest in applying modern system theory to the research of law.

Making Foreign People Pay

ALI CEM BUDAK

Ashgate
DARTMOUTH
Aldershot • Brookfield USA • Singapore • Sydney

© Ali Cem Budak 1999

All rights reserved. No part of this publication may be reproduced, stored in a retrieval system, or transmitted in any form or by any means, electronic, mechanical, photocopying, recording or otherwise without the prior permission of the publisher.

Published by
Dartmouth Publishing Company Limited
Ashgate Publishing Limited
Gower House
Croft Road
Aldershot
Hampshire GU11 3HR
England

Ashgate Publishing Company
Old Post Road
Brookfield
Vermont 05036
USA

British Library Cataloguing in Publication Data
Budak, Ali Cem
  Making foreign people pay
  1.Debt - Law and legislation 2.Debtor and creditor
  3.Collection laws 4.Debtor and creditor - Social aspects
  5.Collection laws - Cross-cultured studies
  I.Title
  346'.07709

Library of Congress Cataloging-in-Publication Data
Budak, Ali Cem.
  Making foreign people pay / Ali Cem Budak.
      p.   cm. -- (Studies in modern law and policy)
  Based on the author's thesis (doctoral)--University of Bremen.
  Includes bibliographical references and index.
  ISBN 1-84014-436-X (hardcover)
  1. Debtor and creditor--Social aspects. 2. Executions (Law)--Social aspects. 3. Conflict of laws--Debtor and creditor.
  4. Collection laws--Social aspects. 5. Debts, External--Social aspects. I. Title. II. Series.
  K1370.B83 1998
  346.07'7--dc21   98-16967
                                                  CIP

ISBN 1 84014 436 X

Printed in Great Britain

Summary of Contents

Table of Contents vii
List of Figures xv
List of Tables xvii
Acknowledgements xix
List of Abbreviations xxi

INTRODUCTION

Introduction 3

PART I   PUBLIC ENFORCEMENT: JUDICIAL METHODS OF DEBT COLLECTION

Chapter 1   Debt Recovery in Germany 21
Chapter 2   Debt Recovery in England 43
Chapter 3   Debt Recovery in Turkey 75
Chapter 4   Results of the Comparison between German, English and Turkish Debt Recovery Law 101
Chapter 5   Role of Lawyers in Cross-Border Debt Collection 113
Chapter 6   Recourse to National Courts in Cross-Border Debt Collection 139
Chapter 7   Factors Impeding Access to Justice in Cross-Border Debt Collection 159
Chapter 8   Conclusions for Part I 175

vi *Making Foreign People Pay*

PART II   PRIVATE ENFORCEMENT: EXTRA-JUDICIAL METHODS OF DEBT COLLECTION

Chapter 9   Routinisation and Privatisation of Debt Collection 179
Chapter 10   Commercial Cross-Border Debt Collection in Germany.... 187
Chapter 11   Commercial Cross-Border Debt Collection in England 211
Chapter 12   Business Organisations of Debt Collection Agencies 243
Chapter 13   Conclusions for Part II 251

PART III   COLLECTION OF DEBTS AND MANAGEMENT OF CREDIT RISKS IN INTERNATIONAL TRADE

Chapter 14   Collection and Security Methods Employed in International Trade 257
Chapter 15   A Survey of the Collection and Security Methods used by Exporters 267
Chapter 16   Conclusions for Part III 301

CONCLUSION

Globalisation of Private Law Enforcement 307

Annexes 319
Bibliography 339
Index 357

Table of Contents

INTRODUCTION

Introduction 3
  A. Legal Sociology of Debt and Cross-Border Debt Collection 3
  B. Scope of Study and Method Used 7
  C. Globalisation of the Economy and Enforcement of Law 14

PART I   PUBLIC ENFORCEMENT: JUDICIAL METHODS OF DEBT COLLECTION

Chapter 1   Debt Recovery in Germany
As Compared with English and Turkish Law, and with Special
Reference to the Execution of Foreign Judgments 21
  A. Legal Basis 21
  B. Civil Execution Officers 22
  C. Basic Rules and Principles: 'Enforceable Title', 'Provisional
     Enforceability', 'Execution Clause', 'Service', 'Exequatur' 23
    1. Enforceable Judicial Acts 23
    2. Provisional Enforceability 24
    3. Execution Clause 25
    4. Service 25
    5. Execution-counterclaim 25
    6. Foreign Judgments / Exequatur 26
  D. Summary Procedures for the Recovery of Debt 29
  E. Enforcing Monetary Claims 31
    1. In General 31
      a) Attachment: execution against movable property 32
      b) Execution against immovable property 34
      c) Garnishee procedure 35

viii *Making Foreign People Pay*

    2. Monetary Claims Based on a Foreign Judgment (or on another Foreign Enforceable Title) 38
F. Protection of the Debtor.. 40
G. Preliminary Remedies for the Protection of the Creditor 41
H. Costs.. 42

Chapter 2   Debt Recovery in England
As Compared with Turkish and German Law, and with Special Reference to the Execution of Foreign Judgments 43
A. Legal Basis... 43
B. Civil Execution Officers 45
C. Basic Rules and Principles: Enforceable Judicial Acts; Effect of the Appeal; Sealing; Service; Leave of the Court; Stay of Execution; Foreign Judgments 48
    1. Enforceable Judicial Acts... 48
    2. Effect of the Appeal 49
    3. Sealing 49
    4. Service 50
    5. Leave of the Court... 50
    6. Stays of Execution... 51
        a) Stay by reason of new occurrences...................................... 52
        b) Stay of execution of writ of *fieri facias* (*i.e.* execution of a High Court judgment against goods)............................ 52
        c) Stay by County Courts 52
    7. Foreign Judgments 53
        a) Statutory law / international agreements 53
        b) Common Law.. 55
D. Summary Procedures for Debt Collection 57
E. Execution for Money Claims.. 58
    1. In General 58
        a) Writ of *fieri facias* and warrant of execution: execution against movable property... 59
        b) Charging orders: execution (obtaining security) against immovable property *etc.* 61
        c) Garnishee procedure: execution against debts.................... 62
        d) Attachment of earnings 65
        e) Equitable execution (appointment of a receiver)................ 67

f) Other methods of execution for judgments for money: judgment summons, County Court administration orders, committal 68
(1) Judgment summonses. 68
(2) County Court administration orders 68
(3) Committal. 69
2. Monetary Claims Based upon a Foreign Judgment (or another Foreign Enforcement Title) 69
F. Protection of the Debtor 70
G. Preliminary Remedies for the Protection of the Creditor 71
H. Costs 73

Chapter 3 Debt Recovery in Turkey
As Compared with English and German Law, and with Special Reference to the Execution of Foreign Judgments 75
A. Legal Basis 75
B. Civil Execution Officers 76
C. Basic Rules and Principles: Enforceable Judicial Acts, Effect of Appeal, Execution Clause, Service, 'Setting Aside' and Stay of Execution and 'Negative Declaratory Action'; Foreign Judgments (Exequatur) 78
  1. Enforceable Judicial Acts 78
  2. Effect of Appeal 78
  3. Execution Clause 79
  4. Service 79
  5. 'Setting Aside and Stay of Execution' and 'Negative Declaratory Action' 79
    a) Setting aside and stay of execution by the Execution Court .. 79
    b) Negative declaratory action 80
  6. Foreign Judgments / Exequatur 81
D. Summary Procedures for Debt Collection 86
E. Execution for Money Claims 88
  1. In General 88
    a) Attachment: execution against movable and immovable property 89
    b) Garnishee procedure: attachment of debts 92
    c) Attachment of earnings 95
  2. Monetary Claims Based upon a Foreign Judgment (or another Foreign Enforcement Title) 96

F. Protection of the Debtor 98
G. Preliminary Remedies for Protection of the Creditor
   (Preliminary Attachment) 99
H. Costs 100

**Chapter 4   Results of the Comparison between German, English
              and Turkish Debt Recovery Law** 101
A. Multiplicity of Legal Sources for Procedural Rules 101
B. Role of Execution Officers and Courts 102
C. Creditor's Control over the Enforcement Procedure 104
D. 'European Summary Procedure for Debt Collection' 106
E. Turkey's Accession to the 1968 Brussels Convention 108
F. Preliminary Remedies for Protection of the Creditor 109
G. Efficiency of Debt Recovery Procedures 110

Chapter 5   Role of Lawyers in Cross-Border Debt Collection 113
A. Need for Representation by a Lawyer 113
B. Lawyers at Cross-Border Debt Recovery Work 115
   1. The Aim of Interviews 115
   2. Selection of Interviewees and the Method Used for
      Evaluating the Information 116
      a) English Law Firm 3: City lawyers 120
      b) English Law Firm 9: Investment lawyers 123
      c) English Law Firm 10: Debt recovery department 125
      d) Turkish Law Firm 1: Traditional lawyers 127
      e) Turkish Law Firm 2: Debt collectors 130
C. Conclusions for Chapter 5 134

**Chapter 6   Recourse to National Courts in Cross-Border Debt
              Collection** 139
A. Generally 139
B. Going to Court in the Home Country 139
   1. Cases for Enforcement of Foreign Judgments in German
      Courts 141
   2. Cases for Enforcement of Foreign Judgments in Turkish
      Courts 142
   3. Cases for Enforcement (Registration) of Foreign
      Judgments in English Courts 144

C. Going to Court Abroad 147
    1. International Cases in the Turkish Courts 148
    2. International Cases in the German Courts.............................. 152
    3. International Cases in the English Courts 155

Chapter 7   Factors Impeding Access to Justice in Cross-Border Debt Collection 159

A. Generally.. 159
    1. Differences Between National Legal Systems? 159
    2. Bias Against Foreigners?... 161
B. Practical and Legal-Bureaucratic Difficulties 163
    1. Tracing the Debtor... 163
    2. Duplication of Lawyer's Fees 164
    3. Service of Documents 164
    4. Translation of Documents 167
    5. Taking Evidence Abroad... 168
    6. Security for Costs 169
    7. International Legal Aid and the Lack of Consumer Advice ... 170

Chapter 8   Conclusions for Part I 175

PART II   PRIVATE ENFORCEMENT: EXTRA-JUDICIAL METHODS OF DEBT COLLECTION

Chapter 9   Routinisation and Privatisation of Debt Collection 179

A. 'The Routinisation of Debt Collection' 179
B. Privatisation of Debt Collection 183

Chapter 10 Commercial Cross-Border Debt Collection in Germany 187

A. Commercial Debt Collection under German Law 187
    1. General 187
    2. Legal Advisory Act 189
    3. Debt Collection Methods... 191
    4. Debt Collection Contract... 194
    5. Costs.. 195
B. Cross-Border Debt Collection in Germany 197
    1. Introduction 197

xii *Making Foreign People Pay*

    2. Annual Number of Cross-border Commercial Debt Collection Cases... 199
    3. Distribution of Cross-border Debt Collection Cases Among Domestic and Foreign Clients in Various Countries 199
       a) Domestic creditors with debtors resident abroad 199
       b) Majority of clients from Europe 200
    4. Characteristics of Parties and Their Receivables 201
       a) Main clientele 201
       b) Types of claims 202
       c) Types of debts collected 203
    5. Debt Collection Methods and International Co-operation 204
       a) Comparison of debt collection methods in cross-border and domestic cases 204
       b) Co-operation with corresponding / sister debt collection agencies and foreign lawyers abroad 205
    6. Difficulties and Success Rates in Comparison to Domestic Debt Collection 207
       a) Difficulties in cross-border debt collection 207
       b) Comparison of the success rates between cross-border and domestic debt collection 207
    7. Costs of Cross-border Debt Collection 208

Chapter 11 Commercial Cross-Border Debt Collection in England 211

A. Commercial Debt Collection under English Law 211
    1. General 211
    2. Consumer Credit Act 1974 212
    3. Debt Collection Methods 213
    4. Costs.. 214
B. Cross-Border Debt Collection in England 214
    1. Introduction 214
    2. Superleague Firms 216
       a) English Debt Collector 1 216
       b) English Debt Collector 12 220
       c) English Debt Collector 13 222
    3. Medium Sized Firms 226
       a) English Debt Collector 6 226
       b) English Debt Collector 11 230
       c) English Debt Collector 2 231
    4. Boutique Type Agencies 234

a) English Debt Collector 7 234
b) English Debt Collector 3 238
5. Conclusions 239

Chapter 12 Business Organisations of Debt Collection Agencies 243
A. National Organisations 243
B. International Organisations 247

Chapter 13 Conclusions for Part II 251

PART III   COLLECTION OF DEBTS AND MANAGEMENT OF CREDIT RISKS IN INTERNATIONAL TRADE

Chapter 14 Collection and Security Methods Employed in International Trade 257
A. Investigating the Creditworthiness of the Debtor 259
B. Standard Collection Methods for Cross-Border Trade 262
C. 'Out-Sourcing' the Cross-Border Collections 263
D. The Standard Contract Terms used in International Trade 264
E. Security Methods Employed in International Trade 265
F. The Export Credit Insurance 266

Chapter 15 A Survey of the Collection and Security Methods used by Exporters 267
A. The Field of Survey and the Method Used 267
  1. The Field of Survey 267
  2. Questionnaire and Information Processing Method 270
  3. The Role of Firm Size 272
  4. Other Important Determinants: Experience in Exports, Export Orientation and Customer Relations 274
B. Relations with the Customers 275
C. Credit Information 281
D. 'Contracting Out' the Risk of Non-Payment 284
E. Securities against the Risk of Non-Payment 287
F. Collection Methods 290
G. Success Rates in Collection of Export Debts 294
H. Disputes Resulting in Non-Payment 296

I. Debt Recovery and Dispute Resolution 298

Chapter 16 Conclusions for Part III 301

CONCLUSION

Globalisation of Private Law Enforcement 307
    A. Thresholds for Thematisation of Law and Cross-Border
       Interactions 307
    B. Substitutes for Thematisation of Law 310
       1. Cognitive Mechanisms Versus Normative Order 310
       2. De-thematisation of Law 311
    C. Cognitive Elements of the New World Order and the Role of
       the Nation-State 313
       1. Legitimacy of Private Law Enforcement 314
       2. Protection of the Small People 317

Annexes 319
    Annex I   Questionnaire on the Collection and Risk Management
              Methods used by Turkish Export Firms 319
    Annex II Questionnaire on 'Cross-Border Debt Collection' 326

Bibliography 339
    I. Literature 339
    II. Statistical Sources and Other Sources of Information 354
    III. Daily and Business Press Reports 355

Index 357

List of Figures

Figure 9.1 Pyramid of Execution.. 183

Figure 15.1 Exporters' first contact with the customers 276

Figure 15.2 Sources of credit information... 282

Figure 15.3 Contracting out the risk of non-payment 283

Figure 15.4 Securities against the risk of non-payment 289

Figure 15.5 Collection methods 291

Figure 15.6 Success rates in collection of receivables arising from export sales.. 295

Figure 15.7 Common reasons for disputes 297

Figure 15.8 Debt collection / dispute resolution practices 299

List of Tables

Table 6.1	Number of 'enforcement of foreign judgments' proceedings at the German first instance courts (1969 – 1981)	142
Table 6.2	Number of orders for registration of foreign judgments in England (1991 – 1995)	145
Table 6.3	German judgments registered in England in 1995	147
Table 6.4	Parties to commercial cases before the Turkish Court of Cassation (1–30 June 1995)	151
Table 6.5	International commercial cases in the Turkish Court of Cassation (1–30 June 1995)	151
Table 6.6	Relative share of international cases in Bremen and Hamburg first instance Courts (1988)	153
Table 6.7	International cases in Bremen and Hamburg first instance Courts (1988)	154
Table 6.8	Amount of claim in national and international cases in Bremen and Hamburg first instance Courts (1988)	155
Table 6.9	Number of English judgments sought to be enforced outside England (1991 – 1995)	157
Table 9.1	Summary debt collection and ordinary court proceedings of civil and commercial law in Germany (1982 – 1991)	181

xviii Making Foreign People Pay

Table 10.1	Fees and costs of cross-border debt collection in Germany (1995)	208
Table 13.1	Regulation of debt collection business in Germany and England	252
Table 15.1	Distribution of respondent export firms according to the firm size	274
Table 15.2	Having old, established customers and firm size	277
Table 15.3	Personal contacts and firm size	278
Table 15.4	Use of agents in Turkey and firm size	278
Table 15.5	Use of agents abroad and firm size	279
Table 15.6	Relations with customers and litigation	281
Table 15.7	Using oral agreements and firm size	284
Table 15.8	Using contracts in writing and firm size	285
Table 15.9	Putting all transactions into writing and firm size	285
Table 15.10	Using standard contracts and firm size	286
Table 15.11	Contracting practices and success rate	287
Table 15.12	Obtaining securities and firm size	288
Table 15.13	Using on sight letters of credit and firm size	292
Table 15.14	Using acceptance letters of credit and firm size	293
Table 15.15	Using documents against acceptance and firm size	293
Table 15.16	Payment methods and export experience	294
Table 15.17	Success rate and firm size	296

Acknowledgements

This book is a doctoral dissertation. I am grateful to Volkmar Gessner of the University of Bremen for his valuable, critical guidance as the Supervisor of my doctoral research.

I am thankful to Hagen Lichtenberg of the same University who was the adviser of my studies during my first year in Germany and the Second Reporter of my dissertation.

I also discussed many of the ideas of the book with Sevim Budak of the Istanbul University, and with Armin Höland, Hanno von Freyhold, Kirstin Grotheer and Enzo Vial of the *Zentrum für Europäische Rechtspolitik* at the University of Bremen. I also thank them.

I must express my gratitude to Ralf Rogowski and the anonymous referees of Ashgate. Before the publication, I edited the dissertation considering their suggestions. Accordingly, the order of the chapters in this book varies from the original version of the doctoral dissertation. Namely, the first three chapters of the dissertation were replaced as chapters 14 – 16, and some new references were inserted into various parts of the book. The main structure and contents of the dissertation remain unchanged.

I wish to thank all the people who have given some of their time for the interviews and questionnaires concerning the empirical part of the research. Several surveys in Germany, England and Turkey would not be possible without the support given by, among others, Baki Kuru of the Ankara University, Mahmut T. Birsel of the Dokuz Eylül University, Halûk Kabaalioglu of the University of Marmara, Ulf Giebel and Carsten D. Ohle of the Federal Association of German Debt Collection Agencies, J. Horsfield of the Judgments/Orders Section in the Action Department of the High Court of Justice, Kurt Obermaier of the Federation of European National Collection Associations and Müjde Oktay of the Istanbul Chamber of Industry.

I thank the Commission of the European Communities acting through the Carl Duisberg Gesellschaft in Germany, for the Jean Monnet Award which supported my studies for my first year in Germany, between August

1994 and July 1995. I also thank the Volkswagen Foundation which supported the empirical part of the research between August 1995 and March 1997, through a major research grant given to the *Zentrum für Europäische Rechtspolitik*.

Last but not least, I thank Balkrishna Isvaran of Isvaran Consultancy of Madras, India for his cooperation in producing the book for publication.

Ali Cem Budak
Istanbul

List of Abbreviations[1]

BGBl, RGBL	German Federal Law Gazette.
CCEB	Turkish Code of Civil Execution and Bankruptcy of 19 June 1932.
CCR	County Court Rules 1981.
ECR	European Court Reports.
German CCP	German Code of Civil Procedure of 30 January 1877.
IPPL	Turkish International Private and Procedural Law of 22 May 1982.
OJ	Official Journal of the European Communities.
Resmi Gazete	Turkish Law Gazette.
Rn.	Marginal paragraph numbers used in German literature.
RSC	Rules of the Supreme Court 1965.
Turkish CCP	Turkish Code of Civil Procedure of 2 July 1932.

---

1 For a list of standard abbreviations of English law reports and journals see Leslie Rutherford and Sheila Bone, *Osborn's Concise Law Dictionary*, 8th ed. (London: Sweet & Maxwell, 1993), pp. 355–88. For a list of standard abbreviations for German law reports and journals see Hildebert Kirchner and Fritz Kastner, *Abkürzungsverzeichnis der Rechtssprache*, 4th ed. (Berlin and New York: de Gruyter, 1992). For a list of commonly used abbreviations for Turkish law reports and journals see Baki Kuru, *Hukuk Muhakemeleri Usulü*, Vol.1, 5th ed. (Istanbul: Alfa, 1990), pp. LIV–LVII. For a general loose-leaf reference book see Igor I. Kavas and Mary Miles Prince, *World Dictionary of Legal Abbreviations* (Buffalo, New York: Williams S. Hein & Co., 1994). In this book, German and Turkish law reports and journals are referred to in full titles.

INTRODUCTION

Introduction

A. LEGAL SOCIOLOGY OF DEBT AND CROSS-BORDER DEBT COLLECTION

The title of this book refers to Paul Rock's 'Making People Pay',[1] which was one of the earliest socio-legal studies concerning debt and debt collection. In the 1970s and 1980s, academic literature covered this subject in some detail.[2] During this period, the law reform commissions in Common Law countries also undertook comprehensive studies in this area.[3] In 1987,

---

1   London: Routledge & Kegan Paul, 1973. See also by the same author 'Observations on Debt Collection', *British Journal of Sociology* 19 (1968), pp. 176–90.
2   See *e.g.* David Caplovitz, *Consumers in Trouble: A Study of Debtors in Default* (New York – London: Free Press, 1974); Klaus F. Röhl, 'Schuldbeitreibung als Kontrolle abweichenden Verhaltens', *Zeitschrift für Rechtssoziologie* 5 (1983), pp. 1–49; Klaus F. Röhl, *Rechtssoziologie – Ein Lehrbuch* (Cologne: Carl Heymanns, 1987), Chapter 35 (pp. 292–9); Günter Hörmann, *Verbraucher und Schulden* (Baden-Baden: Nomos, 1987); Janet Ford, *The Indebted Society – Credit and Default in 1980's* (London - New York: Routledge, 1988).
3   *Report of the Committee on the Enforcement of Judgment Debts* (London: Her Majesty's Stationery Office, 1969); Barbara Doig, *The Nature and Scale of Diligence*, Scottish Office Central Research Unit Papers, Research Report for the Scottish Law Commission No. 1 (Central Research Unit, Scottish Office, 1980); Barbara Doig, *Debt Recovery through the Scottish Sheriff Courts*, Scottish Office Central Research Unit Papers, Research Report for the Scottish Law Commission No. 3 (Central Research Unit, Scottish Office, 1980); Scottish Law Commission, *First Memorandum on Diligence* (Edinburgh: Scottish Law Commission, 1980); Michael Adler and Edward Wozniak, *The Origins and Consequences of Default – An Examination of the Impact of Diligence*, Research Report for the Scottish Law Commission No. 5 (Central Research Unit, Scottish Office, 1981); Janet Gregory and Janet Monk, *Survey of Defenders in Debt Actions in Scotland*, Research Report for the Scottish Law Commission No. 6 (London: Her Majesty's Stationery Office, 1981); Barbara Doig and Ann R. Millar, *Debt Recovery – A Review of Creditors' Practices and Policies*, Scottish Office Central Research Unit Papers, Research Report for the Scottish Law Commission No. 8 (Central Research Unit, Scottish Office, 1981); *Insolvency Law*

the empirical findings of the foregoing studies on the sociology of debt found some theoretical support in Germany when a group of legal sociologists who applied the implementation theory of the political sciences [4] to civil and commercial law [5] published a number of articles on the sociology of debt collection.[6] In these studies on debt and debt collection, the individual debtor was of primary interest, particularly in his role as a credit-using consumer in the 'modern world of credit'.[7,8] As a result, debt and

---

and Practice, Report of the Review Committee (London: Her Majesty's Stationery Office, 1982); *Debt Recovery and Insolvency*, The Law Reform Commission Report No. 36 (Canberra: Australian Government Publishing Service, 1987); *Report on Debt Collection*, The Law Reform Commission, Report No. LRC 27-1988 (Dublin: The Law Reform Commission, 1988); Alberta Law Reform Institute, *Enforcement of Money Judgments*, Volume 1, Report No. 61 (Edmonton: Alberta Law Reform Institute, 1991).

4   See *infra* in this chapter.
5   Erhard Blankenburg, Thomas Gawron, Ralf Rogowski and Rüdiger Voigt, 'Zur Analyse un Theorie der Implementation von Gerichtsentscheidungen', *Die Öffentliche Verwaltung* 1986, pp. 274–85. For an earlier study, see Erhard Blankenburg, 'Die Implementation von Recht als Programm', Renate Mayntz (ed.), *Implementation politischer Programme – Empirische Forschungsberichte* (Königstein: Athenäum, 1980), pp. 127–37. For more comprehensive discussion see Thomas Raiser and Rüdiger Voigt (eds), Durchsetzung und Wirkung von Rechtsentscheidungen – Die Bedeutung der Implementations- und Wirkungsforschung für die Rechtswissenschaft (Baden-Baden: Nomos, 1989).
6   See the contributions in Chapter 3: 'Implementation von zivilgerichtlich legitimierten Geldforderungen', in Erhard Blankenburg and Rüdiger Voigt (eds), *Implementation von Gerichtsentscheidungen – Jahrbuch für Rechtssoziologie und Rechtstheorie* 11 (Opladen: Westdeutscher Verlag, 1987).
7   *Insolvency Law and Practice*, p. 11.
8   It is surprising that debtors who fail to honour their debts have not attracted the interest of sociology for quite some time. Since the earlier writings of Durkheim, 'deviance' has been commonly discussed within the context of criminality. See Emile Durkheim, *The Division of Labor in Society* (1893) (New York: Free Press and London: Collier Macmillan, 1965) (translation by George Simpson), Book One, Chapter 2, pp. 70 *et seq.*; Raymond Boudon and Francois Bourricaud, *Soziologische Stichworte* (Opladen:Westdeutscher Verlag, 1992), article 'Anomie'; H. J. Schneider (ed.), *Kriminalität und abweichendes Verhalten*, Vol. 2 (Weinheim - Basel: Beltz, 1983). Robertson and Taylor state 'We can choose to leave crime and deviance as undifferentiated in those societies... (where) the values are common to controllers and controlled', Roland Robertson and Laurie Taylor, *Deviance, Crime and Socio-Legal Control* (London: M. Robertson, 1973), p. 61. However, 'default' in paying contractual debts or performing other monetary obligations is as common as crime in everyday life and, because it is a 'violation of normative rules of the social system' [Albert K. Cohen, 'Deviant Behavior', in David L. Sills (ed.), *International Encyclopaedia of the Social Sciences*, Vol. 4 (New York: Cromwell Collies and London: Macmillan, 1968), p.148.], can be defined as deviant behaviour. Cf. Theo Rasehorn, 'Der Gerichtsvollzieher als 'Basis-Implementeur'', in Erhard Blankenburg and Rüdiger

Introduction 5

debt collection have been discussed by legal sociologists in the context of national societies and national legal systems.[9]

The frame of reference of this study on the legal sociology of debt differs from its predecessors in its emphasis on the international aspects of debt and debt collection. The debtor and the creditor will be private persons or corporations [10] separated by national borders. As a result, the author gives greater weight to business-to-business (commercial) debts, although a distinction between business-to-business and consumer debts was not made in the course of the research conducted for this book.[11]

Debt means something different in the business world than it does in consumer transactions or in transactions between non-business parties. Notwithstanding the growth of consumer credit and the routinisation of consumer debt,[12] default in the performance of monetary obligations still remains something of an exception for individual non-trade debtors. Except for unforeseen events such as illness, loss of employment, divorce, *etc.*, or fault on the part of the creditor,[13] an individual non-business debtor would pay his debts when they fall due. Commercial debt is different in character. The risk of non-payment is inherent to commercial activities.[14] In contrast

---

Voigt (eds), *Implementation von Gerichtsentscheidungen - Jahrbuch für Rechtssoziologie und Rechtstheorie* 11 (Opladen: Westdeutscher Verlag, 1987), pp. 104–9, p. 107.

9   Private individuals are rarely party to cross-border legal relations. See Volkmar Gessner, 'Institutional Framework of Cross-Border Interaction', in Volkmar Gessner (ed.), *Foreign Courts – Civil Litigation in Foreign Legal Cultures* (Aldershot: Dartmouth, 1996), pp. 15–42, pp. 31–2.

10 This may include public bodies which play a role as an actor of a private law relationship.

11 See *supra* footnote 6.

12 See Knut Holzscheck, Günter Hörmann and Jürgen Daviter, *Praxis des Konsumentenkredits – Eine empirische Untersuchung zur Rechtssoziologie und Ökonomie des Konsumentenkredits* (Cologne: Bundesanzeiger, 1982), pp. 57 *et seq.*; *Insolvency Law and Practice*, p. 11; Caplovitz, *Consumers in Trouble*, p. 1.

13 See Adler and Wozniak, *The Origins and Consequences of Default – An Examination of the Impact of Diligence*, pp. 15–6; Caplovitz, *Consumers in Trouble*, Chapters 4–9 (pp. 47–174).

14 For a commercial undertaking is an 'enterprise' which, as the term suggests, can result in failure. This can most evidently be observed in the institution of limited liability, which is the foundation of company law: 'We have ... too far taken for granted that corporations will have debt as well as equity – creditors as well as shareholders. ... If corporate debt is not essential, it becomes unclear why limited liability is necessary. For if the corporations just had the equity capital, so that they couldn't default on loans, the only thing at risk (unless the corporation committed a tort) would be stockholders' capital contributions.' Richard A. Posner, *Economic Analysis of Law*, 4th ed. (Boston – Toronto – London: Little, Brown and Company, 1992), p. 397.

to a non-business creditor, the business creditor is able to calculate and 'manage' the risk of non-payment.[15] Consumer debt deserves to be dealt with as a social problem which can be, and usually has been, handled from a consumer-protection viewpoint, whereas commercial debt is to be dealt with as an economic phenomenon where the actors (debtor and creditor) deserve to be treated as equal parties to the game.[16] For these reasons, this study will focus on the enforcement of monetary claims instead of debt *per se* as a social problem.

International involvement in economic relations entails both increased risks and benefits.[17] One important element of such additional risks is non-payment of debts: the debtor may feel himself to be safely out of the creditor's reach when he is across a border.[18]

As in crime,[19] social control for the enforcement of monetary claims is achieved by legal enforcement agents in addition to extra-judicial enforcement processes. A socio-legal analysis must deal with the latter as well as the legal form of enforcement.

---

15 However, the distinction between 'consumer debt' and 'commercial debt' is not absolute. A company director who has caused the company to be declared bankrupt fraudulently is deviant and a middle-class individual debtor who defaults on the mortgage payments of his house as a result of an unexpected rise of interest rates is not.

16 The inequality between debtor and creditor in terms of financial resources and experience in judicial proceedings which may be observed in consumer transactions and consumer disputes [Marc Galanter, 'Why the "Haves" Come Out Ahead: Speculations on the Limits of Legal Change', *Law and Society Review* 9 (1974/75), pp. 95–160] is not typical of business transactions and disputes between commercial undertakings.

17 Asterios G. Kefalas, *Global Business Strategy – A systems approach* (Cincinnati, Ohio: South-western Publishing, 1990), pp. 9–13 ('The Internationalization / Globalization Process').

18 Modern trends in the global economy 'from transactions to relationships', that is, from interactions between independent firms to internal relations between related companies [S. Tamer Cavusgil, 'Globalization of Markets and Its Impact on Domestic Institutions', *Indiana Journal of Global Legal Studies* 1, no. 1 (1993), pp. 83–99, at pp. 88–9] are far from diminishing the importance of cross-border monetary payments. Despite the stagnation observed in the export of goods in international trade, and even where the services sector is not taken into account, the ratio of total trade turnover (exports and imports) to national income is still between 15 – 25% in Western European countries. Jürgen Neyer, *Spiel ohne Grenzen - Weltwirtschaftliche Strukturveränderungen und das Ende des sozial kompetenten Staates* (Marburg: Tectum, 1996), pp. 27 and 172.

19 Blankenburg, 'Die Implementation von Recht als Programm', pp. 129–30.

B. SCOPE OF STUDY AND METHOD USED

The enforcement of monetary claims, commonly known as 'debt recovery' or 'debt collection', is distinguished from litigation for payment of money. As will be seen below, according to judicial statistics, in the majority of debt cases the debtor refrains from duly paying the creditor even though there is no (genuine) dispute between the parties.[20] Thus, the term 'debt recovery' in English legal terminology is commonly used for collection of undisputed, liquidated claims, as opposed to litigation and arbitration which are the proper recourse for disputed claims.[21] In addition, some of the recent law reform studies conducted in Common Law countries distinguish between 'formal' and 'informal' methods of debt recovery.[22] Accordingly, summary court procedures for debt collection, enforcement of money judgments and enforcement (registration) of foreign judgments for money are the enforcement methods which are discussed in the context of formal methods of debt recovery. Simple methods used for collection of debts by out-of-court contact with the debtor (telephone, demand letters, personal visits), by the creditor personally or by commercial debt collection agencies,[23] are called informal methods of debt recovery. This distinction between formal and informal debt recovery will be adopted in this study, using the terms 'judicial' and 'extra-judicial' methods of cross-border debt collection.[24]

The distinction between judicial and extra-judicial methods of debt collection is also a distinction between 'public' and 'private' enforcement of

---

[20] See *infra* Chapter 9: Recourse to National Courts in Cross-Border Debt Collection.

[21] Terms similar to the English 'debt recovery' or 'debt collection' also exist in German and Turkish *e.g.*, 'Schuldbeitreibung', 'Forderungseinzug', 'Inkasso' and 'para alacaklarinin tahsili', 'tahsilat'. Some of the law firms interviewed for this study (English Law Firms 3 and 10, German Law Firm 2) have debt recovery departments as well as litigation and arbitration departments. See *infra* Chapter 8: Role of Lawyers in Cross-Border Debt Collection. See also advertisements placed by British law firms in the monthly journal *Credit Management* in 1996 (Leicestershire: The Institute of Credit Management).

[22] For Scottish and Australian law reform commissions, see respectively Doig and Millar, *Debt Recovery – A Review of Creditors' Practices and Policies*; The Law Reform Commission, *Debt Recovery and Insolvency*.

[23] In American English, debt collection by commercial debt collection agencies is called 'third party collection'.

[24] See Parts II and III.

law.[25] As will be discussed later, both public and private enforcers of legal claims (national courts and debt collection agencies) have been participating in cross-border co-operation. A comparison between the functioning and efficiency of public and private enforcement will determine the success of these international efforts to date for international co-operation, and suggestions will be made about what must be done in the future.

As regards methodology, this study belongs to the comparative sociology of law,[26] and adopts the same line of research with the Implementation Theory of the sociology of law.[27] The judicial methods of debt collection

---

25 See Roger Cotterell, *The Sociology of Law: An Introduction* (London: Butterworths, 1984), pp. 259–302; Posner, *Economic Analysis of Law*, pp. 595–611. *Cf. infra* Chapter 12: Routinisation and Privatisation of Debt Collection.

26 Dieter Martiny, 'Rechtsvergleichung und vergleichende Rechtssoziologie', *Zeitschrift für Rechtssoziologie* 1, no. 1 (1980), pp. 65–84; Volkmar Gessner, *Methoden und Probleme vergleichender Rechtssoziologie*, Centre for European Law and Politics 'Discussion Paper 2/83' (Bremen: Zentrum für europäische Rechtspolitik, 1983).

27 The Implementation Theory of the sociology of law is borrowed from the political science. The implementation research in the area of the political science is based on a simple, undisputed conception: the impact of a political programme, say the fight against poverty, illegal drugs or environmental pollution, depends on the implementation of the programme by the relevant administrative agencies. As well as the process of development of a political programme (policy-making), whether it be in the form of a normative regulation or in the form of a political decision within the discretion of the government, the process of implementation is a complex process of various interactions. Just as for political parties, industrial organisations, religious communities and other diverse organised or unorganised social groups or persons taking part in the process of development of a political programme, so various governmental agencies and social groups or persons of different kinds take part in the process of implementation of the political programme. As a result of these interactions, the impact of the political programme may be different (*e.g.*, less successful) than what has been intended by the political decision-maker. See Renate Mayntz, 'Einleitung – Die Entwicklung des analytischen Paradigms der Implementationsforschung', Renate Mayntz (ed.), *Implementation politischer Programme – Empirische Forschungsberichte* (Königstein: Athenäum, 1980), pp. 1–19. For a selected bibliography on the Implementation Research, see *ibid.*, pp. 251–3. For various aspects of implementation of normative programmes in diverse policy areas, see Rüdiger Voigt, *Politik und Recht – Beiträge zur Rechtspolitologie* (Bochum: Universitätsverlag Dr. N. Brockmeyer, 1993); Rüdiger Voigt (ed.), *Recht als Instrument der Politik* (Opladen: Westdeutscher Verlag, 1986). For example, depending on what occurs during the implementation process, which is not completely foreseeable for the decision-maker, a de-criminalisation of the consuming of cannabis products may be an effective method of fight against hard drugs, or it may stimulate the demand for drugs. (For empirical evidence concerning the impact of the prohibition of cannabis products, see Norman Braun, 'Reduziert das Cannabisverbot den Konsum harter Drogen?', *Zeitschrift für Rechtssoziologie* 18 (1997), pp. 106–23.) The implementation research was originally established by the political scientists in the US, concerning the functioning of the implementation of political programmes. See Renate **Mayntz**,

involve enforcement of judgments concerning monetary claims. According to the 'theory of implementation of judicial decisions', the implementation of judicial decisions (court judgments) may be considered as an implementation process, same as the implementation of political programmes. Depending on its nature, each single case before the courts is a social interaction process in which various social groups and persons, related directly or indirectly to the individual conflict, may be involved in various degrees. For example, in a divorce case, family members or colleagues of the parties are heard by the court as witnesses; in criminal proceedings against political extremists, human rights organisations send their representatives to the court hearings; monthly journals of industrial organisations comment on recent judgments rendered by labour courts, *etc.* It is this interaction process that the elements of a normative programme are 'interpreted' and applied to an individual conflict, for the purpose of reaching a 'judgment'.[28]

Furthermore, a court judgment is itself a 'programme' aiming to re-regulate the individual legal relation between the parties. As in the case of political programmes which need to be implemented by the relevant administrative agencies, court judgments do not usually have an automatic effect on the legal relationship between the parties, but rather go through an implementation process. As a result, 'it is often the case that, court judgments are not enforced as such, but give rise to a new interaction process during which the judicial decision may be altered or the conflict between the parties re-negotiated'.[29] That is, the implementation of a judicial decision happens in a new 'implementation arena' where not only the enforcement agents (*e.g.*, a Sheriff's Officer) and the parties to the lawsuit, but also third parties or groups ('the parties behind the parties': *e.g.*, industrial or professional organisations seeking to protect the interest of their member or their collective interests) may be involved.[30,31]

'Die Implementation politischer Programme – Thoeretische Überlegungen zu einem neuen Forschungsgebiet', *Die Verwaltung* 10 (1977), pp. 51–66. Later, a group of legal-sociologists (*supra* footnote 5) applied the same theoretical approach to the implementation of judicial decisions.

[28] See Erhard Blankenburg, 'Die Implementation von Recht als Programm' in Mayntz, *Implementation politischer Programme*, pp. 127–37.

[29] Blankenburg, Gawron, Rogowski and Voigt, 'Zur Analyse un Theorie der Implementation von Gerichtsentscheidungen', p. 274.

[30] See *ibid.*, pp.277–82; Voigt, 'Durchsetzung und Wirkung von Rechtsentscheidungen', p. 28; Gottwald, 'Die Zivilrechts(alltags)praxis', pp. 77–81.

[31] A series of regular judgments (judicial precedents) of courts is – as separate from what is said about single court judgments, but more like the normative programmes of the legislative (laws) – a 'programme' in that, it resolves similar individual conflicts

10 Making Foreign People Pay

In this respect, law enforcement must be considered as a whole interactions process of programme-making and implementation which includes the enforcement of judgments as well as legal proceedings. In the course of this interactions process, non-state actors may also play a central role, either in the implementation of legal norms ('alternatives to justice') or the implementation of the judicial decisions (the 'enforcement').[32]

The legal theoretical discussions concerning the 'theory of implementation of judicial decisions' are outside the ambit of this study. However, the author has applied the approach of the implementation theory in that, the process of debt recovery and cross-border debt collection are considered as an interactions process of various actors, including the judicial methods of debt collection through national courts and civil execution officers [33] as well as alternative (extra-judicial) methods of debt collection.[34] The various

---

  by way of 'value and aim oriented interpretation of the legal provisions' (Blankenburg, Gawron, Rogowski and Voigt, 'Zur Analyse un Theorie der Implementation von Gerichtsentscheidungen', p. 276). Examples of such 'programmes' may be seen in the judicial precedents concerning industrial relations, protection of the environment or consumer protection. For examples of value and aim oriented judicial precedents concerning the protection of the tort victims (the employer's liability without fault), consumer protection (standard contracts), and the economic interests of the business community (pledge on moveable property), see Thomas Raiser, 'Wirksamkeit und Wirkung von Zivilrechtsnormen', Raiser and Voigt, *Durchsetzung und Wirkung von Rechtsentscheidungen*, pp. 46–65. Thus, the judiciary, especially the higher ranking courts conduct 'judicial policies' along with, and indeed relatively independent of, the political programmes of the legislative and executive powers of the state. See *e.g.* Lawrence Baum, 'Implementation of Judicial Decisions – An Organizational Analysis', *American Politics Quarterly* 4 (1979), pp. 86–114; Rüdiger Voigt, 'Durchsetzung und Wirkung von Rechtsentscheidungen – Forschungsansätze und Forschungsstrategien', in Raiser and Voigt, *Durchsetzung und Wirkung von Rechtsentscheidungen*, pp. 11–29, pp. 27–8; Walther Gottwald, 'Die Zivilrechts(alltags)praxis – ein Findelkind der Implementationsforschung?', in Raiser and Voigt, *Durchsetzung und Wirkung von Rechtsentscheidungen*, pp. 67–85, pp. 68–71; Kálmán Kulcsár, 'Politics and Legal Policy', in Peter Koller, Csaba Varga and Ota Weinberger (eds), *Theoretische Grundlagen der Rechtspolitik – Ungarisch-Österreichishes Symposium der internationalen Vereinigung für Rechts- und Sozialphilosophie 1990* (Stuttgart: Franz Steiner, 1992), pp. 17–27; Péter Szilágyi, 'Zur theoretischen Grundlegung der Rechtspolitik de Gesetzgebung', *ibid.*, pp. 104–10. For a comparison between political and judicial policy-making see Martin Shapiro, 'Incremental Decision Making', in S. Sidney Ulmer (ed.), *Courts, Law and Judicial Processes* (New York: The Free Press, 1981), pp. 313–23.
32 See Erhard Blankenburg and Y. Taniguchi, 'Informal Alternatives to and within Formal Procedures', W. Wedekind (ed.), *The Eighth World Conference on Procedural Law – Justice and Efficiency – General Reports and Discussions* (Denever: Kluwer, 1989), pp. 335–60, pp. 352–60.
33 Part I of this book.
34 Part II of this book.

actors in this particular interactions process, such as the parties of cross-border commercial debts,[35] national courts, civil execution officers,[36] lawyers,[37] commercial debt collection agencies,[38] *etc.*, and their respective roles are considered in this study.

The book contains three parts. Part I and Part II consider judicial and extra-judicial methods of debt collection. Part I, on the judicial methods of cross-border debt collection, begins with a comparative outline of German, English and Turkish debt recovery law. The choice of England, Germany and Turkey as countries of comparison was intended to compare, as far as is relevant to this research, the aspects of the Common Law system with the Civil Law system. Rules of civil procedure, organisation of the judiciary and the legal profession in England are different from the two civil law systems, which have more points in common. Just how important these differences actually are in the practice of law enforcement will be explored. In this part, emphasis has been placed on the summary procedures for debt recovery and the enforcement of foreign judgments, the latter including the actual enforcement of the judgment by the Sheriff and the Court (*Zwangsvollstreckung*) as well as the registration of foreign judgments (*Vollstreckbarerklärung*).[39] Further, the cross-border law enforcement between both EU Member States will be compared with the law enforcement between these countries and Turkey. The EU aspect is important for judicial methods of debt collection, for Germany and England are both parties to the 1968 Brussels Convention,[40] whereas there is no agreement for reciprocal enforcement of judgments between either of these two EU countries and Turkey. Empirical data concerning the judicial methods of debt collection will illustrate how far the Brussels Convention has succeeded in improving access to justice for EU nationals. Because the scope of the study has been limited to 'debt recovery', the comparison does not

---

35 Part III of this book.
36 Chapters 6 and 7.
37 Chapter 5.
38 Chapters 10–2.
39 In all three countries, standard literature on international private law concentrates on registration of foreign judgments. The actual enforcement stage is usually not discussed in detail. *E.g.*, Jan Kropholler, *Internationales Privatrecht*, 2nd ed. (Tübingen: Mohr, 1994); Ergin Nomer, *Devletler Hususi Hukuku*, 8th ed. (Istanbul: Beta, 1996); Peter Stone, *The Conflict of Laws* (London: Longman, 1995). For an exception in Germany, see Haimo Schack, *Internationales Zivilverfahrensrecht*, 2nd ed. (Munich: Beck, 1996).
40 Convention on Jurisdiction and the Enforcement of Judgments in Civil and Commercial Matters, *Official Journal of the European Communities* 1968, L 304; 1983 C 97.

12 *Making Foreign People Pay*

include a detailed discussion of various aspects of international litigation and arbitration.[41] International Insolvency Law,[42] which can be taken as a separate topic for socio-legal research, also remains outside the ambit of this study.

Following the comparative summary of debt recovery procedures, Part I discusses the role of courts and practising lawyers and the factors impeding access to justice in the field of cross-border debt recovery. In this section, the author uses his research results in combination with existing statistical material and empirical data provided by earlier studies on international litigation. Numerous interviews were conducted with practising lawyers, judges, sheriffs' officers and other court officers in the three countries.[43] In addition, research was carried out on the records of the High Court in London and the Court of Cassation in Ankara concerning the international cases in England and Turkey. Like New York, London is known as a market place for international litigation. The question whether and how far this assumption is true will also be discussed, using data collected from the High Court as well as English solicitors. As socio-legal studies concerning Turkey are very limited in number,[44] this section will also contribute to

---

41 For international litigation in various countries, see *The International Symposium on Civil Justice in the Era of Globalization – Collected Reports* (Tokyo: Japanese Association of the Law of Civil Procedure, 1993). For recent socio-legal research on international litigation and arbitration, see Gessner, *Foreign Courts*, and Yves Dezalay and Bryant Garth, 'Merchants of Law as Moral Entrepreneurs: Constructing International Justice from the Competition for Transnational Disputes', *Law and Society Review* 29, no. 1 (1995), pp. 27–64. Cross-border enforcement of maintenance claims, which plays an important role in private international law, also remains outside the scope of this study. The enforcement of cross-border child support claims is the subject of ongoing socio-legal research. See Kirstin Grotheer, 'Cross-Border Maintenance Claims of Children', in Volkmar Gessner and Ali Cem Budak (eds), *Emerging Legal Certainty – Empirical Studies on the Globalisation of Law* (Aldershot: Ashgate|Dartmouth: 1998).

42 See Ian F. Fletcher (ed.), *Cross-Border Insolvency: National and Comparative Studies* (Tübingen: Mohr, 1992).

43 Throughout this book, all interviews will be referred to anonymously, by a number, *e.g.*, English Law Firm 1 or Turkish Ministry of Justice, Officer 2. In some of the interviews, more than one interviewee was present. In these cases, reference will be made again to the interview as a whole without distinguishing between individual interviewees.

44 Legal sociologists in Turkey are primarily interested in legal theory rather than empirical sociology of law. See *e.g.*, Ülker Gürkan, *Hukuk Sosyolojisine Giris*, 2nd ed. (Ankara: Siyasal Kitabevi, 1994); Adil Izveren, *Hukuk Sosyolojisi* (Ankara: Dokuz Eylül Üniversitesi Hukuk Fakültesi, 1993); Niyazi Öktem, *Hukuk Felsefesi ve Hukuk Sosyolojisi*, 2nd. ed. (Istanbul: Istanbul Üniversitesi Hukuk Fakültesi, 1985); Tarik Özbilgen, *Elestirisel Hukuk Sosyolojisi* (Istanbul: Istanbul Üniversitesi Hukuk

introducing the legal-cultural environment in Turkey, albeit with reference to one specific area of law.[45]

Inclusion of Part II on 'extra-judicial methods of debt collection' in the study suggests that such extra-judicial debt collection methods are to some degree comparable with judicial enforcement mechanisms. Part II begins with a report on modern developments in the field of debt recovery towards 'routinisation' of judicial debt recovery which, the author believes, laid the groundwork for a successful 'privatisation' of law enforcement in this area. This discussion is followed by the results of a survey on the debt collection business in England and Germany.[46] For this survey, questionnaires were used as well as interviews with commercial debt collection agencies, and activities of the national and international business organisations for debt collection were studied. How important is the role of commercial agencies in cross-border debt collection? What methods do they use to make foreign debtors pay? Who will control debt collectors' activities?

Part III on 'international credit management' aims to consider the discussions in the first two Parts in context. International credit management refers to internationally-standardised collection and risk management methods which are employed by business actors (documentary operations, bank guarantees, export credit insurance, *etc.*). As stated above, most cross-border debts are commercial in nature. From the business creditors' point of view, debt collection is part of the general concept of 'credit management'.

Fakültesi, 1976). Legal sociologists in other countries have shown interest in Turkey's reception of Continental civil law. See *e.g.*, June Starr, 'Turkish Village Disputing Behaviour', in Laura Nader and Harry F. Todd Jr. (eds), *The Disputing Process – Law in Ten Societies* (New York: Columbia University Press, 1978), pp. 122–51; June Starr and Jonathan Pool, 'The Impact of a Legal Revolution in Rural Turkey', *Law and Society Review* 8, no. 3 (1974), pp. 533–60; Ernst E. Hirsch, *Rezeption als sozialer Prozeß – Erläutert am Beispiel der Türkei* (Berlin: Duncker & Humblot, 1981).

45 During this study it became clear to the author that many scholars outside Turkey, unlike foreign lawyers who practise law in cases involving Turkey (see Chapter 12 *infra*), have a rather exotic image of this country. They expect to hear that the judicial system has a very different structure in Turkey, and they are dubious or disappointed upon hearing that law and legal practice is by and large similar to Western European countries. Turkey has had a codified civil law since the second half of the 19th century (*e.g.* Code of Commerce 1850, Rules of Procedure for Commercial Matters 1861, Majalla 1869 – 1876) and completed its reception of Continental law in the second half of the 1920s. The author belongs to the third generation of Turkish jurists following the reception. Unlike what one German scholar suspected, law students in Turkey do not read translations from European textbooks and, unlike what another colleague believes, corruption does not rule Turkish courts.

46 Commercial debt collection does not exist in Turkey.

Credit management involves not only collection of debts, but also management of the risk of non-payment, considering the transaction costs and the costs of law enforcement. Unless observed in this context, the behaviour of the parties to cross-border credit transactions cannot be understood properly. Part III produces the results of a business survey on credit management methods employed by Turkish export firms. What does cross-border debt mean for business actors? How do they protect themselves against the risk of non-payment and what do they do when they actually need debt collection?

C. GLOBALISATION OF THE ECONOMY AND ENFORCEMENT OF LAW

Within its 'international' context, the study aims to contribute to current discussions on globalisation.[47] Although the term 'globalisation' and its analogues such as 'the Global Village', 'World Society', 'New World Order' and so on are applied more than any other concept for explaining modern developments in world history,[48] the definition of such terms remains vague. It has been stated that in the social sciences there are as many concepts of globalisation as there are disciplines, *i.e.*, globalisation in economics, in international relations, in cultural studies, *etc.*[49] Nevertheless, it is common to all definitions of globalisation that the term refers to a worldwide process of integration of national societies into a World Society which is unique for our time in terms of speed and intensity, if not in its very nature.[50] Thus, globalisation can be defined as 'a process in which

---

[47] This study was an individually prepared part of the collective research project 'Global Legal Interaction' directed by Volkmar Gessner at the Centre for Law and Politics at the University of Bremen. The research team was composed of jurists and legal-sociologists from various countries. A book containing the first part of the research project was published in 1996: Gessner, *Foreign Courts, supra* footnote 8. A second book is in 1998: Volkmar Gessner and Ali Cem Budak (eds), *Emerging Legal Certainty – Empirical Studies on Globalization of Law* (Aldershot: Ashgate/Dartmouth).

[48] Already in 1973, Alex Inkeles criticised the banalisation of these concepts. Alex Inkeles, 'The Emerging Social Structure of the World', *World Politics* 27 (October 1974 – July 1975), pp. 467–95, at p. 467.

[49] Jan Nederveen Pieterse, 'Globalization and Hybridisation', *International Sociology* 9, no. 2 (1994), pp. 161–8, at p. 161.

[50] Delbrück makes a distinction between internationalisation and globalisation: 'globalization as distinct from internationalization denotes a process of *denationalization* of clusters of political, economic and social activities. Internationalization, on the other hand, refers to co-operative activities of *national* actors, public or private,

social life within societies is increasingly affected by international influences based on everything from political and trade ties to shared music, clothing styles, and mass media'.[51] It is also generally accepted that 'the most powerful form of globalisation is economic',[52] 'in which planning and control expand from a relatively narrow focus . . . to a broad global focus, in which the entire world serves as a source of labour, raw materials, and markets'.[53]

The advanced form of globalisation in the economy today suggests that there must also exist an infrastructure in the form of legal norms and enforcement mechanisms regulating these economic relations world-wide.[54] The literature on trans-national economic relations, whether written by economists, political scientists or jurists, refers to the law of the international economy as a separate topic of discussion. Reference is often made to the liberalisation of international trade (elimination of tariff and non-tariff barriers, anti-dumping law, *etc.*); trade law applicable to international business transactions (international sale of goods, cross-border payment and security methods, *etc.*); the 'protective law' (intellectual property protection, labour law, the protection of consumers, *e.g.*, product liability,

---

on a level beyond the nation state but in the last resort under its control'. Jost Delbrück, 'Globalization of Law, Politics, and Markets – Implications for Domestic Law – A European Perspective', *Indiana Journal of Global Legal Studies* 1, no. 1 (1993), pp. 9–36, at pp. 10–1. See also Gordon R. Walker and Mark A. Fox, 'Globalization: An Analytical Framework', *Indiana Journal of Global Legal Studies* 3, no. 2 (1996), 27 pages in Internet, <http://www.law.indiana.edu/glsj/glsj/html>.

51 Allan G. Johnson, *The Blackwell Dictionary of Sociology* (Cambridge, Massachusetts: Basil Blackwell, 1995), article 'Globalization'. Similarly, McGrew defines globalisation as 'the multiplicity of linkages and interconnections between the states and societies which make up the modern world system . . . by which events, decisions, and activities in one part of the world can come to have significant consequences for individuals and communities in quite distant parts of the globe'. Antony McGrew, 'Conceptualizing Global Politics', in Antony McGrew and Paul G. Lewis et al., *Global Politics* (Cambridge: Polity Press, 1992), pp. 1–28, at p. 23.

52 Johnson, *The Blackwell Dictionary of Sociology*, loc. cit.

53 See *e.g.*, Tamer S. Cavusgil, 'Globalization of Markets and Its Impact on Domestic Institutions', *Indiana Journal of Global Legal Studies* 1, no. 1 (1993), pp. 83–99 and Walker and Fox, 'Globalization' where the integration of financial markets on a global basis has been regarded as 'the paradigm example of the movement toward globalization'.

54 See Martin Shapiro, 'The Globalization of Law', *Indiana Journal of Global Legal Studies* 1, no. 1 (1993), pp. 37–64, at pp. 38–44. 'Globalization and the Quest for Justice' was the subject of the Joint Meeting of Law and Society Association and the Research Committee on the Sociology of Law of the International Sociological Association, in Glasgow in July 1996, where 1,200 legal sociologists met to discuss different aspects of this issue.

16 Making Foreign People Pay

standards, the protection of the environment, *etc.*) and resolution of disputes in international transactions (international litigation and arbitration).[55] The problem of international public debt, particularly the difficulties experienced by less developed countries in the repayment of loans to international lenders, has also been discussed in detail.[56]

Interestingly, 'cross-border debt collection' as defined above - *i.e.* the enforcement of diverse monetary claims of private individuals and businesses across borders - has remained untouched by academic literature. Enforcement of monetary claims is an important example for enforcement of private law. Due to the conflict of national laws and procedures, judicial enforcement of private law has always been more difficult in the international arena. Globalisation of the modern economy must have further increased the demand for international law enforcement in the area of private law. Efforts have been made by the nation-states to improve the capacity of national courts to resolve international disputes at the national level by means of private international law [57] and at the international level by

---

55 *E.g.*, Cavusgil, 'Globalization of Markets and Its Impact on Domestic Institutions'; Shapiro, 'The Globalization of Law', Delbrück, 'Globalization of Law, Politics, and Markets'; Richard J. Barnet and Ronald E. Müller, *Global Reach – The Power of the Multinational Corporations* (London: Jonathan Cape, 1975); Monir H. Tayeb, *The Global Business Environment – An Introduction* (London: SAGE, 1992); several contributions in Richard Stubbs and Geoffrey R. D. Underhill, *Political Economy and the Changing Global Order* (London: Macmillan, 1994); D. M. Day and Bernardette Griffin, *The Law of International Trade*, 2nd ed. (London, Dublin, Edinburgh: Butterworths, 1993); Jürgen Bellers, 'Nationale und internationale Normierungen auf dem Gebiet grenzüberschreitenden Wirtschaftsbeziehungen', in Klaus Dieter Wolf (ed.), *Internationale Verrechtlichung – Jahresschrift für Rechtspolitologie 1993* (Pfaffenweiler: Centaurus, 1993), pp. 127–46. For a recent discourse of the relevant socio-legal literature (with a bibliography), see Klaus F. Röhl and Stefan Magen, 'Die Rolle des Rechts im Prozeß der Globalisierung', *Zeitschrift für Rechtssoziologie* 17, no. 1 (1996), pp. 1–57.

56 See, *e.g.*, Brian Kettel and George Magnus, *The International Debt Game* (London: Graham & Trotman, 1986); *International Debt and the Developing Countries – A World Bank Symposium* (Washington D.C.; The World Bank, 1986); Darrell Delamaide, *Debt Shock – The Full Story of the World Credit Crisis* (New York: Doubleday & Company, 1984); Christopher A. Kojm (ed.), *The Problem of International Debt* (New York: The H. W. Wilson Company, 1984); Hakan Hedström, *Die internationale Verschuldungskrise* (Heidelberg: HVA, 1985); William R. Cline, *International Debt: Systematic Risk and Policy Response* (Washington, D.C.: Institute for International Economics, The MIT Press, 1984).

57 See *e.g.*, Turkish (1982) and Swiss (1987) acts on private international law for their liberal attitudes with respect to application of foreign law and the enforcement of foreign judicial decisions: *e.g.*, Art. 5 of the former and Art. 194 of the latter, which narrows the possibility of application of the *ordre public* barrier against the choice of law

means of international conventions [58] and the unification of law.[59] Knowledge of the facts regarding the functioning and efficiency of judicial (and extra-judicial) enforcement methods for collection of cross-border debts may illustrate the achieved level of the globalisation of private law, and may suggest what must be done to further improve the legal infrastructure for the global economy. How far has the globalisation process developed in providing the private actors of the global economy with conditions for fair play and legal certainty? How can the nation-state, in its role of law enforcer, meet the new challenge presented by globalisation? These questions will be considered in the concluding chapter.

---

contracts and adopts the liberal rules of enforcement of foreign arbitral awards of the 1958 UN Convention as provisions of domestic private international law.

[58] See *e.g.*, European Convention on Information on Foreign Law 1968, Hague Convention on the Service Abroad of Judicial and Extra Judicial Documents in Civil and Commercial Matters 1965, Hague Conventions on enforcement of foreign maintenance orders dated 1958 and 1973; Brussels Convention on Jurisdiction and the Enforcement of Civil and Commercial Judgments 1968.

[59] *E.g.*, UN Convention on the International Sale of Goods 1980, Convention on the Carriage of Goods by Road 1956.

PART I

PUBLIC ENFORCEMENT: JUDICIAL METHODS OF DEBT COLLECTION

PART I

1 Debt Recovery in Germany

AS COMPARED WITH ENGLISH AND TURKISH LAW, AND WITH SPECIAL REFERENCE TO THE EXECUTION OF FOREIGN JUDGMENTS

A. LEGAL BASIS

Civil execution in Germany (*Zwangsvollstreckung*) is considered to be a part of civil procedure and is regarded as being complementary to the court proceedings (*Erkenntnisverfahren*). The rules governing civil execution proceedings are partly to be found in the Code of Civil Procedure of 1877.[1] Civil execution is however, a separate part of Civil Procedure, and it has special rules and principles that are taught at German law schools separately from Civil Procedure in the strict sense of the word (*i.e.* proceedings before the Court seized of and the courts of higher instance) and together with Insolvency Law ('Law of Civil Execution and Insolvency').

In addition to the German CCP, the Act on Public Auction Sales and Administration 1897[2] and the Under-judges Act 1969[3] are of importance in execution proceedings. The former governs the procedure for the enforcement of money judgments through warrant sales as well as administration orders in the case of immovables, and the latter contains the rules concerning the legal status and duties of the Under-judge (*Rechtspfleger*) who plays a central role in civil execution proceedings.

---

1 Chapter 8 (§§ 704–945) of the 'Zivilprozeßordnung' (hereinafter 'German CCP').
2 Gesetz über Zwangsversteigerung und Zwangsverwaltung.
3 Rechtspflegergesetz.

B. CIVIL EXECUTION OFFICERS

The Court Executor (*Gerichtsvollzieher*), the German equivalent of the English 'Sheriff', is the figure who plays the most central role in civil execution proceedings. The Court Executor, who receives a partial legal training, is in actual fact the official who has the competence to enforce money judgments against movable property (*i.e.* the attachment and sale of goods and chattels) and to execute judgments which concern the delivery of goods or the recovery of immovable property.

Civil execution is deemed in Germany to be a legal process which involves the use of public (sovereign) powers against private individuals. As a result of this, the office held by the Court Executor is a public office. The Court Executor is not an agent of the creditor, rather an assistant (*Hilfsorgan*) of the court. The relationship between the Court Executor and the execution creditor arises out of public law. However, as opposed to the Turkish system but as is the case in England, a German Court Executor maintains his or her own private office outside the confines of the Court, employs his or her own staff, keeps his or her own equipment, and even has in practice [4] his or her own working hours.[5] The State is responsible for paying the Court Executor's salary, but his overheads are nonetheless to be covered by the revenues earned from executing judgments, from which the Court Executor is entitled to a share.

The acts of the Court Executor are subject to the control and supervision of the 'Execution Court'.

The Execution Court (*Vollstreckungsgericht*) has a double function in civil execution proceedings: firstly, it is the court which has competence to hear any objections (*Erinnerung* = reminder) raised against the acts of the Court Executor.[6] Secondly, it is in itself a competent forum for the enforcement of money judgments against debts (*i.e.* for garnishee proceedings), and for the enforcement of money judgments against immovable property (*i.e.* for charging orders) *etc.*

The Execution Court is a civil court, namely an *Amtsgericht* (*i.e.* a Court of first instance in civil matters, in which the dispute may be termed a small claim). Instead of a full-judge, an Under-judge (a *Rechtspfleger*) will usually preside over the proceedings in an Execution Court.

---

4 Interview with the German Court Executor.
5 Cf. Chapter 2: Debt Recovery in England and Chapter 3: Debt Recovery in Turkey.
6 German CCP § 766.

The Court which enforces the judgment is thus different from the Trial Court which delivers the judgment. The Trial Court (*Prozeßgericht*) however, also plays a role in execution proceedings. It is the competent forum in which to execute injunctions, as well as other decrees which force the debtor to take action, *i.e.* to do or to abstain from doing an act.[7]

C. BASIC RULES AND PRINCIPLES: 'ENFORCEABLE TITLE', 'PROVISIONAL ENFORCEABILITY', 'EXECUTION CLAUSE', 'SERVICE', 'EXEQUATUR'

1. Enforceable Judicial Acts

The most important enforceable title (*Vollstreckungstitel*, enforceable judicial act) which entitles the creditor to enforce his claim through the statutory civil execution procedure is a judgment. In Germany however, it is also possible to initiate civil execution proceedings 'without a judgment'.[8]

First of all, an out of court settlement between the parties, made in writing before the competent Court (*Prozeßvergleich*), can be enforced as if it were a Court judgment.

Deeds which have been executed before a court or a notary public in Germany can also be enforced as judgments should the subject matter of the deed be a liquidated sum of money or a specific amount/number of goods or securities. Accordingly, a mortgage creditor whose claim appears as a fixed sum on the mortgage (*i.e.* when the mortgage is not a so-called 'maximal hypothek') does not need to obtain a Court order before his claim can be enforced.

In addition, German Court orders pertaining to periodical child maintenance payments, as well as interim injunctions and 'execution orders' (*Vollstreckungsbescheide*) granted by an under-judge in accordance with the summary procedure for collecting monetary debts [9] are also enforceable without a judgment.[10]

---

7 German CCP § 887 et seq.
8 German CCP § 794.
9 *Mahnverfahren*, German CCP §§ 688 – 733d. See *infra*.
10 For further information and other examples of 'enforceable titles' other than judgments see Othmar Jauernig, *Zwangsvollstreckungs- und Insolvenzrecht*, 20th ed. (Munich: Beck, 1996), § 3 V, pp. 24–25.

Domestic arbitral awards [11] are enforced as if they were Court judgments, provided that the arbitral award has been declared 'enforceable' by the State Court. An arbitral award may be declared enforceable if the subject matter of the award does not fall within the exclusive jurisdiction of the state courts, if recognising the award is not incompatible with the basic principles of German law, and finally, if the award is devoid of any important procedural defects which would otherwise render it invalid *e.g.* an infringement of the defendant's 'due process' rights.[12]

2. Provisional Enforceability

A German Court order can only be enforceable if it is a conclusive judgment in the formal sense (*i.e.* the defendant fails to file an appeal with the appellate court and / or the Court of Cassation or the higher Courts approve the judgment of the first instance Court) *or* it must be declared provisionally enforceable (*vorläufig vollstreckbar*) by the Trial Court.[13] In order for the judgment to be declared provisionally enforceable (*i.e.* before the judgment becomes conclusive), the Trial Court will normally require the plaintiff to make a payment into Court as security. The Trial Court may waive this requirement should the plaintiff be in financial difficulties,[14] or should one of the requirements for exemption listed in § 708 of the German CCP be fulfilled (*e.g.* where the order is granted in accordance with the summary procedure for enforcing the payment of debt in the case of cheques or other bills of exchange).

A provisionally enforceable judgment is enforced in the same way as a conclusive judgment and serves to settle the creditor's claims. However, should the provisionally enforceable judgment be subsequently overruled by a higher Court, then the creditor is obliged to return to the debtor all arrested moneys and other goods *etc.* and is also required to indemnify the debtor against any loss suffered as a result of the enforcement of the original judgment.[15]

---

11   For foreign arbitral awards cf. *infra*.
12   German CCP §§ 1041, 1042.
13   German CCP § 704.
14   German CCP § 710.
15   German CCP § 717.

3. Execution Clause

The enforceability of a judgment or other enforceable title is evidenced by an 'execution clause' (*Vollstreckungsklausel*).[16] An execution clause is an official clause which has to be inserted into an enforceable title (see *supra*) and is evidence that this can be enforced. The Trial Court will grant an execution clause in judgments passed by it and in settlements made before it. In the case of deeds which are executed before a Court or notary public, the execution clause must be issued by that Court or notary public.[17]

4. Service

The decree or other enforceable title must be served on the debtor.[18] Unlike in England, documents in Germany can only be served by the Court Executor and not by the relevant party (here: the creditor).[19]

5. Execution-counterclaim

A title to enforce a claim remains valid even if the judgment creditor's claim has been settled outside the execution procedure *e.g.* if he has received direct payment from the debtor. That is to say, a Court order is not automatically supervened by a subsequent out of Court payment of the debt. There is thus the possibility that the creditor may try to enforce a multiple claim on a debt by initiating civil execution proceedings against a debtor who has already discharged his liabilities.

The Code of Civil Procedure thus allows the debtor relief so that he may protect himself from a second enforcement of a claim for the payment of debt: the debtor is entitled, during the course of the execution proceedings, to raise a counter-action against the enforcement creditor before the Trial Court and have the execution proceedings declared inadmissible.[20]

---

16 German CCP § 725.
17 German CCP § 797.
18 German CCP § 750.
19 See German CCP §§ 166 et seq.
20 *Vollstreckungsgegenklage*, German CCP § 767.

6. Foreign Judgments / Exequatur [21]

A foreign judgment is incapable of being enforced without the judgment creditor first petitioning the competent German Court to grant a decree of recognition: this is termed *exequatur* or *Vollstreckungsurteil*.[22]

a) The basic rules governing exequatur proceedings are to be found in §§ 328, 722 and 723 of the Code of Civil Procedure. Thus, judgments of a foreign civil or commercial Court may only be recognised if they are deemed to be 'conclusive in the formal sense'. That is to say, a foreign judgment cannot be declared 'provisionally enforceable' (*cf. supra*) for the period during which the case is being heard before the appellate Court or the Court of Cassation.

Furthermore, § 328 German CCP lists a number of requirements which must be satisfied before a foreign judgment can be recognised and enforced. Thus,

(i) the foreign court which granted the decree must, *according to the rules of procedure in German law*, be recognised as having been a competent Court with the authority to make such an order;[23]

(ii) the documents initiating the proceedings must have been duly served and the defendant must have had the opportunity to appear before the Trial Court in his defence;

(iii) the foreign judgment must not be incompatible with any order of a domestic German Court (or indeed, with any judgment of another foreign Court which has already been duly recognised in Germany) or come

---

21 The literature relating to exequatur proceedings in Germany is extensive. For a general discussion of the subject (including 'recognition' of foreign judgments) see Haimo Schack, *Internationales Zivilverfahrensrecht*, 2nd ed. (Munich: Beck, 1996), pp. 305–68; Jan Kropholler, *Internationales Privatrecht*, 2nd ed. (Tübingen: Mohr, 1994), pp.529–55 (§60); Reinhold Geimer, *Internationales Zivilprozeßrecht*, 2nd ed. (Cologne: Schmidt, 1993), pp.636–729; Fritz Baur, Rolf Stürner and Adolf Schönke, *Zwangsvollstreckungs-, Konkurs- und Vergleichsrecht*, 11th ed. (Heidelberg: Müller, 1983), pp.22–39 (§3). For another selected bibliography see Peter Hartmann in Adolf Baumbach, Wolfgang Lauterbach, Jan Albers and Peter Hartmann, *Zivilprozeßordnung* (Commentary), 55th ed. (Munich: Beck, 1997), §§ 328 and 722; for an extensive bibliography see Dieter Martiny, 'Anerkennung ausländischer Entscheidungen nach autonomem Recht', *Handbuch des internationalen Zivilverfahrensrechts*, Vol. 3 / 1, Max - Planck - Institut für Ausländisches und Internationales Privatrecht (Tübingen: Mohr 1984), pp. 3–7.

22 See Leo Rosenberg, Hans Friedhelm Gaul and Eberhard Schilken, *Zwangsvollstreckungsrecht*, 10th ed. (Munich: Beck, 1987), pp.107–8.

23 For a similar rule see Chapter 2: Debt Recovery in England *infra*.

into conflict with the subject matter of an action which is still pending before the German courts and which had been raised before the action was brought before the foreign Court;

(iv) the foreign judgment must not be incompatible with German *ordre public*;

(v) between Germany and the country where the judgment was delivered, there must be the possibility that a similar German judgment could be enforced on a reciprocal basis.

Deeds and court settlements (see *supra*) issued in a foreign country may also be enforced in Germany according to the same basic rules.[24] However, the enforcement of foreign arbitral awards is regulated separately.[25]

These basic rules concerning the recognition and execution of foreign judgments are thus applicable to the execution of Turkish judgments in Germany.

The Turkish International Private and Procedural Law Act 1982 (IPPL) lays down an exequatur procedure similar to that in German law. IPPL lays down a 'reciprocity' requirement before foreign judgments can be enforced. Under Art. 38 /a IPPL however, the reciprocity requirement is satisfied even in the absence of an international agreement, where 'legal provisions' or 'actual practice' in the foreign country in question enables the enforcement of Turkish judgments to take place.[26] As a result of this, it is generally accepted in German literature,[27] that although there is no bilateral agreement in existence between Germany and Turkey which would otherwise provide for the reciprocal recognition and enforcement of judgments, the reciprocity requirement in § 338 of the German CCP is satisfied in the case of the enforcement of Turkish judgments in Germany. In addition,

---

24   Kropholler, *Internationales Privatrecht*, pp.537–8.
25   See German CCP § 1044. This provision has little practical importance as a result of the 1958 United Nations Convention on the Recognition and Enforcement of Foreign Arbitral Awards (*BGBl* 1961 II 121).
26   See *infra* Chapter 3: Debt Recovery in Turkey.
27   Hilmar Krüger, 'Das türkische IPR-Gesetz von 1982', *Praxis des internationalen Privat- und Verfahrensrechtst*, 2. Jahrgang (1982), pp. 252–9, at p.258 footnote 65; Rolf Schütze, 'Die Anerkennung und Vollstreckung deutscher Zivilurteile in West-Europa', *Deutsches Autorecht*, 53. Jahrgang (1983), pp. 110–5, at p.115; Dieter Heinrich, Note on the Judgment of the Court of Appeal, 'OLG Nürnberg' dated 20.9.1983, *Praxis des internationalen Privat- und Verfahrensrechts*, 4. Jahrgang (1984), pp. 162–3, at p.163; Martiny, *Handbuch des internationalen Zivilverfahrensrechts*, Vol.3 / 1, p.658 (§ 1508). Cf. Judgment of the Court of Appeal, 'OLG Braunschweig' dated 2.2.1984, *Niedersächsische Rechtspflege* (1984), p.96 (sceptical).

the German Federal Court of Justice (Federal Court of Cassation, *Bundesgerichtshof*) held in 1985, albeit *obiter dictum*, that since the coming into force of the Turkish International Private and Procedural Law Act 1982 (which laid down an exequatur procedure similar to that of German law), the requirements for reciprocal enforcement of judgments between Turkey and Germany have been satisfied and that therefore a Turkish judgment *could* be enforced in Germany under § 722 German CCP.[28] As will be seen below, the Turkish Court of Cassation decided in 1990, with reference to the above judgment of the German Federal Court, that the reciprocity rule concerning the enforcement of foreign judgments in Turkey had been satisfied *vis-à-vis* German judgments and that consequently, a German judgment could be declared enforceable in Turkey under the International Private and Procedural Law Act 1982.[29]

b) Apart from these general rules, Germany is a party to bilateral [30] and multilateral [31] conventions which make provision for the reciprocal enforcement of foreign judgments and which take the place of the above-mentioned general rules within their respective spheres of application. The two most important multilateral conventions are the Brussels and Lugano Conventions of 1968 and 1988 on the Jurisdiction and Enforcement of Judgments in Civil and Commercial Matters.[32] The Brussels Convention is applicable between the EU Member States and the Lugano Convention is applicable among the countries of the EU and EFTA. The provisions of these conventions are *in general* parallel with Art. 328 German CCP.[33] Nonetheless, the conventions allow judgments to be executed much more easily than under the CCP, because they set out uniform rules for a summary procedure including an ex parte application for an order for enforcement of

---

28 German Federal Court, *Bundesgerichtshof* 10.10.1985, *Neue Juristische Wochenschrift*, 39. Jahrgang (1986), pp.2195–6. The main problem dealt with in this judgment was whether a case pending in Turkey was a bar to a fresh action before a German court based on the same course of action under § 261 III of German CCP. For a decision on the same lines see the judgment of the Appellate Court in Düsseldorf dated 20.3.1985: OLG Düsseldorf, *Neue Juristische Wochenschrift*, 39. Jahrgang (1986), p.2202.
29 See Chapter 3: Debt Recovery in Turkey *infra*.
30 *E.g.* German - British Convention of 14.7.1960: *BGBl* 61 II 301.
31 See *e.g.* Hague Convention 1973, concerning the recognition and enforcement of maintenance orders, to which Turkey and Great Britain are also parties (*BGBl* 1986 II 826).
32 See respectively *BGBl* 1972 II 774, *BGBl* 1994 II 2658.
33 See *supra* and cf. Brussel Convention Arts.26 et seq.

the foreign judgment (which can be challenged by the defendant after being served), and it provides standard rules of international jurisdiction for the contracting states. Moreover, the very existence of the conventions guarantees that the requirement for 'reciprocity' can always be satisfied. The conventions also provide for the recognition and enforcement of 'provisionally enforceable' decrees which originate in other contracting states.[34]

English judgments are recognised and enforced in Germany according to the provisions of the Brussels Convention. However, the German-British Convention concerning the recognition and enforcement of judgments on a reciprocal basis [35] still finds application in those cases which are not covered by the Brussels Convention.[36]

D. SUMMARY PROCEDURES FOR THE RECOVERY OF DEBT

The German CCP provides simplified and speedy procedures for the recovery of debts duly payable. These are (1) summary default action procedure (§§ 688 et seq.) and (2) summary procedure on deeds and bills of exchanges and cheques (§§ 592 – 600, §§ 602 – 605 and § 605a, respectively).

---

[34] However, according to the European Court of Justice, *ex parte* orders concerning preliminary remedies for protection of the creditor is outwith the scope of the Convention [1980] ECR pp. 1553–4. See Peter Gottwald, 'Die internationale Zwangsvollstreckung', *Praxis des internationalen Privat- und Verfahrensrechts*, 11. Jahrgang, no.5 (1991), pp. 285–7.

[35] See *supra*.

[36] See Brussels Convention Arts.55–56 and Heinrich Nagel, *Internationales Zivilprozessrecht*, 3rd ed. (Münster: Aschendorf, 1991), Abschnitt XIX; Holger Müller and Götz-Sebastian Hök, *Deutsche Vollstreckungstitel im Ausland – Anerkennung, Vollstreckbarerklärung, Vollstreckung und Verfahrensführung in den einzelnen Ländern* (Frankfurt – Neuwied: Verlag Kurt Gross, looseleaf / 1988), Chapter: 'Großbritannien'; Hellmut Bauer, *Die Zwangsvollstreckung aus inländischen Schuldtiteln im Ausland* (Flensburg: Verlag Kurt Gross, looseleaf / 1994), Chapter: 'Großbritannien und Nordirland'. For further literature see Jan Peter Waehler, 'Anerkennung ausländischer Entscheidungen aufgrund bilateraler Staatsverträge', in *Handbuch des internationalen Zivilverfahrensrechts*, Vol. 3/2, Max - Planck - Institut für Ausländisches und Internationales Privatrecht (Tübingen: Mohr, 1984),pp. 213–306, at p.222; Martin K. Wolff, '*Vollstreckbarerklärung*', in *Handbuch des internationalen Zivilverfahrensrechts*, Vol. 3/2, Max - Planck - Institut für Ausländisches und Internationales Privatrecht (Tübingen: Mohr, 1984), pp. 317–557, at p. 527.

The summary default action procedure can only be made use of provided that the debt due is denoted in Deutschmark [37] and that the obligation to pay has arisen and is not contingent. The creditor – who in this context is referred to as the 'applicant' (*Antragsteller*), instead of the 'plaintiff'– initiates proceedings by filing an *ex parte* petition with the *Amtsgericht*. The Court (presided over by an under-judge) will issue an official reminder (*Mahnbescheid*), demanding him to pay the debt within two weeks or to provide the Court with valid objections. In case the debtor does not (timely) respond to the *Mahnbescheid*, the Court, acting on a petition by the applicant, will serve the debtor with a second official reminder (*Vollstreckungsbescheid*). The *Vollstreckungsbescheid* enjoys the same status as a 'provisionally enforceable' decree granted by default, which thus gives the applicant an enforceable title, but which may nonetheless be revoked by the Court should the debtor raise any objections before the *Amtsgericht*.[38] However, should the debtor object to the *Mahnbescheid*, it will cease to be effective and the creditor will have no choice but to raise a normal action for the performance of an obligation.

A *Mahnbescheid* may, exceptionally, be issued against a debtor outside of Germany, where this is permitted by the Act on the Implementation of the Recognition and Enforcement (of foreign judgments and orders) [39] and where the resulting *Vollstreckungsbescheid* would be given effect to by (*i.e.* the debt to be recovered is one that falls within the scope of) an international agreement on the reciprocal enforcement of judgments and orders to which Germany is a party.[40] In this case, the time limit for raising an objection to the *Mahnbescheid* is extended to one month [41] and the amount demanded need not to be converted into German currency.[42]

The summary procedure on deeds and bills of exchanges and cheques differs from the ordinary procedure in that, should the debtor raise an objection before the Amtsgericht, only documentary evidence (and statements

---

37 As a rule (cf. *infra*), debts denoted in a foreign currency must be converted into DM (*e.g.* German Federal Court Decision of 5 May 1988, *Entscheidungen des Bundesgerichtshofs in Zivilsachen* 104 (1989), p. 268).
38 See CCP §§ 700 and 338 and cf. *supra* 'Provisional enforceability'.
39 See German CCP § 688 III and 'Anerkennungs- und Vollstreckungsausführungsgesetz' of 30. 5. 1988 (*BGBl* I 662) §§ 34, 35.
40 Rolf Wagner, 'Verfahrensrechtliche Probleme im Auslandsmahnverfahren', *Recht der internationalen Wirtschaft*, 41. Jahrgang (1995), pp. 89–97, at p.90.
41 Anerkennungs- und Vollstreckungsausführungsgesetz § 34 III.
42 Hartmann in Baumbach, Lauterbach, Albers and Hartmann, *Zivilprozeßordnung*, § 688, Rn. 2 and 9.

made by the parties) are admissible. In particular, witnesses cannot be examined.[43] This procedure may only be made use of when it is specifically applied for, and where the debt concerns a definite sum of money. The decree which is granted under this summary procedure is enforceable, but it is not a conclusive judgment based on the merits of the case, rather it is a so-called 'provisional order' (*Vorbehaltsurteil*). Thus, the defendant who loses the case may choose to continue the procedure after the provisional judgment in order to obtain a 'final' judgment in his favour (*Nachverfahren*). This is not an appeal, rather the proceedings will continue in the very same Court and are complementary to the summary procedure. At this stage, the defendant is nonetheless permitted to prove his case by any means *i.e.* with evidence other than documentary evidence. Should the final judgment be for the defendant, the plaintiff who has enforced the provisional judgment will be obliged to make restitution and to compensate the defendant for any loss suffered.

E. ENFORCING MONETARY CLAIMS

1. In General

German law provides various ways in which to enforce decrees for the payment of money (or any other 'enforceable title' for the payment of money), and the application of these remedies depends on the type of property against which action is to be taken *i.e.* there are various remedies available depending on whether movable property is to be attached,[44] on whether a so-called charging order is to be issued against immovable property,[45] or whether debts due to the debtor are to be arrested or any other property of the debtor otherwise attached.[46]

As a general rule, the judgment creditor enjoys the right to identify those assets of the debtor which are to be impounded.[47] Where the creditor does not have sufficient knowledge of the debtor's income and assets, and the value of the properties found and attached by the Court Executor does not

---

43   Cf. Turkish CCP (Arts. 288 et seq.) where practically all monetary contractual obligations can only be proved by means of documentary evidence.
44   German CCP §§ 803 et seq.
45   *Ibid.* §§ 864 et seq.
46   *Ibid.* §§ 828 et seq.
47   Jauernig, *Zwangsvollstreckungs- und Insolvenzrecht*, p.130.

cover the outstanding debt, §807 of the Code of Civil Procedure entitles the Execution Court, acting on an application of the creditor, to require the debtor to submit a list of his income and assets (*eidesstattliche Offenbarungsversicherung*). Should the debtor refuse to abide by the Execution Court's order, he is liable to be sent to prison for contempt of Court.[48] The Court keeps a register of the names of those persons against whom an order under § 807 of the Code of Civil Procedure has been made, and their details are kept for three years on this 'black list', during which time people who have legal interest to do so in accordance with § 915 II CCP may examine the register.[49] In practice, § 807 of the Code of Civil Procedure provides an effective remedy. In order to avoid a registration in the black list, the debtor may pay off the debt using his last resources or possibilities to obtain credit.[50]

a) Attachment: execution against movable property

The enforcement of a Court order against movable property for the purposes of the recovery of debts (*Zwangsvollstreckung in das bewegliche Vermögen*) is effected by way of attachment (*Pfändung*).

The attachment of property is carried out by the Court Executor. It is effected when the Court Executor physically seizes the debtor's chattels. As a result of the seizure of the chattels (*Verstrickung*), a statutory charge is created

---

48 German CCP § 901.
49 See German CCP §§ 915–915h, as amended and partly inserted into the Code by an Act of 15.7.1994 (*BGBl* I 1566). Previously, 'debtor lists' were accessible to 'everybody' without any requirement of having a legal interest to do so being present. See Heinz Thomas and Hans Putzo, *Zivilprozeßordnung* (Commentary), 17th ed. (Munich: Beck, 1991), § 915, No.2; Hartmann in Baumbach, Lauterbach, Albers and Hartmann, *Zivilprozeßordnung*, 51st ed. (Munich: Beck, 1993), § 915, Rn.8; cf. Hartmann in Baumbach, Lauterbach, Albers and Hartmann, *Zivilprozeßordnung*, 55th ed., commentary on §§ 915 and 915b; Thomas and Putzo, *Zivilprozeßordnung*, 19th ed. (Munich: Beck, 1995) commentary on §§ 915 and 915b. The new law is criticised by debt collectors. Referring to the recent amendment of § 915, a debt collector complained that because of strict data protection regulations in Germany, there is no legal mechanism by which a creditor can learn about the financial position of his would-be debtor (Interview with the German Debt Collector 2).
50 Prior to the amendment to § 915 of German CCP, 20% of the debtors used to pay off the debt as a result of the request for a declaration of means and assets according to § 807. Jürgen M. Klein, 'Die Vollstreckung von Geldforderungen durch den Gerichtsvollzieher (aus rechtstatsächlicher Sicht)', in Erhard Blankenburg and Rüdiger Voigt (eds), *Implementation von Gerichtsentscheidungen – Jahrbuch für Rechtssoziologie und Rechtstheorie* 11 (Opladen: Westdeutscher Verlag, 1987), pp. 49–71, pp. 51–2.

in favour of the enforcement creditor, which grants him priority against any other unsecured creditor who attempts to attach the same item at a later date [51] (*Pfändungspfandrecht* = attachment charge).[52]

The Court Executor seizes the goods and chattels in the immediate possession of the debtor, without becoming involved in the substantive law question as to whether the debtor is the actual owner of the property. Should the seized chattels actually belong to a third party, then it is necessary for the third party to raise an action *against the enforcement creditor* before the ordinary courts, so that his property be exempted from the attachment proceedings and be repatriated to him (*Widerspruchsklage* [53]).

On the other hand, in case movables owned by the debtor are in the possession of a third party, the creditor cannot have these attached as such, rather he is only able to make a claim against the third party on the basis of his cause of action against the debtor (in strict terms, he can attach the *cause of action* which belongs to the debtor *vis-à-vis* the third party for the recovery of the movables, *i.e. Herausgabeanspruch*). In order to have the movable actually attached and realised, the enforcement creditor has to sue the third party before the ordinary courts and force him to return the goods or chattels to the court executor.[54]

The sale of the movables in order to settle the creditor's claims is carried out by the Court Executor by public auction (*öffentliche Versteigerung* [55]). For the protection of the debtor – and, as the case may be, other parties – the Code of Civil Procedure lays down a minimum sale price (minimum bid, *Mindesgebot*) rule.[56] The minimum sale price is half of the actual market price.[57] Sale by public auction represents a quasi-contract of sale which has its basis in public law and it is concluded when the (highest) bid is formally accepted by the Court Executor (*Zuschlag*). The *Zuschlag* creates only a personal right; the real right in the movables is transferred to the buyer by a separate act of the Court Executor: the delivery (*Ablieferung*). Similarly, the enforcement creditor gains the ownership over the proceeds of the sale when the moneys are delivered to him by the Court Executor.

---

51 Cf. *infra* Chapters 3: Debt Recovery in Turkey, and Chapter 2: Debt Recovery in England.
52 German CCP § 804. The legal nature of the attachment charge is controversial. See Jauernig, *Zwangsvollstreckungs- und Insolvenzrecht*, pp. 70–1.
53 German CCP § 771.
54 German CCP § 846 et seq. Cf. *infra* Chapter 3: Debt Recovery in Turkey.
55 German CCP § 814 et seq.
56 Cf. *infra* Chapter 2: Debt Recovery in England.
57 Cf. *infra* Chapter 3: Debt Recovery in Turkey.

b) Execution against immovable property

Enforcing claims against immovable property (*Zwangsvollstreckung in das unbewegliche Vermögen*) is largely regulated by the Act on Public Auction Sales and Administration 1897 ('Public Auctions Act'). The term 'immovable property' does not only refer to land and related collateral rights (*grundstücksgleiche Rechte, e.g.* right to have a building on land belonging to another, *Erbbaurecht*) but also to ships and aeroplanes.[58]

There are three different ways the creditor can choose from in which to enforce a claim against immovable property. These are (i) Public Auction Sale (*Zwangsversteigerung*), (ii) Administration (*Zwangsverwaltung*) and (iii) creation of a charging order (*Zwangshypothek*).

The Administration method is of practical importance for the enforcement of a claim against commercial and rented property, especially if the creditor is looking to settle his claims through a share in capital or through other periodical payments. The Administrator (*Zwangsverwalter*) is appointed by the Execution Court. The judgment debtor himself will normally be appointed the Administrator of commercial property, and will be placed under the control of a supervisor.[59] The Administrator is bound to continue the business operations which take place on the property and has responsibility for collecting rents and profits on behalf of the creditor. The Administrator has no power to dispose of the land itself.

The creation of a charging order [60] does not immediately settle the creditor's claims, but it will provide him with a real security right in the property concerned and will also secure him a ranking in the list of secured creditors, enabling him to initiate other methods of execution at a more convenient point of time. This method thus only has practical significance for unsecured creditors. The Land-Registrar (*Grundbuchamt*), who is also an Under-judge, is the relevant Execution Officer who is responsible for enforcing a charging order.

Sale by public auction is regulated in detail by the Public Auctions Act. The competent Execution Officer is the Execution Court itself. Upon the application of the creditor, the Execution Court will make an order for public auction, with the effect of preventing the debtor from transferring

---

[58] German CCP § 864, Public Auctions Act §162.
[59] Public Auctions Act §§ 150b, 150c. See Jauernig, *Zwangsvollstreckungs- und Insolvenzrecht*, pp.116–7.
[60] German CCP §§ 866 III, 867–8.

the property to another person.[61] An order for public auction provides the execution creditor with a priority ranking in the case of bankruptcy,[62] but it does not create any security rights *vis-à-vis* other individual creditors of the execution debtor.[63]

The Execution Court will thereafter order and advertise the date of the public auction. A 'minimum sale price', *i.e.* 50% of the market price of the immovable is also applicable here. Nonetheless, this 'minimum price rule' will be waived should a second auction have to be held, the first auction having been unsuccessful.[64] In any case, the immovable property can only be sold once the highest bid made is enough to cover in full all the claims of those other creditors who have a ranking higher than that of the creditor who has caused the auction to be held (*i.e.* creditors whose secured rights in the immovable property have a higher ranking) (Covering Principle, *Deckungsprinzip* [65]). As a rule, the buyer who buys the immovable property will acquire it along with all the existing rights secured in it (*i.e.* security rights of the 'higher ranking creditors' are neither extinguished nor paid out with the execution sale) [66] and he himself becomes liable to these secured creditors. The buyer pays what remains after the total amount of higher ranking debts have been subtracted from the price (the 'transfer principle', *Übernahmeprinzip*).[67]

The (highest) bid made in the public auction sale is accepted by the Execution Court by way of an Order of the Court (*Zuschlag*), which will automatically transfer ownership of the immovable property to the buyer.[68]

c) Garnishee procedure

The competent Execution Officer for garnishee proceedings ('execution against money claims', *Zwangsvollstreckung in Geldforderungen*) is the Execution Court and is again presided over by an Under-judge.[69]

---

61 *Beschlagnahme des Grundstücks*, Public Auctions Act §§ 15, 20, 23.
62 Bankruptcy Act = *Konkursordnung* § 47.
63 Jauernig, *Zwangsvollstreckungs- und Insolvenzrecht*, p. 110.
64 Cf. *supra* 'Attachment' in this chapter.
65 Public Auctions Act § 44.
66 For the exceptions (*inter alia* the wages of employees who are employed on land used for agricultural purposes and the property tax accumulated in the previous two years) see Public Auctions Act § 10 Nr. 1 – 3.
67 Public Auctions Act § 52 I. Cf. *infra* Chapter 3: Debt Recovery in Turkey.
68 Cf. *supra* 'Attachment' in this chapter.
69 German CCP § 828, Under-judges Act § 20, Nr.17.

As a rule, any debt – except for one arising out of tortual liability [70]– can be attached under German procedure, regardless of the reason therefor. Negotiable instruments and securities are however regarded as movables and they are thus subject to the rules applicable to Attachment in ordinary cases.[71] Unlike in England,[72] the 'Attachment of Earnings' is also subject to the general garnishee provisions.[73]

Attaching the debtor's bank accounts is of greatest practical significance. Garnishee proceedings begin with an *ex parte* application by the execution creditor to the Execution Court. The Execution Court will examine the grounds of action to ensure that there is indeed a genuine enforceable claim (*i.e.* whether there is an 'enforceable title' and an 'execution clause' and whether the deed has been served upon the debtor [74]) and, should it be probable that the third party is indeed indebted to the debtor, will grant a garnishee order (*Pfändungsbeschluß*).

The garnishee order is served upon the debtor's debtor (garnishee, third party debtor, *Drittschuldner*) *and* upon the judgment debtor. It orders the garnishee not to pay the debt to the judgment debtor, and the judgment debtor not to receive (or otherwise dispose of) any payments from the garnishee.

The judgement debtor is entitled to object against the garnishee order by using the general Reminder (*Erinnerung*) procedure.[75] On the other hand, as opposed to the case in English and Turkish law, the garnishee himself need not have to object to the garnishee order. A garnishee order does not effect the legal position of the garnishee *vis-à-vis* the holder of the attached claim.[76] That is to say, should the garnishee have reasonable cause not to make a payment to the judgment debtor, then the garnishee is also entitled to assert this right against the judgment creditor who has attached the debt.[77] The garnishee is thus only obliged to make payment to the judgment creditor if and insofar as he would have been liable to make payment to the judgment debtor.

---

70   Jauernig, *Zwangsvollstreckungs- und Insolvenzrecht*, p.86.
71   German CCP §§ 821 – 831. Securities which have a stock market value or market price are sold by the Court Executor by handsale without a public auction being held.
72   Cf. *infra*.
73   For the protection of the debtor in garnishee proceedings see *infra* 'Protection of the Debtor' in this chapter.
74   See *supra*.
75   See *infra*.
76   Jauernig, *Zwangsvollstreckungs- und Insolvenzrecht*, p.91.
77   German Civil Code §§ 412 and 404.

Garnishee proceedings involve settling the creditor's claims by assigning the debt to him. The assignment is made by an order of the Court (assignment order, *Überweisungsbeschluß*) and transfers the legal rights and remedies to the enforcement creditor. In practice, the assignment and garnishee orders are granted together on the same day.[78] Should the garnishee refrain from paying the execution creditor or disputes his liability, the execution creditor has no choice but to sue him before the ordinary courts. If, on the other hand, the garnishee pays the execution creditor without raising any objections, he will be deemed to have discharged his liabilities to the judgment debtor.

Garnishee proceedings against third party debtors resident abroad cause difficulties for the enforcement creditor.[79] It has been reported in the relevant literature that it is very difficult in Germany – if not impossible – to serve a garnishee order abroad. German courts will usually refrain from forwarding garnishee orders to those competent foreign authorities which otherwise have the authority to serve the order on the third party debtor;[80] and, should a garnishee order have been forwarded to the relevant foreign authority, the latter will not serve the order.[81] If a garnishee (and assignment) order is served upon the third party debtor abroad and he refuses to pay the execution creditor voluntarily, the execution creditor's only option is to sue the third party debtor. Initiating such an action against the third party debtor will also pose difficulties. This is so, because if the execution creditor has to sue the third party debtor abroad (*e.g.* because of a jurisdiction clause in the main contract between the judgment debtor and the third party debtor), the foreign court may not recognise his *locus standi* for such a lawsuit.[82]

---

78 Jauernig, *Zwangsvollstreckungs- und Insolvenzrecht*, p.90.
79 See also *infra*.
80 German CCP § 119.
81 See Reinhard Welter, *Zwangsvollstreckung und Arrest in Forderungen – insbesondere Kontenpfändung – in Fällen mit Auslandsberührung* (Frankfurt am Main: Wertpapier - Mitteilungen, 1988), pp. 45–6; Kurt Stöber, *Forderungspfändung*, 10th ed. (Bielefeld: Gieseking, 1993), Rn.39; Baur, Stürner and Schönke, *Zwangsvollstreckungs-, Konkurs- und Vergleichsrecht*, Rn.79; cf. Haimo Schack, 'Internationale Zwangsvollstreckung in Geldforderungen', *Der Deutsche Rechtspfleger*, 88. Jahrgang (1980), p. 175–8; Gottwald, 'Die internationale Zwangsvollstreckung', p. 289; Rolf Stürner, 'Das grenzübergreifende Vollstreckungsverfahren in der Europäischen Union', in Walter Gerhardt, Uwe Diederichsen, Bruno Rimmelspacher and Jürgen Costede (eds), *Festschrift für Wolfram Henckel zum 70. Geburtstag am 21. April 1995* (Berlin and New York: Gruyter, 1995), pp. 863–75, at pp. 865–7.
82 Schack, *Internationales Zivilverfahrensrecht*, Rn.986.

2. Monetary Claims Based on a Foreign Judgment (or on another Foreign Enforceable Title)

As has been discussed above, the enforcement of monetary claims based on a foreign judgment or another foreign enforceable title (*e.g.* a court settlement [83]) is possible, provided that a recognition order has been granted by the competent German Court which has the effect of declaring the foreign title enforceable in Germany.

By its nature, civil execution is said to involve the use of sovereign powers, in that it usually [84] involves the exercise of public authority against the debtor (*e.g.* the seizure of property). For this reason, rules of civil execution are always a part of national domestic law and they can only be applied within national boundaries. It follows that:

(i) a foreign judgment (or another foreign enforceable title) which is declared enforceable under an exequatur-order in Germany will be enforced in the same way as a domestic enforceable title, *and*
(ii) the acts of a German Execution Officer are, *as a rule*, effective and enforceable only within the geographic boundaries of the country, *i.e.* against the property or persons situated within the jurisdiction of German courts.

An important exception to the latter is that an Execution Court in Germany does have the authority to serve a *garnishee order* upon a third party debtor who is resident outside of Germany. This is the case due to the fact that garnishee proceedings in German law do not involve 'the use of public powers' against the third party debtor to make him pay the enforcement creditor, rather will only *inform him* that any payment made to the judgment debtor shall not extinguish the debt. That is to say, the serving of a garnishee order abroad is not a use of sovereign powers outside the jurisdiction of German courts. [85,86]

The international jurisdiction of the German Execution Officer in the enforcement of monetary claims arises out of the movable and immovable

---

[83] See *supra*.
[84] See Schack, *Internationales Zivilverfahrensrecht*, Rn. 957 and cf. *infra* Chapter 9: Routinisation and Privatisation of Debt Collection.
[85] Schack, 'Internationale Zwangsvollstreckung in Geldforderungen', p. 176; Stöber, *Forderungspfändung*, Rn. 38–39.
[86] For problems concerning the serving of German garnishee orders abroad see *supra*.

property, which is to be affected by the enforcement procedure (*e.g.* by attachment), being situated on German territory.[87]

In the case of garnishee proceedings however, the judgment (execution) debtor's having his domicile or some property within Germany suffices to give rise to the international jurisdiction of German Execution Officers.[88]

German Execution Officers will only apply the German law of civil enforcement to proceedings which have been duly initiated in Germany. The question whether a particular movable is exempt from attachment is, for example, answered according to German law.[89]

Similarly, remedies against the acts of Execution Officers which are granted to either of the parties – *i.e.* the *Erinnerung* (reminder) against the acts of the Court Executor, the *Widerspruchsklage* of a third party whose movables have been seized from the judgment debtor [90] and the *Vollstreckungsgegenklage* (execution-counterclaim) which protects the judgment debtor from a repeated debt action should the creditor's claims have been settled out of Court [91] – are fully subject to German law and to the jurisdiction of the German courts.[92]

As a rule, a foreign judgment ordering the payment of a particular sum in a foreign currency is regarded enforceable in Germany as a judgment ordering the payment of money (*i.e.* not as a judgment concerning the 'delivery of goods' or the 'doing of an act').[93] Should the judgment debtor

---

87 German CCP §§ 808 and 866. See Schack, *Internationales Zivilverfahrensrecht*, Rn.960.
88 See German CCP §§ 828 II and 23. In German literature it is further claimed that the fact that the third party debtor has his domicile in Germany will also be sufficient to render the German Execution Officers competent (Schack, *Internationales Zivilverfahrensrecht*, Rn. 982; Schack, 'Internationale Zwangsvollstreckung in Geldforderungen', pp. 175–6; Hartmann in Baumbach, Lauterbach, Albers and Hartmann, *Zivilprozeßordnung*, §828, Rn.4.). This interpretation is not compatible with the wording of §23 German CCP. It is evident that the venue provision in §23 which refers to the 'domicile of the debtor' is aimed at the debtor who is indebted to a creditor who in turn, is intending to sue (*i.e.* it is aimed at the defendant or the execution debtor). The (third party) debtor who is indebted to 'the debtor' is not the debtor within the meaning of § 23; see *e.g.* Stöber, *Forderungspfändung*, Rn. 446.
89 Schack, *Internationales Zivilverfahrensrecht*, Rn.961.
90 German CCP § 771.
91 *Ibid.* § 767.
92 German CCP § 811, *ibid.* Rn. 989–92.
93 Rosenberg, Gaul and Schilken, *Zwangsvollstreckungsrecht*, p.112; Dieter Medicus and Karsten Schmidt, '§§ 243 – 254' in *J. von Staudingers Kommentar zum Bürgerlichen Gesetzbuch mit Einführungsgesetz und Nebengesetzen, Zweites Buch*, 12th ed. (Berlin: J. Schweitzer, 1983), § 244, Rn. 113.

40 *Making Foreign People Pay*

not be in the possession of money in the relevant currency (which could be seized and delivered to the creditor by the Court Executor [94]), the foreign currency debt must be converted into Deutschmark during the execution proceedings.[95] Such a conversion cannot be made earlier in the exequatur-order.[96] So that the judgment creditor can settle his claims in full, the currency is converted according to the exchange rate applicable on the day on which the creditor is paid by the Court Executor, *e.g.* when the proceeds of the warrant sale are paid to the creditor.[97] In practice, the Court Executor will call a local branch of a private bank in order to obtain the conversion rate applicable on the day when the payment is made or the recovery of the debt carried out.[98]

F. PROTECTION OF THE DEBTOR

Enforcing a civil claim (through the Execution Officers) against the debtor's property is only permissible to the extent that it is necessary for the creditor to settle his claims and for the recoupment of the costs involved.[99] Furthermore, the Code of Civil Procedure makes provision for the protection of the debtor against any harshness in the debt recovery process which may cause him severe financial difficulty. Thus, § 811 provides a catalogue of goods and chattels which are exempt from the Court Executor's power of seizure, which includes for example clothing, bedding and tools used at work. Similarly, the debtor's earnings can only be attached insofar as there is no harshness caused to him and his family.[100] German law however, as opposed to Turkish law,[101] does not recognise an 'exemption from execution' as regards immovable property.

---

94 German CCP § 815.
95 See Frederich Arend, *Zahlungsverbindlichkeiten in fremder Währung* (Frankfurt am Main, Bern, New York, Paris: Lang, 1989), pp. 171–87.
96 Hartmann in Baumbach, Lauterbach, Albers and Hartmann, *Zivilprozeßordnung*, § 722, Rn. 3; Schack, *Internationales Zivilverfahrensrecht*, Rn. 963.
97 See German Civil Code § 244 II; Arend, *Zahlungsverbindlichkeiten in fremder Währung*. Cf. Schack, *Internationales Zivilverfahrensrecht*, Rn. 965.
98 German Court Executor.
99 German CCP § 803 I.
100 See *ibid.* §§ 850 et seq.
101 See *infra*.

G. PRELIMINARY REMEDIES FOR THE PROTECTION OF THE CREDITOR

The court proceedings which are required in order to obtain an enforceable judgment against the debtor are time consuming, and during this time it is possible that a debtor may attempt to move his assets out of the creditor's reach. In order to protect the creditor during this period of time, the Code of Civil Procedure provides a provisional remedy for the creditor (Preliminary Attachment, *Arrest* [102]).

Thus, the creditor may petition the ordinary civil courts for a 'preliminary attachment order' and this will initiate summary proceedings. The Court will pronounce judgment either after a hearing or in the absence of the debtor ('the surprise effect'). In the latter case, the debtor may initiate a later hearing by raising an objection against the *ex parte* order.[103]

The creditor is obliged to begin the enforcement procedure for preliminary attachment within one month of the judgment being delivered or the notice of the decision being served on the debtor. The preliminary attachment is made in the same way as an ordinary attachment, but no sale of the attached property takes place. Seizure of movables in preliminary attachment proceedings creates, as is in the case of normal attachment proceedings, a statutory charge on the goods and chattels in favour of the creditor *vis-à-vis* other unsecured creditors (*Arrestpfandrecht*). The preliminary attachment of *immovables* is only possible by registering a so-called *maximal Hypothek* (a mortgage claim in which the claim is not fixed [104]) with the Land Registry.

Should the creditor succeed on the merits of the case, then the preliminary attachment will automatically change to a full attachment and the creditor will be entitled to enforce a warrant sale. However, should the creditor be unsuccessful in his action, the 'debtor' will be entitled to sue him for the losses incurred through the preliminary attachment.[105] The creditor's liability here is strict.[106]

---

[102] German CCP §§ 916 et. seq.
[103] German CCP § 924.
[104] German Civil Code § 1184.
[105] German CCP § 945.
[106] For other remedies for the protection of the debtor in preliminary attachment procedure see German CCP §§ 923, 926 and 927.

H. COSTS

The costs incurred through initiating enforcement proceedings do not form part of the (Trial) Court's costs. These costs – including counsel fees – are nonetheless borne by the debtor in Germany [107] without there being a need to obtain a separate order for costs. However, should a judgment which has been enforced be revoked by a Court of higher instance, then the creditor is obliged to repay these costs to the debtor. [108]

---

107   Cf. *infra* Chapter 2: Debt Recovery in England.
108   German CCP § 788.

2 Debt Recovery in England

AS COMPARED WITH TURKISH AND GERMAN LAW, AND WITH SPECIAL REFERENCE TO THE EXECUTION OF FOREIGN JUDGMENTS

A. LEGAL BASIS

Civil execution in England is the same as that in Germany in the sense that it is considered to be a part of the civil procedure.[1] The applicable rules governing civil execution proceedings are mainly to be found in the Rules of Supreme Court 1965 ('RSC') and the County Court Rules 1981 ('CCR') which govern the procedure in the High Court of Justice ('High Court') and in the County Courts respectively.[2] Thus, in order to distinguish the fields

---

[1] The term 'civil procedure' has a narrower meaning in English compared to the virtually identical terms in German and Turkish legal terminology (*i.e.* '*Zivilprozeßrecht*' and '*medeni usul hukuku*'), because Evidence (*Beweisrecht, ispat teorisi*) – including the doctrine of res judicata (*Rechtskraft, kesin hüküm*) – is a separate discipline in English law and covers both civil and criminal procedures. For a general introduction to English civil procedure see John O'Hare and Robert N. Hill, *Civil Litigation*, 7th ed. (London: FT Law & Tax, 1996) or R. Greenslade (ed.), *Civil Court Practice* (London, Dublin, Edinburgh: Butterworths, 1994) ('Introduction' chapters); John Beechey, 'Litigation', in Barbara Ford (ed.), *Doing Business in the United Kingdom*, Vol. I (New York: Matthew Bender, loose-leaf / 1993) (36 pages); John Fage and Gary Whitehead, *Supreme Court Practice and Procedure*, 5th ed. (London: Tolley, 1992) (a textbook in a nutshell); in German language: Jürgen Bunge, *Zivilprozeß und Zwangsvollstreckung in England* (Berlin: Duncker & Humblot, 1995). For legislative developments: see D. B. Casson, and Ian H. Dennis, *Modern Developments in the Law of Civil Procedure* (London: Sweet & Maxwell, 1982), 'Chapter 6: Aspects of Enforcement' and *inter alia* Courts and Legal Services Act 1991, Supreme Courts Act 1981.

[2] For the texts of the Rules with annotations see two practice books '*The Supreme Court Practice*' ('White Book') and '*County Court Practice*' ('Green Book') which are respectively being published biannually and annually in London by Sweet & Maxwell.

of application of these two sets of rules, it is of importance to acknowledge the respective jurisdictional limits of the aforementioned courts.

In contrast to what the term 'High Court' may suggest, the relationship between the High Court and County Courts is not one of two instances but is a question of jurisdiction (*sachliche Zuständigkeit, görev*). Since 1991 however, the allocation of legal matter between the High Court and the County Courts has been governed by the High Court and County Courts Jurisdiction Order [3] which has to a large extent abolished the previous financial limitations on the County Courts jurisdiction.[4] At present and as a rule, the High Court and the County Courts exercise concurrent jurisdiction thus enabling a plaintiff to commence proceedings in either one of these courts, subject to a personal injury action where if the value of the claim is less than £5000 it must commence in the County Court. However, court proceedings may be transferred from the County Court to the High Court and *vice versa* in light of the financial substance, importance, complexity and speed of the matter at stake.[5]

The High Court and County Courts exercise concurrent jurisdiction not only in the field of main proceedings (*Erkenntnisverfahren*) but also in that of civil execution, *i.e.* for the enforcement of judgments.[6] As a rule, a creditor in both the County Court and in the High Court has the option at his own discretion of either enforcing the judgment obtained in the High Court or in the County Court.[7]

---

3   Statutory Instruments 1991, No. 724 (L 5).
4   See *Osborn's Concise Law Dictionary*, 7th ed. (London: Sweet & Maxwell, 1983), 'County Courts'.
5   High Court and County Courts Jurisdiction Order 1991, sec.7.
6   See Alastair Black and Duncan Black, *Enforcement of a Judgment*, 8th ed. (London: Longman, 1992), 'Chapter 6: Transfer Between High Court and County Court'.
7   The exceptions to this rule are that a County Court judgment for payment of a sum of money which is sought to enforce by execution against goods (see *infra*) shall be enforced only by – and, in case the necessity arises, must be transferred to – the High Court where the sum which is sought to enforce is £5000 or more; and (such a judgment) shall be enforced only by – and, in case, must be transferred to – a County Court where the sum which is sought to enforce is less than £2000. Similarly a charging order (see *infra*) for a sum less than £5000 can only be enforced by a County Court: High Court and County Courts Jurisdiction Order 1991, sec. 8; Charging Orders Act 1979, sec. 1(2). See also Practice Direction [Queen's Bench Division] County Court: Transfer of Action [1991] 1 WLR 643. Besides, County Courts do not have the power to grant some of the remedies for protection of the creditor, namely *Mareva* and *Anton Piller* orders. A creditor who wants to make use of these remedies must choose to commence proceedings at the High Court; see *infra*.

In addition to the provisions of RSC and CCR which are in essence *statutory instruments* [8] made in accordance with the provisions of the Supreme Court Act 1981 (secs. 84, 85, 87) and the County Courts Act 1984 (sec. 75), the Attachment of Earnings Act 1971 and the Charging Orders Act 1979 are of particular importance in connection with execution proceedings. The former governs a special type of garnishee procedure for the attachment of earnings and the latter sets out the procedure for making charging orders against immovable property.[9]

B. CIVIL EXECUTION OFFICERS [10]

The officer who is of central importance in English civil execution proceedings is the Sheriff. Broadly speaking, a Sheriff is the counterpart in English law of the 'Court Executor' and the 'Execution Officer' in terms of German and Turkish law.[11] He has namely the power to execute High Court judgments for money and make orders against movable property as well as being able to enforce the judgments and orders of the same Court concerning the delivery of goods (RSC Ord. 45, r.4) or the recovery of immovable property (RSC Ord. 45, r.3).[12]

A Sheriff is not an officer of the High Court,[13] rather an officer of the Crown who is, in addition to his duties in the area of civil procedure, in charge of parliamentary elections and execution processes from the criminal

---

8 *I.e.* secondary legislation made – in this case – by and subject to the approval of the Lord Chancellor (the Minister of Justice and the President of the Supreme Court).
9 See *infra*.
10 The author conducted an interview with a 'Sheriff Officer' in England on 9.2.1996. The Sheriff Officer was questioned about the practical aspects of civil execution, especially in connection with cases having cross-border elements. Some information below and in the 'Conclusions' (*infra*) are taken from this interview. In addition, a book which has been written by three colleagues of the interview partner (a solicitor and two lately Sherriff's Officers) gives some insight into civil execution in England: J. A. Keith, W. B. Podevin and Claire Sandbrook, *The Execution of Sheriffs' Warrants* (Chichester, West Sussex: Barry Law Publishers, 1996). References to this book are made in the form of quotations, where the relevant information relates to the practical aspects of the Sheriff's work.
11 *Gerichtsvollzieher, icra memuru.*
12 See Black and Black, *Enforcement of a Judgment*, Chapter 5: Remedies Pursued Through the Sheriff.
13 The High Court has no officers of its own for the purpose of executing judgments, D. B. Casson, *Odgers on High Court Pleading and Practice*, 23rd ed. (London: Sweet & Maxwell / Steven, 1991), p.416.

courts *etc.*[14] A Sheriff is appointed for each county for ('no more than') one year [15] and is usually not employed full-time in that office but has in addition a private practice as a solicitor.[16] A Sheriff is assisted in his office by an Under-Sheriff, Deputy Sheriffs and Bailiffs who are appointed by the Sheriff himself.[17] 'To ensure the continuity within the office, it is usual for the Sheriff to appoint an Under Sheriff who is experienced and likewise Officers who are similarly experts in their fields.'[18] However, there is no compulsion for the Sheriff to appoint either the Under Sheriff or the Officers of his predecessor.[19] This in turn motivates the Under Sheriff and the Officers to work more efficiently in order to maintain their employment when the new Sheriff has been appointed.[20] As a result of the annual re-appointment of the Sheriff, the Sheriff himself must also prove a high level of performance. The Sheriff's Offices are usually organised in the form of partnership and sometimes as limited companies.[21]

In the field of civil execution, the Sheriff is under an obligation to obey the 'writ of execution' of the court – commanding him to enforce the judgment [22] – and in addition, the lawful instructions of the creditor.[23] In the case where acts or omissions of the Sheriff are considered to be a breach of law or legal procedure, *e.g.* in the case of wrongful or excessive seizure of the property of the debtor, the Sheriff is liable under the provisions of the law of tort *e.g.*: joint and several liability, as the case may be, together with the creditor.[24] In contrast to the provisions of German [25] and

---

14 *Osborn's Concise Law Dictionary*, 8th ed. by Leslie Rutherford and Sheila Bone (London: Sweet & Maxwell, 1993), 'Sheriff'; Bunge, *Zivilprozeß und Zwangsvollstreckung in England*, p. 24–5.
15 Sheriffs Act 1887, sec. 3.
16 Lutz Krauskopf, 'Das britische Vollstreckungsrecht', *Blätter für Schuldbetreibung und Konkurs*, 42. Jahrgang, no.4 (1978), pp. 97–109, at pp.99–100.
17 Bailiffs who are employed in a Sheriff's Office are also called Sheriff's Officers or Serjeant at Mace. The Sheriff is legally responsible for the acts of his officers. In practice, Sheriffs take out professional indemnity insurance. Keith, Podevin and Sandbrook, *The Execution of Sheriffs' Warrants*, p. 4.
18 *Ibid.*, p. 3.
19 *Ibid.*
20 The interview with the Sheriff's Officer.
21 The interview with the Sheriff's Officer.
22 See *infra*.
23 Black and Black, *Enforcement of a Judgment*, p.46.
24 *Ibid.*, pp. 46 and 48–9.
25 See *supra* and German CCP § 766.

Turkish [26] law, there are no special provisions in English law for setting aside irregular acts of a Sheriff.

In the County Court, duties corresponding to the Sheriff's are performed by the district judge through Bailiffs appointed to assist him.[27] The general rules which are applicable to Sheriffs as to the manner of execution and the property under which may ultimately be subject to an order *etc.* are also applicable to the County Court Bailiffs.[28] As stated above, there is a concurrent High Court jurisdiction for the enforcement of County Court judgments for the value of between two and five thousand pounds. It has been reported that because in practice the Sheriff's officers tend to be more efficient in execution proceedings, it is unlikely that the County Court Bailiffs' machinery is used for execution procedures against goods.[29]

In contrast to the provisions of German and Turkish law, the term 'execution court' (*Vollstreckungsgericht, icra tetkik mercii*) is unknown in English legal terminology. Nevertheless, ordinary courts play an important role in the English execution proceedings and as already discussed above, the civil court which enforces a judgment may not necessarily be the judgment court.

One aspect of English law which has similarity with the provisions of German law is that concerning charging orders made against immovable property, garnishee orders, orders concerning the doing of or abstaining from an act (committal) and the attachment of earnings which are all made by civil courts. Some other forms of enforcement which have no counterpart in German and Turkish law (namely sequestration, administration orders: CCR Ord. 39 and appointment of a receiver [30]) are also exercised by

---

26 See *infra* and Turkish Code of Civil Execution and Bankruptcy, Art. 16.
27 Bailiffs of County Courts are salaried employees of the Court and they are not the same as the Bailiffs who are employed in a Sheriff's office and known as 'bound Bailiffs' or 'bum Bailiffs'; see *Osborn's Concise Law Dictionary* (8th ed.), 'Bailiff'.
28 Black and Black, *Enforcement of a Judgment*, Chapter 7: Analogous County Court Remedies.
29 David Barnard and Mark Houghton, *The New Civil Courts in Action* (London, Dublin, Edinburgh: Butterworths, 1993), p.354; Stephen P. Allison, *Debt Recovery* (London: Longman, 1990), p.42. For the procedure for enforcement in the High Court of County Court judgments see CCR Ord. 25, r.13; Practice Direction [1988] 3 All ER 1084; [1990] All ER 800. It is the usual practice in England that small claims are started at the County Courts and the County Court judgments are transferred across to the High Court for the execution by the Sheriff (the interview with the Sheriff's Officer).
30 See *infra*.

the courts.[31] Except for 'committal', execution cases at the High Court are dealt with not by full judges but by under-judges (Masters and Registrars).[32]

C. BASIC RULES AND PRINCIPLES: ENFORCEABLE JUDICIAL ACTS; EFFECT OF THE APPEAL; SEALING; SERVICE; LEAVE OF THE COURT; STAY OF EXECUTION; FOREIGN JUDGMENTS

1. Enforceable Judicial Acts [33]

The most important enforceable judicial acts are judgments (*Urteile, hükümler*) and court orders (*Beschlüsse, kararlar*; e.g. a maintenance order).[34] English arbitral awards may be enforced similarly to the enforcement of court judgments [35] or (alternatively) the successful party to arbitral proceedings may bring a separate action in the ordinary courts, founded on the contract constituted by the *submission* (*i.e. Schiedsvertrag, tahkim sözlesmesi*).[36]

In contrast to the provisions of the laws of Germany and Turkey, RSC and CCR in their present forms make no provision for the enforcement of deeds executed before a notary public.[37] Similarly, the Continental concept of *court settlements* (*Prozeßvergleich, sulh*) is not known in English law. A settlement between the parties may however be taken as a ground for a so called 'judgment by consent' which can be enforced in the same manner as any other judgment furnished by a court.[38]

---

31 Among these, sequestration is only available in the High Court and the attachment of earnings and administration orders can only be made by County Courts; for the other methods of enforcement there exists concurrent jurisdiction of both.
32 Christoph Graf von Bernstorff, 'Grundzüge des Zivilprozeß-, Zwangsvollstreckungs-, Konkurs- und Vergleichsrechts in England', in Christoph Graf von Bernstorff and H. Reinecker (eds), *Zivilgerichtsbarkeit, Zwangsvollstreckung und Konkurs in europäischen Ländern – Teil I: England, Frankreich und Schweiz* (Stuttgart: Deutscher Sparkassenverlag, 1983), p. 36.
33 Black and Black, *Enforcement of a Judgment*, Chapter 2: Enforceable Judgments and Orders; Bunge, *Zivilprozeß und Zwangsvollstreckung in England*, pp.29–30.
34 RSC Ord.45; CCR. Ord.25; Maintenance Enforcement Act 1991.
35 Arbitration Acts 1950 and 1975; cf. also County Courts Act 1984, sec.64.
36 See RSC Ord.73, r.10.
37 See Wolff, 'Vollstreckbarerklärung', p. 428; cf. Bunge, *Zivilprozeß und Zwangsvollstreckung in England*, p.29.
38 Wolff, 'Vollstreckbarerklärung', p. 428.

2. Effect of the Appeal

The German concept of provisional enforceability (*vorläufige Vollstreckbarkeit*) is not known to English law. An English judgment takes effect from the day of the provided date and this is normally the day on which it is pronounced.[39] Similar to the rule provided under the provisions of Turkish law,[40] an appeal against a judgment as such does not entail a stay of execution and in contrast to the provisions of German law, a judgment against which an appeal is lodged may be enforced without a so-called declaration for 'provisional enforceability'. The Court of Appeal may however stay the execution of the judgment pending an appeal or, in the case of an appeal from a County Court, the County Court judge may stay execution on a deposit or security.[41] In considering whether to grant such a stay of execution pending an appeal, the court must commence on the assumption that there had to be good reason to deny the creditor in the particular case the financial remuneration as prescribed by the provisions of the judgment.[42]

3. Sealing

An 'execution clause' (*Vollstreckungsklausel*) as such does not exist in English legal procedure. However, in order to gain enforceability, a High Court judgment must be *sealed* by an officer of the court.[43] In addition, where a 'writ of execution' is sought (*i.e.* in the case of the enforcement of money-judgments against goods and in the case of recovery of land or delivery of goods *etc.* through the Sheriff [44]), the judgment which is going to be sealed must be firstly entered into the books of the court.[45]

---

39 RSC Ord.42, r.3(1).
40 See *infra* Chapter 3: Debt Recovery in Turkey.
41 See *infra* stay of execution. RSC Ord.59, r.13 and 19(5); *Sewing Machine Rentals v Wilson* [1976] 1 WLR 59.
42 *Winchester Cigarette Machinery Ltd. v Payne (No.2)*, The Times, 15.12.1993, C.A.
43 RSC Ord.46, r.6(4)(a); CCR Ord.42, r.5.
44 See Black and Black, *Enforcement of a Judgment*, p.46 et seq.
45 O'Hare and Hill, *Civil Litigation*, p. 508. Such an entry is not necessary if some other method of enforcement, such as garnishee proceedings, is sought: See *Holtby v Hodgson* (1889) 24 QBD 103; Black and Black, *Enforcement of a Judgment*, p.11; cf. Bunge, *Zivilprozeß und Zwangsvollstreckung in England*, p.27.

4. Service [46]

In contrast to the procedure in Germany, an English judgment does not normally require to be served upon the defendant in order to be enforced. [47] Service of an endorsed copy of the judgment is necessary in order to begin only certain kinds of enforcement proceedings, *i.e.* committal and sequestration. In England, only the County Court judgments are served *ex officio* by the court.[48] The service of High Court judgments must be effected by the plaintiff in one of the accepted methods of service, *e.g.* by personal service, leaving the documents with the defendant or his solicitor empowered to accept service.[49]

5. Leave of the Court [50]

For the enforcement of an English judgment, a leave of court is necessary in certain cases. In order to obtain a leave of court, the judgment creditor must file an application with the High Court or, as the case may be, a County Court. This must be supported by an affidavit to the effect that the judgment debt is due as of the date of the application with the person against whom it is sought, being liable to execution *etc.* The application for leave of court may be made *ex parte*. The court may either grant the application unconditionally or may order a trial on any issue necessarily arising or impose such terms pertaining to the costs of the execution *etc.* Leave in the High Court expires after one year as of the date of the order.

As the judgment creditor must produce an affidavit ensuring the fact that the judgment debt is due, the leave of the court in England in part serves the same function as the German 'execution-counterclaim' (German CCP § 767). That is to say that it acts as a barrier to the enforcement of judgments in the case where the claim has already been extinguished out of court.[51]

In the following cases leave of court is necessary:[52]

---

46 Black and Black, *Enforcement of a Judgment*, pp.11–2.
47 *Land Credit Co. of Ireland v Fermoy* (1870) LR 5Ch 323. Cf. the rules concerning the judgments from EU / EFTA states, *infra* 'Foreign Judgments'.
48 *I.e.* by the court registry. See CCR Ord.22, r.1(1).
49 Cf. *infra* interview with the English Law Firm 3.
50 Black and Black, *Enforcement of a Judgment*, pp. 16–30.
51 See also *infra* 'stay of execution' and cf. *supra* Chapter 1: Debt Recovery in Germany.
52 RSC, Ord.46, r.2; CCR, Ord.26. The list below is not exhaustive; for other cases see Black and Black, *Enforcement of a Judgment*, pp. 16–24.

Debt Recovery in England 51

- Where the effect of a High Court judgment is conditional or contingent, *e.g.* in a vendor's action for specific performance, upon the plaintiff executing an assignment and delivering the deeds.[53] In such cases, the plaintiff who seeks to obtain leave of court must firstly fulfil or await the fulfilment of the condition imposed by the judgment.[54]
- Where there has been a change in the parties (due to death of a party, an assignment of the judgment debt *etc.*).
- Where six years or more have elapsed since the date of the judgment or order.
- Where a High Court judgment or order is made against the assets of a deceased person which shall come into the hands of his executors or administrators.
- Where a judgment or order against a firm is sought to be executed against a member of the firm who has not (or has not given the opportunity) to appear in the proceedings leading to the judgment.[55]
- Where an arbitral award is sought to be enforced as a judgment or order of an English court.[56]

6. Stays of Execution [57]

As previously stated, the enforcement of an English judgment may under certain conditions be suspended pending an appeal.[58] A pending appeal is not the only ground for a stay of execution. There are a number of other special provisions in English law which provide for stay of execution. For example, a petition for the bankruptcy of a debtor normally stays any execution against his property,[59] and an execution on a default judgment against goods stays automatically for fourteen days where the judgment

---

53 *Bell v Denver* (1886) 54 LT 829.
54 For Turkish law cf. Saim Üstündag, *Medeni Yargilama Hukuku*, 5th ed. (Filiz: Istanbul, 1992), pp.786–8; for German law cf. German Civil Code § 322, German CCP §§ 756, 726 II, 731.
55 RSC Ord.81, r.5; CCR Ord.25, r.9.
56 Arbitration Act 1996, sec.66; Arbitration Act 1975, sec.5(1)(a). C.f. German CCP § 1042; Turkish CCP Art.536.
57 Casson, *Odgers on High Court Pleading and Practice*, pp. 29–30; Black and Black, *Enforcement of a Judgment*, pp. 24–25; *Halsbury's Laws of England*, Vol.17, 4th ed. (London: Butterworths, 1976), paras. 451–6.
58 *Supra* 'Effect of Appeal'.
59 Insolvency Act 1986, sec. 285(1)(2); *Re Manning* (1886) 30 ChD 470.

52 *Making Foreign People Pay*

debtor indicates his intention to object against the judgment under a special procedure.[60]

Apart from these special provisions however, there also exists general statutory provisions [61] which enable the Court to grant a discretionary stay upon the cause:

a) Stay by reason of new occurrences

A person against whom a High Court judgment has been made may apply to the Court for a stay of execution of the judgment on the ground of matters or circumstances which have occurred since the date of the judgment. The court may grant such relief on such terms *as it thinks just*.[62]

This provision serves a similar function to the 'execution counterclaims' and the 'setting aside of execution' procedures in German and Turkish law.[63]

b) Stay of execution of writ of fieri facias *(i.e. execution of a High Court judgment against goods)*

RSC Ord. 47 confers a wide discretionary power on the High Court to stay execution against goods either absolutely or for such period or subject to such conditions as the court thinks fit. The Court's discretion here is not limited by precise rules. The execution of a judgment may be stayed, for example, where an informal moratorium is in the interest of all the creditors but where no compromise with those creditors could be achieved under the statutory composition procedure (*gerichtlicher Vergleich, Konkordato*).[64]

c) Stay by County Courts

County Courts have a similar discretionary power to stay the execution of a judgment under the County Courts Act 1984, sec.88.

---

60 See RSC Ord.13, r.8.
61 See *infra*. See also Practice Direction: stay of execution [1984] 1 WLR 1126.
62 RSC Ord.45, r.11.
63 German CCP § 767; Turkish Code of Civil Execution and Bankruptcy Art.71.
64 *Prestige Publications Ltd. v Chelseav Football Co.*, The Times, 28.4.1978.

7. Foreign Judgments [65]

a) Statutory law / international agreements

There are a number of statutory provisions in English law which enable the enforcement of foreign judgments:

The Administration of Judgments Act 1920 applies to the enforcement of judgments for money and arbitral awards of (most) Commonwealth countries, according to which the judgment creditor may apply to the High Court to have a foreign judgment for the payment of money registered in the Court. The High Court will grant registration when it is of the opinion that it is 'just and convenient' to do so, and such a registration renders the foreign judgment enforceable in England.

The Foreign Judgment (Reciprocal Enforcement) Act 1933 applies to the enforcement of judgments for money and arbitral awards of 'recognised courts' of certain other countries [66] – including Israel, Pakistan and parts of Canada and Australia. A foreign judgment for money which the 1933 Act applies to may be registered with the High Court, similar to that for foreign judgments brought within the provisions of the 1920 Act. Under the 1933 Act the High Court however, has no discretionary power to reject the application for such registration.

Prior to the ratification of the 1968 Brussels Convention [67] in England, (the Brussels Convention 1968 took effect in England as of 1.1.1987), as a result of the British-German reciprocal enforcement of the Judgments Agreement 1960,[68] the enforcement of German judgments for money in England was subject to the provisions of the 1933 Act.[69] Since 1987, the

---

65 *Dicey and Morris on Conflict of Laws*, Vol.I, 12th ed. (London: Sweet & Maxwell, 1993), Chapters 14 –15. For a detailed summary see Stuart Mill Duncan and Christopher I. Millar, 'United Kingdom' (national report), in Philip R. Weems (ed.), *Enforcement of Money Judgments Abroad*, Vol. II (New York: Matthew Bender, looseleaf / 1994); or Jeremy Carver and Christopher Napier, 'United Kingdom', in Charles Platto and William G. Horton (eds), *Enforcement of Foreign Judgments Worldwide*, 2nd ed. (London, Dordrecht, Boston: Graham & Trotman / International Bar Association, 1993), pp. 223–52.
66 See 1933 Act sec. 35(1) and Schedule 10.
67 See *infra*.
68 *BGBl* 61 II 301.
69 See Reciprocal Enforcement of Foreign Judgments (Germany) Order 1961; Bunge, *Zivilprozeß und Zwangsvollstreckung in England*, p. 68 et seq.; F. Sonderkötter, 'Anerkennung deutscher Urteile in Großbritannien', *Recht der internationalen Wirtschaft*, 21. Jahrgang (1975), p.370 et seq.; Graf von Bernstorff, 'Grundzüge des Zivilprozeß-, Zwangsvollstreckungs-, Konkurs- und Vergleichsrechts in England', pp. 70–8.

provisions of the 1960 British-German Agreement have been largely superseded by the Brussels Convention 1968. Presently, the 1960 British-German Agreement is practically effective only to such limited extent [70] where the 1968 Brussels Convention is not applicable.[71,72]

The Civil Jurisdiction and Judgments Act 1982 applies to the enforcement of foreign judgments under the 1968 Brussels and 1988 Lugano Conventions on the Jurisdiction and Enforcement of Judgments in Civil and Commercial Matters which apply between the EU and EFTA countries. The concept of *exequatur* in Continental law is not known in English law. The enforcement procedure in the 1982 Act provides for a registration of the foreign judgment in the High Court, similar to the 1920 and 1933 Acts. The registration procedure in the 1982 Act is nevertheless *in its effects* similar to an *exequatur* order of Continental law.[73] This involves an *ex parte* registration of the foreign judgment upon application supported by an affidavit, followed by a service of a 'notice of registration' upon the defendant [74] which enables the latter to file an appeal to set aside the order for registration.

Besides foreign judgments in the narrow sense (*i.e.* conclusive decisions of the foreign courts made after a full trial), foreign court settlements (*gerichtlicher Vergleich*), injunctions, interim awards or *ex parte* orders – including German *Vollstreckungsbescheid* – can also be enforced in England under the Jurisdiction and Judgments Act 1982 (*i.e.* under the Brussels and Lugano Conventions).[75]

---

70 Cf. Christoph Graf von Bernstorff, 'Die Eintreibung von Forderungen durch ausländische Gläubiger in England', *Recht der internationalen Wirtschaft*, 31. Jahrgang, no.5 (1985), pp. 367–73, at p.371.
71 See the Brussels Convention Arts.55–56 and *supra* Chapter 1: Debt Recovery in Germany.
72 For the 1960 German-British Reciprocal Enforcement of Judgments Agreement see Hellmuth Bauer, 'Großbritannien und Nordirland', in *Die Zwangsvollstreckung aus inländischen Schuldtiteln im Ausland* (Flensburg: Verlag Kurt Gross, loose-leaf / 1994); Holger Müller and Götz-Sebastian Hök, 'Großbritannien', in *Deutsche Vollstreckungstitel im Ausland* (Neuwied-Frankfurt: Verlag Kurt Gross, loose-leaf / 1988), pp. 13–8.
73 1982 Act ss.31–45; RSC Ord.71.
74 Cf. *supra* 'Service' in this chapter.
75 Brussels Convention 1968 Art.25; Civil Jurisdiction and Judgments (Authentic Instruments and Court Settlements) Order 1993; Duncan and Millar, 'The United Kingdom', p.16; Wolff, 'Vollstreckbarerklärung', pp.427–8.

b) Common Law

In addition to the statutory provisions, the enforcement of a foreign judgment for money is also possible in England under the general rules of Common Law. The basic rule of Common Law is that [76] any judgment of a foreign court for a debt or definite sum of money which is final and conclusive on the merits may be enforced in England provided that the foreign court could exercise its jurisdiction over the defendant when this matter is construed in terms of English law.[77]

A foreign court is recognised as having jurisdiction over a judgment debtor in the eyes of English law in the following instances:
- if the judgment debtor was, at the time of initiation of the proceedings, present in the foreign country, or
- if he submitted to the jurisdiction of the foreign court either by instituting the foreign proceeding himself or by voluntarily appearing before the foreign court, or by having agreed to submit to the jurisdiction of the same court prior to the commencement of the proceedings.[78]

A foreign judgment is not enforceable at common law as a 'judgment' as such in the literal sense of the word, but is regarded as creating a simple contract debt.[79] Therefore, in order to enforce a foreign judgment at common law, the judgment creditor must bring a fresh action in England. A foreign judgment which is final and conclusive on the merits cannot be reversed in the High Court for any error of fact or of law.[80] Furthermore, since the debt will have been established by the foreign court, the judgment debtor may apply for a summary judgment at the High Court under Ord. 14 of the RSC, pleading the foreign judgment as giving rise to a claim for a debt to which there is no defence.[81]

The High Court may refuse the 'enforcement' of the foreign judgment on grounds of public policy, fraud or natural justice;[82] but under common

---

76 *Dicey and Morris on Conflict of Laws*, Vol.1, Rule 35.
77 Cf. German CCP §§ 723 II and 328 I, Nr.1.
78 *Dicey and Morris on Conflict of Laws*, Vol.1, Rule 36.
79 *Russel v Symth* (1842) 9 M. & W. 819; *Adams v Cape Industries plc.* [1990] Ch 433, at p.513.
80 *Dicey and Morris on Conflict of Laws*, Vol.1, **Rule 41**.
81 *Ibid.*, **Rule 34** (at p.457).
82 *Ibid.*, Rules 43, 44, 45.

law the requirement of reciprocity does not exist between the country of origin of the judgment and England.[83]

The possibility in Common Law of enforcing any foreign judgment under the summary judgment procedure, without going into the merits of the case and without reciprocity being required, may be regarded as a very liberal approach of the English procedure. In practice however, 'it is relatively easy to raise an objection [against such an application for enforcement of a foreign judgment under the common law] asserting a procedural defect' such as the lack of jurisdiction. Thus, it is difficult to argue that the existence of the Common Law method of enforcement of foreign judgments in England as such fulfils the reciprocity requirement on the part of England vis-à-vis third countries under which the rules provided by the provisions of private international law, the enforcement of a foreign judgment is made subject to the reciprocity rule.[84]

Judgments for money from the Turkish civil and commercial courts may be enforced in England under the common law rules.[85] However, (except in most exceptional cases which fall neither within the Brussels Convention nor within the 1960 Reciprocal Enforcement of Judgments Agreement) no action to enforce a German judgment may be brought in England under Common Law.[86] This is because, where a registration is possible under the 1933 or 1982 Acts (*e.g.* under the 1968 Brussels Convention) an action to enforce a judgment under Common Law is inadmissible.[87]

The United Kingdom is a party to the 1958 United Nations Convention on Recognition and Enforcement of Foreign Arbitral Awards.[88] A foreign arbitral award may also be enforced in England by the leave of the High Court in the same manner as a domestic arbitral award [89] or it may constitute the basis for an ordinary action in the English courts brought to enforce the obligations arising under the award.[90]

---

83 *Adams v Cape Industries plc.* [1990] Ch 433, at p.552.
84 Interview with the English Law Firm 8. See *infra* 'Summary Debt Collection Procedures' and cf. *infra* Chapter 3: Debt Recovery in Turkey.
85 See *infra* Chapter 3: Debt Recovery in Turkey.
86 See Müller and Hök, *Deutsche Vollstreckungstitel im Ausland*, pp.18–20.
87 Carver and Napier, 'United Kingdom', p. 226.
88 For the recognition and enforcement of a foreign judgment under the UN Convention see the Arbitration Act 1996, secs. 100–4.
89 Arbitration Act 1996, sec. 66 (4).
90 Mark Huleatt-James and Nicholas Gould, *International Commercial Arbitration* (London: Lovel White Durrant, 1996), p. 11.

D. SUMMARY PROCEDURES FOR DEBT COLLECTION

RSC Ord. 14 (and CCR Ord. 9, r.14 to the similar effect) provide for a speedy procedure for obtaining judgments for the payment of money. Accordingly, a plaintiff who believes that the defendant has no arguable defence may apply to the court for a summary judgment. The application is made to the court on summons supported by an affidavit verifying the claim and stating the belief that there is no defence to the claim. If such application is accepted by the court, a copy of the summons containing the plaintiff's application and affidavit is served upon the defendant not less than 10 days before the return date of the summons.[91] The defendant has to prove to the court that there *is* a dispute or question which ought to be tried.[92] In the case where the defendant remains silent or he cannot satisfy the court that there is a 'triable issue' between the parties, the court will grant a summary judgment.[93] Similarly, where the defendant's case depends on a point of law or construction of a document only, the court may on application decide the case summarily without a full trial.[94]

The summary judgment procedure under Ord. 14 is widely used, particularly for claims which are based on a cheque or bill of exchange where the defendant is not normally allowed to contest the case referring to questions arising from the underlying transaction.[95] In contrast to the *Mahnverfahren*, as well as deeds, bills of exchange and cheque procedure in German Law, the claim to be made in the Order 14 procedure need neither be based upon documentary evidence nor negotiable instruments nor contain a liquidated sum of money which remains outstanding independent from the performance of an obligation on the plaintiff's part. Even if the

---

[91] RSC Ord. 14, rr. 1, 2.
[92] RSC Ord. 14, r.4.
[93] RSC Ord. 14, r.3.
[94] RSC Ord. 14A (came into force 1.2.1991).
[95] Richard Guy and Hugh Mercer, *Commercial Debt in Europe: Recovery and Remedies* (London: Longman, 1991), p.173. 'In practice an application under Ord. 14 based on the dishonour of a cheque may only be defended where the cheque is alleged to have been obtained by fraud or where the defendant has received no consideration at all for the cheque', *ibid*. English Law Firm 3 argues that, because of the lack of a special procedure, enforcing a cheque is still a quite complicated process in England which, he observes, works against the small enterprises in the market: 'large operators who are very strong in the market place say to the customer "we are not going to supply you until you pay this in advance". Of course, they are always paid. This is because, before the goods get out the money is there with them. If you are a small supplier, you do not have the same commercial power...'. Cf. also *infra* Chapter 5: Role of Lawyers in Cross-Border Debt Collection, 'Turkish Law Firm 2'.

58 *Making Foreign People Pay*

claim is for damages, the plaintiff may apply for a summary judgment for damages to be assessed by the court.[96]

As a result of this, the field of application of English summary judgments procedure is theoretically considerably larger than its German (functional) counterpart. However, 'in practice, unless the defendant's case depends on a point of law ... [in which case the above mentioned Ord. 14A may be applied], it behoves [in England] a defendant to serve a well particularised affidavit in order to avoid [a summary] judgment being entered against him'.[97]

E. EXECUTION FOR MONEY CLAIMS

1. In General

Similar to the provisions provided by German law, the methods of enforcement of judgments for money in England vary with the target of the enforcement; namely execution against goods and chattels (RSC Ords. 46, 47; CCR Ord. 26, r.1), charging orders on land and securities (Charging Orders Act 1979, RSC Ord. 50, CCR Ord. 31), garnishee orders against debts due to the judgment debtor (RSC Ord. 49; CCR Ord. 30), attachment of salaries *etc.* (Attachment of Earnings Act 1971; CCR Ord. 27), appointment of a receiver to collect future rents, profits *etc.* (RSC. Ord. 51, CCR Ord. 32).

Similar to the provisions of German law, there are statutory provisions in English law enabling the judgment creditor to discover the means and assets of the judgment debtor (RSC Ord. 48, r.1; CCR Ord. 25, r.3).[98] Accordingly, the creditor applies *ex parte* on an affidavit to the court for an order requiring the oral examination of the debtor before the Court.[99] The order must be served upon the debtor and when the debtor appears before the Court, the creditor is entitled to conduct an exhaustive inquiry into the means and assets of the debtor by examining (and 'cross-examining') the debtor personally.[100]

---

96   Guy and Mercer, *Commercial Debt in Europe*, p. 172.
97   *Ibid.*, p. 173.
98   For details see Allison, *Debt Recovery*, pp. 38–41.
99   Cf. German CCP § 807 which provides for having the debtor produce a written 'inventory of assets' only.
100 *Republic of Costa Rica v Strousberg* (1880) 16 ChD 8, C.A.

a) Writ of fieri facias *and warrant of execution: execution against movable property*

The most common method for the enforcement of judgments for money is the execution against goods which is initiated by the High Court writ of *fieri facias* (literally 'cause to be made', commonly abbreviated to *fi.fa.*) and its counterpart in the County Court procedure, the warrant of execution.[101] This procedure enables the judgment creditor to obtain the seizure and sale of the goods and chattels (movable) owned by the debtor and corresponds to the attachment procedure in German and Turkish law.

In order to initiate the procedure, the creditor petitions the Court in which the judgment was obtained and requests the issue of a writ of *fieri facias* or (in the case where a County Court procedure is utilised, a warrant of execution).[102] Strictly speaking, a writ of *fieri facias* (or a warrant of execution) is an official document made under the Court's seal, commanding the Sheriff (or the Bailiff) to seize and sell the goods of the debtor for the satisfaction of the judgment creditor.

The writ of *fieri facias* (or the warrant of execution) is then delivered to and executed by the Sheriff (or the Bailiff) in the *bailiwick*[103] in which the defendant resides or carries on business. The Sheriff (or Bailiff) armed with the information from the creditor will execute the writ or warrant by entering the debtor's premises. He will either seize the goods or take what is known as 'walking possession' of them.[104,105]

As is similar in German and Turkish law, the seizure of goods owned by the debtor does not cause the property in the goods to pass to the creditor.[106] Furthermore, in contrast to the provisions of German law, it is not the actual seizure of the goods in English law which grants priority to the judgment creditor against other (unsecured) creditors. The priorities among several creditors seeking the execution against goods are determined in the

---

101   RSC Ords. 45 – 47, CCR Ord. 26.
102   As stated above (*supra* 'Civil Execution Officers'), a County Court judgment may – and in practice usually is also enforced at the High Court.
103   'Bailiwick' is the area under the jurisdiction of a Sheriff or Bailiff.
104   That is, an agreement will be made whereby in consideration of the Sheriff's not seizing the goods, the debtor agrees not to remove or otherwise deal with the goods. See Keith, Podevin and Sandbrook, *The Execution of Sheriffs' Warrants*, pp. 63–7; Allison, *Debt Recovery*, p.44.
105   Cf. German CCP § 808 II; Turkish Code of Civil Execution and Bankruptcy, Art.88 II.
106   *Giles v Grover* (1832) 9 Bing 128.

High Court by the order of delivery of the writ to the Sheriff [107] and in the County Courts, at the time the request for an issue for the warrant of execution is delivered to the court.[108] In the case of bankruptcy of the debtor, the execution creditor may only obtain priority against the other creditors (against the trustee in bankruptcy) when the seized goods and chattels have been sold.[109]

If a third party claims the goods found in the debtor's possession which have been taken or are intended to be taken by the Sheriff in execution, the Sheriff may *interplead*. That is to say that he can compel the third party and judgment creditor to take proceedings between themselves to determine whether the judgment debtor or the third party is the owner of the goods. With regard to interpleading, the Sheriff is neutral and retains the possession of the goods pending the proceeding between the creditor and the third party.[110,111]

The sale of the goods seized is normally made [112] by the Sheriff (or the County Court Bailiff) by public auction unless the Court makes an order permitting sale under a private contract. The application for such an order for private sale can be made either by one of the parties or by the Sheriff himself who is under a duty to receive the best possible price for the goods.[113]

In contrast to the provisions of Turkish and German law there does not exist the 'minimum sale price' rule in public auction under execution in England. The court however may set aside a sale it considers to have been badly advertised or where the sale was under-valued.[114] In addition, because the Sheriff's fees are calculated on the amount of the monies recovered,[115] it is also in the interest of the Sheriff not to sell the goods

---

107 See Keith, Podevin and Sandbrook, *The Execution of Sheriffs' Warrants*, pp. 15–8.
108 Supreme Court Act 1981, secs. 103(2), 138; RSC Ord. 46, r. 8(4); CCR Ord. 26, r. 6(2). Black and Black, *Enforcement of a Judgment*, pp. 47–8 and 55–6; Allison, *Debt Recovery*, pp. 49–50.
109 Insolvency Act 1986, secs. 183, 184 and 346.
110 Cf. Turkish Code of Civil Execution and Bankruptcy, Arts. 96 – 97.
111 See RSC Ord. 17 and (for similar procedure in the County Courts) CCR Ord. 33, rr. 1–5. See Keith, Podevin and Sandbrook, *The Execution of Sheriffs' Warrants*, p. 70–114; Black and Black, *Enforcement of a Judgment*, pp. 51–2.
112 *I.e.* where the value of the goods exceeds £20 (Supreme Court Act 1981, sec. 138A (1); Bankruptcy Act 1883, sec. 145).
113 Supreme Court Act 1981, sec. 138A; County Courts Act 1984 secs. 97 and 98; RSC Ord. 47, r. 6; CCR Ord. 26, r. 15.
114 *Edge v Kavanagh* (1884) 24 LR Ir 1.
115 See *infra* 'Costs' in this chapter.

under-value. The purchaser obtains title to the goods, as a rule, against the whole world.[116]

b) Charging orders: execution (obtaining security) against immovable property etc.

The High Court and (where the judgment to be enforced does not exceed the value of five thousand pounds, County Courts [117]) are given power under the Charging Act 1979 to impose a charge on any *land* or *interest in land* owned by a judgment debtor.[118] Similarly, charging orders may be made against securities, such as shares,[119] funds in court [120] and beneficial interest under trusts.[121] In practice, charging orders against land are of most importance.[122]

Strictly speaking, a charging order is not a means of enforcement as such. The effect of a charging order is to give the creditor security for the money due (or to become due) under the judgment. In order to satisfy the judgment, the creditor must cause the sale of the property.[123] Thus, an English charging order is similar to 'hypothecation' under the provisions of German law.[124]

The procedures to be followed for the High Court and the County Courts with regard to charging orders are similar. In both cases there are two stages for the charging order application: an *ex parte* application for the charging order *nisi* (*i.e.* a provisional order effective until the hearing where the debtor will be heard and can object against the same) and, thereafter, an application for the charging order *absolute*. The court has a wide discretion as to the making of both an order *nisi* and *absolute*, and will bear in mind not only the interest of the debtor and the creditor but also (if any)

---

116 Black and Black, *Enforcement of a Judgment*, p. 59; *Curtis v Malony* [1951] 1 KB 726.
117 See Allison, *Debt Recovery*, pp. 52–3.
118 'Interests in land' correspond broadly to the limited ownership rights on land (beschränkte dingliche Rechte, sinirli ayni haklar) in Continental law. For a general introduction to the English law of property in German language see Bunge, *Zivilprozeß und Zwangsvollstreckung in England*, pp. 13–21.
119 See Graf von Bernstorff, 'Grundzüge des Zivilprozeß-, Zwangsvollstreckungs-, Konkurs- und Vergleichsrechts in England', pp. 42–4.
120 See Supreme Court Funds Rules 1975.
121 RSC Ord. 50; CCR Ord. 31.
122 Allison, *Debt Recovery*, p. 52.
123 RSC Ord. 88; CCR Ord. 31, r. 4.
124 See *supra* Chapter 1: Debt Recovery in Germany.

62 Making Foreign People Pay

the interests of the other creditors and joint owners of the land in question.[125]

The creditor who applies for the charging order *nisi* must show *prima facie* proof of ownership of the land proposed to be charged by the debtor. The Land Registry in England has been open to the public since 1990 and an application for a search for such evidence may be made to the Land Registrar.[126]

The effect of an order *nisi* is that the creditor may register the charge [127] so that any person dealing with the land thereafter will be subject to the creditor's rights to enforce his security.[128] The order *nisi* also determines a date for the hearing of the application for a charging order *absolute*, and it must be served upon the debtor who is to attend the hearing in order to show why the order *absolute* should not be made.

Once a charging order *absolute* is made at the subsequent hearing, the creditor may apply for an order of sale under RSC Ord. 88 or CCR Ord. 31(4), as if he was a mortgagee of the land.[129] Alternatively he can apply for appointment of a receiver [130] who may either sell the land or satisfy the creditor otherwise (*e.g.* by collecting rents).[131] Furthermore, if the debtor becomes bankrupt, the creditor will be a secured creditor as of the date on which the charging order nisi was made.[132]

c) Garnishee procedure: execution against debts

A garnishee order involving the courts, in which they divert the payment of monetary debts owed to the judgment debtor to the judgment creditor, is an effective method of enforcement in England. Similar to German and Turkish practice, the garnishee procedure is most commonly used in England in order to obtain money standing to the credit of the judgment debtor in a bank account. This method hereby includes not only current accounts but also deposit accounts and receivables in building societies *etc.* In contrast

---

125 Land Charges Act 1972, sec. 1(5); *Harman v Glencross* [1986] 2 WLR 637; Allison, *Debt Recovery*, p. 59; Black and Black, *Enforcement of a Judgment*, p. 86.
126 See Barnard and Houghton, *The New Civil Courts in Action*, pp. 354–5.
127 Land Charges Act 1972, sec. 6.
128 Barnard and Houghton, *The New Civil Courts in Action*, p. 355.
129 Allison, *Debt Recovery*, pp. 56–7.
130 See *infra*.
131 RSC Ords. 30, 51; CCR Ord. 32.
132 Insolvency Act 1986, secs. 183, 346.

to the procedure in Germany,[133] damages to be paid to the judgment debtor are attachable, as from the time when the amount to be paid is ascertained by a judgment.[134] Attachment of earnings is however, governed by a special law.[135,136]

Garnishee procedures in the High Court and in the County Courts are similar in nature.[137] As with the charging order procedure, there are two stages: an application *ex parte* for a garnishee order *nisi* and thereafter, an application for the garnishee order *absolute*, both orders being against the garnishee, *i.e.* the third party debtor who owes the judgment debtor.

Similar to the procedure in the charging orders, the court has wide discretion as to the making of the orders. In exercising this discretion the court must bear in mind not only the position of the judgment debtor and the judgment creditor, but also the position of the other creditors of the judgment debtor (with a view to ensuring the distribution of the available assets of the debtor among the creditors *parri passu*).[138]

A garnishee order *nisi* is addressed to the garnishee and forbids him from paying the debt over to the judgment debtor and requires him to attend the hearing for the garnishee order *absolute* in order to show why the monies should not be paid to the judgment creditor. If, at this subsequent hearing the Court is satisfied that the garnishee is indebted to the judgment debtor then it will order him to pay over the debt to the judgment creditor (*i.e.* the garnishor).

In the case where the garnishee refrains from effecting payment, the garnishee order *absolute* may be enforced against him in the same manner as any other order for the payment of money as it confers an immediate right to payment on the garnishee creditor.[139]

As with the German procedure,[140] a garnishee order cannot put the creditor in a better position *vis-à-vis* the garnishee than the judgment debtor himself.[141] Thus, a garnishee may set off debts due to him from the

---

133 See *supra* Chapter 1: Debt Recovery in Germany.
134 *Holtby v Hodson* (1889) 24 QBD 103, CA.
135 See *infra* 'Attachment of Earnings' in this chapter.
136 For a list of cases where a debt is not attachable – *i.e.* where a garnishee order is not admissible – see *Supreme Court Practice 1995*, annotation under Ord. 49, r. 1.
137 RSC Ord. 49; CCR Ord. 30.
138 *D. Wilson (Birmingham) Ltd. v Metropolitan Property Developments Ltd.* [1975] 2 All E R 814, CA.
139 *Rainbow v Moorgate Properties Ltd.* [1975] 1 WLR 788, per Buckley L, J. at p. 793.
140 See *supra* Chapter 1: Debt Recovery in Germany.
141 *Loescher v Dean* [1950] Ch 491.

judgment debtor at the time when the order becomes binding.[142] Compliance with the order *absolute* also gives the garnishee a valid discharge against the judgment debtor.[143]

As discussed in Chapter 1 above, the author is of the opinion that a garnishee order can be made against a third party debtor (garnishee), if the original debtor is subject to the jurisdiction of the forum. The garnishee order affects the property rights of the original debtor, and, therefore, it is the original debtor (not the garnishee) who must be subject to the jurisdiction of the court which issues the garnishee order. Provided that the original debtor is subject to the jurisdiction of the English courts, a garnishee order can be made against a garnishee even if he is not subject to the jurisdiction of the English courts, *e.g.* being outside England and Wales.[144,145]

There is no limitation which states that the garnished debt must be properly recoverable (*i.e.* must be paid) within the jurisdiction; but the Court may, as a matter of discretion, not garnish a debt which is recoverable outside the jurisdiction if to do so would expose the garnishee to the risk of having to pay the debt twice.[146] Similarly a garnishee order should not be made in England if, as a result of proceedings in a foreign jurisdiction for the recovery of the same debt, the garnishee faces a risk of having to pay the same debt twice.[147]

---

142 *Hale v Victoria Plumping Co. Ltd. and En-Tout-Cas Co. Ltd.* [1966] 2 QB 746.
143 RSC Ord. 49, r. 8.
144 See *infra* 'Equitable Execution' and 'Money Claims based on a Foreign Judgment' in this chapter.
145 Yet, it is understood that, in English legal practice, in order to issue a garnishee order, it is required that the garnishee (not only the original debtor) is subject to the jurisdiction of the English courts. See *Grahame v Van Biane*, 3.11.1906 (unreported), cited in *the Supreme Court Practice 1995*, Ord. 51, para. 51/1–3/12; *Goldschmidt v Oberrheinische Metallwerke* [1906] 1 KB 373, CA. Thus, referring to the RSC Ord. 81, r. 1, it has been argued that a garnishee order may be made against a firm in relation to debts due from it if the firm carries on business within England and Wales, notwithstanding that one or more of its members are resident abroad. See Black and Black, *Enforcement of a Judgment*, p. 101. However, since Ord. 81, r. 1 governs the jurisdiction of the English court for actions by and against firms within the jurisdiction (*i.e.* it applies to 'firms and single individuals suing or being sued in their firm or trading name': *Supreme Court Practice 1995*, Ord. 81, annotation 81/1/1), this provision is not applicable to the garnishee procedures where no 'action' is brought against a 'defendant', rather the garnishee order is addressed to a third party (debtor to the judgments debtor).
146 *Interpool Ltd. v Galani* [1988] QB 738.
147 *Deutsche Schachtbau- und Tiefbohr GmbH v Shell International Petroleum Co. Ltd.* [1988] 3 WLR 230; [1988] 2 All ER 833, HL.

d) Attachment of earnings

In contrast to the procedure in Germany and similar to the case in Turkey,[148] the attachment of earnings is categorised in English law not as a special variety of garnishee procedure, but as a separate method of enforcement. This particular method of enforcement [149] is only available through the County Courts, *i.e.* a County Court (attachment of earnings) order is required.[150]

The appropriate County Court for application for the attachment of earnings is normally the County Court in the district in which the judgment debtor resides. If the debtor does not reside in England or Wales however, the proper Court is the Court for the district in which the judgment sought to be enforced is obtained.[151]

Before an attachment of earnings order is made, two conditions must be satisfied:

(1) the debtor must have defaulted in paying one or more of the instalments under a judgment ordered to be paid by such instalments;
(2) the debtor must have an identifiable employer from whom he receives *earnings* (*i.e.* salaries, wages or pensions such as for past services or for compensation for loss of office).[152]

In order to obtain an attachment of earnings order, the judgment creditor files a request for the attachment of earnings order in the appropriate Court, where the enforcement of a High Court judgment is sought, supported by an official copy of the judgment and an affidavit verifying the amount due under the judgment.[153]

The Court will then send to the debtor a notice of application together with a reply form (*i.e.* a form for a declaration of the details of employment, earnings, the expenses for the household *etc.*) which he must complete and return to the Court Office within 8 days of receipt of the document. If the employer is in England or Wales but the debtor is not, the

---

148 See *supra* Chapter 1: Debt Recovery in Germany and *infra* Chapter 3: Debt Recovery in Turkey.
149 Attachment of Earnings Act 1971; CCR Ord.27.
150 Judgments and orders of the High Court may also be enforced through County Courts; see *supra* 'Legal Basis'.
151 For other exceptions see CCR Ord. 27, r. 3.
152 Attachment of Earnings Act 1971; secs. 3 and 6.
153 CCR Ord. 25, r. 11.

district judge may allow service on the debtor abroad.[154] In the notice of application, the debtor is informed *inter alia* that he may apply for a 'suspended order' – *i.e.* an order whereby provided he makes regular payments, his employer will not be contacted. Once the reply is received, the Court may make an attachment order and may also at the same time make a further order suspending the attachment order. At this stage, there is no hearing. The creditor or the debtor may however apply, upon service of such order, to the district judge to review the matter.[155] Where a suspended order is made and the debtor fails to comply with such an order, the creditor may apply for the court to send the notice of attachment of earnings order without further notice, to the debtor's employer.

An attachment of earnings order [156] is addressed to the debtor's employer and orders him (on penalty of a fine) to make periodical deductions from the debtor's earnings and to pay such monies over the court. The court which makes the order fixes the amount of the order by determining two 'rates' which it thinks fit, namely:

(1) normal deduction rate, *i.e.* the amount which should be deducted regularly by the employer from the debtor's wages;
(2) protected earnings rate, *i.e.* a minimum amount which in the opinion of the Court the debtor should retain from his earnings, having regard to his (and his dependants') resources and needs.[157]

Accordingly, should the debtor's income fluctuate from time to time (*e.g.* as a result of the availability of overtime working *etc.*), the deduction made from his earnings may not reduce his earnings below the 'protected earnings' level.

The money deducted from the earnings belongs to the judgment creditor as from the date of payment made by the employer to the court.[158]

---

154 CCR Ord. 8, r. 4.
155 If the debtor fails to complete and return the reply form, he will be required after receiving a notice to attend the court to show cause why he should not be committed to prison because of his failure to comply with the order (see *infra*), as a result of which the debtor will normally be persuaded to complete the reply form. In practice a debtor seldom goes to prison. See Barnard and Houghton, *The New Civil Courts in Action*, pp. 365–6.
156 Attachment of Earnings Act 1971, sec. 6.
157 *Ibid.*, s.6(5).
158 *Re Green (A Bankrupt)*, The Times 7.7.1978 (cited in Black and Black, *Enforcement of a Judgment*, p. 98).

e) Equitable execution (appointment of a receiver)

There may be various interests in property to which the judgment debtor is entitled but which cannot be taken in execution by one of the usual legal execution methods. This is the case, for example:

(1) where the judgment debtor is entitled to accruing – but not accrued – rents from tenants *or*
(2) where a debtor of the judgment debtor is outside the jurisdiction of the Court and therefore a garnishee order is not possible but there is evidence to suggest that the money is about to be sent over the judgment debtor.[159]

In such exceptional cases, the enforcement of a judgment or order may be achieved by the appointment of a receiver by the court.[160] That is, equitable execution is a relief obtainable where impediments exist to ordinary execution methods.[161]

Appointment of a receiver is a discretionary remedy, and the Court in exercising its discretion is required to take account of the amount claimed by the creditor, to the amount likely to be obtained by the receiver, and to the probable costs of the appointment *etc.* Application for the appointment of a receiver can be made *ex parte*, supported by an affidavit setting out the judgment debtor's interest in the property and the fitness of the proposed receiver. If the receiver is appointed, the court will normally require him to give security for the proper execution of his duties.

The receiver collects the interests in the property for which he has been appointed as receiver, *e.g.* he receives the rents from the debtor's tenants (see the first example above) or receives the monies sent by the debtor's debtor abroad (see the second example above) in satisfaction of the judgment creditor.

The order appointing a receiver does not as such create a charge on the debtor's property and the judgment creditor does not become a secured creditor for the purposes of bankruptcy.[162] The order operates further as an

---

159 *Grahame v Van Biane*, 3.11.1906 (unreported), cited in the *Supreme Court Practice 1995*, Ord. 51, para. 51/1–3/12; *Goldschmidt v Oberrheinische Metallwerke* [1906] 1 KB 373, CA.
160 RSC Ord. 51; CCR Ord. 32.
161 'Equitable execution is not like legal execution: It is equitable relief, which the court gives because execution at law cannot be had. It is not execution, but a substitute for execution.' *Re Shephard* (1890) 43 ChD 137, per Bower, L.J at p.137.
162 See *Re Whiteheart* (1870) 116 SJ 75; *Re Potts* [1893] 1 QB 648.

injunction to prevent the judgment debtor from receiving or otherwise dealing with the monies to the prejudice of the judgment creditor, *e.g.* from utilising a debt by way of set off or counterclaim.[163]

f) Other methods of execution for judgments for money: judgment summons, County Court administration orders, committal

(1) Judgment summonses   The enforcement of judgments for money by attaching the person of the debtor (*i.e.* imprisonment for debt) was severely restricted in England by the Debtors Act 1869 (sec.4) and by the Administration Justice Act 1970 (sec.11).[164] However, in exceptional cases, a judgment debtor may still be forced to pay under the threat of imprisonment, that is by obtaining a judgment summons.[165] With the exception of matrimonial cases,[166] a judgment summons can only be issued by the County Courts and can only be used to enforce maintenance arrears or certain taxes. Accordingly, the *judgment summons* (*i.e.* a Court document ordering the judgment debtor to attend before the issuing Court) obtained from the local County Court where the debtor resides, is served upon the debtor and on appearing before the Court, the Court will under its discretion (if it thinks that the debtor *can* pay *etc.*) make a committal order suspended for a further time in order to enable the debtor to pay the judgment debt. In the case where the debtor fails to pay the required amount within the prescribed period he will be sent to prison for a period not exceeding six weeks.

(2) County Court administration orders   This method of enforcement is only available in the County Courts and therefore for relatively small debts.[167] This procedure requires the debtor to pay all of his creditors in instalments and in an amount in proportion to the whole amount owing to

---

163   See *Tyrrell v Painton* [1895] 1 QB 206; *Exp. Peak Hill Goldfield* [1909] 1 KB 430.
164   See Casson, *Odgers on High Court Pleading and Practice*, pp. 427–8; Black and Black, *Enforcement of a Judgment*, p. 119; *Supreme Court Practice 1995*, Ord. 45, para. 45/1/35–36.
165   CCR Ord. 28; RSC Ord. 45, r. 1.
166   See Family Proceedings Rules 1991, rr. 7.4 – 7.6.
167   This is because, in order to bring the execution within the jurisdiction of the County Court, the total amount of debt which will be effected by the order must not exceed the value of £5000, see *supra* 'Legal Basis'.

those who are subject to the order. Payment can be made either in full or – similar to *concordat* procedure – at an agreed percentage.[168]

Administration is firstly for the benefit of the debtor. It can be made either on the debtor's application or by the Court on its own motion pursuant to an oral examination[169] or pursuant to an attachment of earnings application where the judgment debtor has other debts.[170] In each case the debtor and each of his creditors are given the opportunity to be heard at a hearing held after the date of notice has been given to them.

(3) Committal [171]   Committal is the sending of a person to prison for a short period of time or temporary purpose.[172] Committal as a method of enforcement is subject to the Debtors Acts 1869 and 1878 which restricted such remedy to a large extent.

Strictly speaking, where the enforcement of judgments for money is concerned, committal is not of itself an enforcement method; but failure to comply with orders in certain enforcement procedures (oral examination, attachment of earnings, judgment summons *etc.*[173]) can – subject to courts discretion – lead to a committal order.

In the case where the enforcement of a judgment for money is concerned, a Court may only make an order of committal when it is satisfied that the debtor actually has the means to pay the debt.[174]

2. Monetary Claims Based upon a Foreign Judgment (or another Foreign Enforcement Title)

As has been seen above, the enforcement of foreign money judgments is possible in England, provided that the foreign judgment be registered in the High Court under the relevant statutory procedures, or a judgment be obtained under Common Law for the enforcement of the foreign judgment.

---

168   CCR. Ord. 39; County Courts Act 1984, secs. 112 – 117; Allison, *Debt Recovery*, pp. 76–9.
169   CCR Ord. 39, r. 2.
170   Attachment of Earnings Act 1971, sec. 4; Black and Black, *Enforcement of a Judgment*, p. 97.
171   See Black and Black, *Enforcement of a Judgment*, pp. 79–82.
172   *Osborn's Concise Law Dictionary*, 8th ed., 'committal'.
173   See *supra*.
174   *Farrant v Farrant* [1957] 1 All ER 204. (The relevant burden of proof lies with the creditor who may also cross-examine the debtor, Krauskopf, 'Das britische Vollstreckungsrecht', pp. 102–3.)

70 *Making Foreign People Pay*

Similar to German law, the civil execution procedures which involve the use of public force against the debtor are governed exclusively by national law and can only be carried out by the English 'Execution Officers'.[175] Powers of the Execution Officers are only applicable to the movable and immovable property within the jurisdiction.[176]

Judgments – including a judgment obtained in the High Court for the 'enforcement' of a foreign judgment under Common Law – and orders can be made in England in a foreign currency.[177] Similarly, a foreign judgment can be registered under the Jurisdiction and Judgment Act 1982 (*i.e.* under the Brussels or Lugano Conventions) in its original currency.[178]

In both cases, the creditor who proceeds to enforce the judgment must convert the foreign currency into Sterling, applying the rate valid at the date of application made to the Enforcement Officer (*i.e.* as the case may be, at the request for issue of a writ of *fi. fa.* to the Sheriff or in the affidavit in support of the application for a garnishee order *etc.*).[179] Once the foreign currency amount is converted into a Sterling figure, this figure remains valid for all stages of the execution procedure.[180]

F. PROTECTION OF THE DEBTOR

The following property of a debtor who is a natural (*i.e.* not juristic) person is exempt from seizure:

(a) such tools, books, vehicles and other equipment necessary to the debtor for use personally in his job or business;

---

175   Duncan and Millar, 'The United Kingdom', p.17; Müller and Hök, 'Großbritannien', pp. 28–30; Bauer, *Die Zwangsvollstreckung aus inländischen Schuldtiteln im Ausland*, pp. 23–4.
176   For garnishee orders, see *supra* 'Garnishee Procedures'.
177   See Practice Direction 18.12.1975 [1976] All ER 699; Black and Black, *Enforcement of a Judgment*, pp. 30–1.
178   *Schorsch Meier GmbH v Hennin* [1975] QB 416; *Milliangos v George Frank (Textiles) Ltd.* [1976] AC 443; Duncan and Millar, 'The United Kingdom', p.11.
179   *Halsbury's Laws of England*, Vol.17, para. 404; Duncan and Millar, *ibid.*; Black and Black, *Enforcement of a Judgment*, pp. 30–1, 85; Carver and Napier, 'United Kingdom', pp. 226–7.
180   The interview conducted with the Sheriff's Officer.

(b) such clothing, bedding, furniture or household equipment necessary for satisfying the basic domestic needs of the debtor or his family.[181]

A practice guide book issued by the Lord Chancellor's Department for the Bailiffs to comment this provision [182] holds that it is for the defendant to satisfy the Bailiff that a vehicle is necessary to allow him to continue his work (a need to get to and from the place of work is not in itself sufficient to constitute a valid ground) and household items such as stereo equipment, televisions or microwave ovens are not considered 'basic needs' of a family.

Furthermore, execution against goods is only allowed to the extent necessary for the satisfaction of the creditor and a Sheriff is liable in tort for excessive levy on the debtor's goods.[183]

Protection of the debtor in the attachment of wages and salaries is governed in English law by a special attachment of earnings procedure outside the usual garnishee orders procedure.[184,185]

G. PRELIMINARY REMEDIES FOR THE PROTECTION OF THE CREDITOR

RSC makes provision for the interim preservation of any property which is the subject matter of an action.[186] Accordingly, where the right to any specific fund is in dispute, the court may order the fund to be paid into court, pending the action. Further and more generally, the High Court has a discretionary power to grant by order (whether interlocutory or final) an

---

181 Courts and Legal Services Act 1990, sec. 15. Earlier there were no statutory provisions in England as to the exemption from execution, and the criteria could only be found in the Common Law. Krauskopf, 'Das britische Vollstreckungsrecht', p. 101. Notwithstanding this new rule, 'the Sheriff has the *prima facie* right, indeed a duty to seize all of the goods of the judgment debtor' and the burden rests on the judgment debtor to raise the issue that the goods are not seizable: *John Kenneth Moffat v Lemkin* (1993), unreported, cited in Keith, Podevin and Sandbrook, *The Execution of Sheriffs' Warrants*, pp. 36–7.
182 See Court User's Guide 1991, Appendix 3 (reproduced in Barnard and Houghton, *The New Civil Courts in Action*, p. 355).
183 See *e.g. Moore v Lambeth County Court Registrar (No.2)* [1970] 1 QB 560; cf. German CCP § 803.
184 See *supra*.
185 For protection of the debtor by 'staying execution' see 'Basic Rules and Principles' in this chapter.
186 Ord. 29.

injunction (*i.e.* a decree by which a party to an action is required to do or refrain from doing a particular thing) in all cases in which it is of the opinion that it is just and convenient to do so.[187]

Under this latter provision, it has been recognised since 1979 [188] that the High Court may grant a preliminary remedy for protection of the creditor in the form of an injunction commanding the defendant to preserve his assets (*e.g.* not to remove from the jurisdiction) pending the court proceedings or pending the execution of the judgment ('Mareva injunction' or 'Mareva order'). A Mareva injunction is usually coupled with an order to the defendant to declare on oath what and where his assets are,[189] and will only be granted upon the condition that the plaintiff makes an undertaking to compensate any loss to the defendant in case it turns out that the injunction should not have been made.[190] Being an order *in personam*, a Mareva injunction does not affect assets as such but it only orders the defendant – under the threat of contempt – to preserve (*e.g.* not remove) such assets. However, a general rule of English Equity is that a third party who knows of (*e.g.* who has been served with a notice of) an injunction is also bound not to impede it. For example, where monies in a bank account are 'frozen' by a Mareva injunction the bank which has been served with the notice of Mareva will be in contempt of a Court order if it pays out the monies in the account.[191]

It is well established that [192] a Mareva injunction can extend to assets situated outside the jurisdiction of English courts and to the bank accounts

---

187 Supreme Court Act 1981, sec. 37(1).
188 *Mareva Compania Naviera v International Bulk Carriers Ltd.* [1980] 1 ALL ER 213.
189 Without such an order for disclosure of assets it is very difficult to ascertain the whereabouts of the debtor's assets. This is the case for example for land owned and bank accounts held by the debtor: unless the place of land or the branch of bank where the debtor's account is held is known, it is very expensive to trace the debtor's money or land in the entire country. (English Law Firm 10.)
190 *Hoffman La Roche v Secretary of State for Trade and Industry* [1975] AC 295.
191 Enforcement of (world-wide) Mareva injunctions outside England and especially against foreign third parties such as foreign banks is highly problematic. See Barbara Dohmann and Adrian Briggs, '"Worldwide Mareva" injunctions and the enforcement of foreign judgments in England', in Peter F. Schlosser (ed.), *Materielles Recht und Prozeßrecht und die Auswirkungen der Unterscheidung im Recht der Internationalen Zwangsvollstreckung* (Bielefeld: Gieseking, 1991), pp. 164–5; Harald Koch, 'Durchsetzung einer "world-wide Mareva order" in Deutschland', in Peter F. Schlosser (ed.), *Materielles Recht und Prozeßrecht und die Auswirkungen der Unterscheidung im Recht der Internationalen Zwangsvollstreckung* (Bielefeld: Gieseking, 1991), pp. 257–8.
192 *E.g. Babanaft v Bassatne* [1990] CH 13; *Derby v Weldon (No.6)* [1990] 1 WLR 1139.

held in foreign countries ('world-wide Mareva orders').[193] However, English solicitors [194] find Mareva procedures cumbersome, the test applied by the High Court for proving the necessity of Mareva as being too high. This results in forum shopping in cross-border cases.[195]

Another remedy for protection of the creditor is the Anton Piller order.[196] Accordingly, the High Court may upon an *ex parte* application of the plaintiff make an order compelling the defendant to permit the plaintiff to enter his premises to discover evidence (*i.e.* documents and articles pertaining to the alleged wrong) relating to the cause of action or essential to execution.[197]

H. COSTS

Similar to the costs of action,[198] as a rule, fees and costs payable to Sheriff [199] can be recovered from the losing party. A writ of *fi. fa.* or other writs

---

[193] Dohmann and Briggs, '"Worldwide Mareva" injunctions and the enforcement of foreign judgments in England'.

[194] English Law Firms 1, 3 and 10.

[195] For example, in a dispute between a British national and an Italian motor racing firm, English Law Firm 1 did not commence the action in England. Considering the 'creditor-friendly' rules of procedure in France which make freezing the debtor's assets very easy, they waited until a race was held in France and then commenced the procedure in France with an order of the local court for freezing assets (motor cars) just before the racing commenced.

[196] *Anton Piller K.G. v Manufacturing Process Ltd.* [1976] 1 All ER 779; RSC Ord. 29, r. 2.

[197] *Distributori Automatici Italia spa v Holford General Trading Co. Ltd.* [1985] 1 WLR 1066. Since German law does not recognise a remedy similar to that of Anton Pillar orders, it is likely that an Anton Pillar order will not be held enforceable within Germany. Thus, a recent appellate court decision held that the so called 'anti-suit injunctions' of English law which orders the defendant to refrain from initiating proceedings against the claimant pending the proceedings in England are, being against the sovereignty of the German state, of no effect in Germany. That is, an order of an English court containing an antisuit injunction may not be served upon the defendant in Germany under the 1965 Hague Service Convention. See OLG Düsseldorf, Order dated 10.1.1996, *Zeitschrift für Zivilprozeß* 109, no.2 (1996), pp. 221–33, with a note by Rolf Stürner.

[198] Supreme Court Act 1981, sec. 51; RSC Ord. 62; see B. Kaplan and K. M. Clermont, *Ordinary Proceedings in First Instance - International Encyclopaedia of Comparative Law*, Vol. XVI, Ch.6 (Tübingen: Mohr / The Hague: Mouton / New York: Oceana Publications, 1984), pp. 39–40.

[199] Sheriffs Act 1887, sec. 20 (2); Order as to Sheriff Fees July 8, 1920, Statutory Rules and Orders 1920 No.1250 (lastly amended by Sheriffs' Fees (Amendment) Order 1982, S. I. 1982 No.89).

requiring the Sheriff to levy money instruct him to levy such fees and charges over and above the sum recovered under the judgment or order. That is to say, the Sheriff's fees and charges are taken into account in the seizure and the Sheriff can take such monies from the property seized when it is sold.[200]

The Sheriff's fees which concern the enforcement of money judgments are calculated, as a rule, as a percentage of the monies recovered, ('poundage'). Accordingly, the Sheriff has a common interest with the execution creditor in the successful conclusion of the execution procedure and, as the case may be, a common interest with the execution debtor in selling the debtor's goods for a high price.

As in Germany, although recoverable from the debtor, the costs of execution are not a part of the costs of action. Strictly speaking, they are not debts due from the judgment debtor [201] but it is the creditor himself who is liable to (and may be sued by) the Sheriff for such costs.[202] In the case, for example, where an execution is stayed before the sale, the execution creditor has to pay the Sheriff fees and costs.[203] Furthermore, where a judgment or order is less than six hundred pounds, the plaintiff is disentitled from recovering the costs of execution by writ of *fi. fa.* from the debtor [204] and remains himself liable to the Sheriff. The Sheriff's fees and costs may reach substantial amounts, especially when the Sheriff's officers take possession of the goods owned by the debtor. Creditors are advised therefore, to take into account those charges when coming into an arrangement concerning the payment of the debt directly with the debtor.[205]

---

[200] See *Halsbury's Laws of England*, Vol.17, paras. 445–50.
[201] *Re Long & Co., ex parte Cuddeford* (1888) 20 QBD 316, C. A.
[202] *Royle v Busby* (1881) 43 LT 717; *Halsbury's Laws of England*, para. 449.
[203] *Ibid.*, para. 450.
[204] RSC Ord.47, r.4.
[205] John K. Gatenby, *Gatenby's Recovery of Money*, 8th ed. (London: Longman, 1993), p. 142.

3 Debt Recovery in Turkey

AS COMPARED WITH ENGLISH AND GERMAN LAW, AND WITH SPECIAL REFERENCE TO THE EXECUTION OF FOREIGN JUDGMENTS

A. LEGAL BASIS

In contrast to the German Code of Civil Procedure and the English Rules of the Supreme Court and County Court Orders, the Turkish Code of Civil Procedure (Turkish CCP) contains no rules concerning civil execution.[1] Civil execution (*icra hukuku*) in Turkey is governed by a separate act, *i.e.* by the Code of Civil Execution and Bankruptcy of 1932 ('CCEB'). CCEB, supplemented by the Rules of Civil Execution and Bankruptcy (Icra ve Iflas Kanunu Nizamnamesi ve Yönetmeligi) issued in accordance with Art. 14 of the Code, covers each and every method of judicial enforcement including for example, civil execution against immovable property and the attachment of earnings. CCEB also governs other related areas such as personal and corporate bankruptcy and concordat (*konkordato, Vergleich*) procedures, *Actio Pauliana* and preliminary attachment (*ihtiyati haciz, Arrest*). Thus, the multiplicity of legislation, which is observed in German and English civil execution law, does not exist in Turkey.

---

1 For a general outline of Turkish civil procedure in English language, see Delmar Karlen and Ilhan Arsel, *Civil Litigation in Turkey*, Ankara 1957 (detailed but relatively dated because of legislative developments); Baki Kuru, Tugrul Ansay and Feyyaz Gölcüklü, 'Civil Procedure', in Tugrul Ansay and Don Wallace (eds), *Introduction to Turkish Law*, 4th ed. (The Hague: Kluwer, 1996), pp. 179–208 (up-to-date summary in a nutshell). In German: Baki Kuru, *Zivilgerichtsbarkeit, Zwangsvollstreckung und Konkurs in europäischen Ländern – Teil II: Griechland, Italien, Jugoslawien, Portugal, Spanien und Türkei* (Stuttgart: Deutscher Sparkassenverlag, 1983), pp. 359–459.

CCEB is to a large extent based upon the Swiss Federal Code on Debt Collecting and Bankruptcy 1899 (*Bundesgesetz über Schuldbetreibung und Konkurs*[2]). The original text of the Code has however been radically altered through a number of amendments made by Parliament, the most important being the 1940, 1965, 1985 and 1988 Amendments.[3,4]

B. CIVIL EXECUTION OFFICERS

The most important officer in Turkish civil execution procedure is the Execution Officer (*icra müdürü*, formerly *icra memuru*). His powers are wider than those of the Sheriff's in English legal procedure and the Court Executor's in German law. Some functions which are fulfilled by the courts in Germany and in England are carried out by the Execution Officer in Turkey. He has competence for example to 'seize' immovable property and to issue garnishee orders.

In contrast to the legal system in England, the Execution Officer in Turkey is a public employee and his acts are subject to the control and supervision of the Execution Court. Accordingly, where he acts contrary to the principles of law or procedure (*e.g.* in the case of wrongful seizure of property), he is, unlike the Sheriff in England,[5] not personally liable against the person who has suffered loss, but, this person must sue the public administrator instead of the Execution Officer.[6]

---

2 The Swiss Code governs, unlike its Turkish counterpart, only the execution of monetary-claims and excludes, for example, the execution for the recovery of goods and chattels and land.
3 For the differences between Turkish and Swiss civil execution and bankruptcy procedures and important amendments made to the CCEB see Baki Kuru, 'Das schweizerische Schuldbetreibungs- und Konkursgesetz in der Türkei', *Zeitschrift für Schweizerisches Recht* 83 (1964), pp. 331–50; 'Die neue Revision des türkischen Schuldbetreibungs-und Konkursgesetzes', *Blätter für Schuldbetreibung und Konkurs*, no.2 (1967), pp. 33–45; 'Wechselbetreibung im türkischen Recht', in *Festschrift zum 70. Geburtstag von Max Guldener* (Zürich: Schultess, 1973), pp. 177–88.
4 It has been argued that these amendments have changed the original system of the Code to a more creditor-oriented debt collecting mechanism. See Saim Üstündag, *Icra ve Iflas Kanunu'nun Dünü ve Bugünü* (Istanbul: Evrim, 1990); Ali Cem Budak, 'Icra ve Iflas Kanunu'nda Borclu Aleyhine Yapilan Degisiklikler', in Ali Cem Budak (ed.), *Türk, Ingiliz ve ABD Hukukunda Isletmelerin Ödeme Güçlügü Sorunlari ve Banka Iliskileri Sempozyumu* (Istanbul: Istanbul Chamber of Industry, 1993).
5 See *supra*.
6 CCEB Art. 5. Similar to German law; see German Civil Code § 839; Jauernig, *Zwangsvollstreckungs- und Insolvenzrecht*, p. 40.

The Execution Court (*icra tetkik mercii*) in Turkey is, unlike the Execution Court in Germany and the ordinary courts of first instance which take part in the execution procedure in England,[7] not of itself an 'Execution Officer'.[8] None of the enforcement methods are to be used directly by or through the 'Execution Court'. Involvement in the execution procedure is however implemented in three ways:

(1) complaints against the acts of the Execution Officer are made to the Execution Court (*sikayet*, CCEB Art. 16);[9]
(2) the Execution Court is the competent court in summary procedures for liquidated monetary obligations, debts due under a negotiable instrument *etc.*;[10]
(3) it is furthermore the competent court for third party oppositions in the seizure of goods allegedly owned by a third party (*cf.* Sheriff's interpleader, *Drittwiderspruchsklage*) and in the public auction sales.[11] It is also competent to set aside or stay the execution where the judgment debt is extinguished outside the court (Turkish counterpart of the German *Vollstreckungsgegenklage*[12]); to hear some of the so-called civil execution and bankruptcy crimes (*e.g.* fraudulent bankruptcy) and committal (*Haftanordnung*) cases.[13]

The Turkish Execution Court is, unlike its counterparts in English and German law, a so-called 'Court of limited competence' which applies simplified rules of procedure and evidence, the decisions of which are not therefore conclusive under the doctrine of *res judicata*.[14]

---

7   See *supra*.
8   As a result of the public law nature of the civil execution procedure, Turkish courts have exclusive jurisdiction for cases concerning execution proceedings in Turkey (CCEB Arts. 69 II, 72 VIII, 89 III, 142 I, 154, 235 I, 258, 259 IV) which may not be avoided by a jurisdiction agreement between the parties. See Nuray Eksi, *Türk Mahkemelerinin Milletlerarasi Yetkisi* (Istanbul: Beta, 1996), p. 196.
9   Cf. '*Erinnerung*' in German law, German CCP § 766.
10 Such summary procedures are provided in the CCEB (not in the Turkish CCP) and are regarded as being a part of civil execution procedure in Turkey.
11 CCEB Arts.96 et seq., Art.134 respectively.
12 See *infra*.
13 CCEB Arts.331 et seq.
14 There is an exception to this rule. Decisions (judgments) made in connection with third party oppositions in public auction sales (*supra*) – where the court applies ordinary rules of procedure and evidence – are *res judicata*. Saim Üstündag, *Icra Hukukunun Esaslari*, 6th ed. (Istanbul: Alfa, 1995), p. 31.

C. BASIC RULES AND PRINCIPLES: ENFORCEABLE JUDICIAL ACTS, EFFECT OF APPEAL, EXECUTION CLAUSE, SERVICE, 'SETTING ASIDE' AND STAY OF EXECUTION AND 'NEGATIVE DECLARATORY ACTION'; FOREIGN JUDGMENTS (EXEQUATUR)

1. Enforceable Judicial Acts

As in German law, execution procedures can be initiated in Turkey either with a judgment (*hüküm*) or order (*karar*) of an ordinary court or with another 'enforcement title'. Among the enforcement titles apart from judgments and orders, are deeds made by and executed before a court or notary public (*re'sen düzenlenen noter senetleri*) containing a liquidated sum of money, court settlements (*sulhler*) and admissions (*kabuller*) made and guarantees (*kefaletnameler*) given before the court or Execution Officer.[15] Mortgages containing a liquidated sum of money [16] and payment orders (*ödeme emirleri*) of the Execution Officers which have become conclusive in the course of summary procedures for collecting money claims (*i.e.* either as a result of failure on the part of the debtor to raise an objection or as a result of an order of the Execution Court setting aside the objection)[17] are also enforceable in the same way as judgments and orders. Domestic arbitral awards are enforceable after an execution clause has been issued by the competent state court.[18]

2. Effect of Appeal

Turkish law does not recognise the German concept of provisional enforceability (*vorläufige Vollstreckbarkeit*). As with the English procedure, a Turkish judgment can, as a rule, be enforced even when an appeal is pending

---

15 CCEB Art.38.
16 CCEB Art.149.
17 See *infra* 'Summary Procedures for Debt Collection' in this chapter.
18 Unlike the position in Germany, Turkish arbitral awards may not be 'set aside', but are rather subject to the control of the Court of Cassation. The grounds of appeal which may be asserted against an arbitral award are limited to exceptional cases, *i.e.* the award having been made after the arbitration period, the arbitrators' deciding a claim or issue which was not submitted to the arbitration or for which arbitration is not permitted and the arbitrators' failing to decide one of the claims which was submitted to arbitration. See CCP Arts. 533 and 536.

against it. There are a number of exceptions to this principle,[19] the most important ones being judgments relating to ownership or other property rights of immovable property and judgments and orders concerning family law.[20] Besides this, as is the case in England, the enforcement of a judgment pending an appeal may be suspended by a 'stay of execution order' obtained upon deposit or security from the Court of Cassation.[21]

3. Execution Clause

The enforceability of a judgment is evidenced by an 'execution clause' (*kesinlesme serhi*) inserted at the end of the judgment. The execution clause is executed by the single judge or by the chief judge of the court and is sealed with the Court Seal.[22] For other titles such as notary public deeds, an execution clause is not required.

4. Service

In contrast to the system used in Germany and similar to English law, a Turkish judgment need not, in order to become enforceable, be served upon the defendant.

5. 'Setting Aside and Stay of Execution' and 'Negative Declaratory Action'

a) Setting aside and stay of execution by the Execution Court

A similar remedy to the German 'execution counterclaim'[23] is provided in Turkey by Arts. 33, 33a (and—in summary procedures—Art. 71) of the CCEB (*icranin geri birakilmasi, takibin merci karari ile iptali*). Accordingly, where the judgment sought to be enforced has already been satisfied by the judgment debtor outside the court and the judgment creditor attempts to

---

19 See Baki Kuru, *Icra ve Iflas Hukuku*, Vol.3, 3rd ed. (Ankara: Seckin, 1993), pp. 2206 et seq.
20 Turkish CCP Art.443 IV.
21 CCEB Art.36; Turkish CCP Art.443. Cf. *supra* Chapter 2: Debt Recovery in England.
22 Turkish CCP Art.443 III.
23 See *supra* Chapter 1: Debt Recovery in Germany.

collect the debt repeatedly by initiating execution proceedings, the former may apply to the Execution Court (unlike in Germany not to the Judgment Court) to have the execution proceedings declared inadmissible.

Similarly, where the judgment debt has come under the statutes of limitations or the judgment creditor has allowed the debtor a grace period, the judgment debtor against whom execution proceedings are initiated may apply to the Execution Court to have the proceedings set aside (because of the bar arising from the Statute of Limitation) or stayed (during the grace period).

Unlike the German execution counterclaim, the fact that the judgment debt has been satisfied or that the judgment creditor has allowed the debtor a grace period can, as a rule, only be proved before the Turkish Execution Court by a deed executed by a notary public or admitted by the creditor; other evidential material such as witness testimonies *etc.* are not admissible.

b) Negative declaratory action

In the case where the judgment debtor does not have a notary public deed to establish his defence at the Execution Court, in order to have the execution proceedings set aside or stayed as discussed above, he may bring an action at the ordinary courts of first instance for declaratory relief (*menfi tespit davasi*), *i.e.* for a declaratory judgment to the effect that the judgment debt which is sought to be enforced by the creditor does not exist any longer or is no longer payable (because of payment after entry of the judgment *etc.*).[24] At such a negative declaratory action commenced before the ordinary courts, ordinary rules of procedure and evidence apply and furthermore, the debtor may also make use of evidential material other than notary public deeds.

The debtor who has commenced a negative declaratory action may also apply for a stay of execution pending the action, provided a security of not less than 15% of the debt has been deposited in the court.

Negative declaratory actions may also be—and usually are—brought by the execution debtors against whom an execution order has been made at a summary proceeding for collecting money claims (*ilamsiz takip*, *Mahnverfahren*).[25] Such orders of the Execution Court are not *res judicata*,

---

24 CCEB Art. 72.
25 See *supra* 'Enforceable Judicial Acts' in this chapter.

and may be invalidated by a judgment of the ordinary courts by a negative declaratory judgment.

6. Foreign Judgments / Exequatur [26]

As with German law, in order to enforce a foreign judgment in Turkey the judgment creditor must obtain a judgment (*exequatur*) from the competent Turkish court to the effect that the foreign judgment is enforceable within Turkish territory.

The basic rules governing exequatur proceedings are to be found in the Act on International Private and Procedural Law of 1982 (IPPL).[27] Accordingly, 'conclusive' foreign court decisions (judgments and orders) of a civil or commercial law nature may be declared enforceable in Turkey, provided that the requirements of Art. 38 of IPPL are satisfied. Thus,

(i) reciprocity must exist between Turkey and the country of origin of the foreign judgment, enabling the enforcement of a similar Turkish judgment in the foreign country in question;[28]
(ii) the subject matter of the foreign judgment must not be one of those within the exclusive jurisdiction of the national courts (*e.g.* disputes regarding ownership or other property rights on land in Turkey);
(iii) the foreign judgment must not 'explicitly' contravene Turkish *ordre public*;
(iv) due process rules in connection with service of the process, representation before the court and (as the case may be) judgments in default must have been satisfied in the foreign proceedings;

---

[26] For further information see Ergin Nomer, *Devletler Hususi Hukuku*, 8th ed. (Istanbul: Beta, 1996); Aysel Celikel, *Milletlerarasi Özel Hukuk*, 4th ed. (Istanbul: Beta, 1995); Baki Kuru, *Hukuk Muhakemeleri Usulü*, Vol.4, 5th ed. (Istanbul: Alfa, 1991), § 83. For a summary in English, see Fadil Cerrahoglu, A. F. Basgöz, and Peter D. Finlay, 'Turkey', in Philip R. Weems (ed.), *Enforcement of Money Judgments Abroad*, Vol.2 (New York: Matthew Bender, loose-leaf / 1994). In German language see Hartmut Bauer, 'Türkei', in *Die Zwangsvollstreckung aus Inländischen Schuldtiteln im Ausland* (Flensburg: Verlag Kurt Gross, loose-leaf / 1994).

[27] For a translation into German see 'Türkei', in *Handbuch der internationalen Zwangsvollstreckung*, Vol.2 (Kissing: Recht und Praxis, loose-leaf / 1994); for extracts translated into English see Cerrahoglu, Basgöz and Finlay, 'Turkey'.

[28] Such reciprocity may exist as a result of an international convention (see *infra*) or as a result of 'legal provisions' ('legal reciprocity') or as a result of 'actual practice' ('*de facto* reciprocity') in the foreign country, which enables the enforcement of Turkish judgments within that territorial jurisdiction (IPPL Art. 38 / a).

82 *Making Foreign People Pay*

(v) where the foreign judgment affects the personal status of a Turkish national, the foreign court must have applied the substantive law which is the proper law according to Turkish rules for the conflict of laws.

(The first three items are to be observed at the court's own initiative.)

Foreign court settlements declared in the form of a judgment are also enforceable, the same as is with other foreign judgments.[29] IPPL makes provision for the enforcement of foreign arbitral awards which are modelled on the 1958 United Nations Convention on Recognition and Enforcement of Foreign Arbitral Awards.[30]

Besides these general provisions in IPPL, Turkey is party to bilateral[31] and multilateral[32] conventions enabling reciprocal enforcement of judgments.

As there exists no bilateral conventions enabling the reciprocal enforcement of judgments as between Turkey and England or Germany, enforcement of English and German judgments in Turkey (except maintenance orders [33]) is to be sought under IPPL.

The General Assembly of Civil Chambers of Turkish Court of Cassation held in 1990 that the mere existence of an enforcement (exequatur) procedure in the German CCP (*i.e.* §§ 722 – 723) which is by nature similar ('parallel') to the enforcement of foreign judgments procedure in IPPL, suffices to satisfy the reciprocity requirement between Germany and Turkey,[34,35] and a German judgment on a civil or commercial matter may be

---

29 Nomer, *Devletler Hususi Hukuku*, p. 385.
30 Arts.43–45. These provisions are however of little practical importance since Turkey became a party to the 1958 United Nations and 1961 European Conventions concerning foreign and international arbitration and enforcement of foreign arbitral awards. See *Resmi Gazete* 21.5.1991, No. 20877; 23.9.1991, No. 21000; 25.9.1991, No. 21001.
31 Conventions made with Italy (1989), Romania (1972), Tunisia (1984), Turkish Republic of Northern Cyprus (1989), Poland (1990), Austria (1991), Irak (1992), Azarbaijan (1993) and China (1994): Nomer, *Devletler Hususi Hukuku*, p.387.
32 Hague Conventions on the Enforcement of Foreign Maintenance Orders of 1958 and 1973 (*Resmi Gazete* 24.12.1971, No. 14052; 16.2.1983, No. 17961).
33 See *supra* previous footnote.
34 To the same effect see (in German literature) Krüger, 'Das türkische IPR-Gesetz von 1982', p. 258 footnote 65; Schütze, 'Die Anerkennung und Vollstreckung deutscher Zivilurteile in West-Europa', p.115; Dieter Heinrich, Note on Judgment of Court of Appeal, 'OLG Nürnberg' dated 20.9.1983, *Praxis des Internationalen Privat- und Verfahrensrechts*, 4. Jahrgang (1984), p. 162, at p. 163; Martiny, 'Anerkennung ausländischer Entscheidungen nach autonomem Recht', p. 658 (§ 1503).
35 Similar for a Zurich (Swiss) judgment, see 11. HD 6.12.1985, E. 857651 1, K. 85/6766, *Istanbul Barosu Dergisi* 60, no. 1–3 (1986), p. 140.

enforced in Turkey provided that the other requirements in Art. 34 of IPPL are also satisfied.[36]

Presently, there are no reported cases enabling an English judgment to be enforced in Turkey. As is discussed above,[37] the Common Law procedure which enables the enforcement of foreign monetary judgments in England is (unlike the case in Germany) not an 'enforcement of foreign judgments' (exequatur) procedure as such, rather the judgment creditor has to bring a fresh action in England for which the foreign judgment creates a cause of action on contracts. Where such a 'fresh action' at Common Law – which requires no reciprocity between the country of origin and England [38] – has been brought, the English court must be basically satisfied that the foreign court had jurisdiction according to the rules of English law (similar: German CCP §§ 722, 328 I Nr. 1). In addition, the foreign judgment for money which is final and conclusive on its merits cannot be impeached by an error of law or of fact.[39] Thus, the 'enforcement' of foreign judgments for money at Common Law is in its effect similar to the Continental enforcement of foreign judgments (exequatur) procedures. However, as discussed above, it is relatively easy, in practice, to raise an objection against such an application for the enforcement of a foreign judgment under the provisions of Common Law asserting a procedural defect in foreign proceedings. Therefore, it is difficult to argue that the mere existence of Common Law rules enabling enforcement of foreign judgments satisfies the '*de facto* reciprocity'[40] within the meaning of Art. 38 of IPPL.

Courts of First Instance which are petitioned to declare a foreign judgment enforceable in Turkey, occasionally require the legal opinion of the International Law Department of the Ministry of Justice [41] in order to clarify

---

36 General Assembly of the Civil Chambers of the Court of Cassation ('HGK') 13.6.1990, no. 13/3–347, *Yargitay Kararlari Dergisi* (1990), pp. 1282–6, reproduced in Kuru, *Hukuk Muhakemleri Usulü*, Vol.4, pp. 4379–80. Similarly 4th Chamber of the Court of Cassation 30.11.1987, no.5472/8787, *Bursa Barosu Dergisi* (1988), pp. 37–9; 4th Chamber of the Court of Cassation, 6.7.1988, no. 3014/6939 (unreported, cited in the 'General Assembly' judgment *supra*). Cf. Holger Müller and Götz-Sebastian Hök, *Einzug von Auslandsforderungen*, 3rd ed. (Göttingen: WiRe, 1989), pp. 191–2 (doubtful about the enforceability of German judgments in Turkey, because of the reciprocity requirement in IPPL).
37 See *supra* Chapter 2: Debt Recovery in England.
38 *Adams v Cape Industries plc.* [1990] Ch 433, at 452.
39 *Dicey and Morris on Conflicts of Law*, Rule 41.
40 See *supra* Chapter 2: Debt Recovery in England.
41 Uluslararasi Hukuk Genel Müdürlügü.

if reciprocity exists between Turkey and the country of origin of the judgment which is to be enforced.[42]

The International Law Department of the Ministry of Justice uses ready-prepared print-outs in reply to enquiries often posed by the courts of first instance. Accordingly, where a district court asks as to the enforceability of a German or English judgment according to the rules of IPPL, the Ministry will send the relevant print-outs, and as the case may be, with the necessary amendments or interpolations. The Ministry of Justice maintains in its present print-out version of its legal opinion on the enforceability of German judgments in Turkey, that the 'reciprocity' requirement is satisfied between Turkey and Germany as a result of the provisions of the German Code of Civil Procedure (§§722, 723) which thus enables the enforcement of Turkish judgments within the jurisdiction of German courts. In addition, a number of reported decisions of German courts (reference has been made to the judgment of German Federal Court of 10.10.1985 [43]) illustrate that Turkish judgments were held enforceable in Germany.[44]

The Turkish procedure for the execution of foreign judgments only applies for civil and commercial court 'judgments'.[45] It has been argued in the academic literature that the term 'judgment' in this context refers not only to judgments in the narrow sense, but refers to all kinds of court decisions delivered concerning the substantive legal rights of the parties.[46] In practice, it has nevertheless been established that 'payment orders' *etc.* made by foreign summary procedure courts or other foreign 'enforceable titles' other than judgments cannot be declared enforceable in Turkey under IPPL. In the year 1987–1988 many enquiries were made to the Ministry of Justice by the courts of first instance, especially by the courts in the Black Sea district Zonguldak, posing the question whether German *Vollstreckungsbescheide* (summary procedure payment orders) could be enforced under the enforcement procedure of the IPPL. The Ministry of Justice (then the Department of Civil and Commercial Matters [47]) answered those questions in the negative on the ground that a *Vollstreckungs-*

---

[42] Interview with Officer No. 2 of the Turkish Ministry of Justice. See *infra* Chapter 7: Difficulties Hindering Access to Justice in Cross-Border Debt Collection.
[43] *Neue Juristische Wochenschrift*, 39. Jahrgang (1986), p. 2195.
[44] *E.g.* Legal opinion addressed to the Court of First Instance in the District Kumru dated 19.10.1992, numbered B030HIG000000 7-2131-1992 (not published).
[45] See IPPL Arts. 34–41.
[46] Nomer, *Devletler Hususi Hukuku*, p.384.
[47] Hukuk Isleri Genel Müdürlügü.

bescheid which had not been made in open Court was not a 'judgment' within the meaning of Art. 34 IPPL.[48]

As regards the enforceability of English judgments in Turkey, the Ministry of Justice uses in its print-out the following legal formulation:

> After consideration ... it is understood that there exists no contractual reciprocity between Turkey and England.
>
> Concerning the actual practice, that is, concerning the question if Turkish judgments are enforceable *de facto* in England, there are no statistics available. Information to such an effect has neither been received from the British authorities or from the Ministry of Foreign Affairs. The Ministry cannot make enquiries or further research the matter itself in order to answer the individual enquiries to establish whether reciprocity exists between a particular country and Turkey.
>
> Accordingly, the burden to establish whether there is a statutory provision or *de facto* practice that makes the enforcement of Turkish judgments possible in the foreign country a court decision of which is sought to be enforced in Turkey, lies with the parties.[49]

That is to say, that the standard legal opinion of the Ministry of Justice does not categorically preclude the enforcement of English judgments in Turkey, rather it leaves the burden of proof on the plaintiff as regards the existence of 'reciprocity' between the two countries.[50]

Complaints to the Ministry of Justice from the courts or from legal practitioners in connection with the statutory execution of foreign judgments procedure are not heard.[51] Possibly, because of that reason, bureau-

---

48 Turkish Ministry of Justice, Officer 1.
49 *E.g.* Legal opinion addressed to the Court of First Instance in the District Konya dated 07.08.1995, numbered B03UIG00000000 4-8-11-ING-1994. (Not published.)
50 A particular mistrust can be observed against English courts as a result of a Court of Appeal decision where the Civil Division of the Court held that a Turkish District Court in Bosphorous was *not* 'a forum ... in which justice can be done between the parties at substantially less inconvenience or expense' regarding a collision which occurred between a Turkish and a Cuban ship in Turkish territorial waters (*The Abidin Daver* [1983] 3 All E. R., C. A. 46, at p. 53 per Dunn LJ.). Although this Court of Appeal decision was reversed by the House of Lords, where the Turkish court was held to be the appropriate forum for the resolution of the dispute (*The Abidin Daver* (HL(e.)) [1984] 1 AC 398) the negative effects of the Court of Appeal decision seems to remain among the officers in the Ministry. Turkish Ministry of Justice, Officer No: 1 is of the opinion that, English judiciary is 'a little snob' and it has prejudice against the quality of the Turkish court system. See *infra* Chapter 7: Factors Impeding Access to Justice in Cross-Border Debt Collection.
51 This observation was shared by all the interview partners at the Ministry of Justice and the Court of Cassation.

crats in the Ministry of Justice find it difficult to convince their foreign counterparts to draft bilateral agreements for reciprocal recognition and enforcement of judgments. Even the ministerial bureaucracies from the countries where a great number of Turkish nationals live, such as Germany, have not yet proved to be willing to co-operate with their Turkish colleagues to draft agreements for reciprocal recognition and enforcement of judgments.[52]

D. SUMMARY PROCEDURES FOR DEBT COLLECTION

It is a peculiarity of Swiss-Turkish civil procedure [53] that a creditor may commence a debt recovery procedure at the Execution Office, without initial application to a law court being necessary (*ilamsiz icra* = 'debt recovery without a judgment'[54]).[55]

In order to commence a debt recovery procedure as such, the creditor need not file documentary evidence (and in particular a cheque or bill of exchange) with the Execution Officer. Furthermore, the debt must be referred to as a definite sum of money in the petition, but it must not necessarily be a sum present and duly payable or be outstanding independent from the performance of an obligation on the part of the creditor.[56] The Execution Officer who receives the creditor's application serves a 'payment order' upon the debtor without being involved in the merits of the case. Should the debtor not object to the payment order within 7 days commencing from the service of the same, then the debt recovery procedure will be regarded as 'finalised'[57] and the creditor may demand the seizure of the debtor's property *etc.*

Where however, the debtor files an objection the recovery process 'stops' and the creditor who wants to get a summary judgment must justify

---

52   Turkish Ministry of Justice, Officer 3.
53   See Krauskopf, 'Das britische Vollstreckungsrecht', p. 98.
54   CCEB Arts. 58 et seq.
55   Turkish summary procedure for debt collection is different from the Swiss Code as a result of amendments made to the CCEB in favour of the creditors in 1940, 1965, 1985 and 1988. See Kuru, 'Die neue Revision des türkischen Schuldbetreibungs-und Konkursgesetzes'; Kuru 'Wechselbetreibung im türkischen Recht'; Budak, 'Icra ve Iflas Kanunu'nda Borclu Aleyhine Yapilan Degisiklikler'.
56   Cf. *supra* 'Summary Procedures for Debt Collection' in Chapter 1: Debt Recovery in Germany.
57   *Ibid.*, Art. 78.

his claim before the Execution Court (not before the ordinary civil courts) by means of documentary evidence. Such documentary evidence must show a definite and unconditional debt; that is to say, the debt must be a sum present and duly payable and must be outstanding independently of the performance of an obligation on the part of the creditor or any other conditions. The debtor may defend himself against such a claim again only with the use of documentary evidence.[58] (In addition, a creditor who does not have such documentary evidence may file an action at the competent ordinary civil court for the purposes of refuting the debtor's objection. In this latter case however, the usual rules of procedure and evidence will be applicable.[59]) The summary judgment passed by the Execution Court is enforceable, but is not conclusive under the doctrine of *res judicata*.

Therefore, the debtor may make resort to the ordinary courts in order to strike down the summary judgment and it is here where he can also obtain a stay of execution. Such a stay of execution is ordered subject to the court's discretion and in any case, a security must be paid into Court amounting to no less than 15% of the value of the debt.[60]

As regards cheques and bills of exchange, CCEB contains special provisions.[61] Accordingly, such negotiable instruments are *prima facie* evidence of a debt even though they are simple documents and the validity of the signature contained in these documents is contested by the debtor. As a result, the debtor cannot stop the recovery process by simple objection; he must bring the case before the Execution Court himself in order to have the bill of exchange or cheque struck down, and this must be within a 5-day period beginning as of the service of the payment order. In addition, the debtor's mere application to the Execution Court does not suspend the execution until the Court has decided the case. This means that the creditor can cause the debtors' property attached and sold, unless the Execution Court decides on application that the debtor has a good cause to stay the execu-

---

58   See CCEB Art. 68 (in case the document submitted to the Execution Court is authenticated or recognised by the debtor); see Arts. 68A, 69 (in case the document submitted to the Execution Court is a simple document); see Art. 68b (where the creditor is a bank, in which case documents which are prepared unilaterally by the bank are also admissible evidence for a summary judgment). All these provisions are made subject to several amendments in Turkey.
59   *Ibid.*, Art. 67.
60   *Ibid.*, Art. 72. See *supra* 'Negative declaratory action'.
61   *Ibid.*, Arts. 167 et seq. (Inserted in the Code by 1965 amendment.) Cf. *supra* Chapter 1: Debt Recovery in Germany.

tion pending the case.[62] In this respect, a bill of exchange or a cheque gives the creditor a stronger position as compared to admission of debt which has been authenticated by a notary public.

In each and every one of the above mentioned alternatives, any initiative taken by the debtor or the creditor in the summary debt recovery procedure is subject to a fine and/or punitive damages amounting to 10 to 40% of the value of the debt. In particular, a creditor or a debtor who cannot justify his case before the Execution Court sitting in summary procedure or before the ordinary civil court in which an action has been brought, such case having the aim of invalidating the summary judgment of the Execution Court, will be obliged by the Court to pay the other party punitive damages of not less than 40% of the value of the debt.[63]

E. EXECUTION FOR MONEY CLAIMS

1. In General

As with German and English law, enforcement methods in Turkish law vary depending upon the subject matter of the enforcement, that is to say, whether it concerns movable or immovable property of or a debt due to the debtor *etc.*[64]

Unlike Germany, the execution creditor in Turkey may not choose the assets of the debtor upon which the execution will be exercised. The Execution Officer decides which assets are to be attacked by the enforcement measures, taking into account (as well as balancing) the interests of both the debtor and the creditor.[65]

The debtor against whom a summary procedure (Execution Court) order has been made or an enforcement of judgment procedure initiated, will be ordered by the Execution Officer to submit to the Execution Office, the particulars and location of his assets which would be sufficient to satisfy the creditor, as well as the particulars of his earnings and other financial means (statement of assets, *mal beyani*).[66] Unlike England and Germany,

---

[62] CCEB Art. 170 II.
[63] *Ibid.*, Arts. 67, 68, 68a, 72, 168, 169A, 170 (as amended in 1965, 1982 and 1985). See Budak, 'Icra ve Iflas Kanunu'nda Borclu Aleyhine Yapilan Degisiklikler', pp. 329–31 (critical).
[64] *Ibid.*, Arts. 74–144.
[65] Baki Kuru, *Icra ve Iflas Hukuku*, Vol.1 (Istanbul: Evrim, 1988), pp. 633–5.
[66] CCEB Arts. 74–7.

the order to make a statement of assets is made in Turkey by the Execution Officer (not by the Court) and without an application of the creditor being required. The debtor is obliged to declare his assets and means, only to the extent as is enough to meet the execution creditor's claim. Upon an application by the creditor, a debtor who does not make a statement of assets may be sent to prison by the Execution Court by way of committal proceedings.[67]

a) Attachment: execution against movable and immovable property

Execution made against movable and immovable property (the latter also including registered ships, CCEB. Art. 23 IV) of the debtor is effected in Turkey by the attachment procedure (*haciz*). *Haciz* (attachment) can be defined as an official act of the Execution Officer by which the right of disposal in (but not the ownership of) a particular item in the execution debtor's assets (whether real or personal) is vested in the Execution Officer, who will then sell the item in order to settle the execution creditor's claim.[68] Thus, the Turkish law of execution does not provide different sets of rules for execution against movable and immovable property. (The term *haciz* is indeed also used for garnishee orders – *alacaklarin haczi*, even although the nature of a garnishee order is different from that of the attachment of movable and immovable property.)

The competent Execution Officer who effects the attachment is the Execution Officer for the area where the enforcement proceedings were initiated or, as the case may be, where the summary (Execution Court) procedure was brought. Should the movable or immovable property which is to be attached lie outside the district where the Execution Officer holds office, the attachment is made by the local Execution Officer where the property is situated upon instruction of the former.[69]

The attachment of movable property is effected by seizing the goods or chattels, or taking 'walking possession'[70] of them. For land and limited ownership rights in land, an 'attachment notice' has to be inserted into the record of the property held by the local Land Registry.[71]

---

67 CCEB Arts. 337–9.
68 Similar, Kuru, *Icra ve Iflas Hukuku*, Vol.1, p.616.
69 CCEB Art.79 II; cf. (for the immovable property) Kuru, *ibid.*, p.650.
70 See *supra* Chapter 2: Debt Recovery in England.
71 CCEB Arts 85–91.

Unlike the provisions of German law, the attachment of movable property of the execution debtor does not provide the execution creditor with a security right *vis-à-vis* the other creditors of the debtor. The German concept *Pfändungspfandrecht* is unknown in Turkish law.[72] Similarly, the attachment of immovable property does not create a security right in favour of the execution creditor.[73] Competing individual creditors who attack the same property gain priority against each other under Turkish law according to the dates of their contract with the debtor (provided such a contract has been carried through or the date of entry of the contract is evidenced by a notary public's seal) *or* according to the date of commencement of the action or summary proceedings underlying their claims.[74]

Should a third party claim that the goods or chattels seized from the debtor's possession actually belong to him (and should such a claim be disputed by the execution creditor who wishes to have the movable attached), the Execution Officer will refer the case to the Execution Court, in which the third party brings an action against the execution creditor so that the Execution Court can pass judgment as to whether the goods or chattels actually belong to him and not to the execution debtor. The judgment of the Execution Court on this matter is binding only between the third party claimant and the execution creditor.[75] This procedure is similar to the English Interpleader, the difference being that the case between the disputing parties is heard not by the ordinary civil courts but by the Execution Court.

Unlike the procedure in Germany, the debtor's 'demand to recovery' of the goods and chattels in possession of a third party (*Herausgabeanspruch* [76]) cannot be attached in Turkey.[77] According to the CCEB, the Execution Officer may also attach movables in possession of a third party, where the execution creditor claims that the owner of these movables is the debtor. (Third party goods or chattels attached may not however be removed, *i.e.* the Execution Officer takes 'walking possession' of the movables.[78]) In such a case, the matter will again be referred to the Execution

---

72 Üstündag, *Icra Hukukunun Esaslari*, pp. 173–4.
73 Cf. 'Hypothecation' *supra* Chapter 1: Debt Recovery in Germany and 'Charging Orders' *supra* Chapter 2: Debt Recovery in England.
74 CCEB Art. 100.
75 CCEB Arts 96 et seq.
76 See *supra* Chapter 1: Debt Recovery in Germany.
77 Üstündag, *Icra Hukukunun Esaslari*, p. 209.
78 Baki Kuru, *Icra ve Iflas Hukuku*, Vol.2 (Istanbul: Evrim, 1990), p. 1111.

Court, so that the execution creditor will have to bring an action against the third party to establish that the movables are owned by the execution debtor.[79]

The sale of the attached movable or immovable property is normally made by the Execution Officer by means of public auction.[80] Exceptionally, where all the interested parties agree or where there is a stock market value *etc.*, goods and chattels and securities may also be sold by the Execution Officer under private contract (*i.e.* 'by bargaining').

As with the provisions of German law, a 'minimum bid' rule applies at public auction. The 'minimum sale price' at which a movable or immovable can be sold is 75% of the estimated market price; if this amount has not been offered in the first meeting for the auction sale and a second meeting is held, the level is decreased to 40% of the estimated market value.

Besides this, the sale price must always meet the claims of those secured creditors who are above the execution creditor (*i.e.* mortgage creditors of due and payable debts and creditors who have a lien over the chattels to be sold). Such creditors are paid off by the Execution Officer from the proceeds of the sale before the execution creditor receives the remaining amount. Unlike the system in Germany,[81] the buyer in the execution sale is not personally liable against the creditors of such due and payable mortgage debts. Should there however be mortgage debts burdening the attached property which are not yet due, the buyer in the auction sale gains the property burdened with these mortgages and becomes personally liable against the mortgagee. In this latter case, the market value of the property will be estimated for the purpose of determining the minimum sale price and will take into account such burdens on the future buyer.[82]

Public auction sale is, similar to the provisions of German law, a quasi-contract of a public law nature and is basically governed by the same principles concerning transfer of property to the buyer *etc.*[83] Should there be any irregularities (*e.g.*, in case the minimum sale price rule has not been

---

[79] CCEB Art. 99. However, see also Art. 89 CCEB *infra* 'Garnishee Procedure' in this chapter.
[80] CCEB Arts 114 et seq., 124 et seq.
[81] See 'Deckungsprinzip' and 'Übernahmeprinzip' *supra* Chapter 1: Debt Recovery in Germany.
[82] See CCEB Arts. 125, 128, 129.
[83] See *supra* Chapter 1: Debt Recovery in Germany.

observed) it may be annulled by an order of the Execution Court upon an application of an 'interested party' Execution Court.[84]

German *Zwangshypothek* and *Zwangsverwaltung* orders and English charging orders have no parallels in Turkish law.[85]

The sale of mortgaged property and pledged chattels for the settlement of the security holder's claim is also made subject to the rules applicable for public auction sale of attached property.[86] Unlike English law,[87] in case of default of payment of the mortgagor, the mortgaged property may not be transferred under Turkish law to the mortgagee, but the mortgagee's claim may only be settled through the sale of the mortgaged property by the Execution Officer.[88]

b) Garnishee procedure: attachment of debts

In Turkish law, there are two separate procedures for the attachment of debts: Art. 120 of CCEB provides, similar to German garnishee procedure, for the assignment of monetary claims owned by the execution debtor to the execution creditor; and Art. 89 of the same Code provides, similar to English law, a special summary procedure diverting payment of debts due to the execution debtor to the creditor.[89]

Art. 120 procedure which is used infrequently in practice, involves the assignment of monetary claims owned by the debtor against third parties to the execution creditor, as with German law, as *datio in solutum* or *datio in solutionis causa*.[90] (Unlike in Germany however, here the 'assignment' is achieved not by a court order, but by an act of the Execution Officer.) If the third party debtor who has been given notice of the assignment refrains

---

84 CCEB Art. 134.
85 See however CCEB Art. 121 according to which 'administration' methods may be applied in connection with the attachment of usufruct rights where the creditor's claims are settled from the rents and profits of land. Üstündag, *Icra Hukukunun Esaslari*, p. 299.
86 CCEB Art. 150g.
87 Law of Property Act 1925, sec. 88 (2).
88 Turkish Civil Code (Türk Medeni Kanunu) Art. 788. Similarly see German Civil Code § 1147.
89 The reason for this dualism is an amendment made in the CCEB in 1965 which laid down the summary procedure in Art. 89, but which at the same time kept the pre-existing attachment of debts method in Art. 120 CCEB.
90 Cf. German CCP § 835 I.

from making payment to the execution creditor, the latter must sue him before the ordinary civil courts.[91]

As is stated above, this enforcement method is, since 1965, largely substituted for by the procedure set out in Art. 89 CCEB. In particular, the attachment of monies in bank accounts, which is of great practical importance, is regularly made under Art. 89.

The procedure in Art. 89 begins with an 'attachment notice' (*haciz ihbarnamesi*) sent to the third party debtor (*e.g.* the execution debtors bank) by the Execution Officer who acts upon an *ex parte* application of the execution creditor.[92] This attachment notice, which is called the 'first attachment notice' orders the third party debtor (garnishee) not to pay the debt to the execution debtor and makes it clear that only payment made to the Execution Office may discharge him from his obligations. The first attachment also gives the third party debtor notice of a seven day period within which he may file an objection with the Execution Office and deny that he owes such an amount to the execution debtor (*e.g.* the bank may object against the attachment notice on the ground that the debtor does not have an account at that bank). If the third party debtor makes such an objection, the execution creditor may bring an action against the third party debtor at the Execution Court and, should he be able to establish that the latter is actually indebted to the execution debtor, he may collect such amount from the third party debtor without any other judgment being necessary.[93]

On the other hand, should the garnishee not file an objection against the 'first attachment notice' within the given deadline he will be served with a second notice from the Execution Officer (*i.e.* 'second attachment notice') declaring that he is from that time on deemed to be indebted to the debtor as detailed in the first attachment notice and must either pay that money over to the Execution Office or bring a negative declaratory action in the ordinary courts *against the execution creditor* in order to establish that he is not indebted to the execution debtor. If the garnishee brings such a negative declaratory action, he cannot be forced to make the required payment until the declaratory action proceeds to judgment. If however, he loses that suit in the ordinary courts he will be fined and have to pay punitive damages

---

91 Cf. *supra* Chapter 1: Debt Recovery in Germany.
92 Cf. *supra* Chapter 2: Debt Recovery in England where the 'garnishee order *nisi*' is made by the court.
93 Cf. *supra* Chapter 2: Debt Recovery in England, where the garnishee order *absolute* is made by the ordinary courts which have a discretionary power to grant or to reject the application.

to the execution creditor of an amount not less than 40% of the disputed amount.

The procedure set out by Art. 120 of CCEB is a real garnishee procedure which is applicable for the attachment of money debts only. Art. 89 may be used on the other hand to attack movable property of the debtor in possession of a third party (*e.g.* jewellery kept in a bank). The procedure to be applied in such a case is parallel to that for the attachment of monetary-debts and is an alternative to the Art. 99 procedure described above.[94] In any case, as with German law, the attachment of securities having a stock market price is regarded as attachment against movable property and is therefore outside the scope of Arts. 89 and 120. Similarly, the attachment of earnings, which is governed by special provisions,[95] is not covered by these provisions.

The attachment of debts under Art. 89 does not as such provide the execution creditor with a security right or a priority for the purposes of bankruptcy. The assignment of debts under Art. 120 as *datio in solutum* on the other hand, makes the execution creditor the owner of the claim, as a result of which such claim will not be vested in the trustees in bankruptcy.[96]

There are no special provisions in Turkish law concerning the attachment of debts due from third parties resident abroad. Legal literature provides no answer to this. The discussions referred to in connection with the German garnishee procedure to the effect that a garnishee order may in principle be made against a third party debtor resident abroad are also applicable to Turkish law. This is because, the only 'execution act' made by the Execution Officer in the procedures provided by Art. 89 or Art. 120, is the service of an 'attachment notice' on the third party debtor abroad, which can by no means be seen as an exercise of sovereign (public) powers outside the jurisdiction of the courts.[97]

The Turkish Court of Cassation has held that an Execution Officer can serve (by post) an 'attachment notice' against a third party who is resident outside the district (Bailiwick) which is under his jurisdiction. That is, an Execution Officer's power to make an attachment of a debt is not limited to

---

94 *Supra* 'Execution against movable and immovable property'.
95 *Infra*.
96 Üstündag, *Icra Hukukunun Esaslari*, p. 295–6.
97 Cf. however the Court of Appeal in Düsseldorf, the judgment dated 10.1.1996 (*Zeitschrift für Zivilprozeß* 109, no.2, pp. 221–33) where the mere service of an English court order *in personam* (*i.e.* an antisuit injunction) upon a person in Germany was regarded as being against the sovereignty of the German State.

the persons (*i.e.* debtors to the execution debtor) who are resident or actually present in person within his own Bailiwick. Even where such third party debtors are (or are resident) outside the district where the Execution Officer holds office, he can make and serve the attachment of debts (garnishee) order himself and does not need to have the attachment of debts made through the Execution Officer where the third party debtors live or are present.[98] Following this precedent, there is no reason not to accept that an Execution Officer in principle also has competence to serve an attachment of debts notice on a third party resident abroad.

c) Attachment of earnings

The attachment of earnings is made under special provisions, separate from the general garnishee procedures in Arts. 89 and 120 CCEB, which provide for both the protection of the debtor [99] and a simplified collection method in favour of the creditor.[100]

According to Art. 83 CCEB, wages, salaries and other earnings of the debtor may only be attached to such an extent that the basic needs of the debtor and his dependants are catered for. The amount of such deductions is to be calculated by the Execution Officer. Unlike the provisions in English law for attachment of earnings and German garnishee procedures, there is no court intervention in this assessment process, unless a 'compliance'[101] is filed with the Execution Court against the decision of the execution creditor. Neither are detailed guidelines to assist the Execution Officer in exercising his discretion included in the CCEB, unlike the German CCP §§ 850 *et seq.* The only limitation is that the amount to be attached from the debtor's earnings may not be less than 25% of the same.[102]

Unlike the position in England and in Germany,[103] not all kinds of pension but only pensions of public employees are covered by the provisions of Art. 83. Pensioners retired from private employers or self employed pensioners receive full protection, *i.e.* their pensions are—except for attachment

---

98   12th Civil Chamber of the Court of Cassation, 20.12.1976, No. 11269/12923, partially reproduced in Kuru, *Icra ve Iflas Hukuku*, Vol.1, p.696.
99   CCEB Art. 83.
100   CCEB Arts 355–6.
101   See *supra* 'Execution Officers', 'Execution Court' in this chapter.
102   The attachment of earnings for enforcement of maintenance orders being the exception, in which case there is no such limit.
103   German CCP § 850 II.

for the satisfaction of maintenance orders—fully exempt from attachment.[104]

The attachment of earnings is achieved by simply serving an 'attachment of earnings notice', issued by the Execution Officer, on the employer of the execution debtor (including a public employer) to the effect that the earnings of the debtor are attached. The employer is obliged to deduct the amount from the debtors salary *etc.* and pay the amount prescribed to the Execution Office. Should the employer (or the public servant employed by the public employer who is in charge of paying the employee and who is served with the attachment earnings notice in the course of his employment) not act in accordance with the attachment of earnings notice, he will be held personally liable to pay the prescribed amount, without a separate judgment or order against such person being necessary.[105]

An attachment of earnings decision of the Execution Officer does not provide a security or priority right for the purposes of bankruptcy.[106] The ranking among various creditors seeking attachment of earnings against the same debtor is determined according to the 'first come - first served' principle; unless a higher ranking creditor's claim is settled in full, then a lower ranking creditor cannot receive payment.[107]

2. Monetary Claims Based upon a Foreign Judgment (or another Foreign Enforcement Title)

As is discussed above and as is also the case with the provisions of German law, a foreign judgment for the payment of money or any other foreign enforcement title such as a court settlement may be enforced in Turkey, provided that the foreign title has been declared enforceable by the competent Turkish court (exequatur).

---

104 Social Insurance Act (SSK Kanunu), No. 506, Art. 121; Self-Employed Persons Association Act (Bag-Kur Kanunu), Art. 67.
105 CCEB Arts. 355–6.
106 Indeed, wage earners and public servants are not subject to bankruptcy in Turkey. Only individuals and corporations running a commercial business ('merchants' within the meaning of Turkish Commercial Code) can be declared bankrupt.
107 CCEB Art. 83 II.

Furthermore, similar to the provisions of German law, civil execution in Turkey is governed solely by national law and can only be made through the national civil Execution Officers.[108]

As is seen above, the powers of an Execution Officer to attach movable and immovable property are limited to the geographical area of the district where he holds office.[109] Thus, it is obvious that movables and immovables situated abroad cannot be attached by Turkish Execution Officers. An 'attachment notice' (garnishee orders) made in accordance with Art. 89 or Art. 120 CCEB can on the other hand, as discussed above, be served by the competent Turkish officers upon the third party debtors (garnishees) resident abroad.

Should the creditor who initiates the execution procedure in Turkey be resident abroad he must, in the application to the Execution Office, give an address within the jurisdiction of the courts where service may be made;[110] should he be a foreign national, he must also make a payment into Court, as a security in favour of the execution debtor, for costs (*catio judicatum solvi*).[111]

As in England and in Germany, in order to enforce a judgment for money in a foreign currency in Turkey, the foreign currency amount must be converted into Turkish Liras. As a result of the high inflation rate in Turkey, the question as to which date is to be taken into account for the conversion is very important.[112] As opposed to the case in England, the judgment

---

[108] 'Foreign decisions [judgments and orders] which have been declared enforceable are enforced in the same manner as decisions made by Turkish Courts.' (IPPL Art. 41 I.)

[109] CCEB Art. 79.

[110] CCEB Art. 58 I.

[111] IPPL Art. 32. See Kuru, *Icra ve Iflas Hukuku*, Vol.1, pp. 210–1; Nomer, *Devletler Hususi Hukuku*, pp. 377–81. *Catio judicatum solvi* may not be applied where there is reciprocity between Turkey and the country of the execution creditor, which enables Turkish nationals to initiate execution procedures in the foreign country in question without making a payment into Court *etc*. Such reciprocity exists between Turkey and Germany according to the Convention dated 28.5.1929 (*Resmi Gazete* 4.6.1930, No.1511; *RGBl* 1930 II p. 6) Art. 2 and between Turkey and England according to the Convention dated 28. 11. 1931 (*Resmi Gazete* 5.7.1932, no.2142), Arts. 12–13.

[112] For various remedies for the protection of the creditor discussed within the context of civil execution law see Üstündag, *Icra Hukukunun Esaslari*, pp. 108–11; Selâhattin Sulhi Tekinay, Sermet Akman, Haluk Burcuoglu and Atilla Altop, *Tekinay Borclar Hukuku*, 7th ed. (Istanbul: Filiz, 1993), pp. 778–9; Birsel and Erdem, 'Yurtdisindan Alinan Yatirim Kredilerinin Cebri Icra Yoluyla Tahsilinde Ortaya Cikan Sorunlar', pp. 129–32 (followed by comments made by the authors and by Hayri Domanic at pp. 142–8); Talih Uyar, 'Yabanci Para Alacaginin Tahsili', *Istanbul Barosu Dergisi* 68, no.7–9 (1993), pp. 572–82.

creditor who seeks to enforce a judgment for money in a foreign currency in Turkey does not have to apply the conversion rate at the date of application to the Execution Office, rather may choose between the contractual maturity date of the debt and the date of 'actual payment'.[113] According to the precedents of the Court of Cassation, established since 1992, the creditor may request the Execution Officer to enforce a claim for a foreign currency amount.[114] In such a case, the conversion must be made by the Execution Officer using the conversion rate applied on the day when the creditor is paid, *e.g.* when the proceeds of the execution sale are paid to the creditor.[115]

F. PROTECTION OF THE DEBTOR

It is a duty of the Execution Officer to refrain from any unnecessary harshness against the debtor, *e.g.* from excessive attachment. The Execution Officer must also decide which assets of the debtor are to be attacked by the enforcement measures, taking into account *inter alia* the interests of the debtor and his dependants.[116]

Besides this, Art. 82 CCEB provides a catalogue of real and personal property which are exempt from attachment. Similar to English and German law, work equipment and basic household appliances necessary for an individual debtor's job and domestic needs are exempt from attachment in Turkey. In addition, unlike the other two jurisdictions, Art. 82 CCEB

---

113 Turkish Code of Obligations, Art. 83 III. Cf. German Civil Code § 244. Cf. Debt Recovery in England (*supra*) where the conversion is made at the request for the issue of a writ of *fi. fa.* to the Sheriff.

114 Although the amount must be converted into Turkish Liras in the application to the Execution Office (CCEB Art. 58, Nr. 3), according to the Court of Cassation, this is only for the purposes of calculating the court (execution) fees; [12th Chamber of the Court of Cassation, 21.3.1995, No. 3581/3982, Talih Uyar, *Gerekceli – Notlu Ictihatli Icra ve Iflas Kanunu* (A collection of the Court of Cassation precedents), Vol.1 (Ankara: Feryal, 1996), p. 910] and the interest to accumulate after the date of application to the Execution Office (12th Chamber of the Court of Cassation, 10.7.1995, No. 9899/10360, Uyar, *Gerekceli – Notlu Ictihatli Icra ve Iflas Kanunu*, Vol.1, p. 901). Cf. Hakan Pekcanitez, *Medeni Usul ve Icra-Iflâs Hukukunda Yabanci Para Alacaklarinin Tahsili* (Izmir:Dokuz Eylül Üniversitesi Hukuk Fakültesi, 1994), pp. 95–105 (critical: the author finds the judicial precedents *contra legem*.). Cf. Üstündag, *Icra Hukukunun Esaslari*, p. 108.

115 *E.g.* 12th Chamber of the Court of Cassation, 29. 12. 1994, No. 16782/17041, Uyar, *Gerekceli – Notlu Ictihatli Icra ve Iflas Kanunu*, Vol.1, p. 910.

116 See *supra*.

provides that the 'exemption from attachment' is also applicable to some immovable property. That is to say, the debtor's house may be exempt, provided that it is just enough to meet his needs and not too luxurious and large, and the land necessary for a farmer's business cannot be attached for the settlement of his debts.[117]

G. PRELIMINARY REMEDIES FOR PROTECTION OF THE CREDITOR (PRELIMINARY ATTACHMENT)

Preliminary attachment (*ihtiyati haciz*) procedure in Turkey is very similar to the '*Arrestprozeß*' of German law. Accordingly, a creditor may, in order to preserve the debtor's assets pending court proceedings (or pending a summary debt collection procedure under CCEB [118]), file an application with the competent ordinary civil court [119] for an order for preliminary attachment. The order may be—and usually is—made *ex parte*. Where there is *prima facie* evidence that there is a debt due and unsecured, the court will grant the order. Should the claim however not have matured, additional evidence will be necessary to show that the debtor is about to remove his assets *etc.* or that he has no permanent place of residence. In each case the creditor must make a payment into Court as a security for any damages which may result to the debtor's property as a consequence of the preliminary attachment, when such measures turn out to be unnecessary.

The preliminary attachment order must be enforced by the creditor within 10 days [120] subsequent to the making of the order. Preliminary attachment is made in the same way as an ordinary attachment, *i.e.* for immovables by inserting an 'attachment notice' into the records held by the Land Registry.[121]

Should the preliminary attachment order be made prior to the court (or summary debt collection) proceedings, the action on the merits (or the summary debt collection proceedings) must be initiated within seven days following the (preliminary) attachment. Similar to the provisions of German law, where the creditor is successful at the proceedings on the merits of the case (or at the summary debt collection proceedings), the prelimi-

---

117 For protection of debtors in attachment of earnings procedure see *supra*.
118 See *supra* 'Civil Execution Officers' in this chapter.
119 CCEB Art. 257.
120 Cf. *supra* Chapter 2: Debt Recovery in Germany.
121 Cf. Germany, where a 'maximal hypothek' is made.

nary attachment changes automatically to a full attachment.[122] Where, on the other hand, the creditor loses at the main proceedings, the debtor can sue him for damages caused by the preliminary attachment; the creditor's liability here is strict.

H. COSTS

The costs of civil execution proceedings are paid in advance by the creditor and if he is successful in the proceedings, will be ultimately borne by the debtor, *e.g.* deducted from the proceeds of the execution sale without a separate order for the costs being necessary.[123] The costs of the execution proceedings include filing fees, the cost of attachment *etc.* as well as lawyers fees' which are fixed in conformity with an official tariff (*i.e.* not the actual amount agreed between the lawyer and his client which is normally higher than the minimum amounts in the official tariff).

---

122   CCEB Art. 264.
123   CCEB Arts 15, 59, 90, 94 V.

4 Results of the Comparison between German, English and Turkish Debt Recovery Law

A comparison between the legal systems in England, Germany and Turkey demonstrates that the procedures for debt recovery are broadly similar in nature to one another. It is particularly noteworthy that the difference between the civil execution procedures of the English Common Law system and the two Continental systems is not as significant as one would find in other areas such as, for example, property law.[1] Thus in essence, the differences between Turkish and English law of civil execution are not more considerable than those between Turkish and German law. Notwithstanding the general similarities, the following points which may have implications for cross-border debt collection are worthy of attention.

A. MULTIPLICITY OF LEGAL SOURCES FOR PROCEDURAL RULES

Civil execution in Turkey and in Germany is governed by codified (in Germany, federal) law, whereas English civil execution law is a composite of statute law, Common Law and secondary legislation. As compared to his colleagues in Germany and England, the Turkish lawyer would experience the least difficulty in explaining his national provisions to his counterparts abroad (*i.e.* a corresponding lawyer or counsel for the other party). Turkish law is simpler, in that all of the substantial provisions concerning enforcement of judgments as well as summary procedures for debt recovery are contained in the same Code. In addition, as opposed to the English Court Rules and German statutes, the provisions of the Turkish CCEB are briefly

---

1 For additional examples of substantial differences between English and German Law, see Murat Ferid, *Internationales Privatrecht*, 3rd ed. (Frankfurt am Main: Alfred Metzner, 1986), pp. 95–9.

formulated. English law is the least straightforward of the three legal systems, for there are two parallel set of rules in the High Court and County Courts, and in many areas, such as remedies for protection of the creditor, a good command of the case law is required.

B. ROLE OF EXECUTION OFFICERS AND COURTS

Turkish law differs from German and English law in that the Execution Officer is provided with extensive discretionary powers concerning all methods of execution.[2] That is, the subject matter and extent of execution measures are decided by the court executor considering the particulars of each case and the need for protection of the debtor or of third parties. This is the case, for example, for attachment of earnings and execution against immovable property: contrary to the case in German and English law, the order for attachment of earnings and attachment and execution sale of immovable property are made not by the Court but by the execution officer. Acts of the Turkish Execution Officer are subject to the control, but never the leave of the so-called Execution Court. A further difference in connection with this latter aspect is that the English Sheriff and, in practice, the court executor in Germany enjoy the position of a self-employed individual, whereas in Turkey the execution officer is an employee of the Court.

In contrast to the provisions of Turkish law, and even more so than in German law, English civil execution law is exercised at the court's discretion when determining the admissibility and/or the extent of the execution measures. This can be illustrated by a comparison between the German and English procedures for execution against immovable property or attachment of earnings. Unlike under German law, English courts have broad discretion as to the making of a charging order against immovable property, and consider not only the interests of the parties but also the interests of other creditors and joint owners of the land in question. Similarly, unlike the provisions of the German CCP, English law does not have detailed rules about the deductions to be made from the debtor's earnings; instead, the county court decides the 'normal deduction' and 'protected earnings rate' at its discretion. Again counter to German and Turkish law, in certain cases, enforcement of an English judgment is either subject to leave of the court or may be 'stayed' by the court. The former is the case, for example,

---

2   An important exception is the attachment of the dwelling house.

where there has been a change of parties, and the latter where an appeal is pending or if the court *thinks it just.*

The German court executor serves not merely as an 'executor' of the judgment, but plays a significant role in the enforcement of judgments for the purpose of ensuring the effective functioning of the enforcement system.[3] This may be explained by the relatively independent position of the court executor from the judgment court, and his own interest in the successful enforcement of the judgment (his share of the collected monies as a collection fee). In particular, the court executor may persuade the debtor and the creditor to agree on a deferred payment plan. In practice, instead of applying the statutory enforcement measures, the court executor may make a short discussion with the debtor (sometimes on the door-step of the debtor) concerning his financial position,[4] and offer him an acceptable payment plan.[5] That is to say, where necessary, he acts as a conciliator or a mediator who has direct contact with the debtor and knows the local community.[6] This way, by reason of the court executor's active involvement in the legal relationship between the parties, the enforcement of a judgment may become a 'dispute resolution process'. It has been stated that, considering the active involvement of the court executors in the debtor-creditor relationship, and the decreasing efficiency of the execution sales in enforcement of judgments,[7] the role of the court executor must be re-defined. The gravity of the activities of the court executor must be shifted from his function of an enforcement agent towards his function as a mediator.[8]

---

3   In an empirical research, Klein observed the activities of the German court executor and considered 501 'execution files' in the court executor's office. For the account of the research results including, inter alia, a description of the daily work of the court executor, see Klein, 'Die Vollstreckung von Geldforderungen durch den Gerichtsvollzieher'.
4   The so-called 'enforcement advice', Vollstreckungsgespräch.
5   Theo Rasehorn, 'Der Gerichtsvollzieher als "Basis-Implementeur"', in Erhard Blankenburg and Rüdiger Voigt (eds), *Implementation von Gerichtsentscheidungen – Jahrbuch für Rechtssoziologie und Rechtstheorie* 11 (Opladen: Westdeutscher Verlag, 1987), pp. 104–9, p. 107.
6   *Ibid.*, pp. 105–6.
7   This is due to decreasing market value for second-hand goods. Cf. Klein, 'Die Vollstreckung von Geldforderungen durch den Gerichtsvollzieher', p. 65; Rasehorn, 'Der Gerichtsvollzieher als "Basis-Implementeur"', p. 106.
8   Ralf Rogowski, 'Implementation von zivilgerichtlich legitimierten Geldforderungen', in Erhard Blankenburg and Rüdiger Voigt (eds), *Implementation von Gerichtsentscheidungen – Jahrbuch für Rechtssoziologie und Rechtstheorie* 11 (Opladen: Westdeutscher Verlag, 1987), pp. 43–8, pp. 45–6.

C. CREDITOR'S CONTROL OVER THE ENFORCEMENT PROCEDURE

Different positions of civil execution officers in the three countries influence the relations between the execution officers, the parties and their lawyers. In each country, creditors have different degrees of control over the execution procedures. It is common in all three countries that the execution procedure is initiated, not by the court ex officio, but rather by the creditor. In Germany, the judgment creditor is in a highly advantageous position, for he identifies not only the enforcement method to be applied (execution against movable property, attachment of earnings, a charging order concerning immovables, *etc.*) but also the assets which are to be affected. In England, the creditor is able to choose the enforcement method to be applied, but not the assets to be covered by the enforcement. Turkish law differs from the German and English systems in that the execution officer decides both the enforcement method and the assets belonging to debtor which are going to be affected.[9]

According to the German court executor, in 70 – 80% of cases, court executors in Germany are instructed by lawyers rather than by judgment creditors.[10] The court executor follows the instructions of the creditor's lawyer. However, as the lawyer is permitted to choose the enforcement measure as well as the assets to be removed, he does not need to convince the court executor on a particular course of action. Lawyers do not meet with the court executor, and only in exceptional cases, where there are special grounds for the creditor's presence, would creditors or their lawyers accompany the court executor during the seizure of goods.[11]

In England, sheriffs' officers have closer ties with solicitors who specialise in debt collection:

> The solicitors, once they obtain the judgment, would follow and track to see what happens to the execution. I know a lot of solicitors in this country, whose mainstream is litigating in the debt collection area. They do actually treat us as

---

9   See Chapters 1–3 *supra*, Jauernig, *Zwangsvollstreckungs- und Insolvenzrecht*, pp. 4 and 130, O'Hare and Hill, *Civil Litigation*, p. 581 and Kuru, *Icra ve Iflas Hukuku*, Vol. 1, pp. 633–5, respectively.

10 According to the results of Klein's study which was published in 1987, 52% of the German enforcement procedures were initiated by a lawyer. The tendency towards the representation by a lawyer was slightly increasing. See Klein, 'Die Vollstreckung von Geldforderungen durch den Gerichtsvollzieher', p. 66.

11 Interview with German Court Executor.

part of the service that they offer to the client. They do follow up, see that the officer is doing what he is supposed to be doing and not letting it lapse.[12]

However, a sheriff's officer rarely meets the debtor's solicitor, and it is rare for a lawyer to accompany him during his visit to the debtor:

> Solicitors know how to communicate in a meaningful manner . . . We go and see the actual debtor and not their legal representatives . . . Solicitors in general do not wish to go see the debtors. They have come along on occasion. We do not encourage it at the debtor's end, because it can cause problems. We spend a lot of time training our officers, so that when they go round to the premises and see the people, they can talk to them in a way, not trying to be the big 'I am' but to try to understand that they have a problem. The last thing we actually want to do is to aggravate the situation, which happens if you have the creditor come along with you and who says 'I want my money back, I want my money back' or the solicitor trying to provide all sorts of legal arguments to the person when all the person actually really needs to be told is can you pay or, if not, can you do something to pay.[13]

In contrast to the case in Germany and much more often than in England, the Turkish execution officer always works with the creditors' 'advocates' or clerks who are employed by these advocates. A Turkish lawyer personally knows the court executors in the district where he practises law. It is important to establish good relations with one or two court executors. A court executor is able to accelerate the execution process and oversee some 'bureaucratic details' to the creditor's advantage. For example, an application for a 'payment order' under the summary procedure for cheques and bills of exchange must be annexed with the original copy of the bill or the cheque.[14] A court executor may accept photocopies instead of the original documents. He may also assess the value of goods which are going to be seized at lower than the actual market price. In such cases, the debtor may apply to the Execution Court for annulment of the act of the court executor. However, although the execution officer is subject to the Execution Court's supervision, with the exception of cases of severe misconduct, disciplinary measures or criminal prosecution do not come into question, and the Execution Court merely declares the act of the execution officer void.[15,16]

---

12 Interview with Sheriff's Officer.
13 *Ibid.*
14 Summary procedures for debt collection are conducted by court executors rather than by courts. See Chapter 3: Debt Recovery in Turkey, *supra.*
15 Interview with Turkish Law Firm 5.

106 Making Foreign People Pay

The creditor's advocate or an advocate's clerk accompanies the execution officer during the seizure of goods. In contrast to the case in England, the presence of the creditor's lawyer during the seizure of goods and chattels plays a constructive role. It is often the case that the creditor's lawyer and the debtor negotiate the matter and agree on an extension of time or instalments [17] when the execution officer and the creditor's lawyer visit the debtor's property in order to seize his goods and chattels.[18]

D. 'EUROPEAN SUMMARY PROCEDURE FOR DEBT COLLECTION'

As will be later discussed, due to recent developments leading to the 'modern world of credit', summary procedures for debt collection constitute a major part of the workload of national courts.[19] Summary procedures for debt collection play an important role in both domestic and cross-border collection of debts.[20] The structure of summary procedures for debt collection differ in each of the three countries. Under the English system, a defendant can avoid a summary judgment by filing an affidavit 'with a very,

---

16   It is customary in large cities such as Istanbul and Ankara to give the office employees in an execution office a small amount of money (*e.g.* 250,000 Liras = $ 2) during any application. However, in small cities, to offer such a tip may be regarded as contempt and may be embarrassing for the lawyer who offers it. (Interview with Turkish Law Firm 5.) Gessner also reports that it is customary in Mexico 'to place in the hand' of court employees 50 or 100 Peso for each application. Volkmar Gessner, *Recht und Konflikt - Eine soziologische Untersuchung privatrechtlicher Konflikte in Mexiko* (Tübingen: Mohr, 1976), p. 146. It is also routine in Mexico to make 'donations' to judges, which is calculated as a part of their income, *ibid*. Unlike in Mexico (*ibid.*, pp. 98–100), a judge is a highly respected person in Turkish society. Only teachers, judges and medical doctors are addressed by the public referring to their professions rather than their name, *i.e.* 'Hakim Bey' (Mr Judge). People may attempt to bribe a judge, as is possible in any other country, but would never attempt to 'donate' money to him. Cf. *infra* Chapter 7: Factors Impeding Access to Justice in Cross-Border Debt Collection, 'Bias Against Foreigners?'.

17   Payment by instalments is also provided for by Art. 111 of CCEB. Should the debtor's immovable property or goods and chattels which have been 'attached' be of sufficient value to cover the whole debt plus interest, the debtor is permitted to effect payment in four instalments, provided that the first instalment has been paid in advance.

18   Interview with Turkish Law Firm 5.

19   *Infra* Chapter 9: Routinisation and Privatisation of Debt Collection.

20   See *infra* Chapter 6: Recourse to National Courts in Cross-Border Debt Collection.

very flimsy argument'.[21] The Turkish system is at the other extreme [22] and is very much oriented to the benefit of the creditor.[23] It is probably unique for Turkish law that the bearer of a negotiable instrument can cause the debtors' property to be attached and sold even if the latter contests the validity of the signature on the document, unless the Execution Court decides upon application that the debtor has good cause to stay the execution procedure.[24]

As a consequence of differences in summary procedures between various European legal systems,[25] difficulties can arise in cross-border collections. During the interviews with commercial debt collectors,[26] it was stated that there is a need for a European-wide summary court procedure for debt collection.[27] Efforts must be made by the European Union and the Council of Europe [28] to harmonise/unify summary procedures for debt collection throughout Europe. The initiative taken by a working group of twelve university professors for a single 'European Model Code of Civil Procedure' for the EU [29] has already resulted in draft model provisions for

---

21 'English Law Firm 10' in Chapter 5: Role of Lawyers in Cross-Border Debt Collection. *Guy and Mercer, Commercial Debt in Europe*, p. 173.
22 For comparative information on summary debt collection procedures in Europe, see 'Commission memorandum to the Council transmitted on 4 January 1985', *Bulletin of the European Communities*, Supplement 2/85.
23 See Budak, 'Icra Iflas Kanunu'nda Borclu Aleyhine Yapilan Degisiklikler'.
24 The execution officer interviewed in Istanbul reported that each year his office receives around 10 applications for summary procedures from foreign claimants, and they almost always depend upon negotiable instruments. Since there are 12 execution offices with the same workload in the Istanbul Court, the annual number of such international cases in Central Istanbul must be approximately one hundred.
25 See *e.g.* Erhard Blankenburg, 'The Infrastructure for Avoiding Civil Litigation: Comparing Cultures of Legal Behaviour in the Netherlands and West Germany', *Law and Society Review* 28, no.4 (1994), pp. 789–808, at pp.799–800.
26 See Chapters 10, 11, 12 *infra*.
27 English Debt Collector 12.
28 For activities of the Council of Europe concerning access to justice, see *Information Bulletin on Legal Activities within the Council of Europe and in Member States* issued biannually by the Directorate of Legal Affairs of the Council of Europe.
29 'Commission on European Law of Civil Procedure'. See Hanns Prütting, 'Auf dem Weg zu einer Europäischen Zivilprozeßordnung – Dargestellt am Beispiel des Mahnverfahrens', in Hanns Prütting (ed.), *Festschrift für Gottfried Baumgärtel zum 70. Geburtstag* (Cologne: Carl Heymanns Verlag, 1990), pp. 457–69, at pp. 460–1. Marcel Storme, 'Rechtsvereinheitlichung in Europa – Ein Plädoyer für ein einheitliches europäisches Prozeßrecht', *Rabels Zeitschrift für ausländisches und internationales Privatrecht* 56 (1992), pp. 290–9, at p. 298. Herbert Roth, 'Die Vorschläge de Kommission für ein europäisches Zivilprozeßgesetzbuch – Das Erkenntnisverfahren', *Zeitschrift für Zivilprozeß* 109, no.3 (1996), pp. 271–313, pp. 271–7.

such a European summary procedure for debt collection.[30] This draft model law must be considered by national legislators.[31]

E. TURKEY'S ACCESSION TO THE 1968 BRUSSELS CONVENTION

The execution of foreign judgments, including those denoted in a foreign currency,[32] is possible in all three countries through court procedures provided for the execution (or 'registration') of foreign judgments. The 'free movement of judgments' which exists between two EU member states finds no counterpart in the case of Turkey. As a result of the *de facto* reciprocity between Germany and Turkey, judgments from a German court may be enforced in Turkey, and *vice versa*. There is, however, neither a legal Treaty basis nor *de facto* reciprocity between Turkey and the United Kingdom which enables reciprocal enforcement of English and Turkish judgments. As it is relatively easy to raise an objection of procedural defect against a foreign judgment, the possibility in Common Law of enforcing foreign judgments under the summary judgment procedure is of little assistance to Turkish creditors seeking debt recovery in Eng-

---

[30] See Prütting, 'Auf dem Weg zu einer Europäischen Zivilprozeßordnung', pp. 461–9; Hanns Prütting, *Die Entwicklung eines europäischen Zivilprozeßrechts*, Vorträge, Reden und Berichte aus dem Europa-Institut - Sektion Rechtswissenschaft, Nr. 271 (Saarbrücken: Europainstitut der Universtät des Saarlandes, 1992), pp. 19–38 (including the text of the model provisions) and Manfred Wolf, 'Abbau prozessualer Schranken im europäischen Binnenmarkt', in Wolfgang Grunsky, Rolf Stürner, Gerhard Walter and Manfred Wolf (eds), *Wege zu einem europäischen Zivilprozeßrecht – Tübinger Symposium zum 80. Geburtstag von Fritz Baur* (Tübingen: Mohr, 1992), pp. 35–68, at pp. 63–5. Eberhard Schilken, 'Die Vorschläge de Kommission für ein europäisches Zivilprozeßgesetzbuch – einstweiliger und summarischer Rechtsschutz und Vollstreckung', *Zeitschrift für Zivilprozeß* 109, no.3 (1996), pp. 315–36, pp. 316–24.

[31] In addition, as regards debt recovery, the European Model Code of Civil Procedure contains provisions concerning the provisional remedies and the enforcement of judgments or orders for payment of money. However, these provisions (sections 10 and 11) state some very general rules and refer for details back to the national legislation. See Schilken, *ibid*. The text of the European Model Code of Civil Procedure is published in *Zeitschrift für Zivilprozeß* 109, no.3 (1996), pp. 345–71.

[32] For the purpose of enforcing judgments, foreign currency amounts must be converted into the national currency. Notwithstanding the devaluation of the Turkish Lira, creditors of hard currency amounts are protected by Turkish legislation and case law, according to which a judgment creditor may choose, for the rate applicable to conversion, either the contractual maturity date of the debt or the date of actual payment by the execution office. *Supra* Chapter 3: Debt Recovery in Turkey.

land. The accession of Turkey to the 1968 Brussels Convention on Jurisdiction and Enforcement of Judgments in Civil and Commercial Matters would be useful to avoid difficulties in enforcing judgments between Turkey and the Convention states, including the United Kingdom.[33]

F. PRELIMINARY REMEDIES FOR PROTECTION OF THE CREDITOR

As a result of the geographical and legal-cultural distance between the parties, preliminary remedies for protecting the creditor are of particular importance in cross-border debt collection.[34] It is no coincidence that modern English case law providing remedies for protecting the creditor (*Mareva* injunctions, *Anton Piller* orders) have been developed within the context of international cases.[35] The preliminary remedies for protection of the creditor (*Arrest*) are effective also in Turkey and in Germany.[36] A major part of the international work conducted by Turkish Law Firm 2, German Law Firm 1 and the German Court Executor concerns preliminary attachments for the protection of creditors.

---

[33] Since the Convention States are also EU Member States, the accession of Turkey to the 1968 Brussels Convention is also a necessary step in the course of the process for full membership of this country to the EU. See 'Ankara Agreement' of 1963, *OJ* L 217, 29.12.1964; *Resmi Gazete*, no. 11858, 17.11.1964, Art. 28; Harun Gümrükcü, 'EU-Türkei-Beziehungen im Spannungsfeld zwischen Assoziation und Vollmitgliedschaft', in Hagen Lichtenberg, Gudrun Linne and Harun Gümrükcü (eds), *Gastarbeiter – Einwanderer - Bürger?* (Baden – Baden: Nomos, 1996), pp.27–60.

[34] Interviews with German Law Firm 1 and German Court Executor. See *infra* Chapter 5: Role of Lawyers in Cross-Border Debt Collection, interview with Turkish Law Firm 2.

[35] See O'Hare and Nill, *Civil Litigation*, pp. 278–311; Dohmann, 'Worldwide Mareva', p. 160.

[36] For a comparison between the German and English procedures regarding protection of the creditor through preliminary remedies, see Jens Grunet, 'Interlocutory Remedies in England and Germany: A Comparative Perspective', *Civil Justice Quarterly* 15 (1996), pp. 19–43. The author compares the two systems with reference to the protection of the rights of the debtor *vis-à-vis* the creditor who is granted interim protection in an *ex parte* process.

110   Making Foreign People Pay

G. EFFICIENCY OF DEBT RECOVERY PROCEDURES

As will be further discussed below,[37] the interviews with lawyers, judges and other court officers in the three countries showed that the debt recovery procedures do not give rise to a large number of special difficulties for foreign creditors as compared to the creditors of fully domestic legal relations. Yet, the judicial debt recovery procedures provided for in these countries are rarely applied by foreign creditors.

Thus, several judges and other officers who were interviewed for this study [38] stated that they do not come across foreign parties frequently. This is the case especially for claims concerning the execution of a foreign judgment. For the Commercial Courts of first instance in Bremen and Istanbul, the figures given for the annual execution of foreign judgments were between 1 – 3 cases for each chamber. One of the four *Amtsgericht* judges in Bremen, who are in charge of civil execution proceedings,[39] stated that in her term of office, which includes the last three years, she has not come across a single foreign judgment. The Chief Judge of the 11th Chamber of the Turkish Court of Cassation (*i.e.* the Chamber which is in charge of commercial matters) said that the number of appeals made to the Court regarding execution of foreign judgments numbers 5 to 10 cases each year.[40]

---

37   See Chapter 7: Factors Impeding Access to Justice in Cross-Border Debt Collection.
38   That is, three *Rechtspfleger*, three *Amtsgericht* judges, two *Landgericht* judges and a Court Executor in Bremen; the Chief Judge in one of the Chambers of the Commercial Court in Istanbul, three senior Judges of different Chambers of the Court of Cassation in Ankara and an Execution Officer in Istanbul, and two court officers in the High Court and a Sheriff's Officer in London. As a result of the differences in legal cultures, the author experienced different levels of difficulties in obtaining appointments to visit judges in three countries. In Turkey, all the judges, including those in the Court of Cassation, were visited without a prior appointment. A judge is always at the 'people's disposal', unless he is in a hearing. In Germany, one who wishes to visit a judge must make an appointment through his/her secretary. For an interview, an official letter from the University, as the case may be, addressed to the Chief Judge ensuring the academic purpose of the research is also necessary. In England, the request for an interview with a High Court Judge must be made in writing to the Court Service at the Royal Courts of Justice. In this case, it took 15 days to receive an answer to the effect that it was not possible to arrange a meeting with a judge.
39   See *supra* Chapter 1: Debt Recovery in Germany.
40   For statistical data concerning the international cases (*i.e.* foreign party proceedings and the execution of foreign judgments) in three countries see *infra* Chapter 7: Factors Impeding Access to Justice in Cross-Border Debt Collection.

It is difficult to draw a general comparison between the levels of efficiency of the three legal systems, considering the position of the foreign creditors seeking debt recovery. It may only be argued that as a result of the 'private' status of the Sheriff's Offices, the civil execution offices which best serve the foreign (as well as domestic) creditors among the three countries are probably in England. This is illustrated by the Sheriff's Officer who was interviewed on an international case dealt with by their 'company'.[41] It is noteworthy how much effort can be invested by the Sheriff's Office in collecting the debt, where the result is also profitable in terms of the Sheriff's fees:[42]

> We are a private company, we only get our appointment by setting a high standard and by being able to do the work. If we did not do the work, then our appointment would be taken away and given to somebody else. So we are constantly under pressure to make sure that we can perform highly . . . We had an interesting case not too long ago where a French judgment was for the seizure of some parts of the Berlin wall, *i.e.*: the concrete blocks in the Berlin wall.
> It was painted up by some painter. It had been given to a foundation. The foundation which was in France had gone into liquidation. But the items were in this country in a bonded warehouse. Because the liquidation did not extend to this country, the items were still seizable under a judgment in this country. So the French side got their solicitors to obtain a judgment in this country for money. The goods were in a bonded warehouse and they had been there for a year. So the tax man wanted to charge import tax on these items, which had a dubious value.
> We saved these items, tried to sell them by public auction, which is the normal way, . . . and couldn't find anyone who wanted to buy them. We found that the only market place for them was actually in France or Germany. . . . But if we had taken them out of this country, for example, to France to sell, they would have been covered by the liquidation. It would have been outside the jurisdiction of our court and inside the jurisdiction of another court. . . . In the end, we managed to attract some buyers in France to come over here. To do that, we had to apply to the court for a private treaty to negotiate with buyers, get a reasonable price and sell to the highest bidder. We had to go for a public auction and put it to an auction; some people in France were interested in it; we got some bids from France. Then having involved them, we only had to deal with the people who ran the bonded warehouse, how much money they wanted, and persuade the tax man. [We argued that, since the goods were] in the bonded warehouse [they] had not entered the country. So the import tax was not applicable,

---

41 The Sheriff's Office in London at that time was a limited company.
42 Sheriff's fees are calculated, as a rule, as a percentage of the monies recovered by the creditor. See *supra* Chapter 2: Debt Recovery in England.

even though the goods were in the country for over a year. So we managed to push back the claim on this basis. We came to a deal with the people running the bonded warehouse, on the basis that we are actually doing them a favour getting rid of these concrete blocks in the warehouse. So we managed to sell the items and the creditors got a fair chunk of their money back. We actually got about a million Francs in the end.

The 'private' nature of the Sheriff's Office in England is balanced by the extensive judicial involvement in the civil execution procedure, where the judge enjoys wide discretion to control the execution procedure.[43] Such (further) privatisation of the enforcement of judgments services could also be discussed in Germany, where there is extensive judicial involvement in the execution process.[44] The same, however, would be dangerous for the debtor in the Turkish system, where the Execution Officer exercises a high degree of discretion in determining the form and the particulars of the enforcement measures.

The aforementioned 'privatisation', will be discussed further in this study [45] as well as how a different and stronger form of 'private' law enforcement replaced the legal debt recovery procedures in cross-border legal relations.

---

43 See *supra* 'Role of Execution Officers and Courts' in this Chapter.
44 The Execution Officers in some French-speaking countries of Continental Europe (*Huissier de Justice*) are in a similar position. That is, they are self-employed and earn their living on the execution fees paid by the parties. In these countries, the term of office of the Sheriff is not limited as in England. Yet there is a competitive pressure on the Execution Officer in that, unlike in England, there is not a single Sheriff in any one district and the creditor may choose his/her Execution Officer. Baudouin Gielen, 'Gerichtsvollzieher in Europa', *Deutsche Gerichtsvollzeiher-Zeitung*, 107. Jahrgang, no. 1 (1992), pp. 6–8.
45 See *infra* Part III: Private Enforcement: Extra-Judicial Methods of Debt Collection.

5 Role of Lawyers in Cross-Border Debt Collection

A. NEED FOR REPRESENTATION BY A LAWYER

A creditor who chooses to use court proceedings for debt recovery needs a lawyer. In Germany this is a legal requirement: proceedings in the civil courts of general jurisdiction (*Landgerichte*) and in the courts of higher instance can only be commenced and further conducted by a lawyer admitted to practise in the relevant district and court instance. Parties must accordingly be represented by an advocate before the relevant court (*Anwaltszwang*, compulsory representation by an advocate).[1] In Turkey [2] and in England [3] a litigant may represent himself in any court and, in the latter, may even be assisted by a friend.[4] In practice however it is unusual even in these countries for a non-lawyer to appear before the court without being represented by counsel.

---

1. German CCP § 78. In international cases, an important exception to the rule in § 78 is petitions for enforcement of a foreign judgment under international treaties, including the Brussels Convention. See *Gesetz zur Ausführung zwischenstaatlicher Anerkennungs- und Vollstreckungsverträge in Zivil- und Handelssachen* of 30th May 1988, BGBl I 662, § 5 II. Jan Kropholler, *Europäisches Zivilprozeßrecht*, 5th ed. (Heidelberg: Verlag Recht und Wirtschaft, 1996), p. 376. Another exception is proceedings in Amtsgerichte where non-lawyers may represent themselves or third parties provided they do so without being paid. Despite this exception private individuals often consult a lawyer: a survey conducted in 1988 showed that from 1985 to 1988, 25% of all private households in Germany had at least once made use of an advocate, Reinhart W. Wettmann and Knut Jungjohann, *Inanspruchnahme anwaltlicher Leistungen – Zugangsschwellen, Beratungsbedarf und Anwaltsimage* (edited by Federal Ministry of Justice and German Law Society) (Cologne and Essen: Bundesanzeiger, Deutscher Anwaltsverlag 1989), p.25.
2. Advocates Act, Art. 35 (3).
3. Ronald Walker and Richard Ward, *Walker & Walker's English Legal System*, 7th ed. (London, Dublin, Edinburgh: Butterworths, 1994), p.209.
4. *McKenzie v McKenzie* [1970] 3 All ER 1034.

Particularly in cross-border litigation, variously regulated substantive and procedural law rules, different court languages and last but not least, differences in legal cultures make it almost impossible for a lawyer to proceed in a foreign country,[5] let alone litigants themselves. Thus, notwithstanding the considerable liberalisation of the legal market in the European Union,[6] none of the lawyers or even the court officers who were recently questioned in connection with a survey conducted for the European Commission [7] could anticipate an application for recognition and enforcement of judgments being made in one of the EU member states by a lawyer from another member state. Another survey conducted in Germany found that, in the 404 international cases which were brought before the first instance courts in Hamburg, Bremen and Bremerhaven between 1988 – 1989, foreign counsel appeared neither in the files (pleadings) nor in the hearings.[8] Unpublished data collected for this research from the High Court (Judgments/Orders Section) in England [9] shows again that none of the German judgments registered in England in the last five years (1991 – 1995) have been submitted by the plaintiff in person; all applications have been dealt with by solicitors in England. In order to understand the functioning and to judge on the efficiency of court procedures in cross-border

---

[5] Suffice it to mention the diversity in the organisation of and the role played by self-employed practising lawyers in various countries. For a comparative study made in France, Germany, England and Italy see Jean-Louis Halperin, 'The Judicial and Legal Professions in Contemporary History: Forms of Organization in various European Countries', in Volkmar Gessner, Armin Hoeland and Csaba Varga (eds), *European Legal Cultures* (Aldershot: Dartmouth, 1996), pp. 371–6. For the legal-cultural aspects of cross-border debt recovery cases see Schinobu K. Garrigues, 'Collecting Beyond Our Borders', *Collector* (July 1995), pp. 12–20.

[6] Council Directive 77/249, *OJ L* 78, 26.03.1977 (amended: *OJ L* 291, 24.05.1979 and *OJ L* 302, 12.06.1985); European Court of Justice Case no. 107/83: *Ordre des Avocats au Barreau de Paris v Klopp* [1984] *ECR* 2971. Martin Henssler, 'Der europäische Rechtsanwalt', *Anwaltsblatt*, 46. Jahrgang, no.7 (1996), pp. 353–65. See *infra* Chapter 7: Factors Impeding Access to Justice in Cross-Border Debt Collection.

[7] Hanno von Freyhold and Enzo L. Vial, 'Report on the Cost of Judicial Proceedings in the European Union', in Hanno von Freyhold, Volkmar Gessner, Enzo L. Vial and Helmut Wagner (eds), *Cost of Judicial Barriers for Consumers in the Single Market*, A report for the European Commission, Directorate General XXIV (Brussels: European Commission, October/November 1995), pp. 15–127, p. 115.

[8] Volkmar Gessner, 'International Cases in German First Instance Courts', in Volkmar Gessner (ed.), *Foreign Courts – Civil Litigation in Foreign Legal Cultures* (Aldershot: Dartmouth, 1996), 149–207, pp. 155, 190, 204.

[9] See *infra* Chapter 7: Factors Impeding Access to Justice in Cross-Border Debt Collection.

debt recovery, it is necessary to have some insight to the work of lawyers in this field.

B. LAWYERS AT CROSS-BORDER DEBT RECOVERY WORK

1. The Aim of Interviews

During the years 1995 – 1996 the author held interviews with privately practising lawyers in the three jurisdictions, *i.e.* solicitors, *Rechtsanwälte* and advocates, in England, Germany and Turkey, respectively. Interviews were not meant to draw a general comparison between the relevant legal professions in three jurisdictions,[10] which may have more in common than not.[11] Interviewees were selected from those law firms in the three countries which are specialised or largely involved in providing international legal services. Nor was the study aimed at collecting information about the 'international law firms' as such, which would be repetitious. For the study of work of lawyers is one of the favourite subjects of legal-sociology, and an extensive literature has already been dedicated, especially in the United States, to various groups or 'types' of lawyers [12] and different areas of work for the legal profession,[13] including the work of international lawyers.

---

10 For such comparisons see Hamish Adamson, *Free Movement of Lawyers* (London: Butterworths, 1992); Halperin, 'The Judicial and Legal Professions in Contemporary History: Forms of Organization in various European Countries' and the three volume work edited by Richard L. Abel and Philip S. C. Lewis (eds), *Lawyers in Society, Vol. 1: The Common Law World* (Berkeley: University of California Press, 1988), *Vol. 2: The Civil Law World* (Berkeley: University of California Press, 1988), *Vol. 3: Comparative Theories* (Berkeley: University of California Press, 1989).
11 See Lawrence M. Friedman, 'Lawyers in Cross-Cultural Perspective', in Abel and Lewis, *Lawyers in Society, Vol. 3: Comparative Theories*, pp. 1–26, 4.
12 Lawyers have been classified according to the size of their law firms, clientele, social backgrounds *etc.*: sole practitioners, small-firm lawyers, mega-lawyers; corporate lawyers, business-, criminal-, personal injury lawyers; rural lawyers, metropolitan lawyers, Washington-, Chicago-, New York-, Wall Street lawyers; black lawyers, elite lawyers, women lawyers and so on.
13 For an introduction to the socio-legal studies on the work of lawyers and a guided bibliography see Roman Tomasic, *The Sociology of Law* (London, Beverly Hills, New Delhi: SAGE, 1985), Chapter 2 (pp. 29–55). For another 'annotated select bibliography' see John Flood, *The Legal Profession in the United States*, 3rd. ed. (Chicago: American Bar Foundation, 1985), pp. 63–79.

116   Making Foreign People Pay

The work of 'mega law firms' with a 'global clientele' has also already been discussed elsewhere.[14]

For the purpose of this study, our aim was modest: an attempt was made only to find out the facts about the work of lawyers in the area of cross-border debt recovery. How often and in which cases are they being called upon to collect cross-border debts? What do they do to overcome difficulties arising from existing 'judicial borders'? How efficient, that is, how cost effective and how successful are they?

2. Selection of Interviewees and the Method Used for Evaluating the Information

London law firms deserved special attention in this part of the study due to their special role in international counselling. England is one of the most important world-wide exporters of legal services.[15] Similar to New York, London is a place where many international law firms have their head offices[16] and the great majority of these firms are resident in the same neighbourhood (the City)[17] which enabled the author to conduct two inter-

---

[14] Yves Dezalay, 'The Big Bang and the Law: The Internationalization and Restructuration of the Legal Field', *Theory, Culture and Society* 9 (1990), pp. 279–93; David M. Trubek, Yves Dezalay, Ruth Buchanan and John R. Davis, 'Global Restructuring and the Law: Studies of the Internationalization of Legal Fields and the Creation of Transnational Areas', *Case Western Reserve Law Review* 44, no.2 (1994), pp. 407–98; Shapiro, 'The Globalization of Law', pp. 54 et seq.

[15] As of 31 July 1995, 66,123 solicitors held practising certificates in England of which 1,363 were employed abroad. The Law Society, *Trends in The Solicitors' Profession - Annual Statistical Report 1995* (London: Law Society, 1995), p. 14.

[16] In 1995, there were 238 foreign lawyers registered with the Law Society (*ibid.*). However, such registration with the Law Society is optional, and there is no general restriction in English law on giving legal advice and establishing offices by overseas lawyers. Edwin Godfrey and Anne Damerell, 'England and Wales', in Edwin Godfrey (ed.), *Law without Frontiers* (London: Kluwer, 1995), pp. 51–73, p. 69. It was reported that, according to an official of the Law Society, the actual number of foreign lawyers in London was estimated to be 1,000: Christopher W. Stoller, *Transnational Mobility of Lawyers and English Law Firms* (not published). A report prepared for the Joint Meeting of the Law and Society Association and Research Committee on the Sociology of Law of the International Sociological Association held on 10 – 13 July 1996). See also Karl-Peter Winters, *Der Rechtsanwaltsmarkt – Chancen, Risiken und zukünftige Entwicklung* (Cologne: Otto Schmidt, 1990), pp. 250–60 and pp. 275–6.

[17] As far as the legal market is concerned, London is one of the 'glocal' places which provides the global economy with a 'service infrastructure' for cross-border interactions. Cf. Vittorio Olgiati, 'Towards a New "Universalis Mercatorum": The Political

views each day during his short visit to London.[18] As regards international lawyering, legal markets in Germany and in Turkey are not comparable with London. In contrast to the country's important role in international trade and service industry in general, German law firms are far behind their counterparts in the United States, England and France.[19] Turkey is only an importer of international legal services.[20]

The number of interviews conducted is 16. During some of the interviews more than one lawyer was present, one partner and one or two less senior members of the firm. The English Law Firm 7 was of importance for our discussion as one of the two interviewees was a Turkish lawyer and the

---

Economy of the Chamber of Commerce in Milan', in Gessner and Budak, *Emerging Legal Certainty*; Röhl and Magen, 'Die Rolle des Rechts im Prozeß der Globalisierung', p. 8.

[18] Some of the law firms which were visited were those law firms which participated in a previous lawyers survey conducted at the Centre for European Law and Politics in Bremen (see von Freyhold and Vial, 'Report on the Cost of Judicial Proceedings in the European Union'). Others were either chosen from the *Martindale-Hubbel Law Directory* 1995, 32nd ed. (Summit N. J.: Martindale-Hubbel, 1995) which provides brief information about the field of activities of each firm advertised in the Directory or they were recommended by an experienced lawyer in Turkey who deals exclusively with international counselling.

[19] Notwithstanding recent developments of 'internationalisation' of larger law firms in Germany (Trubek, Dezalay, Buchanan and Davis, 'Global Restructuring and the Law', pp. 447–8), professional rules applied to lawyers, namely restrictions concerning establishing offices in more than one court district and calculation of legal fees, make international lawyering difficult in Germany. See Wolfgang Kühn, 'Deutsche Anwälte international in der Abstiegszone', *Anwaltsblatt*, 32. Jahrgang, no. 3 (1988), pp.129–32; Hans-Jürgen Hellwig, 'Formen der Gestaltung der Zusammenarbeit mit dem ausländischen Anwalt', *Anwaltsblatt*, 46. Jahrgang, no.3 (1996), pp. 124–9; Carsten Eggers, 'Germany', in Godfrey, *Law without Frontiers*, pp. 80–93; Wettmann and Jungjohann, *Inanspruchnahme anwaltlicher Leistungen*, p. 67. German law firms are amongst the most expensive service providers in the international legal market. See 'Das kostet Recht', *Die Welt*, 29.12.1992; Junda Woo, 'US International Firms may be Bargains', *The Wall Street Journal*, 20.10.1992.

[20] Lawyers who especially deal with cross-border disputes are small in number in Turkey. The number of firms which are included in the Martindale-Hubbell Law Directory 1995 is 31. Also see *The Professional Directory of Lawyers of the World*, 77th ed. (Sacramento, California: Forster-Long, 1995), pp. 3914 et seq.; International Financial Law Review 1000, *A Guide to the World's International Law Firms* (Euromoney Publications: 1995), pp. 349 et seq. Mega law firms with many lawyers in the American fashion do not exist. According to the information given in the same Directory, the average number of lawyers in a law firm with international contacts in Turkey is 5 or 6. A total number of 176 lawyers work in 31 firms. Usually 2 – 4 of these are partners and the remaining 2 – 4 are associates and/or consultants. Of the 31 law firms which are listed in the directory 22 are situated in Istanbul, 7 firms in Ankara, 1 in Izmir and 1 in Mersin.

other a US lawyer who had previously worked in Turkey for many years. Similarly, one of the four law firms visited in Turkey was doing much of its cross-border debt recovery work for English clients and another was working almost exclusively for clients from Germany and other German speaking European countries. One law firm visited in Germany was involved in international counselling in maritime cases. Another was a large firm with international clientele and a separate debt recovery department. In addition, at the time of the research undertaken in Germany, fifty law firms in Bremen had recently been interviewed about their cross-border cases, the results of which have been published elsewhere [21] and used in this study.

The information which was collected through interviews has partly been used in other parts of this study, especially under the Chapters 1 – 4 above and Chapter 7 below on the difficulties hindering access to justice in cross-border debt collection. Five selected interviews have been reconstructed below in some detail with the aim to demonstrate the work of lawyers in the field of cross-border debt recovery.[22]

The three interviews which were selected from the interviews conducted with the English law firms were those numbered (3), (9) and (10) respectively. Each of these three firms represent different groups of English lawyers involved in cross-border debt recovery and will be called 'the City Lawyers',[23] 'Investment Lawyers / US Affiliates' [24] and 'High Street Solicitors',[25] respectively. The City Lawyers are the primary group of solicitors in London who are organised in very large law firms dealing with international litigation and counselling in the American 'mega-law firm' fashion. Among the City lawyers there are some law firms which concentrate on international finance and investments. These firms, typically being affiliates of US firms, may be called 'Investment lawyers / US Affiliates'. They provide for counselling rather than international litigation before English courts. Lastly, where relatively small claims are concerned (small

---

21 See Thomas Schnorr, 'Einzelanwälte und kleine Anwaltsfirmen im internationalen Rechtsverkehr – Eine empirische Untersuchung', *Anwaltsblatt*, 44. Jahrgang, no.3 (1994), pp. 98–104.
22 Some of the interviews were tape-recorded. Quotations below in quotation marks were the actual words spoken by the interviewees which have been transcribed from tape-records. Quotations without quotation marks were reconstructed from memory, using the notes made during the interviews and/or immediately after.
23 English Law Firms, 1, 2, 3, 5, 6, 8.
24 English Law Firms, 4, 7 and 9.
25 Represented by English Law Firm 10.

for international litigation, around £50,000 or less), so called High Street Solicitors, that is, small-sized law firms for general practice, are also involved in international litigation. Even if the High Street Solicitors deal with international cases on an irregular basis, the amount of work provided for by such firms may be considerable.[26]

English Law Firm 3 is a typical 'City firm' with hundreds of lawyers working in various 'units' to serve a large spectrum of business clients in domestic as well as in international matters. English Law Firm 9 is a mega law firm which concentrates more on international counselling, especially for large investment projects involving multinational entrepreneurs and finance institutions. English Law Firm 10 is *not* a small-size firm. Indeed it is one of the largest law firms in England. However for the purpose of this study it has more in common with High Street Solicitors than the City Lawyers. It does not have a single large office in the City (with a few branches or liaison offices in some other large cities), but rather is a network of numerous offices distributed over the country, the central office being in London, and which are structured mainly to serve UK clients for domestic cases. The advantage of interviewing the London office of English Law Firm 10 was to have the opportunity to hear about cases coming to local offices as well as the London office. Since small firms of general practice only occasionally take on international cases, interviews with independent High Street Solicitors would not have been informative.[27]

The interviews conducted with Turkish Law Firm 1 and Turkish Law Firm 2 were of importance for our discussion in that they illustrate two different types of international legal practice in contrast to each other. Turkish Law Firm 1 is a traditional law office whereas Turkish Law Firm 2 represents the modern developments in cross-border debt collection towards routinisation and privatisation which will be further discussed in Chapter 9.

---

26   High Court Officer 2 states that most of the solicitors who apply to the Court for registration of foreign judgments are London firms, but not necessarily the big ones. English Debt Collector 7 who specialises in collection of business claims for foreign firms in England cooperates with two High Street Solicitors.

27   In a report of his interviews with 50 practising individual lawyers and small law firms in Germany, Schnorr states that: 'For the professional practice of most of the interviewees, neither the harmonisation of EU law, the Brussels Convention and the UN Convention on the International Sale of Goods nor any other convention play a role. Many interviewees asked explicitly about the contents of the Brussels and UN Conventions. Other interviewees repeatedly gave the impression that they did not know about the contents of these Conventions' ('Einzelanwälte und kleine Anwaltsfirmen im internationalen Rechtsverkehr', p. 104).

120   Making Foreign People Pay

a) English Law Firm 3: City lawyers

English Law Firm 3 is a large law firm with 560 employees working in London and two district offices. It has 34 'specialist units' covering not only general areas such as banking, construction contracts and employment, but also more specific matters such as defamation, franchising and pensions. Interviews were held with three members of the firm, two partners and a 'solicitor' (a solicitor who is not a partner), from the 'insurance and professional indemnity' and 'commercial litigation' units.

One lawyer from the insurance and professional indemnity unit stated that international debt recovery cases dealt with by them at that time were mostly 'property fraud cases'. Clarification was as follows.

> In the period 1985 – 1988 real estate prices in Britain rapidly increased. At that time there was an easy way of making money in which credit institutions namely, banks and building societies, real estate valuers and speculators were involved:
>
> Speculator finds a property in London say for £40,000. He finds a valuer to assess the value as if it were worth £100,000. He goes to bank which agrees to provide a £90,000 loan on the basis of the security charged on the property. He pays the vendor of the property the £40,000. He waits some time, a year or so, and then he sells the property for £100,000. Prices increase rapidly. He repays the bank loan and keeps the remaining money for himself.
>
> This scenario was functioning successfully, until August 1988 when property prices began to fall. Within the next four to five years, prices decreased by more than 50%. Speculators were unable to repay the banks and some of them left the country with the money. Where a speculator was insured for professional indemnity, the insurer paid the money. Now these insurers (which assert recourse claims against 'speculators') are our clients.

The firm has European connections as well as international connections outside Europe who assist them in collecting overseas debts. Their contacts (with corresponding foreign lawyers) are on a non-exclusive basis: 'I think our clients choose us because we are "horse for the course" ' explains one of the interviewees 'and, in the same way, when choosing our correspondent overseas we would use the horse for the course'.

This was however obviously not always the case. There were difficulties in international cooperation due to a lack of mutual understanding of the different legal systems:

> If you start proceedings in the High Court then you have to serve a sealed copy of the writ.[28] It is not a photocopy. It is an actual copy of the writ which is sealed by the court. I had one experience in Germany where I have been trying to explain to my colleague there what is required under English law in order to satisfy the English court the proper service is taking place. Because generally you are required to produce an affidavit of the service ... One way of effecting the service is by arranging a process server to deliver the documents and, to hand them the defendant.
>
> In this particular case the contact in Germany arranged for the local court officer who is responsible for the service of documents in the German courts. What he got wrong was to ignore my instructions in terms of serving the original writ of summons. What he did was to take photocopies and to serve those. They came back nicely bound up with a lovely cord, stamps and seal, and so forth. But actually what he had got sealed were not the original documents, but photocopies. And, of course, the English court said that it was not good enough. So they had to be re-served. Every single legal system has its own set of rules for service, so difficulties can always arise.

Similarly, in a case for execution of an English judgment in another EU member state, one of the other interviewees had 'spent four to five hours time arguing with a Greek lawyer to explain that the Greek court should not validate the judgment. All that was required was to obtain an order from the court under the Brussels Convention'.

Somewhat paradoxically, language is also a special problem for English lawyers. Even many elite lawyers do not have a good command of a foreign language.

> Another problem I should acknowledge is, as an Englishman, the language. I am afraid my first foreign language is French. But most of the European countries have provided English as their first foreign language. Nevertheless, we are relying on a local lawyer to explain to us in 'his English' what is required. We are not at the moment trained sufficiently to articulate ourselves in their language ... You are dependent upon their ability to translate into English.

Such difficulties in communication with foreign connections, together with the bureaucracy inherent in international litigation, cause delays which in turn give the debtor the chance to escape the creditor.

An example of such legal bureaucratic difficulties is service of process out of jurisdiction. But for the cases falling within the scope of Brussels

---

28   A writ is the first document which is served to the defendant including the claim in summary, but not necessarily the details of the cause of action which could be served later as a separate 'statement of claim'.

122   *Making Foreign People Pay*

and Lugano Conventions,[29] service of process out of jurisdiction is subject to leave of the High Court. Obtaining such a leave from the High Court Master takes two or three days.

> Then documents must be translated and must be sent to the foreign country in question whose local provisions for service of process are not known to us or might have changed since we used them last time. You may do it yourself, if you have served proceedings in that country recently. But there is an element of risk in that. Because rules of procedure are changing all the time. Therefore, one is advised to contact a local lawyer. Such formalities are time consuming.
>
> I was once instructed by an art dealer in London who was tricked by someone, selling two Picassos in return for a cheque. ... We knew that the pictures had gone over Holland. But, by the time we satisfied the court here [30] and I had gone Holland and instituted the Dutch procedure, we knew that the pictures had already left Holland. They were in Germany. And we were always getting further and further behind the pictures until finally the distance was too great. So we lost them. At the end of the day the insurance picked up the loss. However everybody learned a lesson from it.

Among the firm's clients in the area of cross-border debt recovery were also British banks. However, notwithstanding their continuous involvement in cross-border payment transactions, banks have recourse to cross-border debt recovery only in exceptional cases. The partner from the 'commercial litigation unit' explains the situation as follows.

> Banks let rather [their customers] to make the decision to go beyond the shore to recover the money... I think, letters of credit is the case in point. Where you have a British customer of a bank [*e.g.* an importer of electric goods] who wants to do business with someone [an exporter], let us say, in Germany, they normally would use letters of credit. Clearly, the bank, if it lends money as against, say, the receipt of invoices; it is lending money effectively, say, for electric goods [which are going to be delivered by the German exporter]. If something goes wrong, the bank has two options: [1] It would have a counter-indemnity from its customer in relation to the letter of credit. That is, it can go to the [British] customer. It is easier to do so. But [2] if, for any reason, the customer becomes insolvent, this will not work.
>
> Polly Peck International, a personal empire, was a large trading company, and when it went into insolvency procedure, which we call the administration,[31]

---

29   RSC Ord 11, r. 1(2) and CCR Ord 8, r. 2 (2). One of the interviewees was mistaken when he explained that leave of the Court was necessary for serving a writ in Spain or in France.
30   The case must be before Britain's accession to the Brussels Convention in 1.1.1987. See the previous footnote.
31   See Insolvency Act 1986, Part II.

there were enormous conflicts.[32] Because, many banks had lent a lot of money to Polly Peck International. When going into administration, unless the banks were secured creditors, that is, they had a mortgage on the company assets or some other security, they would be forced to litigate abroad in order to recover monies which they had given in relation to the letters of credit. They could not rely on the counter-indemnity from Polly Peck. They would then have to seek to recover the goods that they were financing which very often meant, in my experience, attempting to recover the goods at the port of arrival. Had they been loaded on to the ship and delivered, say [instead of the port in England], to Amsterdam, then you are forced into cross-border litigation.

So it is often the case when a client of a bank has gone into insolvency procedures. ... The bank's first option is to go to its client in Britain. Should this prove unsuccessful then it is forced to go to litigate abroad.

b) English Law Firm 9: Investment lawyers

English Law Firm 9, as is the case for English Law Firms 4 and 7 (both of which are affiliates of US firms), deals with large investment projects as representative of the investors or the institutions financing the project:

> The focus of this firm's work is acting for large institutions, whether they are banks or corporate institutions, generally involved in the provision of money one way or the other; to acquire companies, to develop projects, anything where large sums of money are required or need to be raised. [33]

It is peculiar for these types of cases that, although there is a great deal of money at stake, the particulars of the legal relationship are straightforward. Thus, the debt recovery process does not involve resolution of a complex dispute on the merits of the case. As a result, court proceedings are preferred to arbitration.

> There is a slight prejudice against arbitration... The banks lend the money. If the money is due to be repaid on specific dates in the future, why would you need to arbitrate... So, I think it is true to say that in a typical transaction with which we

---

32 See *Re Polly Peck International plc.* [1991] BCC 503.
33 There are a lot of projects which I get involved in, which are BOT projects. That is, 'Build, Operate and Transfer', which is a system whereby a lot of countries, including Turkey, are trying to privatize building power stations or roads. If the government wants to build a power station or a road, it gives a concession to a company which may be set up with a Turkish and an international partner to build a road or a power station. In return they get the right to run it for, say, thirty years and to take the revenue from it. And the company quite often goes to the bank in order to lend money to that company to enable him to build the power station or the roads or whatever.

are involved, where it is just the provision of money we are talking about, arbitration would not be an appropriate source of resolution of the disputes.

Investment contracts drafted by the firm contain jurisdiction clauses, instead of arbitration clauses. As a rule, they insist upon the right to bring proceedings in English courts, or alternatively New York courts, but recognise that the local courts of the debtor's country would have concurrent jurisdiction.[34]

> We ask our jurisdiction clause to provide that the parties would submit to the non-exclusive jurisdiction of English and/or New York courts. So it is perfectly open to either party to seek to bring proceedings in any other jurisdiction and claim. In most cases you would attempt to bring proceedings in a jurisdiction where once you have obtained a judgment, you will be able to do something with it, and enforce it against the assets ..., [if it] is likely that most of the assets are in Turkey then it would make a great deal of sense to bring proceedings in Turkey in the first place, on the basis that the Turkish judgment could then be enforced against those assets.

Turkish Law Firm 3, which was also involved in international bank loans, had stated that in their experience, most of the litigation concerning international loan agreements arises from disputes which they come across during the enforcement of security rights. In reply to the question whether English Law Firm 9 experienced this type of dispute, the interviewee explained that they avoid such disputes by having 'another international institution within Turkey' involved in the loan agreement.

> It was some years ago in relation to a series of loan transactions, which were structured so that the foreign banks would lend a Turkish bank money in US Dollars and the Turkish bank would then use that money to on-lend their Turkish tobacco growers, to enable them to meet their pre-export finance requirements. The Turkish tobacco growers needed money because they had grown the tobacco, which was sitting in a warehouse being cured, but was not to be exported for another six months. The Turkish tobacco growers needed the money, but the foreign banks were unwilling to lend directly to the Turkish growers, be-

---

34 Two further firms in this group which are also specialised in investment projects and international loans (*i.e.* English Law Firms 4 and 7) stated however that they use arbitration clauses and jurisdiction clauses alternatively. For the jurisdiction clauses, the New York and London courts were preferred. English Law Firm 10 states that, although the majority of construction contracts (*i.e.* not loan agreements financing the contracts, but the contracts concerning construction engineering *etc.*) contain arbitration clauses, it is usual practice for loan agreements to prefer litigation. An exception to this generalisation is defence industry where manufacturers prefer litigation to arbitration.

cause of the difficulty of taking security over the tobacco sitting in a warehouse. Whereas the Turkish bank which is the intermediary between the foreign lenders and the Turkish tobacco growers felt more comfortable, by having the key to the warehouse, in order that it could actually acquire some sort of security interest over the assets, in this case, tobacco. So I think this is an example of a Turkish security law being seen as perhaps rather difficult for foreign banks who are nevertheless happy to lend to a Turkish bank, to enable a Turkish bank to lend to the Turkish growers and so have a local security arrangement between themselves, not involving the foreign bank.[35] This is a typical transaction which still goes on. Many loans in Turkey are structured in that way whereby foreign banks lend to a Turkish bank to enable the Turkish bank to further lend that money to other Turkish enterprises. ...

Of course, the foreign bank feels happier, in dealing with the Turkish bank which will probably itself have access in London or New York and will also accept the need to submit to the jurisdiction of the London or New York courts, as an inducement to get the foreign banks to lend the money in the first place. Whereas the Turkish tobacco grower will say 'I am not interested in submitting to the jurisdiction of London courts or New York courts, why should I?' It is far better to deal with another international institution within Turkey, to accept the need to submit to the jurisdiction of the courts outside Turkey, even when the money is ultimately going to be used directly by Turkish individuals and Turkish entities.

c) English Law Firm 10: Debt recovery department

English Law Firm 10 is in London. It is one of the largest firms in the country. Yet, this firm is not in the City, and it is not a typical City firm. English Law Firm 10 has several domestic and a few foreign offices which are organised in departments, including a debt recovery department. As opposed to City firms, they are involved in routine debt collection services for undisputed business and consumer debts. As was stated earlier, this type of 'litigation' rarely involves resolution of a dispute on the merits of a case, and therefore it differs from usual litigation.[36]

---

35 The regulation concerning security right over tobacco is peculiar. Security right over tobacco leaves, which differs from the usual security right on movables, is recognised by secondary legislation ('tüzük') instead of a public law (Tütün ve Tütün Tekeli Tüzügü, *Resmi Gazete*, 16.03. 1975, no. 15179). Yet, the relevant statutory instrument makes special reference to the banks as security owners. This unusual form of regulation which is safe enough for domestic banks may be regarded insecure for foreign banks.
36 For collection of undisputed claims by non-lawyers cf. *infra* Part III in this book.

126 Making Foreign People Pay

> From a legal point of view, particularly amongst the larger firms, people treat debt recovery with contempt, if you like, because it is not very difficult litigation which is often for very small amounts. It is not very high profile work from the point of view of the London firm. Yes, we do do debt recovery work, and we do have a large number of clients who provide us with some volumes of debt recovery work. We undertake a fair amount of debt recovery work here, and we also have other offices which are instructed, for example, by government departments and large companies, for whom we undertake large volumes of debt collection work. But you will find, due to the cost of trying to recover money, that most of our debt recovery work is carried out in the province, for example [...] has a very large department which does debt recovery work. If a domestic company has many debtors, small debtors, at any one time, it is quite easy for them to send the work here and we will do it easily, briefly, cheaply and quickly.

Easy, brief, cheap and quick debt collection is, however, not practicable for cross-border debts. International debt recovery undertaken by the firm can hardly be defined as usual (routine) debt collection.

> From the point of view of the London office, we are not so much geared up to a specialised debt recovery service, because naturally, being in London, our overheads are greater. The London office, from a litigation perceptive, does have quite a large amount of international litigation at any one time. However, we have already identified [limits] for the purposes of debt recovery. International debt recovery, because of your picking and choosing the jurisdiction according to the contract, tends to be more on a one-off basis. And when you are talking about matters of small tens and thousands of pounds, often the costs of recovering that debt are disproportionately high and therefore you will not find these [sort of small claims in international cases]. I think that is one of the main reasons why, perhaps, courts are not used extensively in connection with the international debt recovery work. Having said that we [the London office] still do what I would call debt recovery, and often for significant amounts of money.

In addition, the interviewee believes that, even for the 'one-off' debt recovery cases, the English procedure is far from satisfactory. This is due to the wide discretion granted to the trial judge for protection of the debtor, and particularly due to the fact that summary procedure for debt collection can easily be avoided by the debtor:

> I have been involved in a number of international debt collection claims and I think Europeans particularly find our litigation system far from satisfactory. There is a perception that we have a very fair system of litigation, it is very just,

the courts of the Rolls Royce system of justice.[37] But it is very time-consuming and expensive. In one recent case all of these issues came to light. We had a client suing for a debt, probably in the £20,000 region. He was Dutch and asked us to commence the proceedings over here because the person who owed him money was English. We asked the court to give us what is known as summary judgment. However, the defendant was able to include sufficient evidence in the affidavit to make the judge say: I am not prepared to grant judgement because there is the barest of arguments which will justify this man should have a trial. It was a very very flimsy argument, but over here, the system dictates that, if you can show an arguable defence you will be entitled to a trial before a judge. We then got to the stage where we continued the proceedings and prosecuted them quite quickly. After the defendant was issued with legal proceedings, we realised that for all costs incurred after that point, even if we were to win at this stage, which was very likely, we would not be able to recover our costs against him. And we also realised that because he has been given a rebate, it is unlikely that we will be able to enforce any judgment brought against him anyway. Now, had the procedure been swifter perhaps and a more paper-based procedure rather than on a discretionary basis,[38] we might have been able to obtain the judgment quicker. Had the rules of court been more rigorous on the defendant to show an ideal defence, we might have been able to get the judgment much quicker and we might have been positioned where we could enforce it. But as it is, when we talk about two or three years down the road, things change and the situation changes. The client decided that he would withdraw from the proceedings and we settled on the basis of each party walking away better off in costs.

d) Turkish Law Firm 1: Traditional lawyers

Turkish Law Firm 1, one of the leading law firms of its kind, is run by four partners and is included in the 'recommended lawyers' list of the German and Austrian commercial attachés in Turkey. Some of the partners are from an academic background. Among the clients of the firm are mostly exporters, export credit insurance companies and commercial debt collectors [39] from Germany, Austria and Switzerland. They come in contact with their

---

[37] Interviewee borrows the term from Lord Woolf, the editor of the report *Access to Justice: Final Report to the Lord Chancellor of the Civil Justice System in England and Wales* (London: Her Majesty's Stationery Office, 1996). See Joshua Rozenberg, *The Search for Justice – An Anatomy of the Law* (London: Hodder & Stoughton, 1987), p. 172.

[38] Cf. *supra* 'Summary Procedures for Debt Recovery' in Chapters 1 and 3, 'Debt Recovery in Germany' and 'Debt Recovery in Turkey'.

[39] *Infra* Part III.

clients through the commercial attachés of the three countries or through their personal contacts.

Occasionally the firm gives legal opinions on Turkish law, but their main field of expertise is litigation. Their practice varies according to the instructions received from the clients: debt collectors and export credit insurers require, firstly, a legal opinion on the enforceability of their claim, expected costs and length of the proceedings, *etc.* Only thereafter will they decide to commence proceedings or not. Exporters, on the other hand, usually aim at commencing proceedings at the outset. They seem not always, however, willing to proceed with the claim energetically. Their attitude suggests sometimes that they are rather more interested in obtaining official evidence to the effect that either the claim is not enforceable in Turkey or the debtor is insolvent. They may need such evidence for tax purposes or to apply to the export credit insurer for indemnity. Sometimes, first the exporter himself and later the export credit insurer come to the firm for collection of the same outstanding debt.

The firm commences handling of the case, *where they feel necessary*, with a telephone call to the debtor. Repeated warning letters are not sent and negotiations are not made on the part of the client. Usually they sue the debtor even without a prior warning. Instead, they commence summary proceedings at the execution office where the debtor will accordingly be served with a payment order:[40]

> The payment order is normally our first contact with the debtor. It serves the function of a warning letter. In this way, we also obtain information about the assets of the debtor. Sometimes they do not raise an objection in due time or they fail to make a statement of assets, in which case we can easily pressure them to pay.

One important difficulty which the firm experiences is locating the debtor:

---

40   As is discussed above in Chapter 3: Debt Recovery in Turkey, the debtor can object to the payment order within a seven day period. If he does not raise an objection, the payment order becomes an enforcement title, equivalent to a final judgment. If he does not object, he must also, within the same seven days, file a 'statement of assets' with the execution office, declaring the particulars and location of his assets sufficient to satisfy the creditor and the particulars of his earnings and other financial means. Failure to make such a statement of assets is a 'civil execution offence' punishable by imprisonment of a minimum of ten days. Such punishment can be avoided by an application of the creditor or by paying the debt in full. (Turkish CCEB, Arts 62 et seq., pp. 74–7, 337 and 354.)

Today, for example, I have studied 32 files, and in 8 of these we cannot locate the debtor.

They sometimes give up with proceeding because they cannot locate the debtor. It is usual practice for some debtors to escape from creditors by closing the company or the partnership (which is also, in some cases, a judicial person under Turkish law) and to transfer the assets to another, in most cases a newly established company. Another frequent 'trick' is to change the address (the registered 'place of business') of the company or partnership, without duly informing the creditors and the Commercial Registry.

In such cases the firm uses all the legal remedies available to protect the rights of the creditor. For the first typical case which has been referred to above, it may be possible, under the substantive law, to make the new company or partnership responsible for the old debts incurred by the previous one.[41] As to the latter case where the debtor changes its address, the Ministry of Commerce and Industry published a communiqué according to which the service made to the original (registered) address is deemed to be valid even if the firm has been moved to another address.[42]

The law firm seldom has recourse to the statutory procedure for enforcement of foreign judgments:

> The enforcement of foreign judgments is not especially difficult. But, it is time consuming. It is better to commence the proceedings in Turkey. A proceeding on the merits of the case itself does not take much longer than the exequatur proceeding.

During the execution (enforcement of judgment) stage no special problems are experienced in connection with the foreign creditors. The petition for a 'payment -' or 'execution order' under the civil execution procedure can also be made in a foreign currency where the debt / judgment is a foreign currency debt / judgment. In that case the claim can be extinguished only with full payment / recovery under the relevant foreign currency. This interpretation of the law which was made by the Court of Cassation first in 1992 was in the meanwhile 'fully understood' by the civil execution officers in Istanbul.[43]

---

41 See Turkish Code of Obligations, Art. 179 and Turkish Commercial Code, Art. 151.
42 *Resmi Gazete*, No. 22373, 13 August 1995.
43 *Supra* Chapter 3: Debt Recovery in Turkey.

130 Making Foreign People Pay

The firm bills its clients on an hourly basis.[44] They are 'doing well' and are very happy with their foreign clients who pay their fees regularly, unlike their Turkish clients who are seldom willing to pay on due time and especially before the proceeding has been completed successfully.

e) Turkish Law Firm 2: Debt collectors

Turkish Law Firm 2 is run by two partners, both younger members of the profession in their early thirties. The firm entered the international legal market two years ago and specialises in 'creditors' rights and debt recovery work:

> At the beginning we stated even in our advertisements that our field of expertise was 'debt recovery'. But we later ceased to use that exclusive formulation, as many people thought that we were only debt collectors and did not provide any other legal services.

The firm's most important clients are export insurers and commercial debt collectors from England. There are more clients in the former group and larger amounts have to be collected. Their contact with England is organised by an ex-officer of the British diplomatic service who served for many years in Turkey and who started to work for the firm after his return to England.

The firm offers both debt collection and consultancy services. They provide consultancy not only on legal matters but also on the business environment in Turkey in general and in particular cases. They advise their clients, for example, on the credit worthiness of Turkish firms or private banks. Similarly, when drafting contracts for their clients, they consider to a certain extent the commercial aspects of the contract as well as the legal framework.

Their approach to the debt recovery work is not different from that to the consultancy practice. Their style is summarised by the interviewee:

> We act in the first place *not* as a legal agent, but as a commercial agent.

Before they take any steps for debt recovery, they contact the debtor and, where necessary, initiate negotiations on the part of the creditor. Where the

---

44   It has been reported that lawyers' fees of international law firms in Turkey range between $250–450 / hour for partners and $100–200 / hour for associates. ('International Financial Law Review 1000 – A Guide to the World's International Law Firms', p. 349.)

debtor is in financial difficulty, he offers a partial payment or requests an extension of time which the firm is always prepared to discuss. This first (negotiation) step of the debt recovery process may be very fruitful. But it is blocked to a large extent where the client is itself a debt collection agency, that is, where the actual creditor is represented by another debt collector, as it is not possible to receive instructions from the original creditor.

The second step in the debt recovery process, following the (unsuccessful) negotiations, is an *ex parte* petition to the civil or commercial courts of first instance for a preliminary attachment order.[45] As a rule, the firm makes a second attempt for a settlement between the parties only after obtaining and executing such an order *and* commencing a summary debt collection proceeding at the execution office.

A third step to recover the debt may be to commence full court proceedings in Turkey which is seldom done.

As with 'Turkish Law Firm 1', they rarely use statutory procedure for the enforcement of foreign judgments. Until now, the firm has sought enforcement of a foreign judgment only in three cases, in two of them for reasons other than debt collection. Again this is because 'the enforcement of foreign judgments is not especially difficult. But, it is time consuming and it is better to sue in Turkey'.

The interviewee said that their firm improved the legal position of its clients in their relations with Turkish parties, by persuading them to change their usual business practices in connection with the Turkish markets. The export credit insurance companies in England, for example, used to cancel a British exporter's insurance policy relating to a Turkish importer in case of a single default in payment on the part of the latter. Considering the business environment in Turkey however, such a reaction is said to be too harsh. Default in payment in due time is common in commercial sales in Turkey, which results sometimes in a chain of defaults in payment among a number of suppliers and purchasers. Such 'chain reactions' are observed more often during times of economic crisis. In these 'difficult times' it may not be possible to protect the liquidity of a firm for a period, but the fact that a firm is short of liquid assets does not necessarily (and does not usually) mean that the same cannot survive the crisis or is no longer a safe

---

45 *Supra* Chapter 3: Debt Recovery in Turkey, 'Preliminary Remedies for Protection of the Creditor'.

132 *Making Foreign People Pay*

trading partner.[46] Accordingly, two major export credit insurers in England changed their practices for the Turkish market regarding the cancellation of insurance policies on the first default of the importer.

Similarly, the firm persuaded its clients to use negotiable instruments more often in their business transactions with Turkish parties. The interviewee stated that negotiable instruments are not used as widely in England as in Turkey. Until recently this had been also the case for the transactions made with Turkish firms.[47] The firm advised its clients repeatedly of the advantages of receiving bills of exchange under Turkish law and convinced them to accept and demand promissory notes more often in Turkey as a mode of payment or, as the case may be, as security.

In contrast to 'Turkish Law Firm 1', the firm finds that locating the unknown addresses of the debtors is relative easy:

> First of all we get information from telephone enquiries. Actually those making the enquiries are not permitted to provide the subscribers' addresses, only the telephone numbers. We know someone in the telephone company who does that for us. If the debtor has a telephone number, we usually have no difficulty in finding him. Secondly, one usual practice in consumer credit sales is that, the seller takes a photocopy of the first page of the buyer's passport if he is a foreigner. This is done especially where Turkish employees living abroad buy durable goods, furniture *etc.* If we have such a photocopy from the passport, we can search for the debtor in Turkey in his permanent domicile provided that the amount at stake is not too small for such an effort.

---

46 See interviews in Oktay, *Turkish Business Life via the Eyes of Foreign Businessmen*, pp. 32, 33, 34, 37, 49, 57.

47 The interviewee explained the reason, stating incorrectly that, bills of exchange under the English law do not have the quality of negotiability. See Code of Civil Execution and Bankruptcy, Arts. 167 et seq. and c.f. Gatenby, *Gatenby's Recovery of Money*, pp. 114–6. The actual difference between England and Turkey lies in the business practices. English Law Firm 10 explained the situation in England as follows: 'If you hold a cheque and that cheque is not honoured, then you are entitled to sue not on the underlying contract, but you sue on the instrument itself. In 90 to 95% of cases, you will be able to get summary judgement, because there is generally no defence to a dishonoured cheque or other negotiable instruments like that. I know a lot of foreign jurisdictions where you may have a post-dated promissory note. Yes, the concept does exist under the English law, but unfortunately we have a system whereby you tend to be given thirty days, sixty days or ninety days credit; there is no promissory note/cheque backing up. There is no law which prevents you from giving a post-dated promissory note or cheque, which you can present at the appropriate time. It is more a question of business practice. The problem is often the underlying contract does not provide for a promissory note to be issued.'

As a last resort the firm asks for assistance from a friend of one of the partners who has access to such information from official sources and who can find a person's address in a surprisingly short time. Until now, the firm has always been successful in locating the addresses of the debtors in Turkey.

The firm bills its clients not on an hourly basis, as is the usual practice in the Turkish legal market for foreign clients,[48] but on a contingency basis, *i.e.* 'no success - no fee'. The interviewee explains their billing practice as follows:

> Some of our clients formerly choose not to proceed in Turkey at all before they started to deal with us, due to the costs involved. We entered the market with a bargain: at the outset we take only an amount equal to 4% of the claim, that is, 3% for the court fees and 1% for other initial expenditure such as translation costs. In case a preliminary attachment is necessary, we ask for an additional 15%, which will be deposited with the court as a security for costs. All other costs we pay ourselves and we ask for our legal fees only if we win the case or otherwise successfully collect the money.

It is worth noting that, contingency fees absolutely dependent on the success of the case is not permitted in Turkey.[49] It is however the standard business practice for British commercial debt collectors that fees are only charged for actual monies collected.[50]

The firm is very proud of its success in debt collection for foreign creditors:

> In the first year of our practice in international debt collection we collected a total amount of $4 million in Turkey for our foreign clients. Last year, even during the 'April crisis',[51] we collected £17,5 million for a single client, which was owed a total outstanding amount of £19 million from debtors in Turkey.

They explain that the reason for their success lies with their innovative practices according to which, they concentrate on 'out of court' debt collection. They do not work as 'lawyers', but rather as if they were commercial 'debt collectors':

---

48 *International Financial Law Review 1000 – A Guide to the World's International Law Firms*, pp. 349–52.
49 Lawyers Act 1969, Art. 69 II.
50 Helen Furniss and Kurt Obermeier, 'United Kingdom' (national report), in Garrigues K. Shinobu (ed.), *Guide to International Collections* (Minneapolis: American Collectors Association, loose-leaf / 1995).
51 At the beginning of February 1994, one US Dollar was equal to 13,000 Turkish Liras, by mid-April 1994 the parity rose by 300%, *i.e.* one US Dollar was then equivalent to 39,000 Turkish Liras.

134   Making Foreign People Pay

Litigation is only a small part of our daily work. Only one of us, who is my partner, deals with court proceedings. All our associates and assistants concentrate on debt collection out of court including summary proceedings or other legal services. Personally, I am mostly occupied with 'wheeling and dealing'.

C. CONCLUSIONS FOR CHAPTER 5

Cross-border debt recovery has different meanings for different types of international legal practice. Following the three groups with which we held interviews in London, three types of cross-border debts may be distinguished: Disputed Trade Claims, Large Claims arising from Investment Loans, and Routine Trade Claims arising from Business-to-Business or Consumer Transactions. These categories are not meant to be exhaustive,[52] but only provide examples of different types of cross-border legal interactions, by means of which the role played by international lawyers in cross-border debt recovery could be better understood.

International law firms are organised in specialised departments (which are sometimes called 'groups'[53] or 'units'[54]) such as litigation, corporate, banking, property and tax departments. Collection of Disputed Trade Claims is not a part of daily work in an international law firm. City lawyers have to deal with a large number of cross-border debt recovery cases only if this is required in a special context, such as 'property fraud' and 'Polly Peck' examples provided by English Law Firm 3. Where they are involved in international debt recovery, they have to overcome difficulties of legal bureaucracy and the lack of understanding of differences in national legal systems, which, coupled with difficulties in communication with foreign connections, raises the costs by a considerable extent.[55]

---

52   To give a few other examples, consumer claims, the claims arising from labour relations and the claims arising from family law may also be taken as separate categories of cross-border monetary claims. See von Freyhold, Gessner, Vial and Wagner, *Cost of Judicial Barriers for Consumers in the Single Market*; Pierre Guibentiff, 'Cross-Border Legal Issues Arising from International Migrations – The Case of Portugal', in Gessner and Budak, *Emerging Legal Certainty*; Kirstin Groother, 'The Enforcement of Cross-Border Maintenance Claims of Children', in Gessner and Budak, *Emerging Legal Certainty*.
53   English Law Firm 6.
54   English Law Firm 3.
55   See *infra* Chapter 7: Factors Impeding Access to Justice in Cross-Border Debt Collection.

Investment Lawyers / US Affiliates deal with cross-border debt recovery even less frequently, but when they do so, it is for larger amounts. In collection of Large Claims arising from Investment Loans, litigation and arbitration are used alternatively, according to convenience. Even in 'huge' international projects, litigation has not been superseded by arbitration. Particularly in the case of international investment loans where repayments are delayed, litigation is preferred to arbitration. For in these type of cases, although the outstanding amounts are considerable, there is usually no genuine dispute which would require involvement of the 'grand old men'. Again, in contrast to the construction industry in general, in the defence industry, manufacturers prefer jurisdiction clauses to arbitration.[56]

Large Claims arising from Investment Loans are invariably secured claims.[57] That is, debt recovery involving enforcement of security rights. However, calling upon real securities, such as mortgages, is usually subject to the national laws and exclusive jurisdiction of the courts of the country where the property bearing the security is situated. To avoid foreign litigation in enforcement of security rights, international finance institutions cooperate with other 'international institutions' having local connections. The money is lent to a third bank which has a local branch at a place which will 'on-lend' it to the final debtor. This latter bank submits to the jurisdiction of London or New York Courts. Thus, the local branch will be able to cope with the enforcement of securities under the applicable national law, and any international dispute will be between repeat players of the finance sector which is much simpler to manage as compared to a dispute between a multinational and a domestic business.[58] This type of 'internalisation' of

---

[56] Although there is evidence that international commercial arbitration is growing in importance, it would be too simplistic to say today that the dispute resolution mechanism will invariably be arbitration, or to explain the resort to litigation by international lawyers as a 'territorial demand' to protect their prestigious and lucrative practice. Cf. Dezalay and Garth, 'Merchants of Law as Moral Entrepreneurs', pp. 27 and 56. Thus, for example, for the growing importance of litigation as against arbitration in the international reinsurance market see, Christine Stammel, 'Back to Courtroom? Developments in the London Reinsurance Market', in Gessner and Budak, *Emerging Legal Certainty*.

[57] See Birsel and Erdem, 'Yurtdísíndan Alínan Yatírím Kredilerinin Cebri Icra Yoluyla Tahsilinde Ortaya Cíkan Sorunlar', pp. 119–23.

[58] See Klaus Frick, 'Third Cultures versus Regulators: Cross-Border Legal Relations of Banks', in Gessner and Budak, *Emerging Legal Certainty*.

disputes [59] is one of the reasons why national courts are not frequently used for international litigation.[60]

Debt recovery for Routine Trade Claims arising from Business-to-Business or Consumer Transactions is not usual for international lawyers. Their fees are too high for such work. In the domestic legal market, some large law firms and High Street Solicitors do collect Routine Trade Claims arising from Business-to-Business or Consumer Transactions. These include what English Law Firm 10 calls 'bulk debt recovery', that is, debt collection for department stores, mail order companies, wholesalers of consumer goods to the retailers *etc.*,[61] as well as collection of claims 'on a one-off basis'. In the case of cross-border debts, however, bulk debt recovery cannot be made cost-effectively even by this latter group of lawyers. Only debts for a 'considerable amount' can be collected on a one-off basis. The definition of 'considerable amount' differs according to the complexity of the case and the lawyer's relations with the client, but any amount which cannot be expressed in tens of thousands cannot be collected.

Although it was difficult for lawyers to determine a threshold value for cross-border debt recovery, German Law Firm 2 and English Law Firm 9 pronounced DM 10,000 and £10,000, respectively, which could only be accepted due to good relations with a client. Ten thousand pounds was also the amount of the smallest cross-border claim which English Law Firm 10 could collect. According to English Law Firm 8, the acceptable limit for a simple cross-border case was £30,000. English Law Firm 4 (a US Affiliate) did not want to hear anything which was not expressed in millions: 'My current Turkish deal is DM 2.4 billion. My smallest Turkish deal is $15 million. So I am not into smaller deals.'

With respect to that, the two interviews conducted in Turkey illustrate that an international lawyer may become a 'debt collector' for a wide range of creditors, including those who need to enforce far more smaller claims, provided he leaves aside the pride of English Law Firm 4 and, together with his pride, the traditional style of international lawyering.

Indeed, a comparison between the two Turkish law firms indicates the differences between a traditional and an innovative approach to the legal

---

59   Cf. *infra* 'Out-Sourcing the Cross-Border Collections' in Chapter 14: Collection and Security Methods Employed in International Trade.
60   See *infra* Chapter 7: Factors Impeding Access to Justice in Cross-Border Debt Collection.
61   See several advertisements made for debt-collector law firms in the British business magazine *Credit Management*, in 1996.

services, in general,[62] and between what may be called 'international counselling' and 'cross-border debt collection business', in particular. Both firms are among the best earning law firms in Turkey. The professional practices used by them however differ from each other. The first law firm surprises the debtor with a 'payment order' from the execution office, without an initial warning letter, whereas the second negotiates with the debtor as if it were a 'commercial agent' of the creditor. The difficulties in locating the debtor are overcome by the first firm through legal remedies provided for the protection of creditors' rights, *e.g.* by making a newly established company responsible for the debts owed by an old one. The second law firm locates the debtors on the other hand, by practical methods, such as obtaining information from a 'good friend' at the telephone enquiries. The difference can also be observed in the billing practices of the two firms. The first one bills its fees by the hour, independent of the success of the claim, whereas the second, which aims to enlarge its share in the market, offers a bargain requiring only the preparation fees and the security for costs to be covered by the client and does not bill a further amount unless the debt has been successfully collected. The partners of the first office have Doctor titles and judges in their families, the lawyers from the second office have, by contrast, relatives in England and friends at the telephone company and the police department.

During the interviews the difference could even be observed externally, from the physical working environment: at Law Firm 1, the interviewee received the author in a typical, traditional 'attorney office', modestly and neatly furnished with a small wooden table, two leather arm chairs and bookshelves with the most essential Turkish legal literature on private law. At Law Firm 2, however, he was received in a modern, well illuminated office with a large glass table, a computer and telephones at the right hand side and two arm chairs for the clients in front of it. Unlike the office in the 'Turkish Law Firm 1', there were no professional books close at hand around the office table. Instead, on a small shelf opposite the table were only some code texts, several business-travel guides and dictionaries.

Thus, Turkish Law Firm 1 is an example of a traditional attorney office which is being run by well educated 'gentleman lawyers' who specialise in international litigation. The Turkish Law Firm 2 is, however, one of the new 'entrepreneurial service providers', which provides an example of the

---

62   That is, using Dezalay's jargon ('The Big Bang and the Law'), the difference between 'the elders' and 'newcomers' or 'yuppie lawyers' in the legal market.

'banalisation' and 'commercialisation of legal practice'. It has discovered a gap in the legal market, the 'debt collection business', where the technicalities of law and litigation are of marginal importance, and took advantage of being one of the first entrepreneurs in this field.[63] Below in Part III, we will return to this type of 'commercial' debt recovery and its importance for cross-border legal relations.

---

63   Cf. generally the observations made by Dezalay (*ibid.*) regarding the modern developments in the international legal market and an interview made with a German debt collector – lawyer in Hörmann, *Verbraucher und Schulden*, pp. 174–8.

6 Recourse to National Courts in Cross-Border Debt Collection

> Miles of book shelves deal with norms to be applied if an international case is taken into court. But the simple question whether this is done ... is not asked.[1]

A. GENERALLY

As far as the rules of jurisdiction of the relevant forum are suitable, a creditor seeking to recover his cross-border claims may sue the debtor either in his own country of residence or in the country where the debtor has assets, *i.e.* where the enforcement of judgment procedure can be effected most swiftly. A further alternative may be to initiate litigation in a third country, that is, neither the debtor's nor the creditor's domicile. This last alternative comes into question as a result of jurisdiction agreements between the debtor and the creditor (typically in the form of a jurisdiction clause in the contract between the parties), the aim being to achieve a neutral forum where neither the plaintiff nor the defendant has the 'home advantage' over the other.[2]

Accordingly, the question how frequently are the national courts used in cross-border debt recovery will be discussed in two parts: 'going to court in the home country' and 'going to court abroad'.

B. GOING TO COURT IN THE HOME COUNTRY

A creditor who has sued his overseas debtors in his own country of residence can enforce the judgment which he has obtained from the domestic

---

[1] Gessner, 'Introduction', in Gessner, *Foreign Courts*, at p. 9.
[2] Such 'neutral forum' is usually one of the market places for international legal business such as New York and London (English Law Firms 9 and 10).

court in the country where the debtor has his assets. As discussed above in connection with England, Germany and Turkey, such 'enforcement of foreign judgments' is possible in most legal systems provided that the competent courts of the country where the judgment is sought to be enforced declare the (foreign) judgment enforceable with a separate decision of its own. Should the reciprocal enforcement be possible, an exequatur order is normally made without re-examining the merits of the original case which has already been heard by the foreign court. Moreover, according to the international private procedural laws of many countries, the reciprocity in enforcement of foreign judgments may be achieved not only by means of bilateral or multilateral international conventions but also as a result of the statutory provisions or *de facto* application in the relevant foreign country which makes the enforcement of the judgments of the enforcement country possible.[3]

Thus, where the contractual reciprocity for enforcement of foreign judgments exists, such as between the EU member states, most of which are also members of the 1968 Brussels Convention[4] on reciprocal enforcement of foreign judgments, cross-border enforcement of domestic judgments is possible under a simplified procedure. Many national courts are willing to enforce the judgments of foreign courts even where no contractual reciprocity for enforcement of judgments exists between the forum state and the state where the judgment has been rendered. As discussed above,[5] English common law rules concerning the execution of foreign judgments do not require reciprocity, and the Turkish Court of Cassation decided that the mere existence of statutory provisions for enforcement of foreign judgments procedure in the German Code of Civil Procedure suffices to satisfy the reciprocity requirement between Germany and Turkey.

Interviews held with practitioners (judges, attorneys, civil execution officers, officers from the Ministry of Justice) in the three selected countries, in Turkey, in Germany and in England indicate that no *legal* complications

---

3 For detailed information on the 'enforcement of foreign judgments' procedures in international conventions and in domestic private international law provisions of various countries see Martiny, *Handbuch des internationalen Zivilverfahrensrechts*, Vol. 3/1 and Martiny, Waehler and Wolff, *Handbuch des internationalen Zivilverfahrensrechts*, Vol. 3/2.

4 The exceptions are new member states, Austria, Finland and Sweden. (Finland and Sweden are however parties to the Lugano Convention aiming to cover relations between EU and EFTA countries, which is almost identical to the Brussels Convention.)

5 See *supra* Chapters 2 and 3: Debt Recovery in England, and Debt Recovery in Turkey.

Recourse to National Courts in Cross-Border Debt Collection 141

exist in the field of execution of foreign judgments which make the same difficult for the foreign judgment-creditors in these three countries.[6] Accordingly, it might be expected that the enforcement of foreign judgments is part of the daily work of the courts of first instance, especially in the countries where foreign trade is of great economic importance. Is this really the case?

1. Cases for Enforcement of Foreign Judgments in German Courts

The statistical data available in Germany show that the use of the judicial 'enforcement of foreign judgments' procedures which are provided by the Federal Code of Civil Procedure and bilateral or multilateral international agreements on the reciprocal recognition and enforcement of judgments are rarely applied.

According to the official statistics which have been published by the Federal Statistical Office in Germany, the total number of cases decided before the German first instance courts (not including ex-GDR states) for enforcement of foreign judgments within the 13 year period 1969 – 1981 is only 22,504. The great majority of these cases (21,393) were based on international agreements on reciprocal recognition and enforcement of judgments;[7] each year, only about 100 persons made use of the procedure for the execution of foreign judgments provided by the Federal Code of Civil Procedure.[8] (Table 6.1.) To give a comparison, the annual number of concluded cases in German (not including ex-GDR states) first instance civil and commercial courts is currently approximately 2,250,000.[9]

---

6   This was stated by virtually all interviewees who were involved in these type of international cases.
7   See Erik Jayme and Rainer Hausmann (eds), *Internationales Privat- und Verfahrensrecht* (Textausgabe), 8th ed. (Munich: Beck 1996).
8   In 1988, of the 320 international cases handled by Hamburg and Bremen *Landgerichte*, only 18 cases were applications concerning execution of a foreign judgment. Gessner, 'International Cases in German First Instance Courts', p. 189.
9   See data provided annually by Statistisches Bundesamt, *Rechtspflege, Fachserie 10, Reihe 2: Gerichte und Staatsanwaltschaften*, booklets dated 1990 – 1993 (Wiesbaden: Kohlhammer) concerning the workload of *Landgerichte, Amtsgerichte, Familiengerichte* and *Arbeitsgerichte*.

142   Making Foreign People Pay

Table 6.1   Number of 'enforcement of foreign judgments' proceedings at the German first instance courts (1969 – 1981) [10]

	Cases based on Code of Civil Procedure (§ 722)		Cases based on international agreements on reciprocal enforcement of judgments *	
	at the *Amtsgericht*	at the *Landgericht*	at the *Amtsgericht*	at the *Landgericht*
1969	92	16	746	118
1970	86	22	1,080	200
1971	82	31	1,310	207
1972	96	19	1,272	222
1973	75	21	1,228	309
1974	225	17	1,246	376
1975	86	18	1,279	382
1976	80	13	1,344	349
1977	72	12	1,265	373
1978	59	9	1,280	414
1979	34	11	1,308	462
1980	52	9	1,523	592
1981	60	14	1,594	714
Total:	1,099	212	16,475	4,718

Source: Statistisches Bundesamt
* Including the Brussels Convention on Recognition and Enforcement of Judgments in Civil and Commercial Matters, 1968

2. Cases for Enforcement of Foreign Judgments in Turkish Courts

The judicial statistics prepared by the Ministry of Justice in cooperation with the State Institute of Statistics in Turkey [11] do not provide data concerning the annual number of the proceedings for the execution of foreign judgments or, more generally, the number of proceedings involving foreign

---

[10]   The table is borrowed from Dieter Martiny, 'Anerkennung ausländischer Entscheidungen nach autonomem Recht', p. 36. More recent figures have not been published by the 'Statistisches Bundesamt'. The Judicial Statistics published after the year 1981 are classified differently and they do not provide separate figures as to the number of cases regarding the execution of foreign judgments. See Statistisches Bundesamt, Rechtspflege, Fachserie 10, Reihe 2: *Zivilgerichte und Strafgerichte* (as from 1990 renamed: Gerichte und Staatsanwaltschaften).

[11]   *Adli Istatistikler*, published annually by 'Devlet Istatistik Enstitüsü' in Ankara.

elements.[12] In order to gain an overall idea on the practical importance of the judicial methods of debt collection for the foreign creditors in Turkey, officers from the Ministry of Justice and judges from the Court of Cassation in Ankara were interviewed.

Numerical data was difficult to collect through interviews.[13] Both an experienced senior officer and four junior officials in charge at the Ministry of Justice, however, stated that first instance courts which are petitioned to declare a foreign judgment enforceable in Turkey occasionally request the legal opinion of the International Law Department of the Ministry of Justice [14] in order to clarify *inter alia* if reciprocity exists between Turkey and the country of origin of the judgment which has been sought to be enforced. The number of such applications to the Ministry of Justice exceeds one hundred per year.[15]

The majority of foreign judgments which are enforced in Turkey are of a non-commercial nature.[16] The annual number of (second instance) cases brought before the 11th Chamber of the Court of Cassation, *i.e.* the Chamber handling the commercial matters concerning execution of a foreign judgment does not exceed ten.[17]

---

12   The Ministry of Justice and the State Institute of Statistics were also requested to provide unpublished figures on this matter, if any. No unpublished information was available.

13   The author was informed that during 1994 the number of requests made to the Ministry of Justice for service abroad of judicial (and extra-judicial) documents according to the Hague Convention 1965 was about 11,000. (Turkish Ministry of Justice, Officer 3.)

14   Uluslararasí Hukuk Genel Müdürlügü.

15   Turkish Ministry of Justice, Officer 2. Obtaining such preliminary legal opinions is not necessary to decide the case, and the opinion of the Ministry of Justice is not binding on the court. Therefore, in the majority of the cases, especially in the larger cities, the first instance courts are not to be expected to request legal opinions from the Ministry.

16   It may be suggested that an important part of foreign judgments enforced in Turkey is related to family matters of Turkish families residing abroad or of the 'divided families', where typically the husband lives as a 'Gastarbeiter' in a European country and the wife and children remain at home in Turkey. One fifth of male Turkish workers in Germany left their wives and children in Turkey, Ursula Pasero, *Familien Konflikte in Migration* (Wiesbaden: Deutscher Universitätsverlag, 1990), pp. 40, 43. Currently, each year more than 2,000 marriages where one or both of the parties is / are Turkish national(s) end in divorce in Germany: *i.e.* in 1991 there were 1,994 divorces; in 1992, 2,184 divorces; in 1993, 2,516 divorces; in 1994, 2,985 divorces. (Source: Statistisches Bundesamt, unpublished data.)

17   Turkish Court of Cassation, Judge 2.

A recent survey made in Izmir, the second largest export harbour and one of the largest tourism centres of the country, produced similar results. Files of 1,075 cases brought before the three commercial courts of first instance of the district in 1993 were examined. Not a single application was to be found seeking the execution of a foreign judgment.[18]

3. Cases for Enforcement (Registration) of Foreign Judgments in English Courts

As discussed above, foreign judgments may be enforced in England either under the statutory law or, where no applicable registration procedure exists, under common law by means of bringing a fresh action against the defendant depending on the foreign judgment. As there is no published data or central registry where all the civil and commercial cases brought in England are classified according to their causes of action, the number of cases which has been brought under common law for enforcement of a foreign judgment in England cannot be so easily determined. Yet, the frequency of the applications for registration of foreign judgments under various statutory procedures (which constitute the majority of the applications for enforcement of foreign judgments) may be calculated by referring to the files kept in the High Court.

In all three registration procedures, the competent court for accepting the applications for registration of foreign judgments in England is the High Court.[19] The applications for registration of foreign judgments made to the High Court are directed to the Judgments/Orders Section of the Action Department.[20] After receiving a High Court reference number, the applications are checked by an Official of the Court and, if they are made in admissible form including all relevant documents, they are forwarded to a

---

18 Hasan Nerad, Selma Baktir, Esin Taylan and Sevilay Eroglu, *Izmir Asliye Ticaret Mahkemelerinde Görülen Davalar ve Hasimsiz Isler Konusunda Arastirma Raporu*, Dokuz Eylül Üniversitesi Iktisadi ve Idari Bilimler Fakültesi, 1995 (not published). See Hasan Nerad, 'International Litigation and Arbitration in Turkey', in Gessner and Budak (eds), *Emerging Legal Certainty*.

19 Administration of Justice Act 1920, s. 9(1), Foreign Judgments (Reciprocal Enforcement) Act 1933, s.2(1), Civil Jurisdiction and Judgments Act 1982, s.4(1).

20 The Judgments/Orders Section of the Action Department at the 'Supreme Court Group' (*i.e.* an administrative unit of the civil courts in London, in the Royal Courts of Justice and Somerset House), Room E19 (in the Royal Courts of Justice), at the address 'Strand, London WC2A 2LL'.

Master of the Court who makes the order for registration.[21] The applications for registration of foreign judgments, together with the orders, are filed in the Judgments/Orders Section in separate files (cardboard boxes). That is, all the orders concerning registration of foreign judgments in England are kept at the same office in the Royal Courts of Justice in London.

For this study, an Official of the Court from the Judgments/Orders Section of the Action Department [22] calculated the number of registered foreign judgments in England in the period 1991 – 1995, as classified according to the applicable statutory provisions. (Table 6.2.)

Table 6.2 Number of orders for registration of foreign judgments in England (1991 – 1995)

	Orders for registration of foreign judgments		
	Civil Jurisdiction and Judgments Act 1982	Administration of Justice Act 1920	Foreign Judgments Act 1933
1991	468	21	15
1992	697	17	29
1993	518	15	15
1994	481	22	12
1995	547	18	9
Total:	2711	93	80

The frequency of orders for registration of foreign judgments in England is even lower than in Germany. Foreign judgments constitute a very small portion of the judgments enforced in the country. The annual number of foreign judgments registered is approximately five hundred, whereas the number of proceedings for enforcement of judgments in the County Courts alone is over a million each year.[23]

The Judgments/Orders Section provided the author with the reference numbers of the German judgments registered in England in the period 1991 – 1995. The annual number of German judgments registered in England during this period was as follows: in 1991, 27 judgments; in 1992, 27

---

21 See the Rules of Supreme Court 1965, Order 71.
22 The author thanks Ms J. Horsfield for her cooperation.
23 In 1994, 1,348,975 (including the proceedings under the Attachment of Earnings Act 1971). Lord Chancellor's Department, *Judicial Statistics – England and Wales* (London: Her Majesty's Stationery Office, July 1995).

judgments; in 1993, 33 judgments; in 1994, 18 judgments; in 1995, 38 judgments.

The author was permitted to study the 38 German judgments registered in 1995 in the Judgments/Orders Section. These 'judgments' were classified according to the German first instance courts which had rendered the judgments, the parties, the types of action and the amounts decided.

Considering the small number of applications for registration of German judgments in England, it may be assumed that such international litigation is accessible only for the persons/businesses having more favourable economic conditions, *i.e.* larger commercial enterprises which are involved in international business.[24] Such assumption has not however proven correct. Of the 38 German judgments registered in England 18 were rendered by Landgerichte or Amtsgerichte in Bonn or in larger cities (*i.e.* 3 judgments in Hamburg, 2 judgments each in Stuttgart, Cologne, Munich and Düsseldorf, one judgment each in Lübeck, Oldenburg, Leipzig, Berlin, Bonn, Lüneburg and Frankfurt). The remaining 20 judgments were from smaller towns across Germany, which suggests that international litigation leading to the proceedings for the enforcement of foreign judgments is not used mainly by or against the commercial enterprises established in larger cities which conduct international business. The average amount decided by German courts in these cases was DM 43,822; the largest amount being DM 500,000 and the lowest DM 326. Fourteen judgments were relatively small claims below the DM 10,000 limit which fall, as a rule,[25] in the jurisdiction of the Amtsgerichte with limited jurisdiction. Similarly, in 14 of the 38 cases, the plaintiff(s) were not companies or partnerships but private individuals. Interestingly, in 17 cases the plaintiffs were banks or businesses which sued individual debtors. Twelve cases were between individual creditors and debtors. In only 9 cases, both parties were companies or partnerships, which suggests business-to-business debts.

Although no data could be collected concerning the types of action of the foreign judgments registered, according to the information provided by the Judgments/Orders Section, virtually all of the judgments registered in England in the relevant five year period were for money amounts, *i.e.* liquidated claims. It is again interesting to see in the High Court files that most of the German judgments registered in 1995 were decisions which

---

24   Yet, considering the small number of cases, it is not possible to speak about 'repeat players'.
25   Cf. Gerichtsverfassungsgesetz, Art. 23 I, Nr. 1.

Recourse to National Courts in Cross-Border Debt Collection 147

had been made in 'routinised' debt collection cases [26] instead of being judgments rendered as a result of a full trial. The great majority of the 38 registrations in 1995 concerned default judgments, summary default judgments (*Vollstreckungsbescheide*), court settlements and other uncontested/summary orders.[27] Only three German judgments which had been registered were judgments rendered as a result of a full trial. (Table 6.3.)

Table 6.3   German judgments registered in England in 1995

Default judgments	15
Summary default judgments (*Vollstreckungsbescheid*)	12
Order concerning service of a *Mahnbescheid*	2 [28]
Judgment on admittance by the defendant	1
Order concerning costs of proceedings to be borne by the losing party (*Kostenfestsetzungsbeschluß*, German CCP § 103)	3
Court settlement (*Vergleich*)	2
Judgment after a full trial	3
Total:	38

C. GOING TO COURT ABROAD

The small number of cases for the execution of foreign judgments in commercial matters may suggest that foreign claimants prefer to sue in the

---

[26] See *infra* Chapter 9: Routinisation and Privatisation of Debt Collection.

[27] The above mentioned survey in German first instance courts showed that summary procedures for debt recovery were used in international cases in Hamburg and Bremen less often than domestic cases. That is, 30% of domestic cases were summary proceedings for debt recovery in comparison to only 10% of international cases. Gessner, 'International Cases in German First Instance Courts', p.174. Yet, petitions for summary proceedings for debt recovery are possibly withdrawn less frequently than proceedings heard in full trial, see *ibid.* p. 186. Thus, one third of German judgments registered in England are summary default judgments.

[28] These two applications for service of *Mahnbescheide* on the debtor were made under the Hague Service Convention 1965 and were addressed to the Senior Master of the Supreme Court of Judicature, Royal Courts of Justice who is one of the authorities under the Convention (Art. 18(1)) designated to receive requests for service. See David McClean, *International Judicial Assistance* (Oxford: Clarendon, 1992), pp. 20–1. Before being served, they were registered in the Judgments/Orders Section as if they were foreign judgments.

148   Making Foreign People Pay

debtor's country. The judicial statistics in the three countries [29] do not provide information on the nationality of the parties in court proceedings. In Germany, the above mentioned survey which was made in three North German cities details information on international cases in German courts.[30] A similar study on a smaller scale was made in Turkey, in the commercial courts of Izmir.[31] The results of these studies are partly reproduced below. In order to determine the frequency of international cases before Turkish and English courts, further data were collected directly from the Turkish Court of Cassation and the High Court.

1. International Cases in the Turkish Courts

In an attempt to ascertain the frequency of foreign parties in commercial cases in Turkey, the practice of the Court of Cassation provides some insight. All Court of Cassation judgments rendered by the 11th (commercial matters) Chamber of the Court in June 1995 (that is, between 3 June 1995 and 3 July 1995) were studied.

Such sampling is of representative value. The Turkish judicial system provides only two court instances, namely first instance district courts and the Court of Cassation in Ankara. There is no third instance between the two where an appeal on the matters of fact or law is possible. In addition, no leave is required to appeal to the Court of Cassation. In practice, an appeal is ritually lodged against most of the first instance judgments, even in the absence of a convincing ground of appeal.[32]

In June 1995, the 11th Chamber decided 1,039 cases, *i.e.* judgments numbered between 1995/4,560 and 1995/5,599. The judgments of the (11th) Chamber are kept at the Chamber's Registry, ordered according to their dates and numbers. Each judgment includes the names (but not ad-

---

29   In Turkey: *Adli Istatistikler*; in Germany: Statistisches Bundesamt, Rechtspflege, Fachserie 10, Reihe 2: *Gerichte und Staatsanwaltschaften*; in England: *Judicial Statistics*.
30   See Gessner, 'International Cases in German First Instance Courts'.
31   See Nerad, 'International Litigation and Arbitration in Turkey'.
32   As a result of its excessive workload, the work of the Court of Cassation becomes a routine process where only those cases with most principle or financial importance can be proved in detail. The Court of Cassation uses even 'master decisions' either approving the judgments of the first instance courts with a general phrase or reproduces the opinion of the court in some frequently appearing legal matters, which may be entered into a computer adding the names of the parties *etc.* and sent back to the district court.

dresses) of the parties on the first page [33] and the subject matter of the proceedings. The subject matter is very briefly referred to and could be misleading. Therefore, where necessary, the texts of the judgments with foreign party names have also been studied. Due to language differences the fact that a commercial firm is a foreign company or partnership can usually be understood from the abbreviation at the end of the name of the company (*e.g.* 'GmbH' or 'PLC' which can be written after the name of a German or an English company respectively). However, for individuals, as a rule, foreign (not Turkish) names have simply been deemed to belong to foreigners.[34] The cases where one or both of the parties are foreign individuals or foreign businesses are defined as 'international cases'. [35,36]

The number of international cases was 36 from a total of 1,039 cases. That is to say, 3.5% of commercial cases were 'international'. (Table 6.4.) Taking into account the different nature of international trade to domestic trade, it is difficult to make a comparison between the frequency of domestic and international commercial cases in relation to the respective number of domestic and international commercial interactions. It may be argued that the absolute number of international commercial transactions in any country is much less than domestic transactions, but the monies involved in international transactions are much higher than the average in domestic transactions. It may also be argued that, should a dispute arise, the commercial transactions where larger amounts are at stake are more likely to end up before the court as compared to small transactions. Thus, the

---

33 The addresses which are given in the judgment text are those of representing counsel.
34 Even identical Muslim names from foreign countries can normally be distinguished from Turkish names due to the difference in spelling. Jewish names which are commonly used in Turkey have been accepted to belong to Turkish nationals.
35 To be fair it must be added that the Turkish nationals residing abroad (currently estimated at 3,000,000 in Europe) and represented by a Turkish lawyer could not be distinguished from the Turkish nationals residing in Turkey, and could not be taken into account as foreign resident parties. According to the unpublished / not yet published data collected from the *Statistisches Bundesamt* in Germany and *Yurtdışı İşci Hizmetleri Genel Müdürlüğü* (General Directorate for Services for Employees Working Abroad) in Turkey, the number of Turkish citizens living in eight EU member states (*i.e.* Germany 1994, Netherlands 1993, France 1993, Belgium 1993, Denmark 1993, Austria 1992, Sweden 1993 and UK 1993) is approx. 2,815,070: Cigdem Akkaya, 'Die Türkei und ihre Migrationspolitik in die EU-Staaten', unpublished text of a lecture held in the Symposium *AusländerIn sein in Österreich in der EU: Perspektiven im Spannungsfeld politischer Veränderung*, 19 – 20.10.1995, Wien.
36 Cf. Gessner, 'International Cases in German First Instance Courts', p. 151. Gessner defined 'international cases' as the cases where one of the parties has his domicile outside Germany.

monetary volume of commerce in domestic and international transactions within a particular country may be taken as a common factor which has an influence on the number of domestic and international court cases in the commercial courts of the same country.

In a comparative study on the historical development of the workload of the civil and commercial courts in Europe, Wollschläger used the increase of the Gross Domestic Product ('GDP') as an indicator for the increase in domestic legal interactions, which in turn give rise to an increase of the conflict potential and the number of court proceedings.[37] As a criterion for defining the share of international trade in the national economy, political economists use the concept of Foreign Trade Share (*Außenhandelsquote*).[38] Foreign Trade Share is the 'ratio of total trade turnover (exports and imports) to national income'[39] which may be mathematically formulated as (import+export)/2*100/GDP. The author assumes that, in an ideal judicial system where international disputes have access to the national courts as much as domestic disputes, there must be a direct relation between the Foreign Trade Share in a country and the share of international commercial cases. In 1993, the Foreign Trade Share of Turkey was 17%.[40] As a result, the share of international commercial cases which rates at 3.5% suggests that, these cases are considerably under-represented in the workload of the Turkish commercial courts.

In the above mentioned 1,039 cases, 37 international cases were identified. In one such case there were two defendants, both foreigners. In all other cases the foreign party was either the plaintiff (27 cases) or the defendant (9 cases). In 15 of the 27 cases where the plaintiff was a foreign company, partnership or individual, it was represented by a Turkish sister company or a commercial agent in Turkey. In such cases the identity of the plaintiff was formulated as 'Company X in a representative capacity, in the name of Company Y'. Similarly, 3 of the 10 foreign defendants were repre-

---

37   Christian Wollschläger, 'Die Arbeit der europäischen Zivilgerichte im historischen und internationalen Vergleich – Zeitreihen der europäischen Zivilprozeßstatistik seit dem 19. Jahrhundert', in Erhard Blankenburg (ed.), *Prozeßflut? - Studien zur Prozeßtätigkeit europäischer Gerichte in historischen Zeitreihen und im Rechtsvergleich* (Cologne: Bundesanzeiger, 1989), pp. 21–114, at p. 48.

38   See Jürgen Neyer, *Spiel ohne Grenzen – Weltwirtschafliche Strukturveränderungen und das Ende des sozial kompetenten Staates* (Marburg: Tectum, 1996), p. 27.

39   See the article 'Außenhandelsquote', Wilhelm Schäfer, *Wirtschaftswörterbuch*, Vol.2, 3rd. ed. (Munich: Verlag Franz Vahlen, 1991).

40   In 1988, the same ratio was 18%. International Monetary Fund, *International Financial Statistics* (Washington, D.C.: IMF, December 1995). Author's calculation using values for export and import of goods and international service transactions and GDP.

sented by their sister companies or commercial agents in Turkey. (Table 6.4.)

Table 6.4 Parties to commercial cases before the Turkish Court of Cassation (1–30 June 1995)

Cases where both parties were Turkish corporations or Turkish nationals:	1,003	(96.54%)
Cases where one of the parties was a foreign corporation or a foreign national:	36	(3.46%)
Foreign plaintiffs:	27	
(in 15 cases represented by a sister company or a commercial agent)		
Foreign defendants:	10	
(in 3 cases represented by a sister company or a commercial agent)		
Total number of cases:	1,039	(100%)

Concerning the subject matter, 10 of the 36 cases were related to carriage of goods by sea, followed by disputes concerning protection of trade marks, patents and unfair competition (9 cases) and disputes between the insurer and the insured or a third party held responsible for damages (5 cases). One of the remaining cases was related to carriage of goods by land.

Table 6.5 International commercial cases in the Turkish Court of Cassation (1–30 June 1995)

Carriage of goods by sea and by land	11
Protection of trade marks, patents and unfair competition	9
Disputes between the export insurer and the insured or the third party responsible for the damages	5
Execution of a foreign judgment	0
Others	11
Total number of cases:	36

That is, not only were foreign parties few in number, but it appeared that international commercial cases before Turkish courts were concentrated on a small number of issues. Transport cases appeared most frequently: 16 of the 37 international cases (43%) were either directly or indirectly (disputes between the export insurer and the insured or the third party sued for damages) related to the carriage of goods by sea or by land. Those cases were

152   Making Foreign People Pay

followed by cases concerning patents, trade marks and unfair competition, *i.e.* 9 cases (24%).[41]

In domestic commercial cases such disputes are less frequent. Namely, the disputes arising from transport and (all kinds of) insurance contracts were represented respectively by 5 and 29 cases among the 525 contested claims before the commercial courts in Izmir in the year 1993, *i.e.* they only amounted to 6% of the cases. Similarly, the number of (domestic) cases concerning trade marks and unfair competition before the same courts was 7, *i.e.* only 1.3%.[42]

Foreign parties having commercial legal relations with Turkey other than those referred to in the Table 6.5 above are less frequently before the courts. For example, disputes before the Turkish courts arising from foreign investments and foreign bank loans [43] are rare.[44]

2. International Cases in the German Courts

A recent empirical study made in Germany shows that the proportion of the 'international cases' (*i.e.* cases in which one party has its domicile outside Germany) in the caseload of the Bremen and Hamburg courts in 1988 was 2.8%, that is, 320 of 12,029 cases.[45] Of these international cases 65%, that is, 209 cases, were initiated by foreigners.[46] (Table 6.6.)

---

41   The Judge who was interviewed in the Commercial Court of First Instance in Istanbul believes that there are intellectual property lawyers in Istanbul who work as 'detectives' as well. When they discover that a foreign trade mark is used without permission, they get in contact with the owner abroad and bring an action against the user in Turkey.

42   Hasan Nerad, Selma Baktir, Esin Taylan and Sevilay Eroglu, *Izmir Asliye Ticaret Mahkemelerinde Görülen Davalar ve Hasimsiz Isler Konusunda Arastirma Raporu*, p. 3.

43   *Supra* English Law Firm 9.

44   On the other hand, the Judge who was interviewed in the Turkish Commercial Court of First Instance stated that his court issues relatively often interlocutory injunctions against Turkish banks containing an order for refraining from honouring a bank guarantee or a letter of credit on the ground that the goods delivered under a contract of sale are defective *etc.* Since no appeal is admissible against interlocutory injunctions, such cases cannot be found in the Court of Cassation files. Similarly, disputes concerning summary procedures for negotiable instruments are decided, as a rule, by the 12th Chamber of the Court of Cassation and therefore cannot be found in the files of the Commercial Chamber.

45   Cases regarding execution of foreign judgments and other cases on enforcement matters are included.

46   See Gessner, 'International Cases in German First Instance Courts', pp. 155 and 157.

Table 6.6 Relative share of international cases in Bremen and Hamburg first instance Courts (1988)

	Bremen			Hamburg (sample)			Bremen and Hamburg		
	All	International		All	International		All	International	
	N	N	%	N	N	%	N	N	%
General	3,605	45	1	6,661	110	2			
Commercial	833	91	11	930	99	11			
Total:	4,438	136	3	7,591	209	3	12,029	320	3

Source: Gessner, 'International Cases in German First Instance Courts'

Owing to the fact that Hamburg and Bremen are traditional import / export cities, international commercial cases may be over-represented in these Court Districts, as compared to the average for Germany as a whole.[47] Therefore, the 'Foreign Trade Share' criterion which was used for Turkey can be applied here more cautiously. In any case, in 1988, when the above survey was made, the Foreign Trade Share in Germany was 27%,[48] with the share of international commercial cases in these two Districts remaining at 10%.[49]

With reference to subject matter, international cases before German first instance courts was again concentrated on a small number of issues.

---

47 Ibid.
48 In 1994, the same ratio was 29%. International Monetary Fund, *International Financial Statistics*. Author's calculation using values for export and import of goods and international service transactions and GDP. (The ratios found are different from those of Neyer, who used only export and import of goods, but not international services in the formula. Cf. Neyer, *Spiel ohne Grenzen*, p. 172.)
49 If, as is assumed, there is direct relation between the relative frequency of international commercial cases with the Foreign Trade Share, international commercial cases must be considerably over-represented in Hamburg and Bremen. GDP values for the State of Hamburg and for the State of Bremen are found in the Annual Statistics of Hamburg and Bremen as compared to the whole of the Federal Republic. However, the values of export and import which are given in these Statistics cover all German export and import trade made from these States, regardless of the origin of the goods exported or the target of the goods imported within the Federal Republic. Therefore, Foreign Trade Shares cannot be calculated for Hamburg and Bremen by using the available data. Suffice it to say however that, in the year 1988, the relative value of imports and exports in Bremen was so high that, the ratio of total trade turnover in Bremen (*i.e.* German exports and imports made through Bremen) to 'national' income of the State Bremen was over 100%. In Hamburg, the same ratio was 40%. See Handelskammer Hamburg, *Bericht 1989* (Hamburg: Handelskammer Hamburg, 1989); Statistisches Landesamt Bremen, *Statistisches Jahrbuch 1992* (Bremen: Statistisches Landesamt Bremen, 1992). Author's calculation.

154 Making Foreign People Pay

Namely, 83 (41.2%) of the cases were related to contract of sales; 51 (25.3%) were related to sea or land transport and 24 (11.9%) concerned contracts for work.[50] (Table 6.7.)

Table 6.7 International cases in Bremen and Hamburg first instance Courts (1988)

Subject matter	%	N
Contract of sale	41	83
Sea/land transport	25	51
Contract for work	12	24
Commission of agents	6	13
Credit	5	11
Family affairs	5	10
Unfair competition	5	10
Road accident	5	10
Tort	4	9
Real estate	4	8
Suretyship	4	8
Maritime accidents	3	6
Agency	3	6
Corporation affairs	2	5
Insurance	2	4
Travel business	1	2
Total:	100	209

Source: Gessner, 'International Cases in German First Instance Courts' [51]

It can be understood from Table 6.7 that most of the international cases before German first instance courts are of a commercial nature.[52] The majority of these cases are possibly dealt with by larger law firms. Most of the international cases from the districts of Bremen and Lower Saxony handled by smaller local law firms concern claims brought by 'involuntary creditors',

---

50   *Ibid.*, p. 164.
51   Table excludes those matters which are only defined in terms of legal procedures: execution of judgment (32 cases), attachment (14 cases), documentary procedure, such as letters of credit and cheques (12 cases), and arbitral awards (5 cases), *ibid.*, p. 164.
52   Yet, most family cases go to family courts which are not represented in the Table 6.7. See *ibid.*, pp. 189–203.

such as claims in connection with traffic accidents abroad, divorce, travels etc.[53]

The survey made in Bremen and Hamburg first instance courts clearly shows that in international cases more money is at stake than in national cases, which suggests that parties to an international dispute rarely go to court in Germany unless a substantial amount is involved.[54] (Table 6.8.)

Table 6.8 Amount of claim in national and international cases in Bremen and Hamburg first instance Courts (1988)

Value (DM)	National %	N	International %	N	Total %	N
Less than 5,000	8	959	2	6	8	965
5,000 – 10,000	37	4,280	21	66	36	4,346
10,000 – 20,000	24	2,792	20	65	24	2,857
20,000 – 50,000	19	2,177	23	72	19	2,249
50,000 – 100,000	7	797	16	51	7	848
More than 100,000	6	704	19	60	6	764
Total %	97		3		100%	
N		11,709		320		12,029

Source: Gessner, 'International Cases in German First Instance Courts'

3. International Cases in the English Courts

A high frequency of foreign commercial cases could be expected to be found in England. In 1994, England had a Foreign Trade Share of 22.5%.[55] In addition, not only is England an export oriented country, but London itself is a well-known marketplace for international litigation.[56] 'Foreign parties are only encouraged.'[57] The Commercial Court Division of the High Court is said to be an 'International Commercial Court' in competition with the courts of other litigation centres of the world for attracting

---

53 Schnorr, 'Einzelanwälte und kleine Anwaltsfirmen im internationalen Rechtsverkehr', p. 101.
54 Gessner, 'International Cases in German First Instance Courts', pp. 167–8. Cf. *supra* Cases for enforcement (registration) of foreign judgments in English Courts.
55 International Monetary Fund, *International Financial Statistics*. Author's calculation.
56 See *supra* Chapter 5: Role of Lawyers in Cross-Border Debt Collection.
57 English Law Firms 1 and 10.

156 *Making Foreign People Pay*

international litigation, which is a profitable service industry in London.[58] The Commercial Court is said to be designed for international litigation, providing the necessary expertise [59] and speed required in such cases:

> The Commercial Court... [is] different from the rest of the building, in that all pre-judgement matters are dealt with by five judges. Now judges tend to be selected from the most senior barristers. These are the most successful crème de la crème people who are chosen. They are actually the most competent ones. The most senior High Court judges are on par with Government ministers in seniority. They automatically receive a knighthood...
>
> The Commercial Court is much smaller when you are down in the central office. We are geared for the commercial work. We are geared for speed, we are very small, very streamlined. We are very very speedy in that applications [for serving a writ outside the country] [the order giving leave of the Court] could come back the same day. We are very keen to catch the time. We are the International Commercial Court. We are very keen to make it as competitive as possible with the other foreign courts. People want to come to us, we do not want to put barriers in their way of dealing. So if they tell us it is an urgent matter, and if they have someone waiting at the airport literally to have this writ taken off to Spain or wherever, we can do that for them. The judges are very flexible.[60]

In order to confirm these statements the question how often the High Court is used by foreign parties must be answered. As stated above, the frequency of international cases in England cannot be found in the Judicial Statistics. However, the files kept at the Judgments/Orders Section of the Action Department of the Supreme Court Group [61] provide a useful source of help.

All English judgments to be enforced outside England go through the files of the Judgments/Orders Section. Under the Civil Jurisdiction and Judgments Act 1982 as well as under the Foreign Judgments (Reciprocal Enforcement) Act 1933 and the Administration of Justice Act 1920, the English judgments which are sought to be enforced abroad must be certified by the High Court. That is, the authenticity of the judgment must be certified by a document sealed and signed by a Master of the Queen's Bench Division. Similar to the registration procedure, an application for certification of an English judgment is made to the Judgments/Orders Section of the High Court. After receiving a High Court reference number and

---

58 Interview with the High Court Officer 1.
59 For the role of the Commercial Court in international cases concerning reinsurance disputes see Christine Stammel, 'Back to Courtroom: Developments in the London Reinsurance Market', Gessner and Budak (eds), *Emerging Legal Certainty*.
60 Interview with the High Court Officer 1.
61 See *supra*.

checked by an Official of the Court, the application for certification is forwarded to a Master of the Court who formally certifies the judgment.[62] The Rules of The Supreme Court also make provisions for the exceptional cases where an application may be made for recognition and enforcement of an English judgment in a country which is not covered by one of the three statutes above, *i.e.* the Civil Jurisdiction and Judgments Act 1982, the Administration of Justice Act 1920 and the Foreign Judgments (Reciprocal Enforcement) Act 1933. That is to say, considering the countries which are neither one of the Commonwealth countries covered by the 1920 Act nor one of the countries which is a party to one of the bilateral or multilateral conventions on reciprocal enforcement of foreign judgments where England is among the contracting states, the Rules of The Supreme Court provide for the parties to an action to obtain a certified copy of an English judgment for use in a foreign court even where none of the above mentioned Acts are applicable.[63] For example, an English judgment sought to be enforced in Turkey will be certified by the High Court Master. The applications for certification of judgments in this latter (exceptional) case are also made to the Judgments/Orders Section.

Accordingly, the figures concerning the certification of judgments in the High Court represent all international litigation in England which has resulted in an application for recognition or enforcement of an English judgment outside England. These figures have been provided by the Judgments/Orders Section. (Table 6.9.)

Table 6.9 Number of English judgments sought to be enforced outside England (1991 – 1995)

	Civil Jurisdiction and Judgments Act 1982	Administration of Justice Act 1920	Foreign Judgments Act 1923	Rules of Supreme Court, Ord. 38, r.10
1991	210	18	23	53
1992	193	29	23	48
1993	169	12	14	23
1994	124	9	12	18
1995	116	17	13	25
Total:	812	85	85	167

Certificates for English judgments sought to be enforced outside England

---

62 See the Rules of Supreme Court 1965, Order 71.
63 *Ibid.*, Order 38, rule 10.

If these figures concerning certification of English judgments are compared with the figures above concerning registration of foreign judgments in England, it may be seen that, the frequency of English judgments sought to be enforced outside England is even lower than the frequency of foreign judgments sought to be enforced in the country. In the five year period 1991 – 1995, 2,884 foreign judgments were registered in England, whereas 1,149 English judgments were certified in the country to be enforced outside England. The number of foreign judgments which have been 'imported' into England is 2.5 times greater than the number of English judgments which have been 'exported' overseas.

Although the number of Commercial Court cases resulting in out-of-court settlements [64] or withdrawal of claim may be substantial, this is also the case for other countries [65] and cannot alone explain the low frequency of English judgments which are enforced outside the country. It cannot reasonably be argued that the judgments which have been rendered by English courts in international cases are obeyed in foreign countries voluntarily, without proceedings for the enforcement of foreign judgments being initiated. As a result, the statements claiming the internationalisation of the Commercial Court in London, which may be true in terms of the quality of the service provided by the Court, are not equally convincing in terms of quantity.

---

64   See Stammel, 'Back to the Courtroom?'.
65   See *e.g.* Gessner, 'International Cases in German First Instance Courts', p. 185.

7 Factors Impeding Access to Justice in Cross-Border Debt Collection

The reason for the infrequent use of judicial methods in cross-border debt collection may be either legal and procedural or concern some practical difficulties discouraging the creditors from suing in national courts. Such difficulties worthy of consideration in some detail which may be supported with references to the situation in each of the three respective countries are dealt with in this study.

A. GENERALLY

1. Differences Between National Legal Systems?

In the post Second World War period, parallel to the growth of international trade, increased efforts have been made by the community of nation states to improve the capacity of the national courts for solving international disputes. These efforts can be seen both *at the national level*, in the form of developments in domestic private international laws [1] and *at the international level*, in the form of numerous international conventions on private international law [2] and unification of laws.[3]

---

[1] An interesting example is the development in the English rules of jurisdiction for private international law cases; cf. jurisdiction rules in common law with provisions of Rules of The Supreme Court, Order 11 and Civil Jurisdiction and Judgments Act 1982: Volker Triebel, Stephen Hodgson, Wolfgang Kellenter and Georg Müller, *Englisches Handels- und Wirtschaftsrecht*, 2nd ed. (Heidelberg: Verlag Recht und Wirtschaft, 1995), pp. 373–90. See also *e.g.* new Turkish (1982) and Swiss (1987) acts on private international law for their liberal attitudes to the application of foreign law and the enforcement of foreign judicial decisions, *supra* 'Introduction', footnote 41.

[2] See *e.g.* European Convention on Information on Foreign Law 1968; Hague Convention on the Service Abroad of Judicial and Extra Judicial Documents in Civil and Commercial Matters 1965; Hague Conventions on enforcement of foreign mainte-

160 Making Foreign People Pay

The information gathered by the author from international law firms and commercial debt collectors by means of interviews and questionnaires [4] suggests that a great deal of the matters described in literature [5] as legal complications in international debt recovery (*e.g.* various regulated national statutes of limitations, domestic security rights having no effect abroad, currency restrictions *etc.*) are indeed not so important in practice. Such 'legal barriers' have been largely overcome by careful contract drafting in the US fashion [6] as well as by amendments to national laws. For example, where the limitation periods are concerned, international debt recovery cases before the English courts had been problematic in the past due to the fact that the English system qualifies limitation periods as a procedural matter. This feature, which is unique to common law systems, was applied in the past to international cases as well as national cases, as a result of which limitation periods were subject to English law (*lex fori*), regardless of the substantive law applied to the merits of the case. That is to say, a claim on a contractual debt could be barred in England, even if it had been valid and enforceable according to the foreign substantive law applicable to the contract. However, in 1984, English legislators remedied this situation with the 'Foreign Limitation Periods Act 1984' [7] and established the principle that limitation periods in private international law cases shall be subject to the substantive law applicable to the merits of the case (*lex causae*) instead of the principle of *lex fori* [8]. Similarly, in international debt

---

   nance orders dated 1958 and 1973; Brussels Convention on Jurisdiction and the Enforcement of Civil and Commercial Judgments 1968.
3 *E.g.* UN Convention on the International Sale of Goods 1980; Convention on the Carriage of Goods by Road 1956. See René David, *The International Unification of Private Law*, International Encyclopaedia of Comparative Law, Vol. II, Chapter 5 (Tübingen: Mohr / The Hague - Paris: Mouton / New York: Oceana, 1971); Gerhard Kegel, *Internationales Privatrecht*, 7th ed. (Munich: Beck, 1995), pp. 60–99.
4 See *infra*.
5 See *e.g.* Horst Piggert, 'Das Auslandsinkasso', *Teilzahlungswirtschaft*, 15. Jahrgang, no.1 (1968), pp. 15–6; Reinhard Böhner, 'Forderungseinziehung gegen Unternehmen in der EG', *Schimmelpfeng-Review*, 24 / 1979, pp. 69–70; Albert Windolp, 'Das Auslandsinkasso in den Ländern der EWG und EFTA', *Teilzahlungswirtschaft*, 16. Jahrgang, no. 2 (1969), pp. 56–60; Albert Windolp, 'Das Inkasso im Ausland', *Schimmelpfeng-Review* 18 (1976), pp. 38–40; Albert Windolp, 'Das Inkasso nach deutschem und ausländischem Recht', in *Aktuelle Beiträge über das Inkasso im In- und Ausland*, 2nd ed. (Frankfurt: Schimmelpfeng, 1977); Hubert Timmermann, 'Die Zwangsvollstreckung im Ausland ist schwierig', *Teilzahlungswirtschaft*, 16. Jahrgang, no. 2 (1969), p. 20.
6 See *infra* Chapter 9: Routinisation and Privatisation of Debt Collection.
7 Foreign Limitation Periods Act 1984, s 1(1).
8 Stone, *The Conflict of Laws*, pp. 254–6.

recovery cases in Turkey, transfer of foreign currencies out of the country had been problematic.[9] In line with the economic liberalisation movement of the 1980s, Turkey relaxed its restrictive monetary laws.[10] At present, foreign currency amounts collected through judicial proceedings can be transferred abroad.[11]

2. Bias Against Foreigners?

Such efforts not only avoided *legal* complications of cross-border litigation by and large, but also created a reciprocal comity between different national courts.

A well-known English judge, Lord Diplock, summarised the latter development with the words 'judicial chauvinism has been replaced by judicial comity'.[12]

---

[9] Bernard R. Dietrich, *Inkasso Unternehmungen* (Munich: Hieronymus, 1986), pp. 146–7.

[10] See General Directorate of Foreign Investment, *Investing in Turkey* (Ankara: Under-Secretariat of Treasury and Foreign Trade, 1993).

[11] As a rule, monies in foreign currencies may be freely transferred outwith Turkey through banks or other financial institutions. Türk Parasinin Kiymetini Koruma Hakkinda 32 sayili Karar (Decree no. 32 regarding the Protection of the Value of Turkish Currency), *Resmi Gazete* no. 20249, 11.8.1989, Arts 4(e), 10, 13, 15(d)(ii), 20 II, 95/6990 sayili Yabanci Sermaye Cerceve Karari (Foreign Capital Framework Decree no. 95/6990), *Resmi Gazete* no. 22352, 23.7.1995, Art. 5. It has been stated in academic litarature that transfer of monies which have been collected through the civil execution procedure (*e.g.* the proceeds of execution sales) in Turkey outwith the country is subject to the permission of the Under-Secretary of Treasury and Foreign Trade according to Art. 20 II of the *Decree no. 32*. (Birsel and Erdem, 'Yurtdisindan Alinan Yatirim Kredilerinin Cebri Icra Yoluyla Tahsilinde Ortaya Cikan Sorunlar', pp. 136–7.) Art. 20 II of the Decree no. 32 is formulated ambiguously and reads as follows 'the execution of the judgments and decisions which have been issued by judicial or administrative authorities concerning the import of goods into the country is effected by the Ministry under the provisions of this Decree'. The practising lawyers and debt collectors interviewed for this study did not mention this provision or any other formalities regarding the transfer abroad of foreign currency amounts which have been collected through the execution procedure in Turkey.

[12] *The Abidin Daver* (H.L.(e.)) [1984] 1 AC 398, at p. 411. In the Abidin Daver Case ([1983] 3 All ER, C. A. 46), a collision had occurred between a Turkish and a Cuban vessel in the Bosphorous. The Turkish ship commenced proceedings in the competent District Court in the Bosphorous. The owner of the Cuban ship, who blamed the owner of the Turkish ship, did not lodge a cross-claim in the proceedings before the Turkish court, but commenced other proceedings in the Admiralty Court in England. The owners of the Turkish vessel applied to the English Court for a stay of proceedings on the ground that the Turkish court was the appropriate forum. The Court of

162 Making Foreign People Pay

No complaints were to be heard in our interviews that Turkish, English or German courts discriminate against foreign parties. In London, which is an important centre for international litigation, 'foreign parties are only encouraged'.[13] An American attorney who worked for five years in the Istanbul branch of a US mega-law firm [14] states that he had never experienced his foreign clients being prejudiced before the Turkish courts.[15]

Appeal held that the fact that there was a proceeding in Turkey did not deprive the Cuban ship owner the right to commence proceedings in England. According to the Civil Division of the Court, a Turkish District Court in Bosphorous was *not* 'a forum [...] in which justice can be done between the parties at substantially less inconvenience or expense' (at p. 53 per Dunn LJ). The House of Lords decision reversed the decision of the Court of Appeal on the ground that 'the Turkish court was a forum in which justice could be done between the parties at substantially less inconvenience and expense' (H.L.(e.)) [1984] 1 AC 398.

13 English Law Firm 1; High Court Officer 1.
14 English Law Firm 7.
15 There is a popular belief (English Law Firms 7 and 10) on the part of foreign investors, especially US multinationals, that the quality of justice is insufficient in the 'Third World Countries', including Turkey, which raises the costs of security in business transactions (English Law Firm 10). However, the level of economic development is not alone a suitable criteria for the quality of judicial system in a country. Notwithstanding similar levels of GDP per capita in Mexico and in Turkey (in 1994, $2,720 in Turkey and $2,910 in Mexico), Turkish legal culture is different from Mexican legal culture. See Statistisches Bundesamt, *Statistisches Jahrbuch 1996 für das Ausland* (Stuttgart: Metzler-Poeschel, 1996), pp. 352–3; Gessner, *Recht und Konflikt*; Chapter 4: Results of the Comparison between German, English and Turkish Debt Recovery Law, 'Creditors control over the enforcement procedure', *supra*. In Germany, in popular language as well as in socio-legal terminology, the term 'Khadijustice' (Kadijustiz) refers to 'irrational', arbitrary decision making based on subjective discretion of the judge rather than application of formal rules and procedures which provides legal certainty for individuals. The spread of the term in legal language is probably due to Weber's writings. See Max Weber, *Wirtschaft und Gesellschaft – Grundriss der verstehenden Soziologie*, 5th ed. (Tübingen: Mohr, 1976), pp. 477, 810, 816–7, 826. 'Kadi' means judge in Ottoman Turkish. Possibly because of this 'etymological prejudice', a colleague of the author stated, 'although empirical evidence may be lacking', according to 'their image concerning Turkey', the justice system in Turkey must be suffering from corruption. However, existing empirical studies and observations made by legal-sociologist do not confirm that Turkish courts are corrupt. June Starr and Jonathan Pool studied the Turkish court practice as they ask the question 'whom do the courts serve?'. That is, whether the courts were used by the government 'to keep down' the citizens; whether the courts were used by the rich to keep down the poor, or whether the courts were used by men to keep down women. They came to the conclusion that the Turkish courts were not used 'to keep down' the citizens, the poor or the women. See June Starr and Jonathan Pool, 'The Impact of a Legal Revolution in Rural Turkey', *Law and Society Review* 8, no.3 (1974), pp. 533–60, at pp. 548–53. Ernst E. Hirsch, who taught in Turkish Universities and 'observed the legal practice' in Turkey for more than twenty years, did not men-

Factors Impeding Access to Justice in Cross-Border Debt Collection 163

The replies supplied by European law firms to a questionnaire on the 'Costs of Judicial Barriers for Consumers in the Single Market' again showed that no such discrimination against foreigners can be found throughout the courts in Europe.[16] Similarly, none of the 50 small law firms which were recently interviewed in Germany had ever been discriminated by foreign authorities or courts where they had to pursue their client's claims.[17]

B. PRACTICAL AND LEGAL-BUREAUCRATIC DIFFICULTIES

The more important reasons for the limited access by foreigners to the judicial methods of debt collection are more practical and may be termed 'legal-bureaucratic' difficulties. Such difficulties have to be overcome by the creditor who seeks cross-border enforcement of a judgment or who brings an action abroad and include the following:

1. Tracing the Debtor

In order to decide whether to bring an action or not, the creditor must have knowledge of the solvency of the debtor, that is, if the judgment obtained against the said debtor will be successfully enforced abroad where the said debtor has assets. Such information may be very difficult or too expensive to obtain abroad, especially where no or no satisfactory registration system exists in the relevant foreign country, as is the case in England [18] and Turkey.[19] German Law Firm 1 complained about shipping companies registered in so-called 'flag countries' such as Malta which could not be found at their official address.

---

tion that Turkish courts were corrupt. See Ernst E. Hirsch, *Rezeption als sozialer Prozeß – Erläutert am Beispiel der Türkei* (Berlin: Duncker & Humblot, 1981).
16 See von Freyhold and Vial, 'Report on the Cost of Judicial Proceedings in the European Union', pp. 15–127.
17 Schnorr, 'Einzelanwälte und kleine Anwaltsfirmen im internationalen Rechtsverkehr', p. 103.
18 Cf. *supra* Chapter 3: Debt Recovery in England, 'Preliminary remedies for protection of the creditor'.
19 See *supra* Chapter 5: The Role of Lawyers in Cross-Border Debt Collection, 'Turkish Law Firm 1'.

164 Making Foreign People Pay

The whereabouts of the debtor and his assets may be ascertained by hiring private detectives or commercial debt collectors.[20] For a creditor in the EU, if the debtor is resident in another EU member state, costs of tracing the debtor's address are between ECU 5 and ECU 100, and searching the debtor's assets costs between ECU 30 and ECU 400.[21] Costs of tracing the debtor and his assets are not strictly a part of court costs and therefore they are not directly recoverable from the losing party at the end of the proceedings.

2. Duplication of Lawyer's Fees

As discussed above,[22] the plaintiff who brings an action or who seeks to enforce a domestic judgment abroad must invariably hire more than one lawyer, *i.e.* a lawyer in the country of domicile and a 'correspondent' lawyer abroad where the action is going to be brought or, as the case may be, where the domestic judgment is going to be enforced. This causes a substantial increase in costs, if not a duplication.

3. Service of Documents

Notwithstanding the widespread application of relevant bilateral[23] and multilateral conventions,[24] service of documents abroad cost substantially more time and money as compared to the case in domestic proceedings.

It was reported that cross-border service of process between EU member states costs approximately ECU 50 and up to ECU 250 in the United Kingdom.[25]

---

20   See *infra* Chapter 11: Debt Collection Business in England, 'English Debt Collector 13'.
21   von Freyhold and Vial, 'Report on the Cost of Judicial Proceedings in the European Union', p. 111.
22   See *supra* Chapter 5: The Role of Lawyers in Cross-Border Debt Collection.
23   *E.g.* see Turkish – German agreement dated 28. 5. 1929, *Resmi Gazete*, 4.6.1930, No. 1511 or *RGBl* 1930 II 6, see for Germany also Jayme and Hausmann, *Internationales Privat- und Verfahrensrecht*, pp. 505–17.
24   *E.g.* Hague Convention on Civil Procedure 1954, Hague Service Convention 1965.
25   von Freyhold and Vial, 'Report on the Cost of Judicial Proceedings in the European Union', pp. 120–2.

An international lawyer in London states that normally one should expect a four month delay in the service of foreign process within the EU. Exceptional is Spain where the authorities are less co-operative. In a recent case, the above lawyer used The Hague Service Convention and has been waiting for thirteen months to hear from the Spanish authorities.[26] A Turkish lawyer reported that, in a case brought before the Istanbul Commercial Court by a Turkish plaintiff against a Saudi Arabian defendant in 1988, service of the statement of claims was effected in 1993.[27]

A clerk in the international legal assistance department of the Hamburg *Landgericht* stated that whereas a complete failure is an exception, considerable delays occur in cross-border service of documents: in Austria, Switzerland and the Netherlands, documents are normally served in three months. In Denmark, France, Britain, Portugal, Sweden, Norway, Poland and Hungary, a period between three to six months must be expected. In Brazil, Argentina, India, Libya and Spain, one can wait for more than six months.[28] Service in Turkey is also slow but reliable.[29]

In Turkey, each year around 11,000 documents are served using the Hague Service Convention.[30] The form used by the Ministry of Justice for the service under the Hague Convention [31] is translated into Turkish and printed in such a poor quality that applicants and addressees dealing with it can experience considerable difficulty. Since the service of documents through the diplomatic channels or the Hague Convention takes too long, the service of foreign documents in England is always [32] made in the form of 'personal service'.[33] Personal service is effected by leaving the document in the possession of the person to be served [34] with the server often

---

26 Interview with English Law Firm 2.
27 See Nerad, 'International Litigation and Arbitration in Turkey'.
28 Spain is a special case where 'the central authority for service of foreign documents is particularly slow and co-operates only with the assistance of the local attorneys who seem to use everything from personal relations to bribes in order to accelerate service'.
29 Gessner, 'International Cases in German First Instance Courts', p. 173.
30 Turkish Ministry of Justice Officer 3.
31 The form numbered 184, printed in Ankara: Adalet Bakanligi Isletmeler ve Isyurtlari Kurumu.
32 English Law Firm 1.
33 RSC Ord 65, r.2; CCR Ord 7, r.2.
34 Although it is sufficient to leave the documents in the presence of the person served, some old customs still find application in England such as 'pressing the documents into the recipient's ribs or tapping him twice on the shoulder with it' which are

166   Making Foreign People Pay

being an agent employed by a solicitor in the relevant district [35] which entails additional legal costs for the serving party. Service of documents outside England may also be made as personal service as long as such method of service is permitted in the relevant foreign country.[36] However, since in most civil law countries personal service by the plaintiff's solicitor is not permitted, local methods must be used [37] and complications experienced in diplomatic channels or Hague Convention system may take several hours for the lawyer, which in turn adds hundreds of pounds to the costs of the client.[38]

Service of documents is an area where the most strict rules of procedure apply. Thus, the service of process which is made in full compliance with the local rules of procedure abroad may not be 'good enough' for the purposes of the national court where the proceedings have been initiated.[39]

Moreover, the lack of full compliance with the service rules cannot be remedied by the addressee later becoming aware of the information contained in the documents to be served and being reluctant to take further steps to protect his rights. The judgment of the European Court of Justice in *Minalmet GmbH v Brandies Ltd.* [40] exemplifies the latter.

> In the Minalmet v Brandies case an English (proceeding) was sent under Article 5(a) of the Hague Service Convention to the German *Amtsgericht*, which certified that service had been duly effected. Accordingly, a default judgment was entered in the High Court and it was declared enforceable by the *Landgericht*. The defendant appealed first to the *Oberlandesgericht* and, following dismissal of the appeal next appealed to the *Bundesgerichthof*, which decided that service did not accord with the provisions of German law [41] but that the defendant had subsequently become aware of the judgment and had taken no steps to set it

---

    merely 'colourful variants' of the personal service method (O'Hare and Hill, *Civil Litigation*, p.125).

35   *Ibid.*
36   RSC Ord. 11, r. 5(2), r. (3)(a).
37   English Law Firm 8, and High Court Officer 1.
38   The same interviewee speaks of 5 – 6 hours of extra work costing £2,000.
39   See *supra* Chapter 5: Role of Lawyers in Cross-Border Debt Collection, 'English Law Firm 3' on service of an English writ in Germany.
40   [1992] ECR I 5661; to the same effect German Federal Court, Decision of 2.12.1992, *Entscheidungen des Bundesgerichtshofs in Zivilsachen* 120 (1993), p. 305.
41   The documents were sent by mail. The defendant was not found at the address and a notice was left in the defendant's place of business to the effect that he could collect the documents from the post office. This was however not sufficient under German rules of procedure; such a substituted service is only valid if the notice is left at the defendant's private address.

aside in England. The *Bundesgerichthof* referred the question to the European Court of Justice whether, under these circumstances, the default judgment should be recognised. The Court of Justice decided the default judgment must be refused enforcement under Article 27(2) of the Brussels Convention.[42] Lack of due service precluded the enforcement of a default judgment even if the defendant had become aware of it and had had the opportunity to set aside the default judgment.[43]

4. Translation of Documents

The costs involved in the translation of documents may be substantial. The above mentioned survey shows that, the costs of translating a single page into the court language ranges between ECU 50 (Luxembourg) and ECU 22 (Italy and Belgium) in EU member states.[44]

In cross-border commercial litigation involving international lawyers, the translation of documents is sometimes only a red tape formality. One interviewee from English Law Firm 1 complained that they have recently paid £400 for the translation of a document which will be sent to solicitors in the Netherlands 'who speak English better than [them]selves'.[45]

---

42 According to Art. 27(2), where the defendant 'was not duly served with the documents which instituted the proceedings ... in sufficient time for him to arrange his defence' a default judgment cannot be enforced under the Brussels Convention.

43 See *ibid.*, paragraphs 5, 8, 18 and 19.

44 von Freyhold and Vial, 'Report on the Cost of Judicial Proceedings in the European Union', pp. 120–3.

45 It has been stated that the 'court divisions and chambers which frequently deal with international cases' must be able and be permitted to accept documents and even hear the parties in 'several' foreign languages; Nagel, *Internationales Zivilprozeßrecht*, paragraph no. 313. The special chamber for international cases at the *Landgericht* in Hamburg and the Commercial Court Division of the High Court in England are examples of such court divisions dealing with international cases. See Kurt Siehr, 'Special courts for conflicts cases: A German experiment', *American Journal of Comparative Law* 25 (1977), pp. 663–80; Gerhard Luther, 'Kollusions- und Fremdrechtsanwendung in der Gerichtspraxis', *Rabels Zeitschrift für ausländisches und internationales Privatrecht* 37 (1973), pp. 660–81 (with a summary in English), pp. 669–76. In Germany, filing documents (only in *Landgerichte*) and court hearings in a foreign language is already admissible, subject to the court's discretion (German CCP § 142 III; *Gerichtsverfassungsgesetz* § 187 II; Rosenberg, Schwab and Gottwald, *Zivilprozeßrecht*, pp. 118–9). See also Brussels Convention Art. 48(2) according to which documents in a foreign language are admissible but the parties may be required by the court to provide the translation. It is rarely possible however to have judges speaking several foreign languages good enough to conduct cases regularly in those languages. It may be realistic to expect only to find a sufficient number of judges with fluent English for a few special courts to be established in Germany which could deal

In addition, regardless of cost, it may in practice be very difficult to obtain a reliable translation, especially of a document written in complicated legal language. Considering the grammatical structure of Turkish a literal translation from English is very difficult. Therefore a loan agreement, intricate in content, for example, prepared by an American bank can only be rendered into good Turkish by an 'amateur' translator who is a lawyer.[46]

5. Taking Evidence Abroad

Similarly, the existence of international agreements [47] concerning taking evidence abroad is not in itself sufficient as such to overcome legal cultural difficulties. Different rules of procedure applicable to taking evidence in various countries may be inconvenient for the foreign parties who are not familiar with the procedure of the forum. For example, in a case before a United States court where a request to obtain evidence was made to a District Court in Istanbul in 1993, counsel for one of the parties was not satisfied with the assistance provided by the Turkish court in taking evidence, as they were not permitted to 'cross-examine' the expert witnesses. A correspondent Turkish lawyer who requested the author's legal advice reported that her US colleagues also wanted to bring in their own secretaries / stenographers to the court room in Istanbul in order to tape-record or in the event that this would not be possible to transcribe the witness testimonies in full.

A senior judge who was interviewed in Istanbul [48] stated that, in commercial matters, one of the most important difficulties for the foreign parties is the fact that they are not able to prove their claims with their own books of accounts, which is permitted in Turkey in controversies arising from commercial transactions between businesses. According to the Turkish law, only the books of accounts which are kept in accordance with the Turkish Commercial Court are admissible as evidence.[49]

---

with international commercial cases. Bilingual lawyers with Turkish or Polish origin could also be appointed as judges in a few German courts which could be established to deal with cross-border family law matters.

46   See Nerad, 'International Litigation and Arbitration in Turkey'.
47   *E.g.* Hague Evidence Convention 1970; Turkish - German agreement dated 28.5.1929.
48   Interview at the Turkish Commercial Court of First Instance.
49   Arts 66 – 86.

Similarly, the common law process of discovery, whereby the parties to an action disclose to each other all dispute related documents in their disposal, causes difficulties for solicitors representing clients from Continental Europe before the English courts.[50] It has been reported from interviews held with British solicitors that 'discovery may cause major difficulties in understanding by the foreign client. Many Continental clients find the disclosure of documents, whether or not in favour of the client concerned, as *Ausforschungsbeweis* (inadmissible inquiry). It may therefore be that clients do not follow solicitors' instructions to collect certain information and send it to the London forum. ... For this reason, many law firms have brochures for their commercial clients to explain the discovery process in detail in their mother tongue'.[51]

6. Security for Costs

In most legal systems,[52] a foreign plaintiff or, as is the case in England,[53] a plaintiff who is resident abroad is required to give a 'security for costs' which will be used to cover the costs of the defendant should the plaintiff lose the case (*cautio judicatum solvi*).[54] Such security for costs is not required where there is a reciprocal agreement between the plaintiff's country and the country where the action is to be brought [55] and, according to the Court of Appeal in England,[56] between the EU member states. Never-

---

50   See Zoe Picton Howell, 'Prozessieren in England and Wales: "Discovery"', *Recht der Internationalen Wirtschaft*, 42. Jahrgang, no.12 (1996), pp. 1011–3.
51   Stammel, 'Back to the Courtroom?'.
52   For exceptions see Nomer, *Devletler Hususi Hukuku*, p. 380, note 193.
53   RSC Ord. 23, r. 1(1)(a).
54   Turkish IPPL Art. 32; German CCP, §§ 110–113.
55   This is the case *inter alia* for the contracting states of the Hague Civil Procedure Convention 1954, between Turkey and Germany (Agreement of 28.5.1929, Art. 2: *Resmi Gazete* 4.6.1930, no. 1511; *RGBl* 1930 II 6), between Turkey and the United Kingdom (Agreement of 28.11.1931, Art. 12, *Resmi Gazete* 5.7.1932, no. 2142), and between Germany and the United Kingdom (Agreement of 20.3.1928, *RGBL* 1928 II, 623, *BGBl* 1953 II 116).
56   *Fitzgerald and Others v Williams and Others*, The Times (C.A.), 3 January 1996. In this case, the Court of Appeal held that 'the English court should not, in the exercise of its discretion, order security for costs ... to be given by an individual plaintiff who was a national of and resident in another member state party to the Brussels Convention ...'. In its decision, the Court of Appeal made reference to the *Mund and Fenster v Hartlex International Transport* judgment of the European Court of Justice ([1994] ECR I 467). In this latter case, the Court held that the application of the German CCP § 917(2) according to which, should a judgment be enforced abroad, the debtor's assets

theless, many cross-border cases still fall in the field of application of *cautio judicatum solvi*.

An American national who commences an action in Turkey, for example, must deposit the security for costs in the court.[57] According to the Turkish CCP, the court decides if the type and form of the security given by the plaintiff is admissible.[58] The Turkish Court of Cassation requires that the security must be given in a foreign currency.[59] In one case, English Law Firm 9 was required to deposit the security in Turkish Liras, as a result of which, until the judgment was obtained, the monies lost their value to a considerable extent due to the devaluation of the Lira against hard currencies.

7. International Legal Aid and the Lack of Consumer Advice

Concerning small claims, national institutions supporting private individuals at the domestic level, that is, *consumer advice* and *legal aid schemes*, cannot provide the same services efficiently for cross-border claims. The reason for the former is lack of sufficient information regarding foreign judicial systems, and for the latter, *inter alia*, the fact that the individuals who cannot benefit from the legal aid, according to the level of their incomes, may indeed require such support where a cross-border claim is concerned where more expenses are involved.[60]

The consumer associations from all EU member states which were interviewed recently unanimously stated that they would not be able to advise or otherwise assist a consumer in a cross-border consumer dispute.[61]

---

may be seized for protection of the creditor, was contrary to the prohibition of discrimination article 6 of the EC Treaty, if the judgment will be enforced in another EU member state which is a party to the Brussels Convention. According to the Court of Appeal, the application of *cautio judicatum solvi* for an EU resident foreign plaintiff would also be contrary to the EC Treaty.

57 Cf. Kuru, *Hukuk Muhakemeleri Usulü El Kitabi*, p. 689.
58 Turkish CCP Art. 96.
59 *E.g.* 12th Civil Chamber, 7. 12. 1983, No.10341/9973, *Yasa Hukuk ve Ictihat Dergisi* (1984), pp.279–80. Cf. Nomer, *Devletler Hususi Hukuku*, p. 379, note 191a.
60 See EU Commission's Greenbook on Consumer Access to Justice of 16 November 1993, *COM(93) 576 final*, pp. 77–8. Cf. *European Consumer Guide to the Single Market* (Luxembourg: Office for Official Publications of the European Communities, 1995), pp. 31–45, 199–208.
61 von Freyhold and Vial, 'Report on the Cost of Judicial Proceedings in the European Union', pp. 115–6.

It is rare for national legal aid provisions in one country to provide funding for suits in a foreign jurisdiction. However, most of the advanced legal aid schemes permit non-resident foreign nationals to benefit from legal aid.[62] Thus, legal aid schemes in Germany, England and Turkey are available to foreign individuals as well as nationals. In Germany and in England, legislation for legal aid does not distinguish between foreign individuals and nationals.[63] In Turkey, legal aid is available to a person from a foreign country only if a Turkish national in a similar position would be granted legal aid in the country where this person comes from.[64] Nonetheless, this requirement of reciprocal application of legal aid to foreign nationals is of marginal importance. This is because various bilateral and multilateral agreements of legal assistance contain provisions for legal aid, which satisfies the requirement of reciprocal application for a large number of foreign countries.[65]

On the other hand, the mere existence of the possibility to make use of the legal aid system in a foreign country is of little practical value for the private individual. A person who wishes to make use of legal aid benefits in a foreign country must firstly be informed about the relevant procedure in that country. He must then make a written application in a foreign language, and attach the necessary documents (*i.e.* documents providing proof of his financial position, family status *etc.*) which must be translated and legalised by the relevant authorities. Lastly, he may be required to attend a hearing where the eligibility of his application will be determined considering his financial position and the reasonableness of the merits of his

---

[62] Alan Peterson, 'Financial Legal Services: A Comparative Perspective', in D. L. Carey Miller and Paul R. Beaumont (eds), *The Option of Litigating in Europe* (London, United Kingdom National Committee of Comparative Law, 1993), pp. 149–73, at p. 159.

[63] See German CCP § 114 and Schack, *Internationales Zivilverfahrensrecht*, Rn. 568–571; Legal Aid Act 1988, sec. 14 and O'Hare and Hill, *Civil Litigation*, p. 41.

[64] Turkish CCP, Art. 465 II.

[65] See German-Turkish Convention on Legal Assistance in Civil and Commercial Matters (*RGBl* 1930 II 6, *Resmi Gazete* no.1511, 4.6.1930), Art. 5; Hague Legal Assistance Convention 1954 (Arts 20 – 24) where Turkey (*Resmi Gazete* no. 14194, 23.5.1972) and Germany (*BGBl* 1958 II 557), and the European Agreement on Transmission of Applications for Legal Aid where Turkey (*Resmi Gazete* no. 17918, 4.1.1983) and the United Kingdom (Treaty Series No. 39 (1978), Cmnd.7179) are among the contracting parties. Cf. Brussels Convention on Jurisdiction and the Enforcement of Judgments on Civil and Commercial Matters 1968, Art. 44.

case.[66] These are important limiting factors for people with little financial means. In addition, in Germany and in England, any person who wishes to benefit from legal aid chooses his own lawyer,[67] which in turn results in foreigners having to find a lawyer in those countries. Again, this is another important practical difficulty for those pursuing small claims.

In this context, the European Agreement on Transmission of Applications for Legal Aid of 27 January 1977 prepared by the Council of Europe ('European Agreement on Legal Aid') deserves closer attention.[68] According to the European Agreement on Legal Aid, each Contracting State designates a 'transmitting authority' and a 'central receiving authority'[69] for applications for legal aid to be transmitted to or received from other Contracting States. Although the decision on granting or refusing the application is made by the 'competent authority' of the Receiving State,[70] transmitting authorities and receiving authorities assist the applicant in making the application in compliance with the legislation of the Receiving State, including the necessary translation of the documents, and they transmit the application to the receiving authority in the Receiving State. The documents forwarded in accordance with the European Agreement on Legal Aid are exempt from legalisation or any equivalent formality, and no charges will be made by the Contracting States in respect of services made under the Agreement.[71]

Thus, the European Agreement on Legal Aid offers a system which could be beneficial in improving the quality of legal aid services in cross-border litigation. The question remains how often and how efficiently this

---

66 For England see Legal Aid (General) Regulations 1989, Part II. In Germany and in Turkey, this procedure may include a preliminary hearing German CCP § 118, Turkish CCP, Art. 469.

67 German CCP § 121 II; Legal Aid Act, s. 32(1). In Turkey, the lawyer is appointed by the Legal Aid Bureau of the local Bar Association where the action will be brought, Lawyers Act 1969, Arts 176–179.

68 Parties to the Agreement are Greece, Luxembourg, Sweden, Norway, the United Kingdom, Belgium, Denmark, France, Finland, Austria, Turkey, Italy, Portugal, Ireland and the Netherlands. Jayme and Hausmann, *Internationales Privat- und Verfahrensrecht*, Text 106, footnote 2.

69 Federal States are free to designate more than one transmitting / receiving authority.

70 Cf. Brussels Convention on Jurisdiction and the Enforcement of Judgments on Civil and Commercial Matters 1968, Art. 44 where an application for legal aid which has been granted for a proceeding by the national authorities of one Contracting State is recognised by other Contracting States for the purposes of enforcement of the judgment which has been given in the same proceeding. See Kropholler, *Europäisches Zivilprozeßrecht*, pp. 405–6.

71 See Arts 1–7.

system is indeed applied. In this regard, interviews held in Turkey and in England [72] proved to be of interest. In Turkey, the Ministry of Justice is both the receiving and transmitting authority under the Agreement.[73] Officer 2 in the International Law (legal assistance) Department of the Turkish Ministry of Justice as well as three other judges [74] in attendance at an interview with the author were not aware of the existence of the European Agreement on Legal Aid. Officer 1, who was a senior Officer of the Ministry could recall only one case he had had in the early 1980s.[75]

In England, the receiving authority is the London Office of the Legal Aid Board and the transmitting authority is the Head Office of the Legal Aid Board also in London.[76] The Officer of the Receiving Authority was aware of the existence of the European Agreement on Legal Aid. Nonetheless, the Agreement was of no practical importance for the work of her office. As was confirmed by the interviewee, there is no statistical data available on the applications for legal aid by foreign individuals in England. She stated however that the Office does receive around 10 applications from abroad each week. Most frequent are the cases concerning traffic accidents and matrimonial matters. A large share of these applications are from the United States, followed by Germany and other European countries. Applications from Turkey are very rare. The Legal Aid Board decides the applications of foreign individuals according to the same criteria which applies in domestic applications. That is to say, provided that the

---

[72] Germany is not a party to the Agreement.
[73] At the address 'Adalet Bakanligi, Uluslararasi Hukuk Genel Müdürlügü, Kizilay, Ankara'.
[74] These three Officers had the title of a judge, but they were dealing with administration of international legal assistance matters in the Ministry of Justice.
[75] He actually mentioned the year as being 1978, which cannot be correct. Turkey ratified the European Agreement on Legal Aid in 1983. The case concerned a traffic accident where a British citizen who spent her holiday in Izmir claimed restitution of damages against a Turkish lorry driver. The Ministry of Justice, acting as the 'receiving authority', forwarded the case to the Advocate General in Izmir ('the competent authority') who in turn arranged a lawyer appointed by the local Bar Association. Acting as counsel for the British woman the lawyer sued the lorry driver and won the case. However, the enforcement of judgment was not successful, because of the fact that the defendant was at the time insolvent. The 'insolvency certificate' was sent to the transmitting authority in England.
[76] The transmitting and receiving authority for England which was designated during the ratification of the European Agreement on Legal Aid ('The Secretary of the Law Society') was changed. The London Office of the Legal Aid Board (Receiving Authority) is at the address '29 – 37 Red Lion Street, London WC1'. The Head Office of the Legal Aid Board (Transmitting Authority) is at the address '85 Gray's Inn Road, London WC1'.

proceedings will be (or have been) initiated in England or Wales, it is not important if the applicant is a British citizen or not. Also of irrelevance is if the applicant is a national of a country which is a party to the European Agreement on Legal Aid, if he is from a EU member state or from another country.

Another Officer who interviewed at the transmitting authority informed the author that there are currently some 200 applications being processed in the Office. The countries which most frequently appear in applications for legal aid were Spain and France, followed by Portugal, Greece and Belgium. As to the subject matter, ranking first again were the personal injury cases as a result of traffic accidents. Matrimonial cases concerning the maintenance and custody of children were also frequent. An application for legal aid in a foreign jurisdiction was concluded in at least three months, although it normally took six months and even two years in some cases. As a result, the European Agreement on Legal Aid is used in England by a limited number of people, mostly for a limited number of typical cases. The potential benefits of the Agreement are not used by the general public.[77]

---

[77] It is interesting that corresponding English literature pays little attention to the European Agreement on Legal Aid. A multi-volume treatise which is held as the Bible of English private international law states that after 15 years since coming into force the Agreement has not been ratified by the United Kingdom, see *Dicey and Morris on Conflict of Laws*, Vol.1, p. 218, footnote 17. A guide for practitioners which was prepared by the Legal Aid Board itself suffices with reminding the practitioners of the existence of the Agreement, see Legal Aid Board (ed.), *Legal Aid – 1994 Handbook* (London: Sweet & Maxwell, 1994), p. 165.

8 Conclusions for Part I[1]

The results of the comparisons made between German, English and Turkish debt recovery law show that differences between the three legal systems as well as between common law and civil law are not so great as to prevent lawyers from each of these three countries from understanding the legal systems of the others. During the last fifty years of the globalisation of law, the developments in private international laws have improved the legal position of foreign litigants in all three countries, as is the case elsewhere in Europe. As far as the substantive law and procedural rules are concerned, in none of the three national systems are foreign creditors disadvantaged *vis-à-vis* the domestic creditors seeking debt recovery. However, in all three countries, the share of international debt recovery cases in the workload of national courts and civil execution officers is marginal. This is also the case for the role of lawyers in cross-border debt recovery, including international law firms.

This picture is explained partly by the international collection and credit management methods which are effectively used by the business community, and partly by practical and legal-bureaucratic difficulties experienced in cross-border litigation which hinder access to justice. The author did not aim to give an exhaustive list of legal and procedural difficulties experienced in international litigation. However, in light of the above discussion, it would be fair to argue that, the efforts made by the nation states to improve the capacity of the national courts to solve international disputes at national level by means of private international law and at the international level by means of international conventions was not successful,[2] at least

---

1   See also Chapter 4: Results of the Comparison between German, English and Turkish Debt Recovery Law, and 'Conclusions for Chapter 5', *supra*.
2   See Volkmar Gessner and Angelika Schade, 'Conflicts of Culture in Cross-Border Legal Relations: The Conception of a Research Topic in Sociology of Law', *Theory, Culture and Society* 7 (1990), pp. 253–77, pp. 261–3.

where cross-border debt collection is concerned, due largely to these practical and legal-bureaucratic difficulties.

Thus, the following must be asked: does the limited use of nation state produced enforcement systems amount to an anomie in the field of international debt collection, which could have resulted in avoidance of cross-border interactions [3] or, are there some other, autonomously created (non-state produced) enforcement systems which govern this area successfully and, if so, which do not require the intervention of the nation state in its role of law-maker and/or law-enforcer? [4] This will be discussed in the following chapters of this book.

As an introduction to this discussion, some aspects of modern developments in enforcement of law in general, and debt collection in particular, must also be considered. For such developments, which may be termed the 'routinisation' and 'privatisation of debt collection', have an influence on the cross-border legal relations as well as domestic legal relations.

---

[3] Generally, for the 'paralysing' effect of 'norm-conflicts' which deprives individuals from actively participating in the social life see Hans Peter Dreitzel, *Die gesellschaftlichen Leiden und das Leiden an der Gesellschaft*, 3rd ed. (Stuttgart: Enke, 1980), pp. 25–6. For an example of such a paralysing effect in the field of cross-border consumer behaviour see the empirical data collected by the EU Commission in the Eurobarometer survey (EUROBAROMETER 43,0 of 17 May 1995) summarised in Volkmar Gessner, 'Consumers in the Single Market – A Legal Sociological Approach', in von Freyhold et al., *Report on the Cost of Judicial Barriers for Consumers*, pp. 5–14, at pp. 10–4. EUROBAROMETER indicates that the consumers in the EU refrain from buying durable goods in member states other than in their country of residence. That is, the share of Single Market purchases of durable consumer goods in the EU is only 3.2%. Similarly, many individual lawyers and small law firms who were recently interviewed in Germany about their experience in international cases stated that they advised their clients to settle out of court or to give up proceeding with the case where the debtor was abroad, one of which even stated that 'it is better to avoid doing business with foreign citizens, firms and organisations': Schnorr, 'Einzelanwälte und kleine Anwaltsfirmen im internationalen Rechtsverkehr', p. 102.

[4] Cf. Volkmar Gessner and Angelika Schade, 'Conflicts of Culture in Cross-Border Legal Relations', p. 254. Gessner suggests that, 'if on the national level state produced norms (law) are dominant and autonomously created norms are complementary ... the reverse relationship [is true for] the international arena', see 'Introduction', in Gessner, *Foreign Courts*, p. 9.

PART II

PRIVATE ENFORCEMENT: EXTRA-JUDICIAL METHODS OF DEBT COLLECTION

9 Routinisation and Privatisation of Debt Collection

A. 'THE ROUTINISATION OF DEBT COLLECTION' [1]

In the strict sense of the term 'enforcement' or 'execution' is complementary to the court proceedings on the merits of the dispute between the parties. That is, the parties to a civil or commercial law dispute first 'go to court' to resolve the dispute and then, should the unsuccessful party refrain from obeying the judgment of the court, enforcement of the judgment becomes necessary.[2] This picture of enforcement does not correspond with reality today, at least where enforcement of monetary obligations is concerned.

In practice, most of the court proceedings and enforcement procedures involving money claims in the industrialised countries appear to be routinised bureaucratic processes in which the debtor does not actively participate.[3] It was reported that at the High Court and county courts in England and Wales the overwhelming majority of judgments are either default judgments or judgments on consent or admission of the defendant: for the years 1956 – 1967 such judgments represented between 62 – 72% and approximately 90% of county court and High Court judgments respectively.[4] There is evidence that the number and rate of contested trial court debt cases in the United States dramatically declined in the post Second World

---

1 The term is borrowed from Robert A. Kagan, 'The routinization of debt collection: An essay on social change and conflicts in the courts', *Law and Society Review* 18 (1984), pp. 323–71.
2 Many standard textbooks explain the function of the law of enforcement in this pattern, *e.g.* see Üstündag, *Icra Hukukunun Esaslari*, p. 2; Jauernig, *Zwangsvollstreckungs- und Insolvenzrecht*, p. 1.
3 See Michael Adler, 'Alternativen zur Zwangsbeitreibung von Schulden', *Zeitschrift für Rechtssoziologie* 5 (1983), pp. 41–9, at p.45.
4 See *Report of the Committee on the Enforcement of Judgment Debts*, §§ 61 – 64 and Appendix 7, Tables 4 and 5.

180 Making Foreign People Pay

War period. The percentage of contested contract cases in two US trial courts (for which published data exist) decreased from 20 – 25% at the turn of the century to approximately 10% in the post war period.[5]

Similarly, the number of summary debt collection procedures in Germany which are mainly designed for the collection of undisputed money-debts [6] is much greater than the number of ordinary court proceedings at the civil and commercial courts of first instance.[7] For the ten year period 1982 – 1991 the ratio of the number of summary debt collection procedures to the number of ordinary court proceedings of civil and commercial law in Germany was approximately 3.6:1. (Table 9.1.) In addition, one third of the Amtsgericht proceedings other than summary debt collection proceedings lead to a default judgment (25%), a judgment on consent (5%) or payment into court (3%).[8] Thus, it has been fairly estimated that each nine out of ten cases before civil and commercial courts of first instance in Germany are non-contested debt collection cases.[9]

---

5 See the table in Kagan, 'The routinization of debt collection', p. 334.
6 'The summary debt collection procedure in Germany (*Mahnverfahren*) is a court procedure only by the letter of law. In practice it appears to be a silent, mechanised, routine, administrative process', Günter Hörmann and Knut Holzscheck, 'Schuldbeitreibung im Konsumentenkredit – Ergebnisse einer empirischen Studie', *Zeitschrift für Rechtssoziologie* 5 (1983), pp. 26–40, at p. 39. See also e.g. Schmid Jürgen, *Elektronische Datenverarbeitung im Mahnverfahren* (Munich: V.Florentz, 1991), 29; Heinz Menne, *Das Mahnverfahren* (Neuwied: Luchterhand, 1979), pp. 8–11.
7 In a considerable number of such summary procedures creditors are not represented by a lawyer. For, if disputes arising from labour law and divorce cases are not included, only 14% of the cases concluded by practising lawyers in 1985 involved summary procedures for debt collection. Rainer Wasilewski, *Streitverhütung durch Rechtsanwälte – Empirische Untersuchung von Umfang, Struktur und Bedingungen außergerichtlicher Beilegung zivilrechtlicher Streitigkeiten durch Rechtsanwälte* (Cologne: Bundesanzeiger / Deutscher Anwaltsverlag, 1990), p. 34.
8 Elmar Steinbach and Rolf Koniffka (eds), Strukturen des amtsgerichtlichen Zivilprozesses, München 1982, p. 88.
9 Günter Hörmann, 'Gerichtliche Schuldbeitreibung und ihre Umwelt – Zur Entwicklung der gerichtlichen und außergerichtlichen Durchsetzung von Geldforderungen in der Bundesrepublik Deutschland', in Erhard Blankenburg and Rüdiger Voigt (eds), *Implementation von Gerichtsentscheidungen – Jahrbuch für Rechtssoziologie und Rechtstheorie* 11 (Opladen: Westdeutscher Verlag, 1987), pp. 72–94, p. 73.

Table 9.1 Summary debt collection and ordinary court proceedings of civil and commercial law in Germany (1982 – 1991)

	Cases brought under the summary debt collection procedure (*Mahnverfahren*)	Cases brought under the ordinary rules of procedure at the *Amtsgericht*	Cases brought under the ordinary rules of procedure at the *Landgericht* (as the court of first instance)	Ratio of columns 2 + 3 (cases brought under the ordinary rules of procedure) to column 1 (summary procedure cases)
1982	5,699,485	1,064,296	400,487	3.9
1983	5,852,927	1,156,884	377,706	3.8
1984	5,898,632	1,209,422	333,196	3.8
1985	6,085,363	1,243,172	338,603	3.8
1986	6,100,865	1,306,628	353,292	3.7
1987	5,609,801	1,314,642	356,950	3.4
1988	5,492,183	1,298,065	359,492	3.3
1989	5,323,288	1,244,608	352,989	3.3
1990	5,145,256	1,202,782	351,083	3.3
1991	5,337,390	1,198,999	358,546	3.4
Total:	56,545,190	12,239,498	3,582,344	3.6

Source: Statistisches Bundesamt [10]

A comparative study made on judicial statistics in twelve European countries spanning 120 – 170 years of judicial history [11] shows that since the 1950s, summary procedures for debt recovery have been increasingly substituting ordinary court proceedings on the Continent.[12] Thus, Wollschläger writes

---

[10] Rechtspflege, Fachserie 10, Reihe 2: *Gerichte und Staatsanwaltschaften* 1991 (November 1994). The numbers in the first column represent the number of summary procedures which have been commenced annually, whereas the numbers in the second and third columns represent the number of completed proceedings. Nevertheless, since the duration of summary proceedings is relatively short, the data are still representative for the purpose of the above comparison. Cf. the table in Georg Holch, 'Mahnverfahren zwischen Schuldnerschutz und Entlastungsfunktion', *Zeitschrift für Rechtspolitik* 14, no.12 (1981), pp. 281–5, at p. 281.

[11] See Christian Wollschläger, 'Die Arbeit der europäischen Zivilgerichte im historischen und internationalen Vergleich', pp. 21–114.

[12] As a result of the variety of summary procedures and of classification criteria used by different national statistics in Europe, it was not possible to work out average figures valid for all twelve countries. Since the summary procedures for debt recovery may be transformed to ordinary court proceedings, it was also difficult to avoid misrepresentations arising from the overlapping figures under the respective categories of summary procedures and ordinary court proceedings, *ibid.*, 33–5. However, the fig-

'the times when the first instance courts were heavily dealing with collection of day-to-day debts belong to history'.[13]

These numbers demonstrate that 'the recovery of debts is largely an administrative process' and that the 'handling of undisputed claims' forms a large part of the everyday work of the courts.[14]

The reason for this phenomenon must be seen, *inter alia*, in the standardisation and simultaneous 'legal rationalisation' of credit transactions, including consumer-credit transactions, by business creditors (*e.g.* banks, finance companies, department stores, mail order companies *etc.*) with the involvement of legal specialists.[15] Thus standardised credit transactions cover virtually all contingencies in detail and leave little room for future dispute on the merits of the legal relationship between the contracting parties to be settled by means of court proceedings.

As a result of the expansion of the number and proportion of undisputed cases, the borderline between the two stages of judicial debt recovery process (litigation and enforcement) became indistinct for those (majority of) debt collection cases where no actual dispute exists on the merits.[16] Thus,

---

ures which were collected from national statistics are still clear enough to justify this statement. See *ibid.* pp. 56–7, 62, 63, 70, 72, 73 for Dutch, Belgian, German, Austrian, French, Swedish and Finnish statistics respectively, cf. *ibid.*, p. 71 for Italy.

13   *Ibid.*, p. 103.
14   *Report of the Committee on the Enforcement of Judgment Debts*, § 64.
15   See Kagan, 'The routinization of debt collection', pp. 341–2; Shapiro, 'The Globalization of Law', p. 62; Christoph Graf von Bernstorff, *Vertragsgestaltung im Auslandsgeschäft*, 2nd ed. (Frankfurt am Main: Firtz Knapp, 1991). For the legal rationalisation in the field of consumer transactions see Hörmann, 'Gerichtliche Schuldbeitreibung und ihre Umwelt', pp. 84–90.
16   In the minority of debt collection cases, where there *is* an actual dispute and litigation between the parties, the procedure for enforcement of judgment is either not at all commenced with or not completed to the stage where the debtor's assets are sold and the proceeds are distributed among the creditors. That is, the debtor voluntarily pays the judgment debt, either just after (notification of) judgment or before the enforcement procedure concluded with an execution sale. According to the results of an empirical research in Germany which were published in 1987, among 501 cases which were brought to a Court Executor, in 97 cases (19.4%) the debtor paid the debt voluntarily, in 59 cases (11.4%) the attachment was made, and only in 3 cases (0.6%) an execution sale happened. See Klein, 'Die Vollstreckung von Geldforderungen durch den Gerichtsvollzieher', p. 65. A more recent file analysis made on 276 cases provided by 23 bailiffs in Belgium showed that only 4% of judgment debts were satisfied out of the proceeds of an execution sale. See Francis Van Loon and Stephane Delrue, "L'huissier de justice et l'exécution des jugements par voie de contrainte", *Droit et Société*, 30/31 (1995), pp. 413–23.

many professional books bear titles such as 'Debt Recovery on ...' or 'Commercial Debt in ...' *etc.*, under which the enforcement and summary debt collection procedures are discussed within the same context.[17]

B. PRIVATISATION OF DEBT COLLECTION

The routinisation of the judicial debt collection procedures made them interchangeable with 'extra-judicial' or 'private' debt collection services provided by commercial organisations.

The oft repeated theory that 'execution' involves an exercise of sovereign powers against individuals, and therefore can be carried out exclusively by the national government through the competent execution officers [18] only holds true for judicial execution procedures.[19] In addition to judicial debt recovery procedures (*i.e.* litigation plus enforcement of the judgment), there is a range of 'privatised' debt collection services which

---

The authors constructed a 'pyramid of execution' (p. 417):

Figure 9.1   Pyramid of Execution

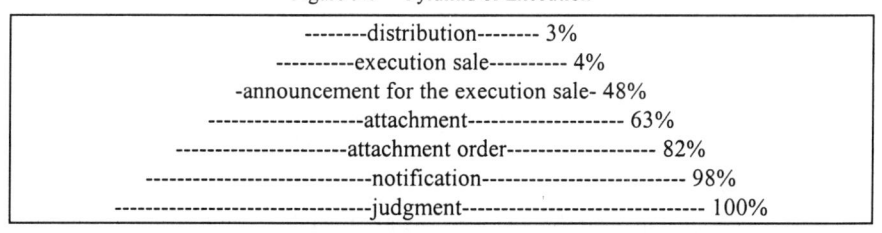

```
            --------distribution-------- 3%
          ----------execution sale---------- 4%
        -announcement for the execution sale- 48%
      --------------------attachment-------------------- 63%
    ----------------------attachment order------------------- 82%
  ------------------------------notification-------------------------- 98%
--------------------------------judgment----------------------------- 100%
```

---

17   See *e.g.* Richard Guy and Hugh Mercer, *Commercial Debt in Europe: Recovery and Remedies* (London: Longman, 1991); John K. Gatenby, *Gatenby's Recovery of Money*, 8th ed. (London: Longman, 1993); Jürgen Capell, *Erfolgreich Mahnen – Handbuch für die Mahn- und Inkassopraxis* (Bonn: Rentop, 1989).

18   See *e.g.* Schack, *Internationales Zivilverfahrensrecht*, Rn. 957; Gottwald, 'Die internationale Zwangsvollstreckung', p.285; Duncan and Millar, 'United Kingdom', p. 17.

19   For a general discussion on the question 'public versus private enforcement' see Posner, *Economic Analysis of Law*, §§ 22.1 and 22.2 (pp. 595–612), at pp. 595–602. See also Roger Cotterrell, *The Sociology of Law: An Introduction* (London: Butterworths, 1984), Chapter 8: The Enforcement and Invocation of Law (pp. 259–302), at pp. 263–4. Posner takes it for granted that the enforcement of law in the fields of torts, contracts and property is entrusted mainly to private persons and discusses the private enforcement with reference to prosecution of criminal offences. However, although violations of private law are not publicly prosecuted, enforcement of judicial decisions in the field of private law is effected mainly by the State (cf. 'Creditor's control over the enforcement procedure' and 'Efficiency of debt recovery procedures' in Chapter 4 *supra*).

184 Making Foreign People Pay

are used by business creditors. Accordingly, the creditor may, for example, sell his receivables to a credit institution which can either be globally for the whole amount of receivables from clients for a certain period of time (factoring) or individually, for a number of individual debts of mid- or long term maturity (forfaiting), or he may retain the title to the debt, but may commission a commercial debt collection agency to collect the debt on his behalf.[20,21]

The latter is of special interest due to the similarity of its function to judicial debt recovery. In Germany, debt collection through agencies goes back more than a hundred years [22] and is a serious competitor to judicial debt recovery.[23] Currently, the annual amount of debts collected by commercial

---

20 See Hoene, *Präventiver Kreditschutz und Zwangsvollstreckung durch Private.* These forms of the private enforcement are comparable but must be distinguished from informal alternatives to judicial conflict resolution (arbitration, mediation, consultation) and private law making (various disciplinary or regulatory procedures which operate in private companies, trade associations, co-operatives *etc.*). In contrast to informal alternatives to judicial conflict resolution, debt collection through commercial organisations does not involve a conflict resolution process. This form of debt collection is used mainly for collection of undisputed debts. In addition, unlike most of other 'alternatives to justice', debt collection through commercial organisations is not only 'extra-judicial' but also a 'commercial' activity. For informal alternatives to judicial conflict resolution see *e.g.* Josef Falke, *Gerichtliche und Außergerichtliche Austragung von Rechtsstreiten – Rechtssoziologische Untersuchungen* (Bremen: University of Bremen, 1984), – including a discourse of the relevant literature at pp. 1–34; Erhard Blankenburg, Walter Gottwald und Dieter Strempel (eds), *Alternativen in der Ziviljustiz – Berichte, Analysen, Perspektiven* (Cologne: Bundesanzeigere, 1982); Andreas Kotzorek, *Private Gerichte als Alternative zur staatlichen Zivilgerichtsbarkeit – Eine ökonomische Analyse* (Tübingen: Mohr, 1987); Walther Gottwald, *Streitbeilegung ohne Urteil* (Tübingen: Mohr, 1981). For private law making see Stuart Henry, *Private Justice – Towards Integrated Theorising in the Sociology of Law* (London, Boston, Melbourne and Henley: Routledge & Kegan Paul, 1983).

21 Blankenburg states that national courts Europe-wide react against an excessive litigation workload in two ways. Firstly, there is a 'tendency towards internalisation', where the State offers summary procedures for the speedy handling of cases. And, secondly, there is a 'tendency towards externalisation' where judicial functions are transferred to out-of-court procedures. Debt collection for credit transactions is an area where commercial institutions are involved extensively as competitors of court services. See 'Prozeßflucht und Prozeßebbe – Über die Fähigkeit der Gerichte mit Rechtsstreitigkeiten fertig zu werden', in Blankenburg, *Prozeßflut?*, pp. 9–21, at p.18.

22 See Nothnagel, *Execution durch sociale Interessengruppe*, p. 10; Bernhard R. Dietrich, *Inkasso-Unternehmungen* (Nürnberg: Hieronymus, 1986), pp. 16–20.

23 In the German business press, which usually refers to the inefficiency of the judicial system, the business community is advised to make use of commercial debt collection agencies: *e.g. Wirtschaft und Markt,* January 1995: 'Mit oder ohne Gerichtsvollzieher – das ist die Frage'; *Wirtschaft in Südwest-Sachsen,* May 1995: 'Offene Forderungen – Was kann ich selbst tun?'; *Handwerk Magazin,* April 1995: 'Der richtige Umgang

debt collection agencies in Germany is three times higher than the amount collected by the court executors. In 1993 the annual amount of debts collected by 330 of 550 German debt collectors (*i.e.* members of the Federal Association of German Debt Collection Agencies) was DM 6.2 billion [24] whereas the amount collected by court executors for the same year was about DM 2.2 billion.[25,26] Moreover, the rate of increase in the business volume of commercial debt collectors is considerably higher than the increase in the workload of the court executors. In 1979, debts collected by debt collection agencies amounted to approximately DM 900 million, whereas the debts collected by court executors amounted to DM 1.1 billion.[27] For the years 1979 – 1993, the amount collected by German debt collection agencies increased sixfold whereas the amount collected by court executors increased twofold.[28]

---

      mit Schulden – Herunter mit dem Außenständen!'. It is also reported that some professional organisations, e.g. the Chamber of Medical Professions, Chamber of Handicrafts, establish debt collection departments in order to serve their own members: *Frankfurter Allgemeine Zeitung*, 16.7.1993: 'Inkasso-Organisationen der Ärzte'; *Norddeutsche Neueste Nachrichten*, 8.6.1995: 'Kammer-Inkassostelle zog Millionenbeträge ein'; *Flensburger Tageblatt*, 15.9.1994: 'Inkasso-Dienst gegen Zahlungssünder'. Lawyers are also advertising against their competitors, debt collectors: see e.g. *Bild am Sonntag*, 15.1.1995: 'Todesangst vor dem - Schuldeneintreiber' and *Fellbacher Zeitung*, 11.1.1995: 'Rechtsanwalt treibt ein'.

24   Data provided by the Federal Association of the German Debt Collection Agencies, in *Frankfurter Allgemeine Zeitung*, 6.10.1992: 'Die Inkasso-Branche profitiert von Rezession'.

25   Exact figure DM 2,194,606,058.48: Information collected by the Deutsche Gerichtsvollzieher Zeitung from the State administration of justice authorities, in 'Übersicht über die Geschäftstätigkeit und den Personalbestand der Gerichtsvollzieher im Jahre 1993', *Deutsche Gerichtsvollzieher-Zeitung*, 109. Jahrgang no. 9 (1994), p. 143.

26   To be fair it must be added that the amount collected by execution officers does not represent the total amount of judgment debts collected through the judicial debt collection procedure, for attachment of earnings and execution against immovable property are made in Germany by civil courts without the involvement of execution officers. In addition, there may be cases where the debtor pays directly to the creditor or his lawyer, after the Court Executor is involved. Cf. Klein, 'Die Vollstreckung von Geldforderungen durch den Gerichtsvollzieher', p. 66.

27   See Hörmann, *Verbraucher und Schulden*, pp. 183–4.

28   If the conflict potential arising from increasing number of economic interactions and the monetary volumes involved in these interactions are considered, the workload of German courts and court executors concerning debt collection cases increases slower than expected. More interestingly, in Britain, the number of court cases for debt collection did not increase in the 20 years between 1960 and 1980, and the number of requests for enforcement of judgments decreased. See Michael Adler and Günter Hörmann, 'Schuldbeitreibung und die Gerichte – Bundesrepublik und Großbritannien im Vergleich', in Erhard Blankenburg and Rüdiger Voigt (eds), *Implementation von*

It has often been stated by sociologists of law [29] that social control against default (*i.e.* the application of legal enforcement measures), unlike the case in crime, is exerted not by the State on its own initiative, but by the creditors. The use of commercial debt collection agencies represents a further step where not only the initiation and development of the debt recovery procedure are caused by the creditor, but also the 'debt collector' is a private firm.[30]

Although the debt collection methods used by the commercial debt collectors [31] may not include enforcement measures as such or, more accurately, debt collectors require the involvement of official enforcement officers in order to utilise or apply judicial enforcement measures (*e.g.* attachment), the persuasion tactics employed by debt collectors (warning letters, telephone calls, personal visits) albeit involve a certain degree of psychological pressure on the debtor.[32]

Considering the routinisation of the debt collection process and special practical difficulties involved in the 'judicial' methods of cross-border debt collection which make going to court even less attractive in cross-border legal relations than domestic legal relations, it may be supposed that privatised methods of debt collection are used more frequently in cross-border legal relations than in domestic legal relations. That is, one may suggest that debt collection methods autonomously created by the business community are utilised in order to compensate for the lack of efficiently functioning enforcement systems in the international arena.

Surprisingly little is mentioned in the literature on this topic. In particular on the role of commercial debt collection agencies in cross-border collections one finds next to nothing [33] in the writings of jurists or legal sociologists.

Gerichtsentscheidungen – Jahrbuch für Rechtssoziologie und Rechtstheorie 11 (Opladen: Westdeutscher Verlag, 1987), pp. 95–103.

29   *E.g.* see Rock, *Making People Pay*, p. 6; Röhl, 'Schuldbeitreibung als Kontrolle abweichenden Verhaltens', p. 13.
30   Hoene refers to commercial debt collection as 'civil execution through private bodies'. Hoene, *Präventiver Kreditschutz und Zwangsvollstreckung durch Private*, p. 129.
31   See Dietrich, 'Inkasso-Unternehmungen', pp. 73 et seq.
32   See Rock, 'Making People Pay', Chapter 4 (pp. 77–106).
33   Otherwise for factoring and forfaiting see *e.g.* Friedrich Graf von Westphalen, 'Rechtsprobleme des Factoring und des Forfait von Exportforderungen', *Recht der internationalen Wirtschaft*, 23. Jahrgang, no. 2 (1977), pp. 80–6; Kurt F. Schär, 'Die wirtschaftliche Funktionsweise des Factoring', in Ernst A. Kramer (ed.), *Neue Vertragsformen der Wirtschaft: Leasing, Factoring, Franchising*, 2. Auflage (Bern and Stuttgart: Paul Haupt, 1992), pp. 275–8.

10 Commercial Cross-Border Debt Collection in Germany

A. COMMERCIAL DEBT COLLECTION UNDER GERMAN LAW

1. General

It was reported that in 1994 an estimated 550 'debt collection agencies' (*Inkassobüros, Inkassounternehmen*) operated in Germany.[1] A debt collection agency is legally defined in Germany as a commercial undertaking, the commercial activity of which is to collect debts which are owed by others or which have been transferred to it by others in order to be collected on the account of the transferor or on its own account.[2] A debt collection agency is therefore (i) a *commercial organisation* and (ii) its field of activity is *collection of debts owed by its clients*. It must be added (and it is a result of its 'commercial' nature) that, (iii) a debt collection agency carries on its business only by *extra-judicial debt collection methods*, or when recourse to the courts is necessary a lawyer must be commissioned.[3]

---

1 'Mehr Insolvenzen, hohe Forderungsausfälle und geringe Zahlungsmoral' (reported from a speech by Ulf Giebel, Chairman of the Federal Associaton of German Debt Collection Agencies, at the annual meeting of the Association in Berlin on 10.11.1994), *Frankfurter Allgemeine Zeitung*, 11.11.1994.
2 'Inkassobüro', in H. Tilch (ed.), *Deutsches Rechts-Lexikon*, Vol.II, 2nd ed. (Munich: Beck, 1992). Similarly see '5. Verordnung zur Ausführung des Rechtsberatungsgesetzes of 29.3.1938', *BGBl* III 303–12–5; 'Grundsätze für Berufsausübung zugelassener Inkassounternehmen in der Bundesrepublik Deutschland' (= Code of Conduct for Admitted Debt Collection Undertakings in Federal Republic of Germany) issued by the Federal Associaton of German Debt Collection Agencies reproduced in Peter David, *Zusammenarbeit mit Inkassounternehmen*, 3rd ed. (Munich, Planegg 1993), pp. 39–43 Art. I(1).
3 The difference between 'factoring' and the practices of debt collection agencies in Germany is that, in factoring the client transfers all of his claims (with a 'global-contract') against a particular third party/third parties to the factor (*e.g.* a bank); and the factor, who becomes the owner of the debts, pays the value of the claims to the

German debt collection agencies find their origin in the 'business information agencies' (*Handelsauskunfteien*) of the second half of the 19th century which commercially provided businessmen with the information concerning financial situation and credibility of their prospective commercial partners.[4]

The majority of debt collection agencies in Germany are individually owned. Most of these firms are run by a small group, usually not more than five people. Firms with 60 employees are among the large sized debt collection agencies. The number of incorporated *Inkassobüros* is relatively small and only large sized firms are incorporated as a limited company.[5]

As stated above, debt collection agencies may use only extra-judicial debt recovery methods and, where recourse to the courts is necessary the co-operation of a professional lawyer is required. Consequently, it has been argued that,[6] a business symbiosis exists between lawyers and *Inkassobüros* rather than competition. Professional co-operation between lawyers and debt collection agencies is legally permitted.[7] Debt collection agencies may also co-operate with private detectives to collect information

---

    client in advance, after deducting its commission. The risk of non-payment may be borne either by the factor (real factoring) or by the client (unreal factoring) in which case he should repay the factor if the debt cannot be collected. See Otto Palandt / Helmut Heinrichs, *Palandt Bürgerliches Gesetzbuch* (Commentary), 56. ed. (Munich: Beck 1997), the commentary on § 398, Rn. 35 – 37; cf. *ibid.* § 398 Rn. 26 – 28. Neither of the two forms of factoring contravene the provisions of the Legal Advisory Act ('Factoring', in H. Tilch (ed.), *Deutsches Rechts-Lexikon*, Vol. I, 2nd ed. (Munich: Beck, 1992)); and a debt collection contract between a debt collection agency and its client under which the agency acquires debts transferred to it by the client and collects such debts on its own account may be a factoring contract according to its contents. See Walter Seitz, 'Materiellrechtliche und prozessuale Probleme des Inkassorechts', in Walter Seitz (ed.), *Das Inkasso-Handbuch - Recht und Praxis der Inkassounternehmen*, 2nd ed. (Stuttgart: Verlag für Wirtschafts- und Steuerrecht, 1985), Rn. 366 – 367.

4   See Dietrich, *Inkasso Unternehmungen*, pp. 16 – 20; Carsten D. Ohle, 'Das deutsche Inkassogewerbe in Vergangenheit, Gegenwart und Zukunft', in *Das Inkasso-Handbuch*, pp. 1 – 43, Rn. 5 – 10.

5   Ohle, 'Das deutsche Inkassogewerbe in Vergangenheit, Gegenwart und Zukunft', pp. 9 –10; David, *Zusammenarbeit mit Inkassounternehmen*, p. 29. For licensing conditions applicable to the debt collection agencies in the form of a limited liability company see 1.Verordnung zur Ausführung des Rechtsberatungsgesetzes; § 19 II and § 3; Michael M. Benninghaus and Wolfgang Moisek, 'Berufsrecht der Inkassounternehmen', in *Das Inkasso-Handbuch*, Rn. 400; Albert Windolph, 'Das Inkasso nach deutschem und ausländischem Recht', p. 53.

6   Ohle, 'Das deutsche Inkassogewerbe in Vergangenheit, Gegenwart und Zukunft', Rn. 4; cf. Dietrich, *Inkasso Unternehmungen*, pp. 45 – 8.

7   Grundsätzen des anwaltlichen Standesrechts § 90 I.

on the address, means and assets of the debtor *etc.* required for the debt recovery process.[8] Further, some of the debt collection agencies in Germany (in particular the larger firms) also operate as business information agencies with their own information files.[9]

The first statutory regulation relating to extra-judicial debt collection practices appeared in the Act on Prevention of the Misuse of Legal Advice 1935,[10] which has been later enacted to the Federal Code of Laws of the Federal Republic [11] under the title Legal Advisory Act (*Rechtsberatungsgesetz*). According to this statute [12] 'collecting someone else's or for collection purposes transferred debts commercially' was 'regardless of its being a main or a secondary professional (activity) or a remunerative or a non-profit making activity' subject to licensing.[13] Yet, this provision had not pronounced the term *Inkassobüro*, which would be inserted in the text [14] later, with an amendment made in 1980.[15]

2. Legal Advisory Act

The licence which is required by Art. 1 of the Legal Advisory Act is granted by the *Landgericht* or by the head of the *Amtsgericht* where the debt collection agency undertakes its business.[16] There is no statutory provision which explains in detail the qualifications required for establishing a debt collection agency.[17] Art. 1, § 1(2) of the Legal Advisory Act only requires the applicant to have 'the reliability, personal suitability and expertise which is necessitated by the profession', although it is clear that a

---

8 David, *Zusammenarbeit mit Inkassounternehmen*, pp. 90–7; Windolph, 'Das Inkasso nach deutschem und ausländischem Recht', pp. 47–9.
9 See Windolph, 'Das Inkasso nach deutschem und ausländischem Recht', pp. 49–50; Ohle, 'Das deutsche Inkassogewerbe in Vergangenheit, Gegenwart und Zukunft', Rn. 5–8.
10 Gesetz zur Verhütung von Misbräuchen auf dem Gebiete der Rechtsberatung, *RGBl* I 1935, p. 1478, *BGBl* III 303-12.
11 Sammlung des deutschen Bundesrechts.
12 Art. 1, § 1(1).
13 Cf. *infra* Chapter 11: Commercial Cross-Border Debt Collection in England; Consumer Credit Act 1974, s.145(7).
14 Art. 1, § 1(1), Nr. 5.
15 *BGBl* I, 1503.
16 1. Verordnung zur Ausführung des Rechtsberatungsgesetzes from 13.12.1935 (*BGBl* III 303-12-1) § 11.
17 David, *Zusammenarbeit mit Inkassounternehmen*, p. 18.

general knowledge of civil and commercial law, civil procedure and business management is also necessary.[18]

Unlike debt collection agencies, 'factoring' business [19] (*e.g.* factoring carried out by commercial banks) is not subject to licensing requirement under the Legal Advisory Act.[20]

It has been argued that debt collection agencies which are based abroad cannot operate in Germany without having a licence under the Legal Advisory Act.[21] Thus the Landgericht in Munich therefore decided in 1978 that an application which had been filed with the court executor by a foreign debt collection agency was inadmissible.[22] A foreign debt collection agency which is professionally recognised under its national laws may collect its clients' debts through civil execution proceedings in Germany. This is however only the case where the foreign debt collection agency is duly represented before the German execution officers either by a German lawyer or by a sister debt collection agency in Germany.

Foreign individuals and legal persons who apply for a debt collection licence in Germany are generally subject to the same requirements as German nationals and corporations.[23]

Debt collection agencies are subject to the supervision of the Chief Judge of the local civil court (*Landgericht* or *Amtsgericht*).[24] The supervision of the court does not involve regular checks but is exercised when

---

18 See *ibid.*, pp. 17–8.
19 See *supra*.
20 See German Federal Court, Decision of 3 May 1972, *Entscheidungen des Bundesgerichtshofs in Zivilsachen* 58 (1972), p. 364; Dietrich, *Inkassounternehmungen*, pp. 33–4. For other exceptional cases where collection of debts owed by others is not subject to the Legal Advisory Act see *ibid.*, pp. 27–33.
21 David, *Zusammenarbeit mit Inkassounternehmen*, p. 26.
22 Decision of the Landgericht in Munich, dated 28.6.1978, *Deutsche Gerichtsvollzieher-Zeitung*, 94. Jahrgang (1979), p. 10.
23 See Benninghaus and Mosiek, 'Berufsrecht der Inkassounternehmen', pp. 350–440, Rn. 397 – 399; the authors argue that, exceptionally, foreign nationals and corporations *from non-EU states* are subject to the so called 'public need' requirement, '*Bedürfnisprüfung*' i.e. the requirement that the need for new Inkassobüros must not have already been satisfied with a sufficient number of existing debt collection agencies in a particular area which is not applicable to EU nationals and corporations as a result of a precedent of the Constitutional Court on 'freedom of choice of work'; cf. the decision of the German Federal Court of Administrative Matters of 10 May 1955, *Neue Juristische Wochenschrift*, 8. Jahrgang (1955), p. 1532 and Art. 52 of the EEC Treaty.
24 2.Verordnung zur Ausführung des Rechtsberatungsgesetzes from 3.4.1936 (*BGBl* III 303 - 12 - 2), § 3.

necessary.[25] If, as a result of these checks circumstances arise which would render the issue of the licence impossible, the debt collection agency's licence will be cancelled.[26]

According to the German Commercial Code § 2 I a debt collection agency is a 'commercial firm' (*Gewerbebetrieb*) and its owners are tradesmen (*Kaufleute*).[27] As a result, unlike lawyers, legal advisors and tax consultants, debt collection agencies may advertise their firms in the media.[28] However such advertising must be 'honest' and suitable (*i.e.* compatible with their professional activity which is to some extent of a legal service nature).[29] Advertising which does not fulfil this criteria can be prohibited by the supervising court and may even result in the cancellation of the debt collection agency's licence.[30] In practice, debt collection advertisements usually appear in publications read by the business community.[31] Again as a result of their commercial nature, debt collection agencies fix (or bargain) their fees freely, without being subject to an official tariff, regulation *etc.* Thus, unlike lawyers, they can determine their fees either on a contingency basis or they can contract a 'success premium' (*Erfolgshonorar*) with their clients.[32]

3. Debt Collection Methods

Under its licence a German debt collection agency can provide the following services:[33]

– Consultancy concerning debt recovery in general: *e.g.* to what extent a particular claim is undisputed or recoverable; whether a limitation period

---

25 Windolph, 'Das Inkasso nach deutschem und ausländischem Recht', p. 57.
26 1.Verordnung zur Ausführung des Rechtsberatungsgesetzes, § 14.
27 Ohle, 'Das deutsche Inkassogewerbe in Vergangenheit, Gegenwart und Zukunft', pp. 5 and 38.
28 3.Verordnung zur Ausführung des Rechtsberatungsgesetzes (*BGBl* III 303-12-3).
29 See David, *Zusammenarbeit mit Inkassounternehmen*, p. 44.
30 Windolph, 'Das Inkasso nach deutschem und ausländischem Recht', p. 57; David, *Zusammenarbeit mit Inkassounternehmen*, pp. 27 and 44; Ohle, 'Das deutsche Inkassogewerbe in Vergangenheit, Gegenwart und Zukunft', pp. 5–6.
31 Ohle, 'Das deutsche Inkassogewerbe in Vergangenheit, Gegenwart und Zukunft', pp. 44–7.
32 See *infra* 'Costs' in this chapter.
33 Günter Rennen and Gabriele Calibe, *Rechtsberatungsgesetz mit Ausführungsverordnungen* (Commentary), 2nd ed. (Munich: Beck, 1992), Rn. 78 et seq.; Capell, *Erfolgreich Mahnen*, pp. 148–56.

exists *etc.* A debt collection agency may not however give full legal advice involving the substantive law aspects of a case. This can only be done by a lawyer.

- Drafting simple 'demand letters' to the debtor (*außergerichtliche Mahnschreiben*).
- Filing an application with the court executor based on an enforceable title.[34]
- Collecting information from 'debtors' lists' kept by execution courts.[35]
- Monitoring of bad debts, enabling the possible recovery of the debt to be quickly executed.

According to the contents of the contract between the agency and its clients, the agency may use one of the following methods in order to provide these services:[36]

- It may act under a power of attorney given by the client, empowering it to represent him for debt recovery purposes (*Einziehung fremder Forderungen*).
- It may acquire the claim transferred to it by the client for a fiduciary purpose (*Einziehung von zu Einziehungszwecken abgetretenen Forderungen*).
- It may purchase debts, enabling the agency to recover the debt on its own behalf (*Einziehung von Forderungen auf eigene Rechnung*).[37]

A debt collection agency may not, however, represent its clients in court proceedings including summary court procedures and proceedings before the execution court.

Although the debt recovery practices used by debt collection agencies in Germany vary from one firm to another, a general debt recovery process may be described as follows:

---

34 See *supra* Chapter 1: Debt Recovery in Germany and cf. *infra*.
35 Debt collectors' access to the debtors' lists was recently restricted to a large extent. See *supra* Chapter 1: Debt Recovery in Germany. Such a list (*Schuldnerverzeichnis*) is a record kept by the execution courts which includes the names of debtors against whom an order has been made requiring them to submit to the court an inventory of their means and assets available for the satisfaction of their creditors: German CCP § 915.
36 Rennen and Calibe, *Rechtsberatungsgesetz mit Ausführungsverordnungen*, Rn. 81; Ohle, 'Das deutsche Inkassogewerbe in Vergangenheit, Gegenwart und Zukunft', Rn. 27; Dietrich, *Inkassounternehmungen*, pp.161–8.
37 Cf. Factoring, *supra* 'General' in this chapter.

The 'debt collection' process begins with a simple demand letter to the debtor. This letter informs the debtor, *inter alia*, that from that date, he should pay his creditor through the debt collection agency. If this first step proves to be fruitless, the debt collection agency commences inquiries in order to collect information about the means and assets of the debtor. Debt collection agencies make use of a wide range of information from telephone directories to court records. Following these inquiries, debt collection agencies may make further contact with the debtor, including individually drafted letters, telephone calls and personal visits. Should these efforts also be unsuccessful, debt collection agencies may choose to initiate court proceedings through a lawyer.[38] This lawyer is usually a practitioner with whom the debt collection agency is in continuous co-operation. Where the debt to be recovered has been acquired by or for collection purposes transferred to the debt collection agency, the lawsuit is brought in the agency's name; where, on the other hand, the client has not transferred his claim to the debt collection agency, the lawyer must act in the name of the client.[39] Lastly, should the debt collection process be unsuccessful, the debt collection agency remains in contact with the debtor and makes periodic inquiries on his assets until the recovery is possible.[40]

Debt collection agencies must refrain from using debt collection methods against good faith and particularly offensive methods of pressure.[41,42]

---

[38] For the discussions on the question whether Art. 1 § 1 Nr.5 of the Legal Advisory Act to the effect that debt collection agencies use extra-judicial ('out of court') debt recovery methods preclude the debt collection agencies to initiate court proceedings even through a lawyer see Rennen and Calibe, *Rechtsberatungsgesetz mit Ausführungsverordnungen*, Rn. 83 – 85 and David, *Zusammenarbeit mit Inkassounternehmen*, pp. 65–6.

[39] Cf. David, *Zusammenarbeit mit Inkassounternehmen*, p. 48 and Windolph, 'Das Inkasso nach deutschem und ausländischem Recht', p. 59.

[40] David, *Zusammenarbeit mit Inkassounternehmen*, p. 68.

[41] Windolph, 'Das Inkasso nach deutschem und ausländischem Recht', pp. 55–6; see also former (no longer in force) 'Ausführungsverordnung des Reichsjustizministeriums' dated 24.10.1941, reproduced in *Das Inkasso-Handbuch*, pp. 290 et seq., Title 'A', Paragraph '3'.

[42] A debt collection method may be regarded as offensive even where only an undue psychological pressure is brought to bear on the debtor. Cf. Karin Güthlein, 'Rote Zahlen ziehen "Schwarze Schatten" an', *Süddeutsche Zeitung*, 11.11.1994. It was reported that a newly established debt collection agency in Germany pressured the defaulting debtors of its clients into making payment, by making its employees wear black suits (known as 'Black Shadows'), to follow the debtors in public.

4. Debt Collection Contract

The debt collection contract (*Inkassovertrag*) is a special type of contract for the provision of services.[43] Under a debt collection contract, the debt collection agency undertakes, as an independent contractor (*Inkassomandator*), to collect a particular debt and the client (*Inkassomandat*) on his part undertakes to pay the debt collection agency its fees and, when necessary, a success premium.

In addition to the debt collection contract which states the rights and obligations of the parties, a power of attorney (*Inkassovollmacht*) must be prepared and /or executed by the client, empowering the debt collection agency to act on his behalf. However, as mentioned above, instead of providing a power of attorney, the client may choose to transfer his claim to the debt collection agency, in which case the latter would act on its own behalf.

In practice, debt collection agencies use standard contract terms and enter into so-called 'blanket contracts' with their regular clients, which include, *inter alia*, provisions prohibiting the client from dealing with his debtor personally, providing the debt collection agency with a partial discharge from contractual liability, and determining the conditions for cancellation of the contracts *etc.*[44] The contents of such standard contracts (*i.e.* validity and construction of their terms) are subject to the provisions of the German Standard Contract Terms Act, which protects the interests of the individual clients.[45]

---

[43] Entgeltlicher Geschäftsbesorgungsvertrag, German Civil Code § 675; David, *Zusammenarbeit mit Inkassounternehmen*, p. 48; Windolph, 'Das Inkasso nach deutschem und ausländischem Recht', p. 58; Dietrich, *Inkassounternehmungen*, p. 157.

[44] See David, *Zusammenarbeit mit Inkassounternehmen*, pp. 48–59; Windolph, 'Das Inkasso nach deutschem und ausländischem Recht', p. 60; Dietrich, *Inkassounternehmungen*, pp. 157–9.

[45] Gesetz zur Regelung des Rechts der allgemeinen Geschäftsbedingungen from 9.11.1976 (*BGBl* I, p. 3317), §§8 et seq.

5. Costs [46]

As mentioned above, debt collection agencies in Germany are free to set their own rates without being subject to an official tariff. The federal rules concerning lawyers' fees are not applicable to debt collection agencies.[47] Debt collection agencies use various methods to calculate their fees and costs. Nevertheless, it has been reported that,[48] according to the usual commercial practices, debt collection costs can be itemised as follows:

- *Processing costs* (general expenditure of processing the debt collection case, including preparation of the file and the initial examination of the facts of the case) amount to 5 – 6% of the total cost of the claim (minimum DM 10 – 15).
- *Debt collection fees* (fees concerning real debt collection service, excluding general processing costs) amount to 3 – 4% of the total cost of the claim.
- *Fees for various accounting services* (*e.g.* long term instalments) amount to 2 – 4% of the total cost (maximum DM 50 – 80 per month).
- *Costs for correspondence, telephone etc.* amount to 1 – 3% of the claim (maximum DM 50).
- *Success premium* [49] amounts: (i) for the claims based on a judgment or another enforceable title – up to 20%; (ii) for claims without a judgment or an enforceable title – up to 30% (where there has been no previous attempt to collect the debt) *or* up to 50% (where there has been a previous attempt to collect the debt); *(iii)* for claims against debtors abroad, – up to 40%; (iv) for claims based on a judgment or another enforceable title, in case of the risk of an unsuccessful debt collection attempt being borne by the debt collection agency, up to 60% of the amount of the claim.[50]

---

46   The subject 'debt collection (agency's) costs' has been discussed in German literature in detail. Indeed a great part of the literature concerning debt collection agencies (see Dietrich, *Inkassounternehmungen*, pp. VII – XXXV) is devoted to this topic. See, for example, Wolfgang Jäckle, *Die Erstattungsfähigkeit der Kosten eines Inkassobüros* (Berlin: Duncker & Humblot, 1978); Dietrich, *Inkassounternehmungen*, pp. 169–79; Seitz, 'Materiell-rechtliche und prozessuale Probleme des Inkassorechts', Rn. 76 – 295; Capell, *Erfolgreich Mahnen*, pp. 160–207.
47   5. Gesetz zur Änderung der Bundesrechtsanwaltsgebührenordnung, Art. IX(2).
48   Ohle, 'Das deutsche Inkassogewerbe in Vergangenheit, Gegenwart und Zukunft', Rn. 41.
49   See also David, *Zusammenarbeit mit Inkassounternehmen*, p. 79.
50   Cf. *infra* 'Costs of cross border collection' in this chapter.

196 Making Foreign People Pay

The question as to whether and to what extent the costs of a debt collection agency (*i.e.* the costs and fees paid to the debt collection agency by the creditor) are recoverable by the creditor is highly controversial in Germany.[51] For the purpose of this study, without becoming involved in the theoretical discussions, the present law can be summarised as follows:[52]

a) As a rule, the costs paid to a debt collection agency cannot be recovered by the creditor as part of the costs of the court proceedings (German CCP §§91 *et seq.*) which are awarded by the court in favour of the successful party.[53]

b) The debt collection agency's costs are however actionable as a separate substantive law claim (albeit together with the main claim), *i.e.* as a part of the damages suffered as a result of the default on the part of the debtor (German Civil Code §286). The pre-condition for such a claim is that, resort to a debt collection agency could be deemed reasonable. For example, if the amount of the claim was disputed between the parties and it was therefore apparent from the beginning that the attempts of the debt collection agency out of court would be futile, resort to a debt collection agency would be of no use. In such a case, the creditor, who is under a statutory obligation to keep his financial losses to a minimum (German Civil Code §254) is denied a course of action to recover the costs paid to the debt collection agency.[54]

c) The so-called 'success premium' is not recoverable from the debtor, as the creditor can by no means extend the amount of the liability of the

---

51   General information provided in the widely used commentaries and handbooks varies surprisingly. Cf. for example, the discussions by Wolfgang Grunsky, Vor §249, Rn. 66a and Reinhold Thode, §268, Rn. 8 in *Münchener Kommentar zum Bürgerlichen Gesetzbuch*, Vol. II, 3rd ed. (Munich: Beck, 1994); Reinhard Bork, §91 IV, Rn. 41 and 92 in *Stein-Jonas Kommentar zur Zivilprozeßordnung*, Vol. II, 21st ed. (Tübingen: Mohr, 1994); Rudolf Althenhoff, Hans Busch and Jürgen Chemnitz, *Rechtsberatungsgesetz* (Commentary), 10th ed. by Jürgen Chemnitz (Münster: Aschendorff, 1993), Art.1 §1, Rn. 177 – 181; David, *Zusammenarbeit mit Inkassounternehmen*, pp.78 – 87.

52   For a full discussion of the subject see Jäckle, *Die Erstattungsfähigkeit der Kosten eines Inkassobüros*, in particular pp. 51–80 and pp. 120–4.

53   Bork, *Stein-Jonas Kommentar zur Zivilprozeßordnung*, §91 IV, Rn. 41 and 92. Cf. David, *Zusammenarbeit mit Inkassounternehmen*, p. 79; Hartmann in Baumbach, Lauterbach, Albers and Hartmann, *Zivilprozeßordnung*, §91, Rn. 108.

54   See and cf. Grunsky, *Münchener Kommentar zum Bürgerlichen Gesetzbuch*, Vor §249, Rn.66a; Thode, *Münchener Kommentar zum Bürgerlichen Gesetzbuch*, §268, Rn. 8; Chemnitz in Althenhoff, Bush and Chemnitz, *Rechtsberatungsgesetz*, Art. 1 §1, Rn. 171 – 172; David, *Zusammenarbeit mit Inkassounternehmen*, pp. 80–1.

debtor by entering into a contract with a third party (*i.e.* by promising a success premium to a debt collection agency).[55]

d) As a rule, the costs of a debt collection agency are only recoverable up to the amount which would have been paid in counsel fees if the creditor had collected his claim through court proceedings.[56]

B. CROSS-BORDER DEBT COLLECTION IN GERMANY

1. Introduction

In a recent study analysing the economical efficiency of German debt collection agencies it was reported that cross-border debt collection by commercial debt collectors is becoming more important in Europe as a result of increasing trade within the Single Market.[57]

One of the larger debt collectors in Germany confirms that 'there is an increasing demand for cross-border debt collection services especially directed to internationally serving debt collection agencies'. A senior officer of the Federal Association of German Debt Collection Agencies similarly states:

Cross-border debt collection has a growing importance in practice. The historical phase which we are going through is comparable with the 'founding years' of Germany in the nineteenth century. In those days, political and technological developments (unification of Germany and industrialisation) stimulated the expansion of local German business environments to a nation-wide economy. Today we are experiencing a similar development throughout Europe. Even medium sized undertakings are looking for markets and business contacts in other European countries. Parallel to the growing volume of cross-border trade, the demand for cross-border debt collection is also growing. I suppose, in recent years the number of cross-border debt collection cases has grown dramatically.[58]

---

55 Chemnitz in Althenhoff, Bush and Chemnitz, *Rechtsberatungsgesetz*, Art. 1 §1, Rn. 177; David, *Zusammenarbeit mit Inkassounternehmen*, p. 78. Cf. Thode, *Münchener Kommentar zum Bürgerlichen Gesetzbuch*, §268, Rn. 8.

56 Chemnitz in Althenhoff, Bush and Chemnitz, *Rechtsberatungsgesetz*, Art. 1 §1, Rn. 179; Thode, *Münchener Kommentar zum Bürgerlichen Gesetzbuch*, §268, Rn. 8; David, *Zusammenarbeit mit Inkassounternehmen*, pp. 83–7.

57 Cora Stahrenberg, *Effektivität des externen Inkassos – Ein Beitrag zur Ausgliederung betrieblicher Funktionen* (Berlin: Dunker & Humblot, 1995), p. 200.

58 Interview conducted in June 1995.

In consumer credit and debt collection business periodicals, 'cross-border debt collection' occasionally appears as a separate topic of discussion.[59] The way these articles approach the subject suggests that the activities of debt collection agencies in the field of cross-border debt collection consists of the collection of commercial debts (Böhner) as well as consumer debts (Scholten, Garrigues). These articles highlight the peculiarities of and difficulties experienced in cross-border debt collection,[60] thus enabling the author to draft 'Questionnaire on Cross-Border Debt Collection',[61] for the response of German debt collection agencies.[62]

The first draft of the questionnaire was corrected and finalised with the assistance of the Federal Association of German Debt Collection Agencies.[63] This organisation informed the author that cross-border commercial debt collection is carried out in Germany only by a very small group of (3 or 4) debt collection agencies, which may also work on behalf of other (domestic) debt collectors on a commission basis. These debt collection agencies are affiliates or sister companies of international debt collection and credit reference agency concerns. The questionnaire was accordingly distributed in August 1995 to 11 German debt collection agencies, that is, to the four debt collection agencies named by the Federal Association and also to those debt collection agencies which, according to their size or international contacts, may also be involved in international debt collection.

During the period August to October 1995, seven replies were received; one simply informed that the firm does not carry out cross-border debt collection; one of the larger firms apologised 'on grounds of business administration' for being unable to complete the questionnaire and the remaining five returned the completed questionnaire with a request for anonymous processing of the data and information provided.

---

59   See e.g. Piggert, 'Das Auslandsinkasso', pp. 15 et seq.; Windolp, 'Das Auslandsinkasso in den Ländern der EWG und EFTA', pp. 56–60; Böhner, 'Forderungseinziehung gegen Unternehmen in der EG', pp. 69 et seq.; Schinobu K. Garrigues, 'Collecting Beyond Our Borders', *Collector*, July 1995, pp. 12–20.

60   See also Windolp, 'Das Inkasso im Ausland', pp. 38 – 40; Windolp, 'Das Inkasso nach deutschem und ausländischem Recht'; Timmermann, 'Die Zwangsvollstreckung im Ausland ist schwierig', p. 20.

61   See *infra* Annex II. The original text in German can be obtained from the author.

62   The same questionnaire was also used in the survey made in England. See *infra*.

63   With thanks to Dr. Carsten C. Ohle, the General Secretary of the Association for his comments on the first draft of the questionnaire. With thanks also to Mr. Ulf Giebel, the Chairman of the Association for his support in bringing the author in to personal contact with the German debt collectors, without whom the survey would not have been possible in Germany due to confidentiality concerns.

All of the respondent firms were larger debt collectors, three of them [64] being mainly involved in cross-border collection, that is, dealing either exclusively or predominantly in cross-border debt collection. Taking into account the small number of German debt collectors which carry out cross-border collection, the replies received were not only informative, but also representative.[65]

2. Annual Number of Cross-border Commercial Debt Collection Cases

With the available data it is not possible to determine the annual number of cross-border debt collection cases in Germany. Only two of the (specialised) firms provided such figures. In 1994, one of the firms dealt with 7,100 cross-border cases and the other 6,300. Their business has been increasing during the last decade, the annual figures being 3,450 and 2,318 in 1985, and 6,200 and 4,601 in 1990, respectively.

3. Distribution of Cross-border Debt Collection Cases Among Domestic and Foreign Clients in Various Countries

a) Domestic creditors with debtors resident abroad

The five debt collection agencies collect both receivables of German creditors abroad and receivables of foreign creditors resident within Germany. It is understood however that specialised cross-border debt collectors work more frequently for domestic creditors who seek to collect debts abroad.

Thus, 90% of the cross-border cases received by Debt Collector 3 involve domestic clients with the remaining 10% involving creditors resident

---

[64] *I.e.* German Debt Collectors numbered 3, 4 and 5 below. Together they are referred to as 'specialised firms', 'specialised debt collectors', *etc.* To secure anonymity, each of them is referred to as 'one of the three specialised firms'. Where the data obtained from specialised firms are presented, the order is not necessarily 'Debt Collector 3, Debt Collector 4 and Debt Collector 5'.

[65] The debt collection market in Germany is highly concentrated. Although an estimated 550 debt collection agencies operate in Germany ('Mehr Insolvenzen, hohe Forderungsausfälle und geringe Zahlungsmoral', *Frankfurter Allgemeine Zeitung*, 11.11.1994), a study of the income and corporation tax statistics for 1986 showed that 12 firms represent approx. 80% of the branch's turnover in the country. See Stahrenberg, *Effektivität des externen Inkassos*, pp. 120–2.

abroad. Corresponding statistics for Debt Collector 4 are: approximately 80% domestic clients (having receivables abroad) and 20% foreign clients (having receivables from German resident debtors). For the years 1985, 1990 and 1994, the figures for the foreign creditors with domestic debtors of Debt Collector 4 were 20%, 15% and 25% respectively. With regard to Debt Collector 5, the figures provided for the years 1985, 1990 and 1994 suggest that in only 10% of the cross-border cases dealt with the creditor was resident abroad.

Accordingly, it may be presumed with some caution that, in the overwhelming majority of cross-border debt collections carried out by German agencies (perhaps 80 – 90%), the creditor is resident in Germany and the debtor is resident abroad.

b) Majority of clients from Europe

The majority of foreign creditors served by the German debt collection agencies are from continental Europe. All three specialised debt collectors and Debt Collector 2 named their five most important foreign countries in their cross-border collection activities. The Benelux countries (especially the Netherlands), France, Switzerland, Austria and Italy were the 'top five' for both outgoing and incoming cross-border debt collection cases in Germany.

Only Debt Collector 2 (one of the not specialised firms) named England [66] as the fifth most important debtor country. However, further questioning on the number of cases relating to England revealed that England was also of importance for the cross-border debt collection market in Germany. All three specialised debt collectors collect debts from debtors resident in England. That constitutes 10 – 15% of their outgoing cross-border collection activities.[67]

For one of the specialised firms the United States was the fifth important creditor's country. The US was not listed as one of the five most important

---

[66] England (not the whole of the UK) was taken as one area of empirical research. Therefore, the questions in the questionnaire referred to 'England'.

[67] For one of the three specialised firms, the proportion of debtors from England in their total workload has remained at 10% since 1985. For the remaining two firms the proportion of outgoing debt collection for England for the years 1985, 1990 and 1994 were 15%, 15% and 17% for one firm and for the other 13%, 10% and 5%. For incoming cross-border cases from England the figures for one specialised firm for the years 1985, 1990 and 1994 were 10%, 14% and 16%, whereas the other two firms had no English clients at all.

markets by the other firms. It is worth noting that other non-European countries, including the United States and Japan, with which Germany currently carries out approximately 40% of its foreign trade [68] are underrepresented in this context. This is of particular interest when one considers that as a result of a lack of bilateral conventions on reciprocal enforcement of judgments, 'judicial debt collection methods' are more difficult in cross-border legal relations with these countries.[69]

4. Characteristics of Parties and Their Receivables

a) Main clientele

The clients of one of the three specialised debt collection agencies are always other (foreign or domestic) debt collection agencies which have no cross-border debt collection departments. As a result, it becomes impossible to ascertain the characteristics of creditors. One of the remaining two specialised debt collectors obtains its foreign and domestic cross-border debt collection clients exclusively from import and export business. The third one obtains most of its domestic cross-border debt collection clients from mail order companies and exporters, whereas its clients resident abroad are exclusively exporters who export goods to Germany. Debt Collector 2 (one of the not specialised firms) lists the following lines of business: mail order companies, banks, insurers, publishers, individual traders, credit-card institutions.

---

[68] See *Zahlen zur wirtschaftlichen Entwicklung der Bundesrepublik Deutschland 1995* (ed.: Institut der Deutschen Wirtschaft) (Cologne: Deutscher Instituts-Verlag, 1994), Tabelle 35: Außenhandel nach Ländern und Ländergruppen.

[69] The fact that debt collection cases in relation to Japan are small in number may be partially explained by the legal culture in Japan, where individuals and businesses are less litigious than in Europe and in the US [Horst Raabe, 'Die japanische Zivilprozeßordnung und die Zwangsvollstreckung in Japan', *Deutsche Gerichtsvollzieher-Zeitung*, 102. Jahrgang, no. 1 (1987), pp. 5–7, including comparative statistical data from 1971] and because Japanese multinationals have their own subsidiaries abroad, which therefore limits their involvement in 'cross-border' disputes. Hanno von Freyhold, 'Cross-Border Legal Interactions in New York Courts', in Volkmar Gessner (ed.), *Foreign Courts – Civil Litigation in Foreign Legal Cultures* (Aldershot: Dartmonth, 1996), pp. 43–148, p. 69.

202 Making Foreign People Pay

b) Types of claims

The average amount of cross-border debt collected by Debt Collector 2 does 'not differ from the average amount of a domestic claim'.[70] That is, DM 1,000 for debts arising from the sale of goods and DM 6,000 for debts arising from loans.

The three specialised firms provide different figures. The average amount of cross-border debt collected by one is DM 9,000. This figure may appear too small for cross-border commercial transactions, which could suggest that the majority of the debtors are non-trade debtors. However, with regard to the characteristics of debtors in England (around 10% of all the foreign debtors) the debt collection agency noted that 'frequently the debtor-firm is a limited liability company', which implies that commercial debts due from foreign debtors are also frequently collected through the agency. In fact, the average amount of debts collected by this firm on behalf of foreign creditors is higher than the average amount of debt collected in domestic debt collection cases. One of the two other specialised firms stated that the average amount of a claim in an outgoing cross-border collection is DM 10,000 – 20,000. The average amount of an incoming claim is however not different to a domestic claim. One specialised firm provided more precise figures: the average debt in outgoing collection cases was DM 830 and the average debt for incoming cases was DM 1,300. Most of the English and Turkish debtors with whom the firm dealt were NATO personnel (who return home after completing military service in Germany) and other individual debtors (possibly Turkish employees who return to their country). This confirms the assumption that cross-border consumer debts are also collected by commercial debt collectors.

This data indicates that the average amount of debt collected in cross-border cases is generally higher than that in domestic debt collections. Both consumers and commercial firms are among the debtors. Consequently, unlike judicial methods of debt collection, commercial cross-border debt collection is also suitable for small claims. A recent survey [71] showed that commencing a cross-border lawsuit or cross-border enforcement of a

---

70 Average domestic claim collected by debt collection agencies is DM 1,000 – 1,500 (reported by the Vice-President of Federal Association of the German Debt Collection Agencies, in *Frankfurter Allgemeine Zeitung*, 6.10.1993; *Neues Deutschland*, 26.4.1994).
71 von Freyhold and Vial, 'Report on the Cost of Judicial Proceedings in the European Union'. See *supra* Chapter 7: Factors Impeding Access to Justice in Cross-Border Debt Collection.

domestic judgment is unpractical for any claim for less than ECU 2,000. Such a debt collection through 'judicial methods' will cost an average of ECU 2,489 at the debtor's place of residence and at the creditor's place of residence an average of ECU 2,437 in EU countries. The duration of the proceedings would be an average of 23.5 months and 29 months in the debtors' and creditors' countries, respectively.

c) Types of debts collected

The debt collectors were asked how frequently judgment debts appear in cross-border debt collections compared to domestic debt collections. It was assumed that once a creditor had hired a lawyer, gone to court and obtained a judgment, he would prefer to further utilise the judicial enforcement mechanism, that is, he would seek to enforce the judgment after having obtained an exequatur order from the competent court in the debtor's country of residence. This assumption however proved to be incorrect. Both judgment debts and non-judgment debts are collected across borders. However, the business practices vary between the debt collection agencies. One specialised firm collects a negligible amount of judgment debts; the others collect considerably more.

In response to the above question ('whether judgment debts more frequently appear in cross-border debt collections') Debt Collector 2 replied to the effect that their share of judgment debts is *higher* in cross-border debt collection compared to their domestic debt collection. The three specialised firms gave varied responses. One stated, unlike Debt Collector 2, that with regard to the receivables of German creditors abroad and the receivables of foreign resident creditors in Germany, the percentage of judgment debts (and debts evidenced by a summary -procedure default order) in cross-border debt collection is lower than compared to the same percentage in domestic debt collection cases. One of the remaining two specialised firms accepts *only* non-judgment debts for outgoing cross-border debt collections. For incoming collections it also accepts judgment debts, but the number of judgment debts from foreign creditors is negligible: 0.5% in 1985; 0.7% in 1990 and 0.4% in 1994. The share of judgment debts collected by the same firm in domestic debt collections was however 15% in 1985; 17% in 1990 and 8% in 1994. The last specialised debt collector was not asked by its clients resident abroad to collect judgment debts in Germany. With regard to the outgoing cross-border debt collections, 35% of the debts are collected abroad through court proceedings with the assistance of a foreign lawyer.

204   Making Foreign People Pay

Non-judgment debts are then more frequent in both cross-border debt collections and domestic debt collection cases. This supports the assumption that debt collection agencies do not have a complementary, but rather an alternative debt recovery method to the judicial debt recovery procedures.

5. Debt Collection Methods and International Co-operation

a) Comparison of debt collection methods in cross-border and domestic cases

With the exception of 'personal visits' to the debtor's home or work place which cannot be made in some foreign countries (Debt Collector 2 and one of the specialised firms), all debt collectors state that the methods used in cross-border debt collection are not different from those used in domestic cases. As stated above, court proceedings are also used.

The summary debt recovery procedure provided by the German Code of Civil Procedure [72] is unpopular among cross-border debt collectors in Germany despite the positive provisions made in the 1968 Brussels and 1985 Lugano Conventions on reciprocal enforcement of foreign judgments among the EU and EFTA countries.[73] Two of the specialised firms do not use the procedure as, in cases involving the courts, they prefer to sue the debtor in his home country. Two other specialised firms find the cross-border enforcement of summary court orders 'difficult' and 'economically not feasible'. This is due to the fact that in order to have a German summary court order declared enforceable under the Brussels (or Lugano) Convention, the order and the relevant documents must be translated into the court language and that should the debtor raise an objection against the 'decision authorising enforcement', additional court proceedings are necessary. This enforcement then becomes very expensive and time consuming. In addition, in many such cases the creditor is not able to provide the documents proving the service of process abroad.[74]

---

72   See *supra* Chapter 1: Debt Recovery in Germany.
73   See German CCP §688 III, Brussels Convention Art. 25; Rolf Wagner, 'Verfahrenrechtliche Probleme im Auslandsmahnverfahren', *Recht der Internationalen Wirtschaft*, 41. Jahrgang (1995), pp. 89–97.
74   Additional information collected through telephone conversations with the debt collectors who completed the questionnaire. See Brussels Convention, Arts. 36 and 46, 47, 48(2), respectively.

b) Co-operation with corresponding / sister debt collection agencies and foreign lawyers abroad

'Cross-border debt collection' is not necessarily executed by the German debt collectors themselves, but rather, the German debt collection agencies co-operate with corresponding or sister debt collection agencies or lawyers in the relevant foreign country. As one of the firms stated:

> Only competent service provided on location can secure the client a return commensurate with the fees paid. Thus, neither [the Debt Collection Agency] nor the client has to deal with foreign legal systems, lawyers, enforcement difficulties *etc.* in each individual case, which would not be economical.

Accordingly, three of the five larger debt collectors never provide cross-border debt collection services directly through their offices in Germany. One of the two non-specialised debt collectors and one of the specialised firms work exclusively in cooperation with corresponding debt collection agencies abroad. The other unspecialised firm has sister debt collection agencies in some foreign countries and corresponding debt collectors in others. The remaining two specialised firms handle some of the cross-border cases through their own offices in Germany, as well as having sister and corresponding debt collection agencies in some foreign countries. Not only neighbouring countries such as Austria and France, but also Turkey is among the countries where debt collection services are provided through German offices of one specialised firm.

With regard to incoming cross-border debt collection, one of the three specialised firms establishes initial contact with most of its clients directly through its offices in Germany. One of the others obtains its clients regularly through corresponding debt collection agencies abroad. Another specialised firm obtains its clients both directly through their office in Germany and through corresponding or sister debt collection agencies abroad.

None of the five debt collectors work with German lawyers for cross-border debt collection. However, two of the firms co-operate with foreign resident lawyers regularly either directly or through their sister collection agencies, and two of the remaining firms only occasionally. One of the former generally prefers to co-operate with foreign lawyers where the debt

206 Making Foreign People Pay

is contested by the debtor. This is always the case in Turkey where this collection agency regard the co-operation of a lawyer as a necessity.[75]

However, with regard to the incoming cross-border debt collection cases, where court proceedings are necessary, all debt collectors co-operate with lawyers resident in Germany.

The information collected above indicates that international co-operation is of great importance for cross-border debt collection. Without well organised business contacts with sister or corresponding debt collection agencies and foreign lawyers abroad, cross-border debt collection is neither commercially feasible nor professionally practicable. This explains why most of the transnationally organised credit reference agencies [76] also have debt collection departments [77] and sometimes even a special department for cross-border collections.

International co-operation among debt collectors is also supported by international professional organisations, which will be discussed below.

It is also noteworthy that the co-operation of a German lawyer is never required by a commercial debt collector for debt collection abroad. Even in most of the disputed cases, the services which a domestic law firm can offer for an outgoing debt collection case (*i.e.* preparation of proceedings abroad for a foreign lawyer), can also be provided by the debt collector himself. Accordingly, a creditor may reduce his costs by going to a commercial debt collector instead of a lawyer. The legal fees for preparation of the foreign proceedings may be extremely high, especially with respect to some Northern European countries: for a claim of ECU 2,000 for example, ECU 750 in United Kingdom, ECU 800 in Sweden and ECU 1,300 in Finland.[78]

---

75 In fact, commercial debt collection agencies do not exist in Turkey. Whether establishing such undertakings would be against the statutory monopoly of lawyers to provide legal services in Turkey (Lawyers Act 1969, Art. 35 I) is questionable.
76 *E.g.* Dun and Bradstreet (Schimmelpfeng), Credit Reform, Bürgel, LIC.
77 Generally see Günter Döhler, 'Außergerichtliches Mahn- und Inkassowesen - Arbeitsteilung mit den Unternehmen', *Die Welt*, 21.12.1981.
78 von Freyhold and Vial, 'Report on the Cost of Judicial Proceedings in European Union', p. 123.

6. Difficulties and Success Rates in Comparison to Domestic Debt Collection

a) Difficulties in cross-border debt collection

Two of the three specialised firms experience difficulties in locating the debtor's address in the foreign country, mainly due to an inadequate registration system in some countries (*e.g.* England and Turkey). Two of the three agencies also complain about the loss of security rights, *e.g.* reservation of title in the cross-border sale of goods. In particular, reservation of title clauses which are incorporated in standard contract terms in Germany are regarded as void in many foreign jurisdictions unless a document containing the standard contract terms is separately signed by the debtor.[79] Other difficulties reported by the debt collectors include currency restrictions (one of the non-specialised firms) and converting the debt in DM into foreign currencies (one non-specialised and one specialised debt collector). None of the debt collectors reported other difficulties or ticked more than three out of five 'difficulties' listed in the questionnaire. Differences in statutes concerning limitations in various countries are not seen as a problem, although this is mentioned as a difficulty in the literature.

b) Comparison of the success rates between cross-border and domestic debt collection

It may be assumed that, taking account of the barriers of legal and cultural differences, the success rates in cross-border debt collection are lower than the success rates in domestic debt collection. This is, however, not the case.

One of the three specialised firms finds neither the debtors resident abroad who owe creditors in Germany, nor the debtors resident in Germany who owe creditors resident abroad less co-operative than the debtors in domestic debt collection cases. One of the remaining two firms states that the success rate in outgoing cross-border debt collection cases (*i.e.* where the debtor is abroad) is lower, but the success rate in incoming cross-border cases does not differ from that in domestic cases. The other specialised firm's success rate in outgoing and incoming cross-border debt collection is equal and even higher than the same in domestic debt collections.

---

79 Additional information collected through telephone conversation with debt collectors who completed the questionnaire.

7. Costs of Cross-border Debt Collection

The terms of a debt collection contract between the debt collection agencies and their clients do not differ from those in a domestic debt collection contract. However, the form of power of attorney obtained from the creditor varies in different countries and the purchasing of bad debts is not always permitted. Three specialised firms provided information about cross-border debt collection fees and costs, as summarised below (Table 10.1).[80] The numbers separated with a stroke refer to the fees charged by different firms.

Table 10.1 Fees and costs of cross-border debt collection in Germany (1995)

JUDGMENT DEBTS

Creditor in Germany / Debtor in England:

Debt amounts to	DM 500.-	DM 5,000.-	DM 50,000.-
Debt collection fee	DM 100.- / none	DM 100.-	DM 100.- / none
Success fee	50%	50% - 20%	35% / 15%

Creditor in Germany / Debtor in Turkey:

Debt amounts to	DM 500.-	DM 5,000.-	DM 50,000.-
Debt collection fee	DM 100.-	DM 100.- / DM 150-	DM 100.-
Success fee	50%	50% / 15%	40%

Creditor in England / Debtor in Germany:

Debt amounts to	DM 500.-	DM 5,000.-	DM 50,000.-
Debt collection fee	DM 40.- / DM 60.- / DM 75.-	DM 40.- / none	DM 3,500.- / subject to negotiation / none
Success fee	50% / 30% / none	50% / 30% / 10%	subject to negotiation / 10%
Expected external costs	DM 20.- / none	DM 300.- / none	DM 500.- / none

---

80 Not all parts of the relevant questions were answered by all three firms. In addition, some questions were inapplicable for some of them. For example, one firm does not collect judgment debts in foreign countries.

Creditor in Turkey / Debtor in Germany:

Debt amounts to	DM 500.-	DM 5,000.-	DM 50,000.-
Debt collection fee	DM 40.- / DM 60.-	DM 40.- / DM 300.-	DM 3,500 / subject to negotiation
Success fee	50% / DM 30.-	50% / 30%	subject to negotiation
Expected external costs	DM 20.- / none	DM 300.- / none	DM 500.- / none

NON-JUDGMENT DEBTS

Creditor in Germany / Debtor in England:

Debt amounts to	DM 500.-	DM 5,000.-	DM 50,000.-
Debt collection fee	DM 100.- / DM 60.- / none	DM 200.- / DM 300.- / DM 100.-	DM 500.- / DM 3,500.-/ none
Success fee	18% / 30% / 50%	18% / 30% / 20%	subject to negotiation / 30% / 15%
Expected external costs	DM 100.- / none	DM 300.- / none	changeable / none

Creditor in Germany / Debtor in Turkey:

Debt amounts to	DM 500.-	DM 5,000.-	DM 50,000.-
Debt collection fee	DM 100.-	DM 200.- / DM 150.-	DM 500.-
Success fee	30%	30% / 25%	subject to negotiation
Expected external costs	DM 100.- / none	DM 300.- / none	changeable / none

Creditor in England *or* in Turkey / Debtor in Germany:

Debt amounts to	DM 500.-	DM 5,000.-	DM 50,000.-
Debt collection fee	DM 48.- / DM 60.-	DM 315.- / DM 300.-	DM 3,500.- / subject to negotiation
Success fee	5% / DM 30.-	5% / DM 30.-	DM 30.- / subject to negotiation
Expected external costs	DM 20.- / none	DM 20.- / none	DM 20.- / none

The following conclusions can be drawn from these figures:

(a) Cross-border debt collection between Germany and Turkey is not more expensive than between Germany and England. Considering the lack of a bilateral convention for reciprocal enforcement of judgments between

Germany and Turkey and the lack of commercial debt collection agencies in Turkey (resulting in the necessary assistance of a lawyer), it was expected that debt collection (particularly the collection of non-judgment debts) in Turkey would be more expensive for the German creditors than the collection of debts in England. However, this was only the case for one of the firms. For the other two specialised firms, fees charged in both outgoing and incoming cross-border collections involving Turkey were not higher than the same charged for cases in connection with England.

(b) Notwithstanding the oligopolist nature of the cross-border debt collection market in Germany, fees and costs vary considerably from debt collector to debt collector. Each debt collector uses different tariffs. The combination of costs and fees also varies from one firm to another: for example, one collector charges higher standard fees but lower success fees and another vice versa.

(c) The above conclusions confirm the commercial nature of the debt collection agencies. Services offered by debt collection agencies are not 'legal services'. Debt collection, including cross-border debt collection, is a service industry. In order to be sold, debt collection service must be priced reasonably; that is, the fees and costs involved must be commensurate with the service provided and each debt collector must avoid pricing itself out of the market. This explains why a cross-border debt amounting to ECU 2,000 cannot be economically collected by a law firm, but can be collected by a debt collector.

11 Commercial Cross-Border Debt Collection in England

A. COMMERCIAL DEBT COLLECTION UNDER ENGLISH LAW

1. General

Commercial debt collection agencies are widely used in England as an alternative to going to court.[1] The actual number of English debt collection agencies is not known.[2] The number of debt collection agencies in the London area is estimated to be around 200. As a result of developments in computer technology, which facilitates the debt collection process (filing, accounting and document production), the number of agencies has been on the increase.[3]

Most of the debt collection agencies in England operate all over the country, although some of the small firms are local debt collection agencies.[4] Commercial firms are advised to opt for the nation-wide debt collection agencies for long term contracts as local debt collection agencies are more suitable for individual cases.[5,6]

---

[1] Practitioner guides refer to debt collection agencies as an alternative to the legal profession in England. See *e.g. Gatenby's Recovery of Money*, pp. 1–2; James Richardson, *Debt Recovery in Europe* (London: Blackstone 1993), p. 156.

[2] As will be seen below, this is because not all debt collection agencies are subject to licensing or registration in England. And the 'consumer credit licence' which is necessary for some of the debt collection agencies is not only required for the debt collection business.

[3] See *Gatenby's Recovery of Money*, pp. 257–60.

[4] A lecture given by Kurt Obermaier, the President of Federation of European National Collection Associations, at the annual meeting of Federal Association of German Debt Collection Agencies in Bonn on 5 May 1995. (Hereinafter 'Obermaier, 5.5.1995'.)

[5] Obermaier, 5.5.1995.

[6] Debts due to German creditors can also be collected in England through the debt collection bureau of the German Chamber of Trade and Industry in London. See Müller

2. Consumer Credit Act 1974

In contrast to Germany, there is no detailed legislation relating to debt collection agencies in England. Nevertheless, since the Consumer Credit Act 1974 came into force, a licence is required to carry on debt collection for consumer credit.[7]

For the purpose of the Consumer Credit Act 1974 debt collection is defined as the taking of steps to procure payment of debts due under consumer credit agreements and consumer hire agreements.[8] Only such persons or firms dealing in debt collecting within the meaning of the 1974 Act are subject to the licensing requirement under the Act. Not only debt collection agencies as such are however confined to the licensing; it suffices that the debt collecting activity is carried on in the course of some other business. Solicitors collecting debts for clients without recourse to proceedings and professional receivers and liquidators of companies are, for example, covered by the licensing requirement.[9]

Commercial purchasers of bad debts, firms dealing with instalment sales or rental agreements, and factors who factor debts outstanding from individual traders or partnerships [10] are, if they are involved in collecting debts due under consumer credit or consumer hire agreements, among those who are subject to the licensing.[11] A debt collection company which is based or incorporated outside England is also required to hold a licence in England if it is involved in collecting consumer debts in this country.[12]

---

and Hök, 'Großbritannien', *Deutsche Vollstreckungstitel im Ausland*, pp. 30–2. The German Chamber of Trade and Industry in London is incorporated as a limited company. Information collected from the Chamber showed that the debt collection service of the Chamber is not different from or less expensive than that provided by other private debt collectors.

7   Consumer Credit Act 1974 s. 145(7).
8   A consumer credit agreement is a credit agreement (*i.e.* a cash loan or any other form of financial accommodation agreement such as hire purchase, credit sale, *etc.*) in which the debtor is an individual (or an unincorporated group of individuals *e.g.* a partnership) and the credit provided does not exceed £15,000. A consumer hire agreement is similarly defined: it is a hire agreement made with an individual for the hire of goods which is capable of lasting more than three months and which does not require the hirer to pay more than £15,000. (Consumer Credit Act 1974 ss 8 and 15.)
9   R. M. Goode, *Consumer Credit Law* (London: Butterworths, 1989), pp. 188 and 776.
10 Cf. *supra* Chapter 10: Commercial Debt Collection in Germany.
11 Goode, *Consumer Credit Law*, p. 777.
12 See *ibid.*, p. 804.

Application for a licence is made to the Director of Fair Trading under the provisions of Part III of the Consumer Credit Act 1974,[13] with appeal allowed to the Secretary of State against the licensing decisions of the Director of Fair Trading.[14] Unlike in Germany, the debt collecting licence in England is granted not to a debt collector personally, but to the company which carries out debt collection.[15]

3. Debt Collection Methods

Debt collection methods which are used by British debt collection agencies are, in general, similar to those used in Germany. Initial contact with the debtor is made by a simple demand letter which is normally followed by a telephone call and, when necessary and economically feasible, by court proceedings.

As a result of the efficient 'postcode' system, it is not difficult to locate the debtor if only the postcode is known. A practical difficulty in 'collecting' debts is that, more than 5% of employees in England do not have a bank account, as a result of which some local debt collection agencies have to employ persons to collect instalment payments by going door-to-door 'the same as the milkman does'.[16]

English debt collection agencies' power to initiate and conduct court proceedings is greater than that of German debt collection agencies. That is, English debt collection agencies do not so often require the assistance of a lawyer. *Firstly*, although the practice varies from court to court, summary procedures in county courts may, in many districts, be initiated by a debt collector by having a county court summons issued, without legal representation.[17] *Secondly*, once a judgment in favour of the creditor is obtained, the debt collection agency may always represent its client before the court (even before the High Court) throughout the execution procedure.[18]

---

13   Consumer Credit Act 1974, s. 147.
14   *Ibid.*, s. 150.
15   Dietrich, *Inkasso-Unternehmungen*, p. 148.
16   Obermaier, 5.5.1995.
17   Only some of the county courts reject such applications which are made by the debt collection agencies, on such grounds as 'this court does not accept applications from debt collectors', *ibid.*
18   *Ibid.*

4. Costs

Debt collection fees in England are, as is the case in Germany, not subject to an official tariff. According to the market practices and subject to various factors, such fees can amount to between 10 – 35% of the debt to be collected. A single debt of less than £500 is not worth collecting through a debt collection agency.[19]

The debt collection agency's costs cannot be recovered from the debtor, unless such recovery of costs has been contractually agreed between the debtor and the creditor, and the relevant amount has been claimed in the court proceedings. Such contractual provisions sometimes appear in standard contract terms which are used in international trade, but in domestic contracts are quite rare.[20]

B. CROSS-BORDER DEBT COLLECTION IN ENGLAND

1. Introduction

One characteristic of the cross-border debt collection market in England [21] which distinguishes it from the German market is its diversity. As discussed above, cross-border collections are carried out in Germany only by a handful of larger agencies which are affiliates of international concerns. In contrast, debt collectors in England which provide overseas services are more in number and various in types.

Only a few of the English debt collection agencies which are involved in cross-border debt collection are larger international firms on the German model. The majority are medium sized agencies handling both domestic and cross-border collections and small independent firms which specialise

---

19 *Ibid.*
20 Obermaier, 5.5.1995.
21 Two debt collectors who were interviewed in England criticised the term 'cross-border': in good (British) English one should use the word 'overseas' ('overseas collections'). Again, English Debt Collector 2 was using the term 'export collections'. When writing about English debt collection agencies the author usually preferred the term 'overseas collections'. 'Export collections' was not suitable, since not all cross-border debts collected by agencies arise from export trade, *e.g.* see English Debt Collectors 1 and 11 below. With respect, the term 'cross-border' was also kept in this study, since 'overseas' may sometimes be meaningless for Turkey and Germany which are not island states. See also, *Cross Border Debt Recovery: A manual for exporters and importers* (London: Lawyers International Inkasso, 1996).

in cross-border collections as their main business. Borrowing the terms from one of the interviewees [22] and to adopt US legal jargon,[23] the first group will be named 'superleague agencies' and the third group will be named 'boutique type' agencies. The second group will be called simply 'medium sized' agencies.

Superleague agencies are those firms with numerous affiliates or correspondent agencies in various countries. As in Germany, these larger firms are few in number [24] with some also belonging to international networks of agencies for credit reference. English debt collection agencies providing 'full international service', that is, literally for all countries except those at war, do not number more than three.[25]

Medium sized agencies are normally designed for domestic debt collections.[26] Some of these firms do however handle overseas collections occasionally, especially at the request of a regular client. The reason why a medium sized debt collector in England, unlike a German counterpart, does not forward such cross-border cases to a specialised firm, may be the advantage of using his own language in communication with the debtor. This is the case at least for most of the business-to-business collections.

Boutique type agencies deserve this name due to being small debt collectors (firms run by 2 – 3 persons) who provide a small number of clients with a high quality specialised service for overseas collections. Their clients as well as their debtors are usually customers and suppliers from the same branch of the economy and may even be exclusively from a single line of business.

During January – February 1996 the author visited 14 debt collection agencies in the Greater London area, Kent, Leicester and Cheshire. In addition, some debt collectors were interviewed on 22 February 1996 at the annual 'Meeting of Members' of the Credit Services Association [27] in Leicester, and a debt collector from Cheshire was interviewed in London

---

22   English Debt Collector 1.
23   See Flood, *The Legal Profession in the United States*, p. 15.
24   According to English Debt Collector 6, the number of these firms is six.
25   English Debt Collector 13.
26   According to English Debt Collector 6, these number approximately 100 throughout the UK.
27   See *infra* Chapter 12: Business Organisations of Debt Collection Agencies.

216 Making Foreign People Pay

during a weekend visit for a conference. Most of the interviewees also completed the questionnaire [28] during or after the interview.

As for the interviews conducted with lawyers, the information which was collected through interviews has been used in other parts of this study, namely under 'A' in this Chapter and under Chapter 2 (Debt Recovery in England) and Chapter 7 (Factors Impeding Access to Justice in Cross-Border Debt Collection). Eight selected interviews have been reconstructed below in full in an attempt to present an accurate picture of the work of English debt collectors in the field of cross-border debt recovery. These interviews are divided into three groups according to the distinction made above, that is, superleague firms, medium sized firms and boutique type agencies.

In contrast to the case for lawyers and law firms, the work of debt collection agencies has not been discussed exhaustively in socio-legal literature.[29] Therefore, the interviews held with English debt collectors are reported differently from those held with lawyers, in an attempt to provide a more comprehensive study of the debt collection business. Such study will also include the physical working environment. The author believes such details are important, for the differences between a law office and the office of a debt collector mirror the differences between the debt collection business and the work of lawyers.[30]

2. Superleague Firms

a) *English Debt Collector 1* [31]

English Debt Collector 1 is an example of a superleague agency. It was established in 1993, originally as a boutique type, 'truly international' collection agency for overseas debts with the aim to:

---

28   See *supra* Chapter 10: Commercial Cross-Border Debt Collection in Germany; *infra* Annex II.
29   Rock, *Making People Pay* (pp. 76–106) includes the most detailed discussion, but it refers only to the domestic collections, with emphasis on consumer debts.
30   The author believes that 'animation' is acceptable in scientific literature, especially concerning empirical research, as far as it serves a faithful representation of facts.
31   The interview was not tape-recorded. A record sheet was prepared from memory immediately after the interview. Quotations below were also reconstructed from memory using notes made during the interview. They represent the interviewee's choice of words to the best of the author's memory.

fill the vacuum behind the 'superleague' agencies by providing a high quality personal service to a selected client base.

However, since then the firm has grown to become a large agency with world-wide connections (with offices in North America, Korea, Mauritius and Bahrain and affiliates in more than 100 countries) and has also expanded into the international credit information business. It currently employs fifteen persons in the UK offices and a further 100 persons in its foreign branches. Among its clients are many important multinationals and credit insurance corporations as well as many international freight companies. Currently, two thirds of the company's turnover comes from overseas collections.

English Debt Collector 1 is situated outside central London in a residential area where there are few office buildings. As an interview was requested, one of the two directors suggested to meet 'somewhere in the City'. This director and two of his colleagues would be in London the next day and it was suggested to meet near an Underground station. Two directors and the 'company secretary' were interviewed in a public house, which saved time. They forwarded the completed questionnaire afterwards. Pragmatism is part of the business culture of debt collectors. An English solicitor for whom time is money would never arrange such a 'pub meeting'.

The public image of the firm is very important. It is a member of the American Collectors Association,[32] which according to the interviewee means,

> that the company has to operate to a stringent code of practice, and is part of a drive to improve an industry which does have its share of twilight areas and dubious operators.

The company secretary is a credit manager who is a member of the Institute of Credit Management (ICM),[33] which entails being personally under the control of a professional organisation. National or international organisations of which they were not members were deemed to be either 'unimportant' or 'not useful'.

In its advertisement leaflet, the firm has drafted a 'Client Charter' according to which,

> any client who receives less than the promises embodied in this Charter is urged to call the undersigned on: (telephone number).

---

32   See *infra* Chapter 12: Business Organisations of Debt Collection Agencies.
33   See *infra* Chapter 12: Business Organisations of Debt Collection Agencies.

218 Making Foreign People Pay

The interviewees were apparently concerned about the negative public opinion of the debt collection industry and were attempting to convey the message that they were not one of 'those firms'. They complained about the lack of compulsory insurance for professional liability of debt collectors in England: when a debt collection agency goes bankrupt, monies owed to clients are vested in the trustee in bankruptcy and clients remain at the bottom of the rank of creditors as unsecured creditors.

The interviewees also supported the idea of EU-wide regulation of the debt collection industry, which would not only bring discipline to the market but could also improve the legal rights of debt collectors in England. They believe debt collectors in the UK to be disadvantaged in that they are not, like for example their colleagues in Holland or Germany, able to charge the debtor with interest payments [34] and their fees are not recoverable from the debtor.

In the years 1993, 1994 and 1995, English Debt Collector 1 had 200, 350 and 600 cross-border cases respectively, which represented 10%, 15% and 20% of the number of cases dealt with, but 10%, 30% and 74% of the annual turnover. Most of the business of English Debt Collector 1 is outgoing in that the firm works more frequently for domestic creditors which are owed by debtors resident abroad rather than the converse. In 1995, the firm collected some £8,000,000 in cross-border debts. Of this sum, £500,000 was collected for foreign clients. Eastern Europe, the Far East and Middle East are more important for business than Western Europe and the US. The amount of German related cases in its annual turnover from 1993 – 1995 was between 0.25 – 1.5%. Clients are from various lines of business, all of which are typical for cross-border transactions, *i.e.* export trade, insurance, banking and tourism sectors. The reason for default is according to the interviewee, that 'the client has not properly credit vetted the debtor prior to supply'.

The average amount of foreign debts is greater than in the UK (domestic) cases and the percentage of judgment debts is lower: in the years 1993 – 1995, 5% of domestic debts collected in the UK were judgment debts; in cross-border collections the same was between 1 - 1.5%.

Cross-border claims are handled regularly by foreign branches or affiliates abroad. Especially in Far East collections, the lack of personnel who speak the local languages and the time difference make direct telephone contact from London impractical.

---

34   See *Gatenby's Recovery of Money*, pp. 116–25, esp. pp. 123–4.

It is never necessary to consult English lawyers for overseas collections, but they do occasionally deal with foreign lawyers normally through their foreign agents. This is also the case for Germany. In Turkey, where there are no debt collection agencies as such, the firm deals directly with Turkish lawyers.

'Collection techniques' employed by the firm or its foreign contacts are similar world-wide. Legal action outside Europe is only conducted if the case is substantial. They regard legal action as a last resort of little efficiency. Debtors are aware of this and they dispute the claim in order to force the creditor to sue: 'a high proportion of Far Eastern claims are' for example 'contested as not being due, due to quality of goods supplied'.

The same is true for taking legal action in Britain, be it against a debtor resident in the country who owes to a foreign creditor or against a foreign resident debtor who owes to a British creditor.

> Where the client is outside the European Union, many thousand miles away, should the case proceed to legal action, the debtor will invariably insist on the client lodging security for costs with the (English) court. This may amount to many thousands of pounds. Should the debtor provide even the sketchiest of technical defences, the client then has to make himself available for attendance at court. Invariably the costs and time involved do not make it viable, when this situation occurs, for the client to attend and the debt is written off.

They simplify their experience abroad in execution of English judgments as follows:

> in Western Europe, except Spain: satisfactory / Far East and the US: sketchy / South Africa and Eastern Europe: unsatisfactory / in West Africa: impossible.

The only difficulties which English Debt Collector 1 ticked in the questionnaire are those difficulties arising from currency restrictions and converting the foreign currency into Sterling. This is most probably due to the fact that its main areas of business are Eastern Europe, the Far East and Middle East.

Although there is no registration system in Turkey, for example, the firm has not encountered difficulty tracing debtors in Turkey.[35] In Turkey, the firm suffers most from devaluation of the Turkish Lira:

---

35 One of their corresponding law firms in Turkey is 'Turkish Law Firm 2'. See *supra* Chapter 5: Role of Lawyers in Cross-Border Debt Collection.

220   Making Foreign People Pay

> Recently, a legal debt due to a client was US $15,000. Once converted into local currency, due to devaluation, the amount actually recovered for the client was US $9,000.

Debtors are not less co-operative in cross-border cases:

> Not really, as soon as we get involved, the debtor realises that the creditor is no longer thousands of miles away.

The firm uses the same standard terms of contract throughout the world. They do not purchase bad debts. Collection fees are success fees only and are solely based on the age of the debt. The amount of debt or the fact that a judgment has already been obtained makes no difference. They are however always prepared to bargain with their clients when this is requested. Their tariff is as follows:

Age of debt	Europe - excl. UK	US / Canada	Elsewhere
up to 180 days:	18%	20%	22%
6 months – 1 year:	25%	27%	30%
1 year + :	30%	32%	35%

In addition to these 'fees', external costs must be expected; where the debtor is in the UK, £75 additional costs for a £500 claim; £300 for a £5,000 claim and £2,000 for a £500,000 claim. Where the debtor is in Turkey or in Germany the additional costs would be:

for a claim of	£500	£5,000	£500,000
in Turkey	(no action)	£750	£5,000
in Germany	£100	£200	£1,000[36]

b) *English Debt Collector 12* [37]

After meeting the 'client services director' of English Debt Collector 12 at the 1996 annual meeting of the Collection Services Association, the author interviewed the 'managing director' of the firm at his office.

The firm was located on the second floor of a two storey pre-fabricated building in a less pleasant area not far from a train station in a London suburb. Between 10 and 15 people were working in a large hall at desks fully

---

36   Additional costs for a collection in Germany may be less than a domestic collection.
37   Interview was not tape-recorded.

packed with computers and dossiers. The managing director was using one of two small offices separated with large glass windows from the main hall. He welcomed the author at the entrance and showed him out at the end of the visit, as is done in law firms and in other larger collection agencies, as he explained, not only to be courteous but also because it is required under data protection regulations.

The firm is the English affiliate of the 'European Collectors Association' (ECA) and a member of the Credit Services Association (CSA). The interviewee is a member of the Institute of Credit Management (ICM).[38] However, the firm resigned from a well-known 'superleague' of international debt collection agencies, as that particular organisation 'made it very easy to become members'.

English Debt Collector 12 started up as a credit reporting agency. For many years, they produced 'in depth' credit reports for a small number of clients. Over time, this type of credit reporting became less popular so they began to carry out debt collection as their main business. They still do credit reporting for some clients, but this has become a secondary activity.

Originally they used to collect business-to-business debts only. For some years they have also been collecting individual (consumer) debts. They entered this area of business due to a debtor company going bankrupt, leaving individuals who had given personal guarantees for company debts. They therefore began to deal with people who were not businessmen and later continued to collect non-business debts for other clients. Due to the expense involved, overseas consumer debts are not collected.

Of the firm's total business 40% is international. Yet only three persons, including the director himself, deal with overseas collections.

They collect overseas debts world-wide. They are also specialised in East European countries. The firm's client base is 'both extensive and varied, from the entertainment industry to high street banks'.

For the debtors in Eastern Europe, collections are made from their office in London, where they have employees who speak the languages of these countries. For other overseas collections they regularly employ corresponding agencies.

Their collection methods [39] include telephone calls ('if necessary outside normal day time hours providing that the attempts to contact the

---

38   See *infra* Chapter 12: Business Organisations of Debt Collection Agencies.
39   English Debt Collector 12 prepared a booklet 'Collecting of Outstanding Debt in the UK by Debt Collecting Agencies'. Some quotations below are taken from this booklet.

debtor are at reasonable times') and periodical letters ('increasing in determination and being carefully worded for maximum impact'). 'A response or proposal from the debtor is of utmost importance, *i.e.* the maximum payment or instalment is sought and further dialogue is encouraged.' Personal visits to the debtor can also be effective not only when collecting debts from private individuals, but 'also when there is a large amount of money involved in commercial debt'.

English Debt Collector 12 has developed its own software programme for the administration of debt collecting work. According to the advertisement booklet:

> this programme categorises and prioritises accounts according to the average number of credit days taken. These credit days are further reviewed according to the credit limits granted and the number or value of disputed transactions. This enables the firm to concentrate on the whole or part of an account which is most collectable. The payment profiles, ageing lists and collection histories are all available 'at a glance' so that work is not duplicated and a clearer picture presented for whoever deals with the account next time.

The firm avoids using legal processes as far as is possible. 'But in certain instances this is necessary.' In such a case, as a first step, they gather what they call 'pre-sue information', that is, information about the address and solvency of the debtor and of its directors, if the debtor is a company. They then send a lawyer's letter to the debtor which they term 'letter before action'.

> This letter is a last tool for collection as it could place the creditor in a position of either deciding on taking legal action or writing off the debt.

The firm has an in-house lawyer to whom they refer the case after collecting the pre-sue information.

English Debt Collector 12 is, according to the director, an expensive agency, but its success rates are higher than average which makes it economic.

c) English Debt Collector 13 [40]

English Debt Collector 13 is a wholly owned subsidiary of a British credit insurance company ('parent company'). Each year the parent company underwrites more than £50 billion of credit risks world-wide, which amounts

---

[40] The interview was not tape-recorded.

to 60% of the export credit market in the UK. It is also the principal credit insurer in New Zealand and Australia, and enjoys a significant market share in Canada. In broad terms 90% of the group's work is credit insurance and 10% is debt collection.

Two senior members of the firm (the 'managing director' and the 'international supervisor', who spoke fluent German) were interviewed at their office in London.[41] The office was located in a newly built skyscraper with extensive security measures. The author was received with the usual 'prestigious firm' ceremony which he also experienced in City law firms: reception in a waiting room in the main entrance where two well presented female secretaries (middle aged [42]) sat behind an unnecessarily large reception desk, his coat was taken, he had to put on the security card upon which his name was already printed, somebody from the office came to meet him to show the way in *etc.* As will be mentioned below, its prestige is of a positive, commercial value for the firm:

> (the firm's) name alone is very effective at prompting slow payers.

English Debt Collector 13 has its head office and five 'regional offices' in Britain, four offices in Canada, three in Australia and one each in Italy and New Zealand.

The managing director explained that, under the export credit insurance policies of the parent company, it was the client who was responsible to make efforts to collect the debts owed to it. In other words, before claiming for an indemnity from the insurer, the client must have taken all steps to recover the debt, including going to a debt collection agency and/or lawyer where necessary. The debt collection agency employed by the client may be any commercial debt collector, but the parent company also offers its own debt collection service through its subsidiary, *i.e.* English Debt Collector 13. Where the debtor is not insolvent, the client must, as a last resort, commence legal action.

This legal action can also be conducted by the subsidiary firm, through its own 'litigation resources'. Thus, under its 'legal contribution scheme',

> the firm pays the majority of any legal fees and expenses which may be incurred by the client, if an account (which has been insured by the parent company) proved impossible to collect any other way than through legal action. ... The

---

41 The author was given a colourful information booklet about the firm and its collection services which was titled 'Collections: working in harmony to meet your collection challenge'. Some quotations below are taken from this booklet.
42 That is, 'inexperienced people are not employed even as doormen'.

proportion of the firm's contribution will be equal to the terms of the (parent company's) credit insurance policy. If, for instance, the level of indemnity (provided by the parent company) is 80%, then the firm pays (bears) 80% of the client's legal fees.

Of English Debt Collector 13's clients 60% are also clients of the parent company for export credit insurance. Parallel to the parent company's export credit insurance service, the firm provides a world-wide debt collection service, with the one exception of countries at war.

The firm collects not only overseas debts but also debts owed to foreign creditors by British debtors in the UK.

> Customers are drawn from throughout the industry and business spectrum and include established companies as well as thousands of growing businesses.

Textiles, electronics, food and timber exports are the businesses with which the firm deals with most frequently.

The number of overseas collections made in 1995 was less than 1,000. The US, France, Germany, Italy and the Scandinavian countries are, respectively, the five most important debtor countries. The average amount of overseas debts collected by the firm is between £10,000 to 15,000. In most cases, non-payment is either a result of cash flow problems or where there is a dispute about the quality of goods supplied by the creditor.

Overseas collections begin in the London office whereby initial contact is made with the debtor. This may be either by mail, telephone or fax. The firm employs multi-lingual staff. Such direct contact with the debtor is more efficient than 'going through the chain' (of a foreign debt collector and his lawyer). It can take 7 to 8 weeks to receive the first response from the debtor and to commence with negotiations. Foreign debtors are not less co-operative than debtors in Britain. Should these initial attempts prove futile, the next stage involves referring the case to a local debt collector or lawyer, depending on the nature of the case and the country. This two-track system enables the firm to collect easier accounts from England and for the difficult cases to be referred to overseas agents.

In some countries, *e.g.* Portugal and Turkey, the corresponding debt collector may be a lawyer who offers debt collection service as a 'pre-litigation service'. The firm uses foreign law firms 'occasionally'. Unlike in Turkey where language problems can be encountered, the firm always contacts the German lawyers directly from the London office without the involvement of an English law firm.

Before initiating a legal action, the client will be asked for instructions. Recently, the firm started a new 'experiment' for overseas litigation. Instead of suing the debtor abroad in his own country (which was the normal practice until recently), they bring legal actions in England, serving proceedings out of jurisdiction. After obtaining the judgment, they will seek enforcement abroad. The managing director is personally sceptical about the success of this experiment.

English Debt Collector 13 makes collections for foreign resident clients by employing the usual debt collection methods. The firm also has a separate 'letter service' which is designed *only* for issuing collection letters to 'slow payers'.

> The letter service is available for low value commercial and consumer accounts of up to £750... Two collection letters are sent to the debtor and, if the account is not paid within 10 days after the second letter then a solicitor's letter of intent is issued.

Interestingly, the firm is not actually serious about the warnings it makes in these letters:

> This is the last stage of the process and many debtors will settle the account upon receipt of the solicitor's letter if they have the funds available. [The firm's prestigious name] alone is very effective at prompting slow payers.

Where necessary, they initiate legal action or apply for registration of foreign judgments in England. However, enforcement of foreign default judgments can be especially slow.

The firm charges clients a standard placement fee of £35 for each debt. In addition, the following fees are charged on monies actually collected ('no collection - no charge').

Europe (incl. Turkey), USA, Canada, Scandinavia, Australia	Charge on first £5,000 recovered	16%
	Charge on next £5,000 recovered	8%
	Charge on balance	3%
Middle East, Africa	flat rate	22%
Japan, Taiwan, Hong Kong	flat rate	30%
Other countries	by quotation	

Most problematic in cross-border debt collection is the tracing of 'gone away' debtors. This also applies to commercial collections and is even more problematic in those countries where there is no registration system, such as Turkey. The UK also has no registration system. In domestic collections the firm offers a separate 'Tracing Service' which costs £40 for each address successfully located in the country.

Language also poses a difficulty in telephone collections:

> Debtors, especially from some Mediterranean countries, Spain, Italy, Greece and Turkey are suddenly unable to speak English when asked to repay their debts.

3. Medium Sized Firms

a) English Debt Collector 6 [43]

English Debt Collector 6 has a very special client base: it collects debts owned by bankrupts.[44]

In order to clarify the situation succinctly, for the reader who may not be familiar with English insolvency law, it must be explained that, in England (and Wales), insolvency procedures, including procedures aimed at rehabilitation of an insolvent debtor as well as liquidations,[45] are carried out by 'insolvency practitioners' or 'official receivers'.[46] Their duties involve the collection of debts *owed to* the company or to the individual bankrupt's estate with which they are dealing. Insolvency practitioners and official receivers may collect these debts by contacting the debtors and, where necessary, by taking legal action. Alternatively, however, they may forward this collection work to a professional debt collection agency.

Not long after being established as a small sized firm for small collections, English Debt Collector 6 commenced with this type of collection commissioned by insolvency practitioners or official receivers.

---

43 The interview was not tape-recorded.
44 Cf. *infra* English Debt Collector 7.
45 For a brief summary on English insolvency law see O'Hare and Hill, *Civil Litigation*, Chapter 26 (pp. 601–34); Geoffrey Morse, Enid A. Marshall, Richard Morris and Crabb, *Charlesworth & Morse Company Law*, 5th ed. (London: Sweet & Maxwell, 1995), Chapters 24 – 29 (pp. 657–804).
46 Insolvency practitioners are professional persons who are qualified to act as insolvency liquidators or as officers conducting corporate rescue schemes under the Insolvency Act 1986, for re-organisation of insolvent companies. (Insolvency Act 1986, Part XIII.) Official receivers are civil servants under the control of Secretary of State for Trade and Industry and at the same time officers of the courts having insolvency jurisdiction, who are constituted receiver and manager of a bankrupt's estate or assets of a company in liquidation. (*Ibid.*, ss 399–401.)

Insolvency practitioners who commission English Debt Collector 6 are liquidators in court insolvency procedures as well as voluntary liquidation of companies, accountants dealing with creditor voluntary arrangements (*i.e.* supervisors of composition agreements with creditors) and receivers appointed by fixed or floating charge holders for the management of property of a company which is in default of payment for the relevant secured claims. Administrators who are appointed by the court for the rehabilitation of an insolvent company or for securing the most profitable realisation of a company's assets are also among their clients, but they are few in number: under the Administration procedure, the company structure remains unchanged, therefore companies subject to this procedure maintain their credit management departments and thus carry on pursuing their own debts instead of hiring a debt collector. Insolvency practitioners are usually members of accountancy firms. Twelve top chartered accountancy firms in England are among the firm's clients.

In February 1996 the firm had some 50,000 pending insolvency collection files forwarded by official receivers. Most of these cases however were individual bankruptcies where the debtor had no receivables to collect.

The firm is still a relatively small business with 7 employees. The interviewee works on overseas collections. They use also outside assistance where necessary, especially for tracing the debtor and his assets.

The office is located on the first floor (c. 100 m²) of a two floor building rented on a narrow street connected to the high street in a London suburb. Paper blocks and computers filled the office. Like other debt collection agencies, there were no separate rooms for receiving clients. It was clear that they do not hold business meetings in their office. The telephone and fax are used for all business contact. Telephones were inter-connected so that, 'everyone can answer any telephone call, but has his or her own work'. Thus, throughout the interview with the author the interviewee ignored the constant ringing of the telephone. The interviewee used his computer to answer some of the author's questions and spoke fluent English with a clear French accent.

The firm developed its overseas collection service in 1992, when a great number of UK export firms went bankrupt. At that time they handled a case for collection of debts owed to an insolvent company which was a producer and world-wide distributor of records and CDs. In this first case with major overseas involvement, the firm collected UK-debts only, overseas debts being collected by English Debt Collector 13. Thereafter, the firm began to collect all overseas as well as domestic debts owned by insolvent estates. In

1992, overseas collections made for insolvency practitioners and official receivers amounted to 15% of the annual turnover; in 1995, this increased to 33%.

Business-to-business collections accounts for 90% of the firm's work with the remaining 10% being consumer collections. Among the latter, overseas debts forwarded by a British bank:

> We collect all debts owned by the bank due from (individual) debtors having moved abroad. These may be British soldiers serving abroad, some professionals who find better paid jobs overseas, say, engineers and consultants working in Europe and some people moving abroad with their partners.

They also collect receivables of French companies in the UK. They are in contact with 70 debt collectors in France who forward them collection cases. In Germany, a major producer of electronic devices is among their regular clients.

Yet, the firm prefers insolvency practitioners to these 'commercial creditors':

> Commercial creditors are very curious about our work. They want quick money. They are on your back every other minute. Insolvency practitioners trust us, give us time and are happy with our service.

The average overseas debt collected by English Debt Collector 6 is five times greater than that in domestic collections, that is, £5,000 to £10,000. Judgment debts constitute 10% of debts collected by the firm, in overseas as well as domestic collections, with the exception being US collections where 50% or more of cases include judgment debts. These figures also apply to cross-border cases where the creditor is abroad and the debtor is in the country.

For overseas collections the firm makes the first attempt from the London office, by telephone or mail. Should this prove unsuccessful, the case is forwarded to local debt collectors abroad.

> Personal contacts are very important. In a few years you know who is good and who is bad, also in foreign countries. When we have to do business in a country for the first time, we consult our colleagues in order to obtain the address of a reputable debt collector. International meetings are also very important to establish and maintain contacts abroad.

The firm and the interviewee are members of the Credit Services Association (CSA) and the Institute of Credit Management (ICM). They also support the activities of the Institute of Licensed Debt Practitioners (ILDP).[47]

The methods employed for collecting debts owed to foreign creditors by debtors in the country are the same as those used in all domestic collections, *i.e.* telephone and mail collections:

> If the debtor agrees to pay, but cannot for whatever reason, we obtain detailed information about his financial position, any offer for instalment payments *etc.* Then we prepare a detailed report and take instructions and approval from the client in order to agree a payment plan with the debtor.

Unlike some other English agencies,[48] they do not believe in door-to-door collections:

> If the debtor responds, he responds to a letter or telephone call. If not, it is pointless to go to his address and knocking on the door as this only provokes him.

Success rates in overseas collections are comparable with domestic collections. Where the creditor is abroad and debtor is in the UK, the latter is even more co-operative and success rates are higher than in domestic collections where both parties are in the country.

The firm does not enter into written contracts with clients, but requires simple letters of instruction. Fees and other charges applied by the firm are independent from the fact that the debt is a judgment debt or a simple debt. Where the debtor is in Germany, costs of collection for a client in the UK are as follows:

Amount receivable	£500	£5,000	£500,000
Standard fee:	£20	N/A	N/A
Success fee:	20%	20%	5% (average)
External costs:	£70	£500	£12,500

Conversely, where the creditor is abroad and the debtor is in the UK, the following table applies:

Amount is	£500	£5,000	£500,000
Standard fee:	N/A	N/A	N/A
Success fee:	15%	15%	3% (average)
External costs:	N/A	N/A	N/A

---

47   See *infra* Chapter 12: Business Organisations of Debt Collection Agencies.
48   *E.g.* see *supra* English Debt Collector 12.

230 Making Foreign People Pay

Due to different criteria applied by each firm, these charges are difficult to compare with those charged by superleague firms. It seems however that the external costs may be considerable.

b) English Debt Collector 11 [49]

English Debt Collector 11 is a middle-sized 'credit management' agency which supplies the UK market with business information, account management and litigation services as well as debt collection.[50] The author visited an officer of the firm in their office on a busy street in central London. Aside from the location, the office environment was comparable with that of English Debt Collector 6.

With regard to debt collection services, the firm's principal clients are English banks which provide consumer credit in the form of medium term loans. Where these loans are not repaid on due time, the banks first attempt to recover their money by using out-of-court collection methods. Should these attempts fail, and only when the debt is already 12 to 18 months old, they forward accounts to the firm, 'before writing them off'.

The great majority of these consumer debts are UK debts although there are some overseas debts among them. The firm deals with these overseas cases in addition to the usual domestic cases with marketing concerns, that is, so that it is not necessary for clients to go to other agencies. In 1994, the firm dealt with 60 cases where the debtor was outside Britain. Most of these debtors were from the United States or Europe, *viz.* France, Germany (10 cases in 1994) Italy and the Scandinavian countries. These debts were always greater than in the UK, *i.e.* between £10,000 and £25,000. Virtually all overseas collections made by English Debt Collector 11 were consumer loans provided by banks:

> These debts never start off as cross-border debts. But, the debtor moves abroad after getting the money. Typically, the debtor is somebody who came to England for good work, who lived in the country for a while, incurred debts and, for some reason, left the country without paying. Sometimes they are 'habitual debtors' having unpaid debts in several countries.

---

49   Interview was not tape-recorded.
50   The firm published a brochure introducing its services, all of which were 'available both in the UK and world-wide'.

The interviewee was critical about the credit management practices of British banks:

> Banks do not take steps to check the creditworthiness of consumers. Even people who are in the country for a short time can obtain credit. In a recent case, a famous golfer from Argentina who was in London was granted a loan of £25,000. As he was a well known sportsman, no security was required but he failed to repay the loan after leaving the country.
>
> Banks write off money easily. They do not really expect overseas debts to be collected. Therefore, they do not invest enough funds. The bigger the debt, the easier it is to get away with it. Banks allocate a fixed sum of money for each consumer account, no matter how high the amount of claim may be. For example, in some cases where the claim is relatively a large one and the debtor's whereabouts are not known, tracing the debtor abroad may be economical. But we cannot undertake this, since the bank does not pay the costs which may be around £250.
>
> It is difficult to satisfy a bank bureaucracy that they should invest some more money for collection of consumer debts abroad: senior members do not mind consumer debts of £10,000 to £25,000, but lower ranking members do not have additional means at their disposal to spend for this purpose. So they write the debts off.

As with other firms, they make telephone and mail collections partly from their London office. In addition, they have corresponding agencies abroad.

> One difficulty is that, when a corresponding collection agency asks for our instructions, we must then ask our client (the bank). Going up and down this chain can be very time consuming.

The costs charged by the firm for overseas collections are 35% success fee and an additional £75 standard fee, independent from the amount or age of debt. This may be explained due to the fact that the firm's client base for cross-border collections and cases dealt with do not vary; they are always 12 – 18 months old consumer loans for between £10,000 – £25,000.

c) *English Debt Collector 2* [51]

English Debt Collector 2 has its office in a small town not far from London. The office is the same size, and indeed, surprisingly similar to that of English Debt Collector 6: the neighbourhood, the building; the office and furniture; busy office workers and telephones ringing constantly, *etc.*

---

51   The interview was not tape-recorded.

In spite of the title of the firm's advertisement booklet (which has the words 'International', 'Debt Collection' and 'Credit Information' printed around a map of the world in blue colour), English Debt Collector 2 deals mostly with domestic (but not local) collections: 'most of (their) clients are publishers who sell books to bookshops throughout the country'.

As with English Debt Collector 11, the firm make overseas collections especially when regular clients (publishers) require such service. However, the debts collected by Debt Collector 2 are cross-border debts from the beginning. That is, the debtors are bookshops abroad which sell books in English.

According to the interview the basic advantage of using a debt collection agency in overseas collections is to save costs, by 'cutting down the paper work', such as translations, service of documents *etc.*

The advertisement booklet describes the process as follows:

> On receipt of your instructions the debt is entered onto our system and a demand letter is immediately sent to the debtor. Where a fax number is supplied a copy of both the letter and statement of account will also be faxed.
>
> Depending on the country in which the debtor trades, we allow a maximum of three weeks for reply. If no reply is forthcoming we send or fax a reminder and at the same time ask for your instruction to pass the account to our collection agent in the debtor's country.

The firm's 'agent' in Germany, for example, is 'German Debt Collector 4'. After the first unsuccessful attempt they forward the case to the agent, who then deals with everything, mostly out of court. Only 10% of overseas cases go to court, and then only in the country where the debtor has his assets: a foreign debtor is never sued before the English courts.

The costs charged by English Debt Collector 2, for 'export collections', are a success fee of 8% on the first £1,000 and of 6% on the balance above £1,000 collected. 'Where no commission is appropriate', *i.e.* where the debt could not be collected, there is an administrative charge of £15. These modest fees are however only applicable if the debt could be collected at the first stage in England, before the involvement of a foreign debt collection agency. Where a foreign debt collector is employed, 'agent charges are in addition to (the firm's) commission charges'.

Success rates in overseas collections are 65 – 70%, whereas the firm is able to collect 80 – 85% of debts in the UK. Language can cause difficulties in overseas collection. Debtors from Greece, Spain and Turkey in particular speak very poor English.[52] Therefore, in 'export collections', fax and mail are preferred to the telephone.[53]

In Turkey, they work with the 'Turkish Law Firm 2' [54] but rarely go to court: the inflation rate is very high in Turkey, as a result of which a legal action of long duration makes it inconvenient to sue.

The publishing industry, like any other line of business, has its own characteristics and peculiarities in domestic as well as in international trade.[55] The publishers are usually unsecured creditors.[56] Thus, where a shop owner is declared bankrupt, they are particularly disadvantaged. The retention of title, which is a popular form of security in the commercial sale of goods in England cannot be used by publishers

> because a book does not have an identification number which could be used to distinguish it from other books in the bookseller's stock. It is very difficult to distinguish if a book in the window display is supplied by a publisher or by a wholesaler.

Similarly, in international sales, export credit insurance is seldom used by publishers:

> Some years ago there was an increase in premiums. Publishers dropped export credit insurance, because it turned out to be too expensive.

---

52   Cf. *supra* English Debt Collector 13.
53   However the use of collection letters is not without problems: 'Once I received a letter from a feminist in Canada who was not at all pleased with our warning letter which began with the words "Dear Sir". She wrote that when she had last looked in the mirror, she had been a woman. Of course, I replied, not to make the things more complicated.'
54   See *supra* Chapter 5: Role of Lawyers in Cross-Border Debt Collection.
55   For example, in the UK market at present, an ever increasing number of clients find themselves in financial difficulties and are unable to pay their debts owed to publishers: 'Until recently, there used to be a so-called "Net-Book Agreement" in the market, according to which a bookshop was obliged to sell books at the cover price. This has been invalidated. Bookshops may offer discount prices. As a result, small bookshops are under great competitive pressure from the larger bookshops such as D... and F... which offer very low prices. In turn, they are not in the position to pay the publishers who supply their books.' For the same reason, there is a large number of individual insolvencies among small bookshop-keepers in the country. In February – June 1996, the author purchased books at large bookshops in London which offered discounts of up to 15% for newly published books. There were also many newly opened 'bargain bookshops' *e.g.* on Liverpool Street, Goodge Street, Queensway, Bayswater, which sell books only at reduced prices.
56   For the consequences of being an unsecured creditor in insolvency procedures and the debt collectors function in such cases see, *infra* English Debt Collector 7.

234 Making Foreign People Pay

As a result, credit information becomes very important for publishers. However, due to the characteristics of this particular market where most of the regular customers are relatively small enterprises (bookshops), the usual credit information service supplied by credit reference agencies is of little help. Thus, publishers in Britain have developed their own credit information system which has been discussed below.[57]

4. Boutique Type Agencies

a) English Debt Collector 7 [58]

English Debt Collector 7 specialises in 'international (debt collection) services'. Although the firm is a limited company, it is practically owned by an individual (a Greek businessman) and run by a single person; a British gentleman in his mid-sixties. The firm also employs an external accountant and co-operates with a firm of solicitors. They previously had an in-house lawyer, but later decided to employ outside solicitors to be more cost-effective.

English Debt Collector 7 was on the third floor of an old apartment house in a hotel district in central London. There were no signs of the firm on the windows or on the front of the house, apart from a single capital letter written on the doorbell in the main entrance. English Debt Collector 7 received the author in his office which contained three simple office desks, a small set of drawers and bookshelves along the walls. Many cardboard files could be seen on the shelves, one of which contained newspaper cuttings of the Financial Times currency exchange rates; some foreign language dictionaries; old editions of the Supreme Court Practice (1988) and the County Court Practice (1987) and numerous copies of the 'Yellow Pages' for various districts in the country.

Behind the interviewee's desk was a calendar on the wall, a chart of 'Royal Mail International Price Guide' and a map of the world. There were telephones and fax machine, a typewriter, but no computers. All communications were filed and mental notes were made manually: as with some

---

57 See *infra* Chapter 14: Collection and Security Methods Employed in International Trade.
58 This interview was not tape-recorded. The interviewee spoke slowly enabling the author to take notes. The interview lasted more than two hours. Quotations below were partly taken directly from notes which the author made during the interview, and partly reconstructed from memory with the aid of the same notes.

good boutiques in other businesses, everything was done 'by hand'. Therefore, in contrast to superleague and middle sized agencies, Debt Collector 7 was not suited for processing a large number of cases mechanically (*e.g.* by means of sending a series of standard warning letters formulated according to the 'types' of debtors [59]), but each case was dealt with individually.

English Debt Collector 7 collects both incoming and outgoing cross-border commercial debts, *i.e.* where the debtor or the creditor is a UK firm. The majority of debts collected are larger debts (large for the debt collection business), between £20,000 and £50,000 owed to foreign creditors by UK debtors.

'Collection orders' are forwarded in part by foreign debt collection agencies (in Germany, by German Debt Collector 3 which is the 'German associate' of the firm) and in part directly from creditors abroad.

Before accepting a case, the firm requires, as a condition, sufficient documentation proving the debt. This includes invoices, statements of account and any correspondence with the debtor. Commercial firms have no problem in producing these documents. A debt without documents is a 'hopeless case'.

Upon receipt of a collection order, Debt Collector 7 first inspects the arithmetic on the account, then the debtor's address. However, tracing the debtor can be problematic even with such large commercial accounts.

> Sometimes, especially when a collection order comes from a German creditor, the address is not correct. In that case I do two things. First I contact the Post Code Unit. If you give them both the name and the address containing insufficient or contradictory information, they give you the correct address. If this does not work, and if, as usual, I have a telephone number of the debtor, I call directory enquiries. The directory enquiries unit is not permitted to give the address of a customer. But I talk round the telephone people. I tell them I have such and such an address, but it is somehow incorrect *etc.*, and persuade them to correct the address. If even this attempt is not successful, I do what I call – do not use this expression in your thesis – 'playing the silly bugger', that is, 'send a letter, shot in the dark, maybe you get an answer'.

The actual collection process begins with a demand letter. The letter sets out the facts, but it is not threatening.

> No reply, ... I am on the telephone to them. Sometimes, first at this stage, you may learn that there is a dispute. Then I say: 'Let me have something in writing'. And I report to my client abroad. Sometimes the client confesses the dis-

---

59   See *supra* English Debt Collector 13.

236 Making Foreign People Pay

pute. Say, the clothes exported are not, allegedly, in the required colour. Our clients expect us to resolve such disputes. How can we do that? If they are willing to bring an action, we forward the case to our solicitors. But we never push our client to sue.

If the claim is not disputed but the debtor gives excuses, we have to judge on the validity of these excuses. In case a debtor offers deferred payment, we ask our client for instructions before accepting it. 'The sending the gorillas' method is not a method we use.[60] If we are not satisfied with the excuse, we send a 'letter before action' or a 'seven-days letter'. I do not write such letters unless I mean it.[61]

We have our solicitors working for a fixed fee for debt recovery. That is, when we instruct them we pay a fixed amount which covers issuing fees and basic solicitor's costs as allowed by the court. If they win the case, we pay an additional success fee also permitted by the court.

Before deciding to proceed, Debt Collector 7 advises his clients on the expected costs of the litigation and, where necessary, obtains a legal opinion on the merits of the case from their solicitors. 'We have a duty to our client; we do not take a case without good prospects.'

Unlike most other debt collectors,[62] the firm does not accept judgment debts. For larger debts, where the debtor, despite being ordered to pay by a judgment, is not willing to pay, the firm's involvement would also not be of much assistance. Thus, for judgment debts, creditors are advised to employ solicitors directly.

In contrast to other English debt collectors, Debt Collector 7 does not work on a 'no success - no fees' basis. They charge clients a non-returnable 'handling charge' (£50 + VAT) and commission, the interviewee declined to state how much. In addition, all expenses are paid by the client, which include, *inter alia*, lawyer's fees for legal action or a preliminary legal opinion.

The firm is not a member of the Credit Services Association or any other debt collectors' association.[63] Until some time ago they were a member of an association of the textile industry in Germany. This association decided to restrict its membership to textile exporters and so they had to withdraw their membership.

60	Cf. *supra* English Debt Collector 12.
61	Cf. *supra* English Debt Collector 13.
62	See *e.g.* English Debt Collectors 1 and 6 *supra*.
63	Cf. *infra* Chapter 12: Business Organisations of Debt Collection Agencies.

Textile exporters from Germany were among the best clients. English Debt Collector 7 gave examples from some concluded and pending debt collection cases, more than half of which concerned UK debts arising from textile imports from Germany. He leafed through 11 example cases, each filed in a separate cover. Each file had a few pages of hand written notes containing a detailed summary of the case and contents of the file, which was placed on the top of other documents.

The interviewee complained about his German clients on two points: 'Germans (were) very determined to take legal action', even where it was economically not worthwhile. And they were unnecessarily 'tough' when small amounts were concerned such as small amounts of interest payments.

> Germans are quite tough on exchange rates. It is very difficult to collect small amounts arising from different exchange rates used. If we can, we try to impose 'Financial Times' exchange rates.

Enforcing claims for interest is especially difficult in England. There is no statutory interest for late payments. German textile exporters base their claims for interest usually on standard contract terms, *i.e.* 'general terms of trade of the German textile industry', which they attach to the invoice. English debtors are likely to object to these interest claims which they have not explicitly accepted.[64]

A further complaint about clients, not only about 'Germans', was that they often provided inadequate or even incorrect information about the underlying transaction.

> In a recent case, for example, which had been going on for 10 months, the creditor did not forward the contract in writing which he had made with the debtor to the firm. Debt Collector 7 started the case with some invoices. Later,

---

[64] In one case, the debtor agreed to pay DM 50,000, but without interest. The German creditor decided to take legal action. In the court proceedings, the debtor produced a defence against the main claim, which resulted in a long and costly process. In another German – English case, the creditor first claimed a small amount of DM 1,300 with a statutory interest of DM 750. The debtor objected to paying interest on the ground that they had never received the original invoices for goods which had been supplied. 'If the invoice had been sent, they would have paid.' At the end, the client chose to settle for half of the interest. Just after this first case had been concluded, the same client claimed a further DM 103,000 against the same debtor, which included accrued contractual interest as well as the main claim. Interestingly, the facts of this second case were identical, the only difference being that a far larger amount was claimed. Although the creditor had waived half of the interest in the first case, this second time they were claiming interest calculated on the same rate they had originally used in the first case. The debtor paid DM 99,000 of the DM 103,000. But the client insisted on further payment.

notwithstanding the threatened counterclaim, the client instructed him to take legal action against the debtor. Only when the action was brought and the debtor filed a counterclaim did the debt collector learn that there was a written contract. 'Either they have very bad records or they are playing with it', explained Debt Collector 7.

Apparently, some creditors abuse the 'third party effect' created by involvement of a debt collection agency, at the cost of the debt collector who finds himself face-to-face with the debtor.

English Debt Collector 7 was also dealing with many insolvency cases. Unlike Debt Collector 6 who was working for insolvency practitioners and official receivers in collecting debts owned by the insolvent debtor, Debt Collector 7 was on the side of insolvency creditors to whom the insolvent debtor owes money. In these cases, the firm files the claim with the relevant insolvency administration (*e.g.* the receiver or the liquidator) and represents the client in creditors' meetings. They follow the insolvency procedure to the end, which normally lasts two to three years.

Clients are usually unsecured trade creditors,[65] as a result of which they rank below the preferential and secured creditors and do not usually receive any dividends. In such a case however they need a document prepared by the insolvency administration to the effect, which enables them to claim the amount from 'bad debt insurers' (export credit insurers). Official receivers and insolvency practitioners, especially receivers appointed by a security holder, are not always willing to produce such a document. 'Sometimes (they) have to threaten them with legal action.'

b) English Debt Collector 3 [66]

As with Debt Collector 7, Debt Collector 3 is a small debt collection agency. The owner was formerly a credit manager in a large publishing company where he worked with Debt Collector 2. He is now 'semi-retired' and works as a 'specialist in the recovery of overseas debts'. He has his office at home, in a small, pleasant town not far from London. His wife helps him with the paper and computer work. It is obvious that the firm does not receive business visitors and everything is done by telephone and fax. They are also assisted by an outside accountant.

---

65 Cf. *supra* English Debt Collector 2.
66 Interview was not tape-recorded.

As a result of his previous work experience, Debt Collector 3 has many overseas contacts, including debt collectors in small English speaking countries in Africa. He deals with the collection of relatively large amounts, that is, £20,000 and above. His clients include all kinds of exporters of goods and freight companies.

Debt Collector 3 deals exclusively in overseas collections. He begins the collection with a fax from the England office. The letter-head which includes the information that they are overseas debt collectors and are served by local lawyers and collection agencies world-wide, has quite an effect on the debtor. If there is no response from the debtor within 21 days, they instruct their local agents in the debtor's country. Collection fees charged by the Debt Collector 3 are 9% for the first £900 and 6% on the balance. This does not include the commission charged by overseas agents which varies between 10 to 25%. However, if an overseas agent is employed, his own commission is reduced to a flat 5%.

In spite of the modest size of the firm, the amount of work and the success rate recorded by Debt Collector 3 is impressive. According to his own calculations, in the last 1,500 collection cases he handled, only 107 files have not been cleared, 3 of which are bankruptcy cases, 34 are part paid and the remainder are still in process.

5. Conclusions

Debt collectors in England, one may suggest similar to their colleagues in other countries, are pragmatists. This was apparent from the physical working environment and how the interviewees treated their guests as well as from the contents of the interviews. (To save time, English Debt Collector 1 met the author in a public house.) Unlike lawyers, debt collectors were easy to approach. When they were called on telephone, they were never 'in a meeting'. (All telephones in English Debt Collector 6 are interconnected.) They spoke in an informal, but direct and clear manner. During the interviews they took the opportunity to ask questions as well as answering them. (How long is the limitation period under Turkish law? How much do German debt collectors charge their clients?)

Debt collectors are businessmen. They are not interested in legal intricacies. They may not be sufficiently informed about the latest developments in law. (English Debt Collector 7 uses older editions of the Supreme Court Practice.) Their closest 'relatives' in the market for 'credit management services' are not lawyers, but credit reference agencies (English Debt Collectors 1, 12, and 2). In the course of their business, they try to avoid litigation as far as possible; where they have to go to court they make use of professional lawyers.

The collection methods used by debt collectors are simple (telephone, mail, door-to-door collections). Their efficiency depends on the so-called 'third party effect', that is, the debt collector's involvement in the collection process as a third party who is not party to the main contractual relationship. Thus, numerous 'excuses' and objections which may be asserted to the original creditor / trading partner, cannot be so easily directed towards the debt collector.[67]

The difficulties experienced in cross-border collections are more practical rather than legal. Tracing the debtor abroad and difficulties in communication, including the language barrier, are the most frequently named difficulties stated by the interviewees (English Debt Collectors 2, 7, 11 and 13). These difficulties are managed by using a corresponding collection agency (English Debt Collectors 1, 2, 6, 7, 12, 13) or by establishing affiliates (English Debt Collectors 1, 12, and 13) in the relevant foreign countries, which can contact the debtor there. Unlike the cross-border co-operation between national courts and lawyers, such co-operation is effected in a simple and informal way, which saves costs by 'cutting down the paper work' (English Debt Collector 2), such as translations, service of documents, *etc.*

In addition, debt collectors treat various 'types' of debts and debtors differently, using the methods which prove to be most successful in each case. Each debt collection agency has its own methods which have been developed over the years. For some medium sized and boutique type agencies, such collection methods are specially designed for a specific clientele. That is, consumer loans provided to (foreign) individuals (English Debt Collector 11), debts owed to bankrupts' estates (English Debt Collector 6), receivables of English publishers from bookshops in foreign countries (English Debt Collector 2), receivables of German textile exporters in England (English Debt Collector 7) are collected by different firms, each specialised on the characteristics of its own type of debtor. For example, before accepting a case, English Debt Collector 7 insists that sufficient documentation is provided by the creditor, which is not required by the

---

67   See advertisements published in the *Credit Management* (July 1996) where the debtor is portrayed as Collodi's fictional character Pinocchio.

English Debt Collector 13 for its 'letter service'. English Debt Collector 2 sues debtors, where necessary, exclusively in the country where the debtors have their assets, whereas English Debt Collector 13 initiates legal action in England, serving the proceedings out of jurisdiction. Door-to-door collection methods are used by English Debt Collector 12 even for commercial debts, whereas English Debt Collector 6 does not believe in 'knocking on the door' 'which only provokes the debtors'. English Debt Collector 7 'do[es] not take a case without good prospects', which is not the case for English Debt Collector 11, who collects 12 – 18 month old consumer accounts for banks, which are forwarded to the same only 'before being written off'.

Similarly, the billing practices of debt collection agencies differ. Most of them (*i.e.* all interviewees except English Debt Collector 7) charge their clients on a 'no collection - no fee' basis, together with a fixed 'placement fee' (English Debt Collector 6) or in addition to the 'costs', the amount of which is not fixed at the beginning (English Debt Collector 1). They usually use a price schedule for their 'success fees'. Such schedules offer different prices for different groups of countries which also vary according to the age (English Debt Collector 1) or amount (English Debt Collector 13) of the debt to be collected. This variety which makes a price comparison difficult indicates also that the debt collection market in England is a highly competitive one.

Offering lower fees and charges is not sufficient to bring and maintain success in this market. A good public image is also important. Interviewees were very anxious to have a good public image, which means their firms do not use illegal pressure methods against the debtors and they are in good financial position, able to carry their professional liability, including not going bankrupt with the monies in their possession belonging to their clients. English Debt Collector 1 issues a 'Client's Charter' in its advertisement leaflet. English Debt Collector 13 uses the good name of its parent (credit insurance) company, the name of which was 'alone very effective at prompting slow payers'. Being member of a professional organisation with a Code of Conduct (ICM, CSA) is also seen and presented to the clients as a symbol of good business ethics (English Debt Collectors 1, 6, 11, and 12). English Debt Collector 12 attempts to distinguish itself from other debt collectors asserting its membership of a 'very exclusive club' of European debt collection agencies. In this context various organisations of debt collection agencies deserve to be referred to separately.

12 Business Organisations of Debt Collection Agencies

A. NATIONAL ORGANISATIONS

On 15 January 1995, the German tabloid *Bild Zeitung am Sonntag* published the following story:

> SHE FEARED FOR HER LIFE!
> More and more people are finding themselves unable to repay their debts. Yet the creditors are merciless: many send debt collectors who employ all kinds of tricks. The hunt for debtors can even end in a killing. / 'What do you want?' asked Katherina B. (34), when two young men (wide-shouldered, with shoulder-length hair, leather jackets, jeans, cowboy boots) entered her cosmetics shop in South Potsdam. / They introduced themselves as . . . representing a debt collection agency. 'We want the 5,000 marks the butcher owes, and we want 'em now.' / Katherina reminded them of the letter from the lawyer. 'I've still got 12 weeks to pay . . . . My husband's in prison under suspicion of tax evasion . . .' stammered the mother of three . . . . The debt collectors eventually set a 24-hour deadline. But when the time was up, she didn't pay, and so it happened, two days later: her shop windows were smashed . . . .

This is a typical example of a 'debt collectors story' appearing in a daily newspaper.[1] There can be little doubt: the debt collection industry has a very poor public image.[2]

---

1   Harsh or unlawful methods used by some 'black sheep' in the debt collection branch are frequently reported in the daily press, especially in the form of 'tips' for consumers. Consumers are warned, for example, against 'horror letters' and uninvited personal visits of some debt collectors who threaten debtors with criminal prosecution or publicising their default among neighbours or at their place of work. (*Mitteldeutsche Zeitung*, 23.9.1993: 'Manche verschicken Horrorbriefe'.) They are advised never to acknowledge a debt, to always insist that debt collectors produce a power of attorney before dealing with them, and not to pay excessive 'fantasy debt collector fees'. (*Mitteldeutsche Zeitung*, 13.7.1995: 'Geldeintreiber greifen oft zu rüden Methoden'; *Welt am Sonntag*, 22.01.1995: 'Inkassobüros verlangen Phantasiepreise, für die es

244 *Making Foreign People Pay*

The need to improve the business ethic standards of the debt collection industry, *inter alia* by separating the 'black sheep' from the other members of the industry, as well as by improving their public image, are the main motives which led debt collectors to form national business organisations.

In Germany, 330 of 550 debt collection agencies – which carry on 80–85% of all the debt collection business in the country – are members of a nation-wide business association: the Federal Association of German Debt Collection Agencies (*Bundesverband deutscher Inkassounternehmen, BDIU*).[3] The aims of this organisation are to foster professional co-operation and information exchange between the members, provide information on professional problems, vocational education and dispute resolution facilities between members, and represent the professional interests of the same before the general public, governmental bodies, courts, *etc.*[4] In 1979, the Association issued, as a self-control initiative, a 'code of conduct' which detailed the professional rules to be followed by debt collection agencies in the course of their business.[5] According to the Association's Code of Conduct, a debt collection agency must *inter alia* keep all its relevant books and records open for examination by the client and hold professional indemnity insurance against pecuniary damages for itself and for its office employees in favour of its clients.[6] Debt collection agencies must treat debtors 'properly' and may charge the debtors with the costs of the debt collection process only to the extent that it is 'usual in the market'.[7] In 1994, an ombudsman was appointed by BDIU with the aim of

---

    keine Rechtsgrundlage gibt'; *Bauern Zeitung – Landwirtschaftliches Wochenblatt*, 28.10.1994.) In case of 'old debts', recourse to a lawyer is suggested in order to find out if the debt or, as the case may be, the accumulated interest has come under the statute of limitations. (*Nordwest-Zeitung*, 15.5.1994.) A press release from the Consumer Centre in Hesse providing such consumer tips was reported by more than twenty newspapers and periodicals including advertisers (*e.g. Bergsträßer Anzeiger*, 20–21.8.1994), weekend newspapers (*Welt am Sonntag*, 14.8.1994) and TV magazines (*Funk-Uhr*, September 1994).

2   A leaflet published by the American Collectors Association (see *infra*) complains that public opinion is 'blinded by the misconceptions and stigmas surrounding the (debt collection) industry'.

3   At the address 'Brennerstraße 76, 20099 Hamburg'.

4   See Statutes of the Federal Association of German Debt Collection Agencies = 'Satzung des Bundesverbandes Inkassounternehmen', reproduced in David, *Zusammenarbeit mit Inkassounternehmen*, pp. 31–9.

5   I.e. *Grundsätze für die Berufsausübung zugelassener Inkassounternehmen in der Bundesrepublik Deutschland*, reproduced *ibid.*, pp. 39–43.

6   Code of Conduct, ss 2.4 – 2.6.

7   Code of Conduct, ss 3.1, 3.2.

resolving the differences which may arise between debtors, clients and members of the Association.[8] BDIU is also trying to improve the public image of German debt collectors via press releases and conferences. In 1995, the annual press conference of the BDIU on rates of insolvency and 'payment morality' in the country was reported by 146 newspapers and periodicals throughout Germany,[9] including many local [10] as well as nationally distributed [11] newspapers. Two court judgments declaring the above 'Black Shadows' practice [12] unlawful were welcomed by the Association with a press release.[13]

In England, the counterpart of the German Association is the Credit Services Association (CSA).[14] In May 1995, CSA had 130 members.[15] Members of CSA are not individual debt collectors as such, but debt collection agencies as firms. The condition for becoming a member of the Association is two years' experience in the debt collection business. Similar to the ombudsman at BDIU, CSA has a complaint procedure for complaints coming from clients and debtors.[16] Again, like BDIU, CSA has a 'Code of Practice' for its members. However, the Code of Practice of CSA is more comprehensive than the BDIU Code of Conduct. For example, the CSA Code of Practice requires that members provide advisory services to the debtors who are in financial difficulties,[17] and that they submit to the Association on request proof of their financial solvency.[18]

In 1994, some CSA members established a second association, the Institute of Licensed Debt Practitioners (ILDP),[19] the members of which are not companies but individuals. The aim of ILDP is to secure for English

---

[8] *Leipziger Wirtschaft*, May 1995: 'Ombudsman vermittelt bei Streitfällen in der Inkasso-Branche'.
[9] The author thanks *Bundesverband deutscher Inkasso-Unternehmen* for having been allowed to use the private newspaper cuttings archive of this institution in Bremen.
[10] See *e.g. Aachener Nachrichten*, 5.5.1995; *Badisches Tagesblatt*, 5.5.1995; *Bonner Rundschau*, 5.5.1995.
[11] See *e.g. Handelsblatt*, 5.5.1995; *Süddeutsche Zeitung*, 5.5.1995; *Die Welt*, 5.5.1995.
[12] See Chapter 10: Commercial Cross-Border Debt Collection in Germany.
[13] *Rhein-Neckar-Zeitung*, 18.3.1995: 'Schwarze Schatten sind sittenwidrig'; *Ludwigsburger Kreizzeitung*, 22.3.1995: 'Inkasso begrüßt Urteil gegen "schwarze Schatten"'.
[14] At the address 'Queens House, 123/9 Queens Road, Norwich NR1 3PL'.
[15] Obermaier, 5.5.1995.
[16] Code of Practice, s 5.
[17] Code of Practice, s 3(h)(ii).
[18] Code of Practice, s 6.
[19] At the address 'Greytown House, 221/7 High Street, Orpington, Kent BR6 0NZ'.

debt collectors the right to represent their clients before law courts, the condition being successful completion of the training course offered by the ILDP itself.[20] If this can be achieved, the result will be the creation of a new 'profession'.[21] ILDP – together with CSA – is already discussing with the Office of Fair Trading about an official tariff for debt collection fees, which will be legally recoverable from the debtor.[22]

In addition to CSA and ILDP, some debt collectors in England are members of the Institute of Credit Management [23] (ICM). ICM has a training programme similar to ILDP. However, the members of ICM include not only debt collectors but also credit managers employed by commercial firms. ICM membership was being used as a prestige symbol by interviewees having such status.

---

20   The reason for establishing ILDP was the coming into effect of the Courts and Legal Services Act 1990, which gave the Lord Chancellor the discretionary power to grant right of audience to lay representatives. (Courts and Legal Services Act 1990, s 27. See O'Hare and Hill, *Civil Litigation*, pp. 496 – 497.) As a result, it became possible for debt collectors to obtain the right to represent their clients before courts, at least in certain cases, provided that the Lord Chancellor allows such representation by debt collectors who are not lawyers. In 1992, a group of debt collectors made an application to the Lord Chancellor, requesting such a right for representation, albeit restricted to undefended cases and the administration of the preparation of the case for the law suit. Lord Chancellor made the debt collectors initiate negotiations with an Advisory Committee of the Lord Chancellor Department, as a result of which the latter would submit a report to the Lord Chancellor. In order to persuade the Advisory Committee and the Lord Chancellor, debt collectors established the ILDP, which offers a training programme for the office employees of debt collection agencies. The training programme takes three years, and the curriculum includes (inter alia) basic courses on contracts and civil litigation. (Information given by English Debt Collector 14, the President of ILDP.)

21   Medium-sized firm Debt Collector 5 is strictly against such a regulated business practice: 'It's an old boys' network, which is founded for certain aims . . . In actual fact what they're trying to do is promote the business of credit control into something like the Institute of Chartered Accountants, and that'll never happen because, basically, credit control isn't a very complex matter. It's really quite a simple business. And there's really only so much you can learn about it. Okay, at some ends of the business it's far more complex than others, but it'll never achieve the status of the accountancy profession, simply because the very nature of the business is much more simple . . . That is absolute nonsense. As I say, they're trying to make it a profession and build up their own empire.'

22   English Debt Collector 14, English Debt Collector 12.

23   At the address 'The Water Mill, Station Road, South Luffenham, Oakham, Leicestershire, LE15 8NB'.

B. INTERNATIONAL ORGANISATIONS

Similar to BDIU and CSA, national debt collectors' associations also exist in other European countries. In January 1993, debt collectors' associations from nine European countries [24] came together to form a 'Federation of European National Collection Associations'. Currently the Federation of European National Collection Associations (FENCA) [25] has twelve members,[26] that is, twelve national debt collectors' associations representing 745 debt collection agencies in Europe. The aims of FENCA are

1. [to] protect and take care of the interest of the member associations, within Europe and in international institutions public or private and promote the development of European legislation in favour of the collection industry;
2. [to] promote the development within the member associations and their members of the following:
- keeping the collected means for clients separated from the company means (client accounts),
- having special insurance for the protection of the clients,
- establishing a committee for complaints – to mediate in disputes between agencies and their clients or debtors,
- establishing trading facilities (schools/seminars) for their members,
- introducing basic rules and guidelines for contracts and agreements between the agencies and their clients.[27]

As provided in its statutes, FENCA promotes higher business standards for the European debt collection industry by serving as a common forum and a pressure group at the European level. Debt collectors from the member national associations come together in annual meetings of FENCA and discuss the problems of the industry. FENCA is supporting the idea of a regulation for cross-border data security concerning information regarding clients and debtors and it is lobbying in Brussels for uniform EU-wide rules for licensing and qualification requirements for the debt collection agencies.[28]

---

24   Germany, England, France, Italy, the Netherlands, Norway, Austria, Sweden and Switzerland.
25   At the address 'P.O. Box 311, 3201 Sandefjord, Norway'.
26   In February 1996.
27   Statutes of FENCA, § 3.
28   English Debt Collector 12; 'Europäische Inkasso-Branche schließt sich zusammen - Gleiche Richtlinien vom Nordkap bis Sizilien gefordert', *Bilanzbuchhalter*, no.10 (1993), p. 238.

248 Making Foreign People Pay

Another European organisation of debt collection agencies is the 'European Collectors Association' (ECA). ECA is a group for elite cross-border collection agencies having members in 32 countries. According to the English Debt Collector 12, the President of ECA, ECA is 'a very exclusive club' with strict professional rules. They have only one member agency in each country and they are very selective. However, not all members are super league agencies. One member processes 700,000 cases annually, whereas the member in Hungary has only 500 cases a year. All member collection agencies apply same rates and are subject to the same statute and code of conduct of the ECA. Each member must submit ECA annual solvency reports and any member against whom more than three complaints have been filed by customers 'is out'. Unlike FENCA, ECA is 'not politically minded'. They do not actively take part in lobbying in Brussels. However they support stricter licensing requirements throughout Europe.

Last but not least, some of the debt collectors in Europe [29] are members of the American Collectors Association (ACA). The ACA, with its 3,700 members in more than 50 countries around the world, is the largest trade association in the debt collection business. According to its information booklet, the ACA [30] was formed in 1939 with the aim of 'helping the third-party collection business (*i.e.* debt collection agencies) provide the best services to their clients . . . ؛ ' establishing nation-wide professional and ethical standards for the collection industry'. Similar to the BDIU and the CSA, the ACA defines itself as the 'voice for the collection industry', 'the nation's most misunderstood profession'.[31]

ACA 'promotes professionalism in collections' by offering 250 seminars a year for up-to-date training on collection regulations, and it administers certification and degree programmes 'for advanced training in professional collections'. In the last ten years, around 55,000 people have attended these programmes.

The ACA's Code of Ethics (which has been amended seven times since its adoption in 1971) and Code of Operations are more detailed than the CSA and BDIU codes of conduct, and the Code of Ethics provides various levels of discipline, including expulsion from the organisation.

---

29   *E.g.* English Debt Collector 1, *supra*.
30   At the address '4040 West 7th Street, Minneapolis, MN 55435'.
31   Information below collected from 12 leaflets and booklets provided by the 'Communications Coordinator' of the ACA.

Within the United States, the ACA is 'involved in the legislative process' at both the federal and states level. This means it is in continuous contact with the Federal Trade Commission and the relevant state authorities concerning legislative developments in the fields of debt recovery, debtor protection and creditors' rights. The ACA has supported *inter alia* passage of the Fair Debt Collection Practices Act [32] which imposed numerous restrictions on consumer collections, such as prohibiting harassment of debtors, providing special rules for obtaining debtor location information and communicating with consumer debtors, *etc.* [33]

ACA publishes a comprehensive loose-leaf guide for cross-border collections which includes information about various legal systems in the form of national reports.[34]

---

32 15 United States Code § 1692, effective March 20, 1978. See Douglas J. Whaley, *Problems and Materials on Consumer Law* (Boston, Toronto, London: Little, Brown and Company, 1991), pp. 606–24.
33 ACA also published a leaflet for consumers entitled 'Your rights under the Federal Fair Debt Collection Practices Act'.
34 Shinobu K. Garrigues (ed.), *Guide to International Collections* (Minneapolis: Debt Collectors Association, loose-leaf / 1995).

13 Conclusions for Part II

The results of the survey carried out in Germany and England confirmed our initial suggestion that commercial debt collection is widely used in cross-border legal interactions as an alternative to the judicial debt recovery methods. Litigation (together with international commercial arbitration) plays an important role in the collection of disputed debts. However, for the vast majority of undisputed debts, commercial debt collection proves to be more effective than court proceedings. This applies not only for business-to-business debts but, provided the amount is not too small, also for the collection of consumer accounts of businesses. It is however impractical for small claims of consumers and other economically weak actors (*e.g.* maintenance creditors) to be recovered by debt collection agencies. A single small claim cannot be economically collected by debt collectors.

With any sector of the private economy, debt collection business requires regulation in order to prevent any abuse of enforcement methods against the debtor. This applies in particular to 'one-shotters' who default due to financial difficulties. Public regulation of debt collection in Germany is more comprehensive than in England. (See Table 13.1.) The German model should be considered by the legislators in England with a view to improving their own regulations.

Table 13.1 Regulation of debt collection business in Germany and England

	GERMANY	**ENGLAND**
Legal Provisions	Legal Advisory Act (*Rechtsberatungsgesetz*) 1935: Licensing and supervision by the local civil court.	Not regulated generally. Only the collectors of consumer debts are subject to licensing under the Consumer Credit Act 1974. Unfair debt collection methods are prohibited under the Administration of Justice Act 1970 (s.40).
Commercial Nature	A debt collection agency is a commercial firm: *e.g.* it may advertise its business and determines its fees commercially.	The same as in Germany.
Services / Debt Collection Methods	Besides general consultancy and monitoring bad debts, a debt collector may (in its representative capacity) only use extra-judicial debt collection methods (simple demand letter, telephone, personal visits), with the exception of merely 'filing an application' with the court executor. For court proceedings, the assistance of a lawyer is necessary.	In addition to the services provided by German debt collectors, an English debt collector may generally initiate summary court procedures in county courts and may represent his client before the courts (including the High Court) throughout the execution of judgment procedures: the assistance of a lawyer is less vital.
Costs	Vary according to the nature and amount of the claim. Can be recovered from the debtor as a separate substantive law claim up to such amount which would be paid in counsel fees had the creditor collected his claim through court proceedings.	Vary according to the nature and amount of the claim. Can be recovered from the debtor as a separate substantive law claim if and only if the same has been contractually agreed between the debtor and the creditor.

Associations of debt collection agencies at national and international level attempt to bring a certain discipline to the sector. Their activities must be supported by national governments. The status of national debt collection associations must be legally defined and regulated. As with insolvency practitioners in England,[1] such regulation may require the compulsory membership of the national debt collector's association as a prerequisite for obtaining a debt collector's licence. Provided that this condition is satisfied, debt collectors may also be permitted to represent their clients in summary court procedures for the collection of undisputed debts.

Due to the increasing cross-border activities of commercial debt collectors, EU-wide regulation of the business has become a necessity. Such regulation may take the form of a directive, laying down the principles of national rules applicable to the licensing of debt collection agencies and their activities at domestic as well as at cross-border level.

Similar regulations for the debt collection sector should also be enacted in Turkey and the provisions of any future EU directive should also be adopted. Article 35 of the Lawyers Act 1969 should be amended to enable qualified non-lawyers to carry out debt collection for undisputed debts. Graduates from Justice Colleges are the most suitable candidates for such commercial activity in Turkey.[2]

---

[1] The Insolvency Act 1986 regulates insolvency practitioners by ensuring that they are qualified within the terms of s. 308 of the Act. To act as an insolvency practitioner when not qualified to do so is a criminal offence under s. 309. According to s. 309, only an individual can qualify as an insolvency practitioner. He must be authorised to act as an insolvency practitioner either by virtue of membership of a recognised professional body (*e.g.* Law Society or Insolvency Practitioners Association) or by direct authorisation granted by the Secretary of State, and he must have provided the requisite security for the proper performance of his functions. See also Insolvency Practitioners (Recognised Professional Bodies) Order 1986, *Statutory Instruments* 1986, No. 1764.

[2] Turkish Justice Colleges are attended by non-lawyer court or office employees for a period of two years after high school.

PART III

COLLECTION OF DEBTS AND MANAGEMENT OF CREDIT RISKS IN INTERNATIONAL TRADE

14 Collection and Security Methods Employed in International Trade

The subject 'cross-border debt collection' cannot be discussed in isolation from the legal relations operating in cross-border debts. As in domestic legal interactions, cross-border debts may arise on various legal grounds, *e.g.* torts, contracts and the obligations of family law. Probably the most frequent source of cross-border (private) debts is to be found in international business transactions.[1] Thus, in order to place the subject cross-border debt collection in the appropriate context, it is imperative to consider some of the characteristics of international commercial transactions.

As a result of risks inherent in cross-border legal interactions, international commercial transactions are more secured against the risk of non-payment than domestic legal transactions.[2] At the outset of a continuous cross-border relationship, credit reference agencies are used to investigate the creditworthiness of the foreign businesses. Due to problems encountered in communicating in foreign languages, it is customary to use written documents. Standard contracts prepared by international organisations, such as standard commodity contracts issued by trade associations and standard contract forms of the United Nations Economic Commission for Europe, are widely used.[3] International collection and security methods which are standard in almost all countries ensure payment largely due to the intermediary role of credit institutions; *e.g.* bills of exchange, letters of credit, bank guarantees, factoring and forfaiting. Credit insurance facilities, including export credit insurance from government agencies, are regularly used. Real and personal securities, *e.g.* associated/parent company guarantees, retention

---

1 See Volkmar Gessner, 'Introduction', in Volkmar Gessner, *Foreign Courts*, pp. 1–14, at p. 2.
2 D. M. Day and Bernadette Griffin, *The Law of International Trade*, 2nd ed. (London, Dublin, Edinburgh: Butterworths, 1993), pp. 10 and 150.
3 See Clive M. Schmitthoff, *Schmitthoff's Export Trade – The Law and Practice of International Trade*, 9th ed. (London: Stevens, 1990), Chapter 3.

of title agreements are also used. For investment credits, security types provided by national laws of the debtor's domicile are also widely used by foreign creditors. The business community is widely aware of these collection / security (risk management) methods and how to apply.[4]

The wide variety of collection and security methods used in international trade is the fact that debtors with differing risks levels must be dealt with separately. For example, the credit limits drawn by an expert firm to a particular customer depend on its creditworthiness, and the modes of payment and securities required from different customers vary depending on the level of the risk of non-payment.

An exhaustive description of the international collection and security methods (which combined may be termed 'international credit management' [5]) would be beyond the aim and scope of this study. In order to give an introduction to the empirical research which has been conducted in this area, only the most important collection and risk management methods are briefly discussed below. It must be added at the outset that all of these methods are usually only available for businesses and, even for business creditors, it is often the case that these methods are not available nor enforceable by the creditor. Firstly, standard collection and security methods are used mostly in commercial transactions. Where the debt does not arise from a 'transaction', *e.g.* in tort cases (a traffic accident during a holiday abroad), the creditor can neither obtain a security nor can he impose on the debtor a payment method such as letters of credit or bills of exchange. This is the case for most 'involuntary creditors' [6] such as employees demanding redundancy payment from their ex-employers in a foreign country; cross-border child support claims or consumers of imported medicaments containing harmful substances. Secondly, even in contract cases, the contracting party with the weaker economical position cannot always benefit from

---

4   See 'Introduction', in James Richardson (ed.), *Debt Recovery in Europe* (London: Blackstone, 1993), pp.1–6, at p.4; Burt Edwards, 'Risk Management', in Brian W. Clarke (ed.), *Handbook of International Credit Management*, 2nd ed. (Aldershot: Gower, 1995), pp. 98–110.

5   For the role of an 'international credit manager' in an export firm see Brian Clarke, 'Responsibilities, Expertise and Resource', *Handbook of International Credit Management*, pp. 11–5. Indeed, 'international credit management' does not differ in nature from the usual credit management. It is routine work for any supplier of goods or services to manage the risk of non-payment, that is, to be conscientious concerning their accounts, the 'largest and riskiest asset' of the firm. Burt Edwards, 'The Range of Risks', *Handbook of International Credit Management*, pp. 43–56, at p.43.

6   See Hans-Bernd Shäfer and Claus Ott, *Lehrbuch der ökonomiscen Analyse der Zivilrechts*, 2nd ed. (Berlin: Springer, 1995), pp. 535–6.

international collection and security methods. This can occur for example, where a consumer makes a payment to a mail order company abroad but fails to receive the goods ordered. Lastly, it must be considered that not each and every security included in international contracts is enforceable. This may be due to differences in national laws (*e.g.* the non-enforceability of the German retention of title clauses in standard contract terms in many foreign countries, where the retention of title clause must be signed separately [7] and the non-enforceability of English floating charges over goods and chattels in Civil Law countries where such security rights are not recognised by law [8]) or practical difficulties (*e.g.* the costs involved in returning the goods exported under a retention of title clause).[9]

A. INVESTIGATING THE CREDITWORTHINESS OF THE DEBTOR

There are various methods used in international business to investigate the creditworthiness of a prospective customer or borrower.

The creditor may make use of commercial institutions which are called credit reference agencies.[10] There are a number of international credit reference agencies [11] which are transnational concerns with numerous affiliates in various countries.[12] The information provided by credit reference

---

7   See *supra* Chapter 10: Commercial Cross-Border Debt Collection in Germany, 'Difficulties in cross-border debt collection'.
8   Manfred Wenckstern, 'Die englische Floating Charge im deutschen internationalen Privatrecht', *Rabels Zeitschrift für ausländisches und internationales Privatrecht* 56 (1992), pp. 624–95.
9   Another important practical difficulty for retention of title clauses is that some other parties who have also been involved in the export of goods, *e.g.* the carrier who has not been paid for the freight or the warehouseman who has not been paid for storage charges may intervene to claim a right to deal with the goods under local law. Mark Hoyle, 'Legal and Regulatory Issues', *Handbook of International Credit Management*, pp. 363–70, at p. 367.
10 Also called credit rating agencies.
11 *E.g.* Credit Reform (Germany) and Dun & Bradstreet (United States). The German affiliate of the latter is called Schimmelpfeng.
12 International activity of the credit reference organisations in Europe goes back more than a century. In 1898 one German organisation had 58,000 members and offices in eleven countries including Britain and Turkey. Walther Nothnagel, *Execution durch sociale Interessengruppen* (Wien: Alfred Hölder, 1899), pp. 70–1. There are also domestic trade associations for credit reference (which are sometimes called trade protection societies or credit default registers) which offer credit information about consumers as well as businesses. However, these associations are designed for the

agencies is mainly collected from official sources, the most important being various types of company registers. A 'credit report' is a standard form which provides some general introductory information about the firm (*e.g.* registered address, age, legal status, capital structure, directors *etc.*) and a general judgment about its creditworthiness.[13] Since these credit reports depend heavily on official sources which may not be actual, and which may not include some important information about the past of the firm as a result of data protection regulations, according to which some negative records about the firm must be 'cleaned' periodically (*e.g.* records of protests or records of insolvency proceedings), the credit information collected from credit reference agencies must be considered with caution.[14]

In addition to large international credit reference agencies are what may be called 'boutique type' agencies which provide more detailed but more

---

    needs of domestic businesses. They usually work on a regional or sector basis where members of the association exchange information about their customers through a central data bank, which contains information provided by the members personally. Thus, these trade associations are seldom used by foreign businesses. An example of such a domestic credit reference association is the German 'Schutzgemeinschaft für allgemeine Kreditversicherung', commonly known as 'Schufa', which is a federal association of 13 regional credit reference institutions. In 1985 Schufa provided over 16 million business and consumer credit information references and held recorded credit information on over 23 million consumers. Fred Zeyer, 'Datenschützer fordern mehr Informationen von der Schufa', *Frankfurter Allgemeine Zeitung*, 6.3.1985. Credit information agencies keep their records and sometimes provide information to their clients by means of computer networks. Heiner Sieger, 'Wirtschaftsauskunfteien – Hacker dringen ein', *Focus*, no. 23 (1993); Norbert Robers and Olaf Wilke, 'Größter Daten-Klau', *Focus*, no.17 (1995), pp. 28–34. For a socio-legal study on the German credit reference associations see Eberhard Hoene, *Präventiver Kreditschutz und Zwangsvollstreckung durch Private* (Berlin: Duncker & Humblot, 1971), pp. 46–81. See also Jürgen Capell, *Erfolgreich Mahnen – Handbuch für die Mahn- und Inkassopraxis* (Bonn: Rentop, 1989), pp. 38–43. A number of trade associations and commercial firms for domestic credit reference also exist in England. See Rock, *Making People Pay*, pp. 30–1 and Andrew Bogle and John Fuller, *Successful Debt Collecting* (Bristol: Jordans, 1996), p. 11. In Turkey, there is no credit reference sevice as such. In the past, there have been unsuccessful attempts to establish 'credit default registers' at the local chambers of commerce. Presently, a group of textile firms in Istanbul have made an informal application to the Istanbul Chamber of Industry for a credit default register on the model of the Dutch association 'Dutch Convention on Payments' (NKC). (Information provided by an official of the Istanbul Chamber of Industry, 17.7.1996).

13   See Paul Pitts, 'Customer Risk Assessment', *Handbook of International Credit Management*, pp. 74–97, at pp. 92–5. For examples of standard forms for credit reports used by commercial credit reference agencies see Hoene, *Präventiver Kreditschutz und Zwangsvollstreckung durch Private*, pp. 30–2 and Capell, *Erfolgreich Mahnen*, p. 39.

14   Rainer Chr. Rudolf, 'Wie liest man eine Handelsauskunft richtig?', *Internationale Wirtschaft*, 13.2.1986. English Debt Collectors 3 and 12.

Collection and Security Methods Employed in International Trade 261

expensive 'in depth' credit reports. Investigations conducted for such reports can take two to three weeks and may include 'unofficial' information, for example, on the personal careers of the directors of the firm investigated.[15]

A further method for examining the creditworthiness of prospective clients is to obtain information from the debtor's bank abroad, usually through the creditor's own bank in the creditor's country.[16] Although banks are subject to data protection regulations, it is a commercial custom that they provide such general information about the financial standing and creditworthiness of their clients.[17]

In some branches of the economy, personal contacts prove to be an important source of credit information. The method used by British publishers is illustrative of this. A relatively small group of large British companies publish books in English which are distributed both at home and abroad. Clients are local distributors of international publishers. These clients keep permanent business relations with the publishers and each client purchases books from several publishers. The books kept in a bookshop's or distributor's stock may not be supplied by one or two publishers only. Thus, in the publishing industry, the same markets (and clients) are shared by the same group of suppliers. Clients are typically small or medium sized businesses which may easily fall into financial difficulties. In this context, referring to a credit reference agency at the outset of a business transaction or periodically will be of little use. Instead, a group of credit managers of the British publishers meet once a month under the chairmanship of a retired former colleague [18] and they exchange their experience concerning the previous month's business, paying much attention to the overseas clients.

---

15   English Debt Collector 12 (see *supra* Chapter 10) stated that he recently discovered on behalf of a client that one of the directors of a target company was also the director of twelve other companies which had all gone bankrupt within the last three years, and that, this information was not given to the said client by one of the well-known international credit reference agencies.

16   See Pitts, 'Customer Risk Assessment', pp. 76–7 and Hoene, *Präventiver Kreditschutz und Zwangsvollstreckung durch Private*, pp. 37–45.

17   Clients often supply details of their trading banks as a source of reference (Bogle and Fuller, *Successful Debt Collecting*, p. 10). Although credit managers advise that the bank references can be trusted, 'it is not uncommon for business concerns to maintain a number of active bank accounts, one of which will be kept in credit and used when references are requested, whilst others may be overdrawn and reflect a truer picture of the business and its ability, or otherwise, to meet its liabilities as they fall due'. Pitts, 'Customer Risk Assessment', p. 76.

18   This person is presently in the debt collection business and his firm exclusively deals in cross-border collections.

During such meetings all publishers become informed where a client is in financial difficulties or has accounts overdue. As a result of the special nature of the market for books this is the most efficient method of collecting credit information.[19]

B. STANDARD COLLECTION METHODS FOR CROSS-BORDER TRADE

Cross-border collections are made by means of collection methods [20] which have been standardised world-wide. Documentary operations are widely used, that is, letters of credit (Ls/C) and documentary collections.[21] Both collection methods depend on the intermediary role of the banks. In both cases, payment by the importer is made against the shipping (transport) documents produced by the exporter, which secures both parties against the risk of non-performance.[22] Again in both cases, bills of exchange are widely used to facilitate additional guarantee (*i.e.* the 'acceptance credit' where the acceptance of a time bill is substituted for payment in cash) and/or credit possibilities (*e.g.* the 'avalised bills' where a third person, typically a bank, guarantees payment). Where documentary operations are made with cash, the Ls/C and documentary collections are called 'sight L/C' and 'cash against documents' (CAD) respectively. Should bills of exchange or promissory notes be issued the terms

---

19   English Debt Collector 2.

20   The terms 'collection', 'settlement' and 'payment' are used interchangeably in this context.

21   See Publication nos.500 and 522 *Uniform Customs and Practice for Documentary Credits* (1993), and *Uniform Rules of Collections* (1995), Paris: International Chamber of Commerce. Two useful commentaries on these documents are: Charles del Busto, *ICC Guide to Documentary Operations* (Paris: International Chamber of Commerce, 1994) and *ICC Rules for Collections – A Commentary* (Paris: International Chamber of Commerce, 1995).

22   There are various types of letters of credit and documentary collections which cannot be discussed in detail in this context. However, the same principle applies to all documentary operations. For letters of credit, the importer instructs its bank to place an agreed sum (to be paid in cash or by means of a negotiable instrument) at the disposal of the exporter, which can be collected by the latter, *inter alia*, by handing over to the bank the documents representing the goods which have been shipped to the importer. In documentary collections, it is the exporter who instructs its bank to collect a certain sum from the importer against the transfer of the shipping documents. See Schmitthoff, *Schmitthoff's Export Trade*, Chapters 20, 21 and 22 (pp. 379–445); Jacques Lardinois, 'Documentary Collections', *Handbook of International Credit Management*, pp. 196–221; Brian Clarke, 'Documentary Letters of Credit', pp. 222–42.

'acceptance Ls/C' and 'documentary bills' (documents against acceptance, D/A) are used. Other commonly used collection methods for export sales are advance payment ('cash in advance') and payment after delivery ('cash against goods', 'open account') which depend on mutual confidence between parties to the contract.

C. 'OUT-SOURCING' THE CROSS-BORDER COLLECTIONS

A growing tendency in modern business is the hiring of external debt collectors and credit controllers as opposed to employing in-house credit managers, *i.e.* 'out-sourcing' credit management.[23] This applies in particular to international credit. In addition to the possibility of employing commercial debt collection agencies which work for commission (to be discussed in Part IV), the collection of cross-border payments may be effected by selling these accounts to a bank or other finance institution. The sale of receivables arising from cross-border trade may be either globally for the whole amount of short-term debts due from particular customers for a certain period of time (export factoring) or individually, for a number of individual debts of mid- or long term maturity (forfaiting).[24] In both cases, the bank or other finance institution relieves the exporter from the burden and/or risk of cross-border collections.

---

23 Interview with the President of the European Debt Collectors Association (English Debt Collector 12).
24 In the former case, the bank or the other finance institution is called the 'factor'; in the latter case, it is called the 'forfaiter'. In export factoring, according to the contract between the parties, the risk of non-payment may or may not be borne by the factor. A factor also maintains the client's sales ledger. In forfaiting the risk of non-payment is borne by the forfaiter, but the debt must normally be expressed in a negotiable instrument avalised or backed by a separate bank guarantee by another bank. Although forfaiting was originally applied only to medium and long term credit ranges, it is now quite often the case in Europe that it is applied to credit terms as little as 90 days in individual transactions as low as £50,000 (Gray Sinclair, 'Terms and Conditions for International Trade', *Handbook of International Credit Management*, pp. 133–50, at p.143). See *Schmitthoff's Export Trade*, Chapter 24 (pp. 471–87); Hoene, *Präventiver Kreditschutz und Zwangsvollstreckung durch Private*, pp. 95–110; Kurt F. Schär, 'Die wirtschaftliche Funktionsweise des Factoring', in Ernst A. Kramer (ed.), *Neue Vertragsformen der Wirtschaft: Leasing, Factoring, Franchising*, 2nd ed. (Bern, Stuttgart: Paul Haupt, 1992), pp. 275–8; Friedrich Graf von Westphalen, 'Rechtsprobleme des Factoring und des Forfait von Exportforderungen', *Recht der internationalen Wirtschaft*, 23. Jahrgang, no. 2 (1977), pp. 80–6; Mehmet Tomanbay, *Dis Ticaret Rejimi ve Ihracatin Finansmani* (Ankara: Hatipoglu, 1995), pp. 177–207; Hans-Werner Hauck and W. Beat Haenni, 'Export Finance Techniques in Europe', *Handbook of International Credit Management*, pp. 303–15, at pp. 309–12.

'Out-sourcing' may also be undertaken through agency and distributorship agreements. A distributorship agreement relieves the exporter from the burden and risk of cross-border collections in that the distributor stocks the goods for his own account and sells the goods on to the final customers against the orders which are placed directly with him. An agent abroad (or even in the creditor's place of residence) may also serve such a function if he agrees to take the *del credere* risk, *i.e.* to underwrite the credit risk and, in the event of non-payment by the client, to reimburse the principal.[25] The so-called export trade finance houses (or 'export houses') in Britain provide, *inter alia*, such agency services commercially while at the same time being insured by credit insurers.[26]

Exported goods may also be sold on the foreign market by a local subsidiary or related company, in which case the risk of non-payment remains within the same group of companies but the legal complications arising from cross-border collections are eliminated.[27]

D. THE STANDARD CONTRACT TERMS USED IN INTERNATIONAL TRADE

To avoid disputes arising from misunderstandings, the trade terms used in international trade have been standardised. Standardisation has been achieved to a large extent due to the conventions and publications drafted by the United Nations Commission on International Trade Law (UNCITRAL) and the International Chamber of Commerce in Paris. Two such examples are the so-called 'Hamburg Rules' (Convention on the Carriage of Goods by Sea) [28] and the International Rules for the Interpretation of Trade Terms (1990) ('Incoterms').[29] In addition, international trade institutions in various branches and the United Nations Economic Commission for Europe issued various standard contract forms to be used in international contracts, *e.g.* commodity contracts issued by the Federation of

---

25 See Don Nelmes, 'Agency Representation', *Handbook of International Credit Management*, pp. 16–28.
26 Hauck and Haenni, 'Export Finance Techniques in Europe', pp. 308–9; Brian Clarke, 'Sharing the Risk', *Handbook of International Credit Management*, pp. 113–7, at p.114.
27 See Robert Lambert, 'Operating through Subsidiaries and Affiliates', *Handbook of International Credit Management*, pp. 29–39, at pp. 35–7; Cavusgil, 'Globalization of Markets and Its Impact on Domestic Institutions', pp. 88–9.
28 [1978] *Lloyd's Maritime and Commercial Law Quarterly*, pp. 439–55.
29 Publication no. 460 (Paris: International Chamber of Commerce, 1990).

Oil, Seed and Fats Association (FOSFA) and the standard form no. 188 'For the Supply of Plant and Machinery for Export' of the Economic Commission for Europe. Lastly, many commercial firms which are involved in cross-border business have their own standard contracts to be used in their own business transactions. These standard contracts are drafted using the standardised language and trade terms referred to above [30] and have been widely 'standardised' as a result of the fashion of American contract drafting brought by the 'global Americanisation of commercial law'.[31]

E. SECURITY METHODS EMPLOYED IN INTERNATIONAL TRADE

It is common practice in international trade to use contract guarantees to avoid the risk of non-performance. The contract guarantees which are used in international trade take different forms (*e.g.* bank guarantees, corporate guarantees given by a third company or suretyship provided by associated/parent companies). They provide different degrees of protection to the creditor ranging from simple suretyship, where payment by the guarantor is conditional on the established default, to demand guarantees, whereby a written statement by the beneficiary suffices for calling upon the guarantee. These different forms of guarantees are again elaborated by standardised commercial customs [32] and may be more efficient than those given in domestic transactions.[33]

---

30 For further information see Antonio Boggiani, *International Standard Contracts – The Price of Fairness* (Dordrecht, Boston, London: Graham & Trotman / Martinus Nijhoff, 1991); *Schmitthoff's Export Trade*, Chapter 3.
31 See Shapiro, 'The Globalization of Law', pp. 38–44.
32 For the guarantees typically given to the buyers by guarantors acting on behalf of sellers, see International Chamber of Commerce, Publication no. 325: *Uniform Rules for Contract Guarantees* (Paris: International Chamber of Commerce, 1978); Publication no. 458: *Uniform Rules for Demand Guarantees* (Paris: International Chamber of Commerce, 1992) and Publication no. 524: *Uniform Rules for Contract Bonds* (Paris: International Chamber of Commerce, 1993); Martin Shaw, 'Bonds and Guarantees', *Handbook of International Credit Management*, pp. 151–63.
33 The English term 'guarantee' often has a different meaning in international trade than in domestic transactions. That is, the guarantor's obligation vis-à-vis the creditor is not secondary to the main contract; but, provided that the conditions of the guarantee are satisfied (*e.g.* a document is produced by the creditor), the guarantor is under a primary and independent undertaking to pay the creditor, regardless of the fact that, for example, the principal contract between the debtor and the creditor is invalid. *Schmitthoff's Export Trade*, pp. 446–7.

In addition, real securities used in domestic transactions are also used in international trade. The reservation of title clauses, for example, is applied in the international sales of goods as well.[34] In Turkish law there are a number of special provisions which enables land-, ship- and aircraft-mortgage in a foreign currency where the mortgagee is a foreign creditor.[35] Turkish Law Firm 3 which was interviewed for this study stated that most of the international litigation which they were involved in before the Turkish courts concerned cases on the enforcement of such real security rights.

F. THE EXPORT CREDIT INSURANCE

Export credit may be insured against the risk of non-performance.[36] As a rule, export credit insurance policy covers the so-called 'political risks' as well as the commercial risks of international trade. That is, the exporter is protected not only against the risk of non-payment as a result of insolvency or unwillingness on the part of the debtor but also against the risk of the debtor's government preventing him from honouring the debt.

Since this kind of insurance is not attractive for commercial insurers, in many countries there exist state-owned or state-controlled export credit insurance companies/departments [37] aiming to encourage the exports by providing a government guarantee.[38]

---

[34] Thus, the International Chamber of Commerce issued a book on the reservation of title clauses in 35 countries, *Eigentumvorbehalt in 35 Ländern*, Publication no. 501 (Paris: International Chamber of Commerce, 1993).

[35] See Mahmut T. Birsel and Ercüment Erdem, 'Yurtdísíndan Alínan Yatírím Kredilerinin Cebri Icra Yoluyla Tahsilinde Ortaya Cíkan Sorunlar', in Ali Cem Budak (ed.), *Türk, Ingiliz ve ABD Hukukunda Isletmelerin Ödeme Güclügü Sorunlari ve Banka Iliskileri Sempozyumu* (Istanbul: Istanbul Chamber of Industry, 1993), pp. 103–48, at pp. 119–23.

[36] Export credit insurance (also called 'export guarantee') must be distinguished from insurance against losses as a result of loss or damage occurring to the exported goods.

[37] For example, Hermes Kreditversicherung-AG in Germany and Eximbank in Turkey. British 'Export Credit Guarantee Department' of the Department of Trade and Industry was taken over by a Dutch group (*i.e.* privatised) in 1992. However, the Export Credit Guarantee Department continues at present to re-insure the risks. See Day and Griffin, *The Law of International Trade*, pp. 146–9; *Schmitthoff's Export Trade*, Chapter 25 (pp. 471–87); Tomanbay, *Dis Ticaret Rejimi ve Ihracatin Finansmani*, pp. 156–76.

[38] In recent years private credit insurers began to offer credit cover to foreign companies applicable in their own countries thereby extending their market share against public export credit insurers. For international developments in the export credit market see Paul Dawson, 'Credit Insurance', *Handbook of International Credit Management*, pp. 118–31.

15 A Survey of the Collection and Security Methods used by Exporters

A. THE FIELD OF SURVEY AND THE METHOD USED

1. The Field of Survey

Information concerning business practices used in international commerce for cross-border payments could only be collected by means of a business survey made among a selected group of actors participating in cross-border legal interactions. For this study, export manufacturers of textiles, leather and clothing – collectively 'textiles' – in Istanbul [1] were chosen as a target group for a survey on the above-mentioned topic.[2]

Numerous factors influenced this choice. The region where the survey was made, *i.e.* the area of Greater Istanbul, is the most important centre for industry and the export trade in Turkey. The members of the Istanbul Chamber of Industry ('ICI'), which is a public institution with compulsory membership, accounted for 33.9% of the country's total exports in 1995. In the same year, 691 members of the ICI registered at least one export amounting to a total of $7,330,410,000.[3] Of these 691 exporter firms, 363

---

[1] The export of clothing accounts for 69.8% of Turkish textiles exports. (Unpublished data provided by the Research Department of the Association of Textile and Clothing Exporters of Istanbul, 1996.)

[2] A similar business survey at the level of domestic commercial transactions was published in the *World Development* after this research had been completed. See Marchel Fafchamps, 'The Enforcement of Commercial Contracts in Ghana', *World Development* 24, no.3 (1996), pp. 427–48. Although Fafchamps' study deals mainly with domestic contract enforcement, it refers also to export trade (pp. 437, 445–6), and the results are similar to the results of this study.

[3] *Directory of Exporting Industrialists 1996* (Istanbul: Istanbul Chamber of Industry, 1996), pp. 430–1.

or 52.5% are manufacturers of textiles, clothing ('wearing apparel'), leather and leather products.[4]

In 1995, textiles constituted 41.49% of the value of Turkish exports.[5] As a rule, textile manufacturers are a diverse group. Throughout the year (including low and high seasons) different firms export goods of various types, quality and quantity to buyers with different needs and expectations, rather than producing goods of a similar type and quality to be sold to a certain (more or less homogeneous) group of customers. For both importers and exporters in the textile branch there exist not only small and medium-sized enterprises but also larger enterprises, including manufacturers as well as trading companies.[6] Turkish textile exporters are not concentrated in a single market, but rather undertake business in a number of European countries, the Middle East or the United States.[7] Therefore, to select the textile industry as a sample for this survey provides a relatively large number of examples of cross-border interactions between numerous diverse commercial actors involving the sale of a large variety of products. The value of this sample may be better appreciated if textiles are compared, for example, to other export branches of the Turkish economy *e.g.* traditional agricultural products (nuts, tobacco), petroleum products, cement, electrical machinery, *etc.* which provide less diversity.

The survey was conducted by means of a questionnaire entitled 'Questionnaire on the Collection and Risk Management Methods Used by Turkish Export Firms' (hereinafter 'the questionnaire')[8] which was prepared

---

4   *I.e.* main groups 321, 322, 323 in the 2nd Revision of the 'International Standard Industrial Classification of all Economic Activities' of the United Nations (ISIC Rev.1).

5   Unpublished data provided by the Research Department of the Association of Textile and Clothing Exporters of Istanbul, 1996.

6   Although the majority of textile exporters are small and medium-sized firms, no classified data are available on the size and firm structure of Turkish textile exporters. (Information in writing provided by the Association of Textile and Clothing Exporters of Istanbul on 8.7.1996.) In Istanbul, approximately one-half of textile exporters are small firms with fewer than 50 employees and the other half are medium to large-sized firms with between 51 and 500 employees. See *infra*.

7   In 1995, according to the value of the exported goods, the 15 most important importers of Turkish wearing apparel were Germany, the United States, the Russian Federation, France, the United Kingdom, Poland, Austria, Italy, the Benelux countries, Switzerland, Hungary, Denmark, Saudi Arabia and Libya. (Unpublished data provided by the Research Department of the Association of Textile and Clothing Exporters of Istanbul.)

8   See Annex I for English translation of the original Turkish text. Original text is available from the author.

during August – October 1995 in Bremen and Istanbul.[9] A 'pilot survey' was then performed in November 1995 among nine larger textile exporters from the ICI.[10] After considering the results of this pilot survey and making some minor changes to the questionnaire, it was distributed among the remaining ICI textile exporters.[11] By March 1996, 55 completed questionnaires had been returned to the ICI. Also in March 1996, 30 copies of the questionnaires were sent a second time to a group of large-sized exporter firms [12] which had not responded to the first request. As a result, two more answers were received, making a total of 57 answers (including the pilot survey). Thus, a total of 17% of the firms questioned replied.

The firms which replied to the questionnaire represent different branches of the textile export industry in Turkey: for the export of clothes, 41 firms are represented; 10 firms represent textiles manufacturing, and 4 firms for leather products and shoes.[13] The same holds true for firm size: of the 57 firms which replied, 15 employ fewer than 50 employees; 30 employ between 51 and 500; 4 firms employ between 501 and 1000, and 4 firms employ more than 1000 employees.[14] For more than one-third of the firms which replied, business is exclusively in exports, *i.e.* 100% of their products are exported. A further third exports between 80 – 99% of their prod-

---

9   The author's first draft was improved after discussions with a number of academicians and industrialists in Turkey. The author thanks Hasan Nerad of Dokuz Eylül University, Haluk Kabaalioglu of Marmara University, Müjde Oktay and Ayhan Öztürk of ICI and Tuncer Ögün of the Association of Textile and Clothing Exporters of Istanbul. The following reference books on the law and regulations for export trade in Turkey were also helpful in drafting the questionnaire: Ahmet Kizil and Macide Sogur, *Ihracat-Ithalat Islemleri ve Muhasebe Uygulamasi* (Istanbul: Der, 1995), Mehmet Tomanbay, *Dis Ticaret Rejimi ve Ihracatin Finansmani* (Ankara: Hatipoglu, 1995).

10 To ensure responses, these nine firms were selected from the businessmen personally known to an officer of the Chamber, who in turn signed the cover letter which accompanied the questionnaire.

11 The questionnaire was annexed to a cover letter from the Centre for Law and Politics at the University of Bremen. A second cover letter by ICI referring to a Board of Directors' decision of the Chamber supporting the survey was enclosed. In order to encourage replies, the exporters were requested to send the answers back to a senior officer at ICI instead of to the author directly. Some replies were mailed or faxed to ICI. Other exporters chose to send their replies by registered mail or delivered them personally with a request for absolute business confidentiality. ICI forwarded the completed questionnaires to the author in Bremen.

12 *I.e.* thirty firms from ICI's list of 'Outstanding Exporting Industrialists 1993' totalled textile exports of more than $10,000,000 in that year.

13 Two firms did not answer the relevant question.

14 Four firms provided no answer to the question regarding the number of employees.

ucts, and the remaining third have lower rates of export, evenly distributed between 10 and 75%. With regard to the export markets, the majority of exports for 44 firms are to EU and EFTA countries; for 6 firms, exports are mainly made to the Middle East, and for 4 firms the United States and Canada rank first in their client portfolio. (The countries other than these three groups are mentioned, if at all, as the second or third major export markets, *i.e.* by 8 and 11 different combination of firms, respectively.[15]) As will be seen below, some of these characteristics of the textile exporters have been taken into account when analysing the survey results, as far as an association or relationship can be established between these characteristics and the firm's behaviour concerning the collection and the risk management methods.

Although the survey was on a modest scale, the export-orientation and diversity observed in the Turkish textile industry, in conjunction with the variety of firms responding to the questionnaire, enabled the results to be generalised to some extent as a representative sample of the export industry in Turkey.[16] However, the number of replies received (57) does not permit the author to draw detailed conclusions expressed in definitive numerical terms.[17] Thus, even though the survey results were computer-processed, which reduced the paperwork,[18] the conclusions drawn are not meant to provide precise statistical data.

2. Questionnaire and Information Processing Method

The questionnaire consists of 18 questions in two parts. The first part seeks to obtain information about the firm. This part contains questions about the field of commercial activity, size of the firm, the degree of export orientation, experience in exports, and the foreign markets where the firm carries out business.

The second part includes questions on the subject matter of the research. Question II(1) aims to collect information on the exporter's customer relations. The firms were asked how they initiate business relations with their

---

15 Two firms provided no answer to the question on export markets.
16 See, *e.g.* Jürgen Friedrichs, *Methoden empirischer Sozialforschung*, 10th ed. (Opladen: Westdeutscher Verlag, 1982), pp. 125–6.
17 Therefore, except for in the tables and figures, the conclusions below are expressed in approximate terms, such as 'half of the exporters' instead of, *e.g.* '47%' or '54%'.
18 See *infra*.

clients, which, the author believed, may have an influence on the firm's behaviour relating to credit management in export sales. Questions II(2) and II(3) refer to the methods used (if any) for acquiring credit information on the importers. Question II(4) aims to establish whether, and to what extent, contracts are used to avoid possible conflicts between the exporter and the importer, which may result in non-payment of the sale price. Questions II(5) and II(6) concern the security (risk management) methods used by exporters against the risk of non-payment. Question II(7) refers to collection methods and question II(8) to the success rates in collections. The following four questions, *i.e.* II(9), II(10), II(11) and II(12) concern the possible disputes arising between the exporter and the importer which may result in non-payment, and the subsequent dispute resolution methods. In the last two open questions, the exporters are invited to comment on possible 'difficulties' (or particular problems) and to provide examples based on their own experience.

With the exception of the last two questions, all questions are in multiple-choice or 'fill in the blank' form. Some of the multiple-choice questions contain a final choice of 'others', where the exporter may insert a short comment. In addition, other multiple-choice questions require the exporter to answer by listing in order of preference. For example, in question II(7), the exporter may answer that, for his firm, the most commonly used collection method is letters of credit providing for payment on sight, and their second most favoured method is 'cash in advance', and so on.[19]

The answers were processed using a commercial computer programme.[20] Firms were numbered 'Exporter 1', 'Exporter 2', *etc.* The answers, including some of the answers to the open questions [21] or the

---

[19] Six firms (*i.e.* Exporters 12, 13, 24, 26, 30 and 44) answered the preference questions with 'ticks' instead of numbers. In addition, some preference questions were answered with more than one '1' or '2', which signifies that the firm regards more than one of the choices as being of equal value (*e.g.* Exporter 1, in questions II(1) (3) (7) and (10) and Exporter 23 for question 23). In these cases, all the multiple choices marked with '1' are regarded as the most common practices.

[20] *I.e.* SPSS/PC+. See Gerhard Broius, *SPSS/PC+ Basics and Graphics – Einführung und praktische Beispiele* (Hamburg: McGraw Hill, 1988). In a small-scale study with 57 cases, the 'significance test' which is provided by SPSS/PC+ is not workable. Therefore, the significance of the data and the correlations for the cross-tables have been controlled manually, taking into account the contents of the questions and answers as well as the quantitative significance.

[21] Some of the answers to the open questions which are repetitive (usually due to the fact that the person completing the questionnaire inserted a comment before reading the following questions) were simply ignored. On the other hand, other answers to open questions were attributed to one of the existing categories (multiple-choices) or

questions where blanks had to be filled in, were coded with variable numbers. The answers to the preference questions were processed under two files which have been studied separately. The first file includes information concerning the preferences.[22] The second file, which aims to provide a more accurate overview, ignores the 'preferences' and considers each answer (*i.e.* each mark made for a multiple-choice) as a tick in the box at the margin of the question.[23] For convenience, the first and the second file have been used interchangeably. Where the terms '(most) common practice' *etc.* are used, the first file has been taken as a basis; where the terms 'common practice' and 'no common practice' are used, the second file is at issue.

3. The Role of Firm Size

It is said that the size of the firm plays an important role in defining the legal relations between the actors in international business:

> The big multinational enterprises . . . [which], seen economically, are by far the most important actors, . . . tend to push their legal claims into the background and work on the basis of mutual trust or economic interdependence . . . The medium-sized firm, on the other hand, lacks the dominant position to make state law superfluous, [but] is strong enough to go into the global market and use all necessary legal means to pursue its economic interests . . . The role of small firms in global legal interaction generally seems to be more difficult to define, since their participation in the global (legal) market depends very much on the support structures (chambers of commerce, consulates, governmental legal information services, and so on) they find in their home country.[24]

Large-sized firms have more financial means to remedy the difficulties of enforcement of the law resulting from differences in the legal systems involved in international legal transactions. Yet larger firms do not necessarily have better credit management for international sales:

---

    collated into groups and considered as if there were multiple-choices involving the relevant information. As a result of the latter, the figures below contain some information which was not expressly asked for in the questionnaire.

22   The 'most common practice' is given the value '1', the second common practice is given the value '2', and so forth.

23   A box which has been marked is given the value '1' regardless of the fact that it shows the first, second or third common practice. An empty box is given the value '2'.

24   Gessner, 'Introduction', *Foreign Courts*, p. 2.

[Although] a large firm has the benefit of large-scale operation, . . . it suffers from a number of disadvantages because of its sheer size. Communications can never be as good as in a small company, and business activities tend to be compartmentalised, with nobody seeing the overall picture in anything but superficial detail.[25]

In the following analysis, considering the possible influence of the size of the firm on its behaviour, the answers given to the questions on cross-border collections and the management of credit risk are compared with the firm sizes. That is, the firm sizes are used as a general reference point to check the results of the survey. Where the answers to the questions are not evenly distributed among the respondent firms, as a result of the fact that the exporters with different firm sizes tend to answer differently, these differences are made clear.

Since all the firms which replied belong to the same industry, which employs a relatively large workforce, the number of employees working in a firm is taken as a basis for defining the firm size. Thus, the export firms are divided into four categories according to their number of employees. Firms with 0 – 50 employees are referred to as 'the smallest firms'; firms with 51 – 500 employees plus the smallest firms are referred to as 'the smaller firms'; firms with more than 1,000 employees are referred to as 'the largest firms' and firms with 501 – 1,000 employees plus the largest firms will be called 'the larger firms'.

With regard to firm size, a comparison between the distribution of the firms which completed the questionnaire and all the textile exporters registered with the ICI in 1995 showed that, when compared to the whole group, the smallest firms were under-represented and the larger firms were over-represented among the respondents to the questionnaire. In order to improve the representative quality of the survey results, the values in single figures or calculations were multiplied by a 'correction figure' where necessary.[26]

---

25 Brian W. Clarke, 'The role of credit in world trade', *Handbook of International Credit Management*, pp. 3–10, at p. 9.
26 In the tables where firm size was taken as one variable, such 'correction' was unnecessary.

Table 15.1 Distribution of respondent export firms according to the firm size

	Respondent firms		All textile exporters		Correction figure
Number of employees	count	%	count	%	
1 – 50	15	28%	170	47%	47/28
51 – 500	30	56%	172	48%	48/56
501 – 1000	4	8%	12	3%	3/ 8
1000 – 3000	4	8%	8	2%	2/ 8
Total:	53	100%	362	100%	

Missing Observations: 4.
Source: Unpublished ICI computer records. (Author's calculation.)

Thus, if all the firm-size groups had been equally represented and 100 firms had completed the questionnaire, the respondent firms would have been distributed according to the firm size as follows:

$\quad$ 1 – 50 employees : $\quad$ 15 * 47/28 * 100/54 = 47 firms.
$\quad$ 51 – 500 employees : $\quad$ 30 * 48/56 * 100/54 = 48 firms.
$\quad$ 501 – 1000 employees : $\quad$ 4 * 3/ 8 * 100/54 = 3 firms.
$\quad$ 1001 – 3000 employees : $\quad$ 4 * 2/ 8 * 100/54 = 2 firms.

The figures below will be constructed based on this assumption, *i.e.* as if the questionnaire had been completed by 100 firms and as if all firm sizes were distributed in accordance with the actual distribution of firm sizes among the textile exporters. Thus, single figure values will be in percentages rather than absolute numbers.

4. Other Important Determinants: Experience in Exports, Export Orientation and Customer Relations

In addition to firm size, three other hypothetical determinants have also been taken into account in the process of drawing conclusions and information from the survey results. After initial study of the completed questionnaires, the export firms were divided into categories relating to their experience in the export business, their degree of export orientation, and the nature of their customer relations.

Firms which have been in the export business since 1985 (or longer) are referred to as 'the experienced exporters', while firms which have been in the export business only since 1991 are called 'the less experienced exporters'.

As already stated, all firms which completed the questionnaire were export firms, *i.e.* they are registered with the Istanbul Chamber of Industry and listed in the Directory of Export Industrialists. However, some of these export firms have a considerable domestic customer portfolio, which may have an effect on their behaviour in that they are less likely to have permanent business contacts abroad, and their credit managers are in a position to consider domestic sales as an alternative to exports. The firms which export more than 85% of their products are referred to as 'export-oriented firms' while the remaining group is referred to as 'less export-oriented firms'.

Two groups of textile exporters in Istanbul could be identified from the information provided in the questionnaires. One group establish contact with their customers through their personal relations and reputation in foreign markets or already have established customers,[27] and the second group employ commercial agents in order to reach their customers abroad.[28] The first group is referred to as 'the firms depending on personal relations / regular customers' and the latter as 'the firms co-operating with agents'.[29] The results of this distinction are discussed below.

B. RELATIONS WITH THE CUSTOMERS

Despite the distance and national borders (or, possibly because of the lack of legal certainty created by them), personal relations depending on mutual confidence and prestige of the firm play an important role in the business relations of textile exporters in Istanbul. The firms were asked how they first establish contact with importers abroad.[30] Almost one-half who replied that most of their customers are regular established customers seldom do business with new customers.[31] (Figure 15.1.)

---

27   *I.e.* the firms which marked the multiple-choices (f) and (g) in the Question II(1).
28   *I.e.* the firms which chose the multiple-choices (c) and (d) in the Question II(1).
29   See *infra* 'Relations with Customers' in this Chapter.
30   See the Questionnaire, II(1).
31   Questionnaire, II(1)(g).

276 Making Foreign People Pay

Figure 15.1

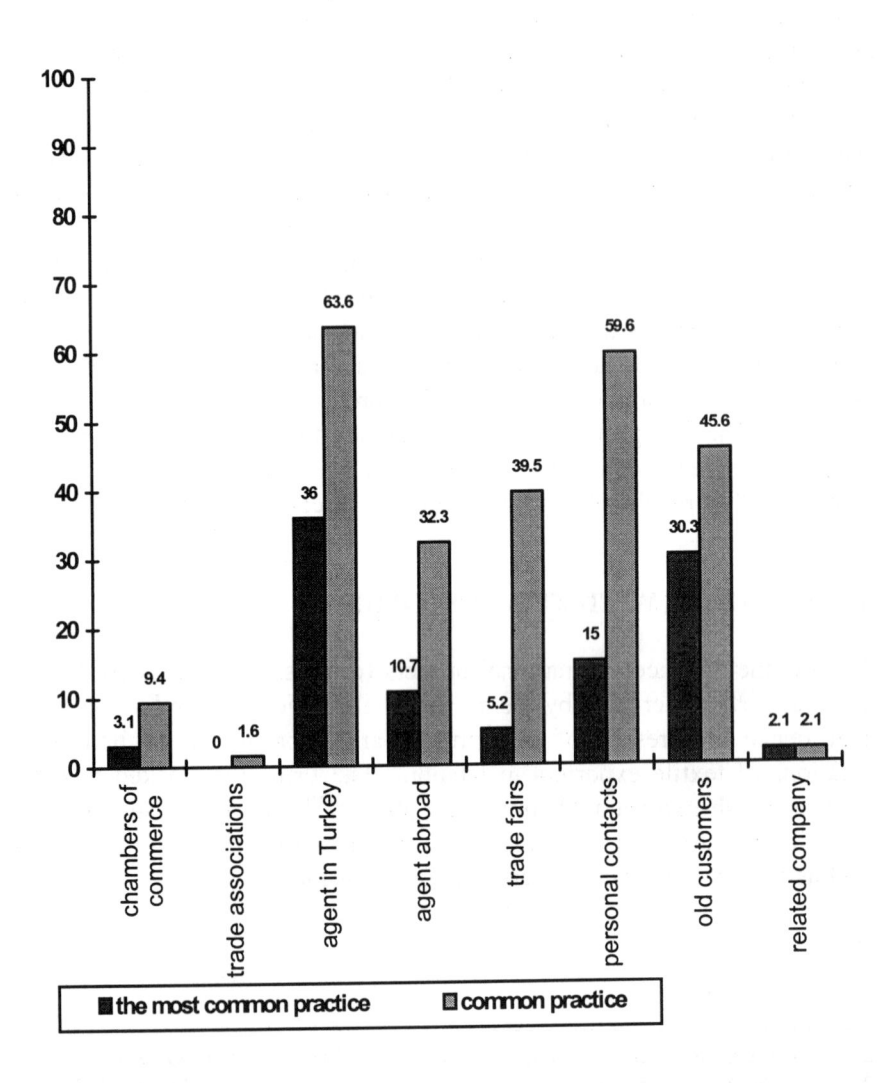

Exporters' first contact with the customers
(Values in percentages*)

	the most common practice	common practice
chambers of commerce	3.1	9.4
trade associations	0	1.6
agent in Turkey	36	63.6
agent abroad	10.7	32.3
trade fairs	5.2	39.5
personal contacts	15	59.6
old customers	30.3	45.6
related company	2.1	2.1

Valid cases: 53. Missing cases: 4.
(*) Values have been corrected regarding the actual distribution of firms according to firm size.

Unsurprisingly, the experienced exporters have established customers more often than do the less-experienced exporters. The 7 out of 12 experienced exporters have 'old, established customers', whereas for the 18 less-experienced exporters, only 8 firms have established customers.

The primary role of personal relations is valid not only for small firms, where personality of the owner of the business may be of greater importance, but also for the largest firms, where the business contacts may remain relatively anonymous to the customers. Half of the larger textile exporters have old established business relations, and they seldom do business with new customers (Table 15.2).

Table 15.2 Having old, established customers and firm size

Count Row Pct Firm size (no. of employees)	Established customers common practice	not common practice	Row Total
0 – 50	5 33.3	10 66.7	15 28.8
51 – 500	17 56.7	13 43.3	30 56.6
501 – 1000	2 50.0	2 50.0	4 7.7
1001 – 3000	3 75.0	1 25.0	4 7.7
Column Total	27 50.9	26 49.1	53 100.0

Number of Missing Observations: 4.

Again, for 60% of the export firms, it is common practice to get in touch with the importers for the first time through their personal contacts, or be contacted first as a result of their reputation in the foreign market (Table 15.3).

Table 15.3 Personal contacts and firm size

Firm size (no. of employees)	Count / Row Pct	Personal contacts — common practice	Personal contacts — not common practice	Row Total
0 – 50		7 46.7	8 53.3	15 28.8
51 – 500		21 70.0	9 30.0	30 56.6
501 – 1000		3 75.0	1 25.0	4 7.7
1001 – 3000		3 75.0	1 25.0	4 7.7
Column Total		34 66.0	19 34.0	53 100.0

Number of Missing Observations: 4.

Table 15.4 Use of agents in Turkey and firm size

Firm size (no. of employees)	Count / Row Pct	Agent in Turkey — common practice	Agent in Turkey — not common practice	Row Total
0 – 50		11 73.3	4 26.7	15 28.8
51 – 500		18 60.0	12 40.0	30 56.6
501 – 1000		1 25.0	3 75.0	4 7.7
1001 – 3000			4 100.0	4 7.7
Column Total		30 56.6	23 43.4	53 100.0

Number of Missing Observations: 4.

The fact that the smallest firms contact their customers less often through personal contacts may explain why these firms more often need a commercial agent in Turkey for marketing their products (Table 15.4) whereas larger firms have agents abroad (Table 15.5). A commercial agent in Turkey having connections in different foreign markets does not provide marketing service on site, but it offers a better-known 'address' for the customers abroad.

Table 15.5 Use of agents abroad and firm size

Count Row Pct Firm size (no. of employees)	Agent abroad common practice	Agent abroad not common practice	Row Total
0 – 50	3 20.0	12 80.0	15 28.8
51 – 500	13 43.3	17 56.7	30 56.6
501 – 1000	3 75.0	1 25.0	4 7.7
1001 – 3000	2 50.0	2 50.0	4 7.7
Column Total	21 39.6	32 60.4	53 100.0

Number of Missing Observations: 4.

Indeed, it might have been assumed that small enterprises often use their personal contacts, whereas for the larger firms business relations remain more anonymous. This is not the case, however, possibly because it is more difficult for a small firm to establish personal contacts and reputation abroad. A larger firm, which is able to reach the foreign market directly, depends more heavily on its reputation and personal contacts.

It may be assumed that the firms depending on personal relations / old customers rely on the personality of their business contacts, whereas the firms working with agents prefer to protect themselves by means of legal / commercial mechanisms available for risk management in international sales. One may expect to find that the firms depending on personal relations / old customers are more likely to do business at an informal level, *e.g.* making oral agreements instead of contracts in writing, using the collection methods which are based on mutual confidence (that is, advance payment and cash against goods) instead of the collection methods which are based on the intermediary role of the banks (*i.e.* documentary collections or documentary credits), preferring to resolve disputes by means of negotiation instead of litigation, *etc.* Similarly, the firms working with agents may be expected to require more often securities from the customer, to use contracts in writing and safer collection methods, *etc.* The survey results have been processed in order to find out if there exists such a relationship between the customer relations and the firm behaviour concerning the collection and risk management methods in international sales.

The comparison between the firms depending on personal relations / old customers and the firms working with agents shows that the nature of customer relations has an influence on (but does not necessarily determine) firm behaviour concerning collections and risk management in international sales. The firms depending on personal relations / old customers use credit information services as often as all the other firms (including the firms working with agents), *i.e.* around 60% of the firms. The same was true of the rates for using contracts in writing (around 50%), oral agreements (around 40%) and the use of security methods in the form of bank or corporate guarantees (around 60%). The collection methods based on the intermediary role of the banks are commonly used by both the firms which depend on personal relations / old customers and the firms which work with agents to the same extent, *i.e.* around 90%. Last but not least, the firms depending on personal relations / old customers and the firms working with agents share the same success rates in collecting their receivables arising from export sales, which is the same as the general average, *i.e.* around 75% of the firms are able to collect more than 95% of their receivables.

However, there are also distinctions between the two groups which confirm the initial assumptions. Firstly, open accounts ('cash against goods') which are based on the seller's confidence in the buyer are provided to the foreign customers more frequently by the firms depending on personal relations / old customers (around 75%), as compared to the general average around 60% (which is also applicable to the firms working with agents).

Secondly, and more importantly, there are differences in dispute resolution practices. Whereas negotiations are used by around 90% of the firms working with agents (which also represents the general average for all textile exporters), it is common practice for all the firms depending on personal relations / old customers (with a single exception) to resolve the disputes giving rise to overdue accounts by means of negotiations without resorting to litigation. As a result, the firms working with agents use litigation more often than the firms depending on personal relations / old customers and the general average (Table 15.6). In Table 15.6, the figures represent the percentages of firms belonging to the relevant group and describing litigation as a common practice for dispute resolution.

Table 15.6 Relations with customers and litigation

	All exporters *	The firms depending on personal relations / old customers		The firms working with agents	
		Old customers	Personal contacts	Agent in Turkey	Agent abroad
In-house lawyers	8.2%	4.3%	6.1%	6.7%	15.8%
Lawyers in Turkey	8.2%	4.3%	6.1%	13.3%	21.1%
Lawyer abroad	34.7%	39.1%	39.4%	40.0%	47.7%

Number of Missing Observations: 9.
* Also including those firms which do not fall into either of the two categories.

C. CREDIT INFORMATION

Textile exporters in Istanbul inquire about the commercial creditability and solvency of the importer before they initiate business contacts. The most favoured method – similar to the case for establishing first contact with the customers is to use personal contacts to investigate the creditworthiness of the customer. This is followed by bank information and the credit rating obtained from the commercial credit reference agencies. The answers given to the open questions and the multiple-choice 'others' show that export credit insurance and factoring companies are also used as sources of credit information.[32] That is, the 'credit limits' determined by the state-owned export insurance company (*i.e.* the Türk Eximbank) and the factoring companies

---

32   Exporters numbered 2, 16, 21, 24, 28 and 29.

282 *Making Foreign People Pay*

are considered by the majority of their clients as a reliable credit reference.[33] (Figure 15.2.)

Figure 15.2

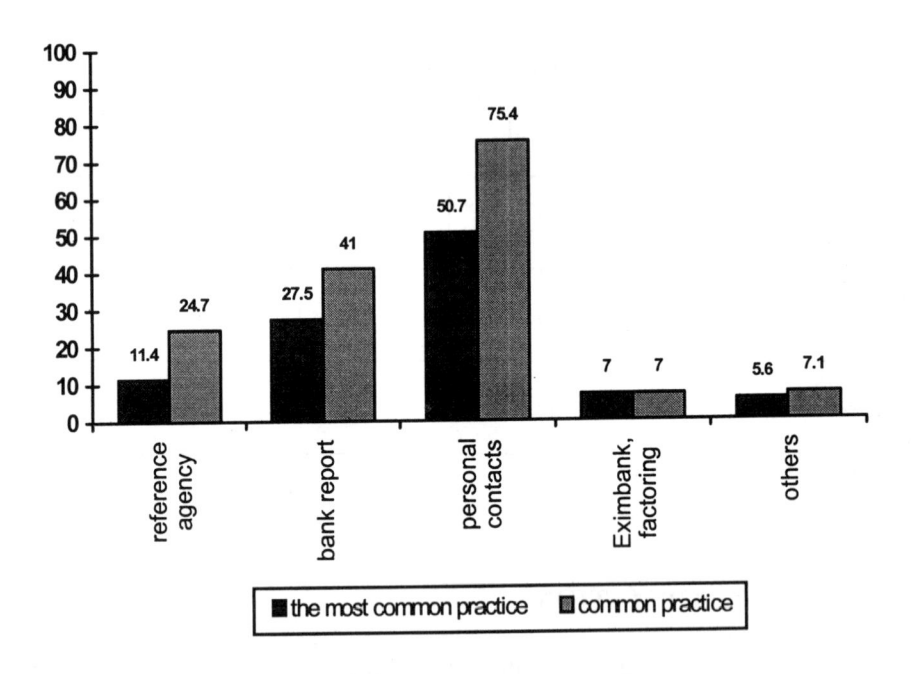

Sources of credit information
(Values in percentages*)

Source	the most common practice	common practice
reference agency	11.4	24.7
bank report	27.5	41
personal contacts	50.7	75.4
Eximbank, factoring	7	7
others	5.6	7.1

Valid cases: 49. Missing cases: 8.
(*) Values have been corrected regarding the actual distribution of firms according to firm size.

Smaller firms use credit information regularly as well as the larger firms. The less-experienced exporters use credit information more regularly than

---

33 On the other hand, Exporter 12 states that factoring companies who are anxious about the credit risk set the credit limits too low. Recently, for a customer who has always paid Exporter 12 on time for 8 years during which he has regularly bought goods worth a value of $3,000,000, the factor drew a credit limit as low as FFR 50,000. Exporter 27, who comments on the usefulness of Türk Eximbank guarantees, uses commercial credit reference agencies for credit vetting, and he does not mention the credit limits set by Türk Eximbank as a source of credit information.

the experienced firms. The 10 out of 17 less-experienced exporters use credit information regularly ('always') and the remaining 7 firms 'where necessary'. For the 12 experienced exporters, the corresponding figures are respectively 5 ('always') and 6 ('where necessary').

Figure 15.3

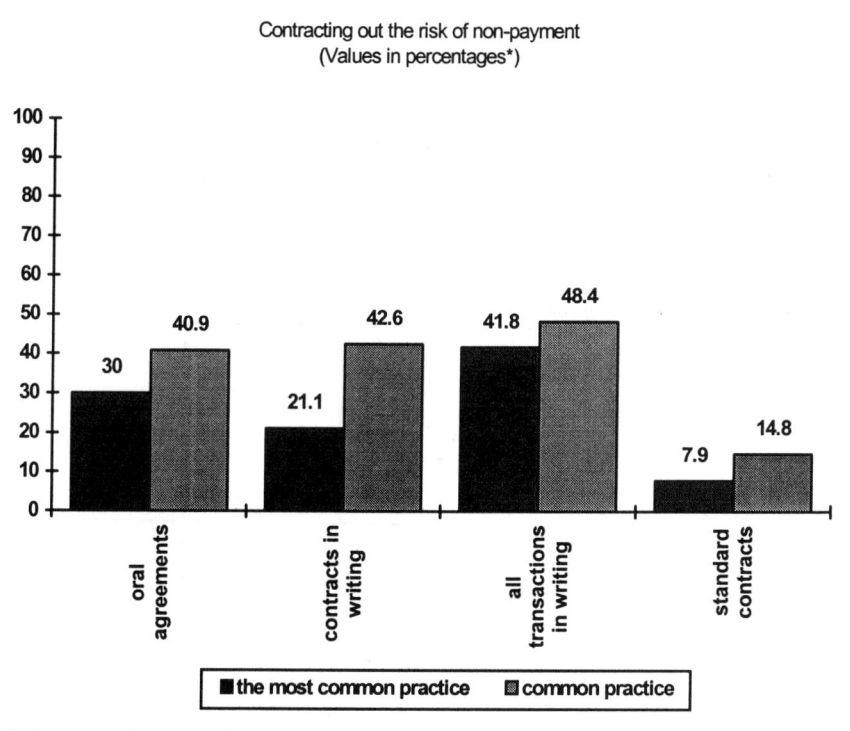

Contracting out the risk of non-payment
(Values in percentages*)

	the most common practice	common practice
oral agreements	30	40.9
contracts in writing	21.1	42.6
all transactions in writing	41.8	48.4
standard contracts	7.9	14.8

Valid cases: 53. Missing cases: 4.
(*) Values have been corrected regarding the actual distribution of firms according to firm size.

Interestingly, there exists no clear relation between the use of credit information and the success rate in collection of export sale accounts. Yet the firms which use credit information experience fewer disputes which may result in non-payment of the sale price. That is, more than one-third of the firms which use credit information regularly ('always') never experience disputes leading to non-payment, whereas for the firms which use credit information 'where necessary' the same rate is somewhere below 20%.

D. 'CONTRACTING OUT' THE RISK OF NON-PAYMENT

After checking the customer through the credit vetting process, the textiles exporters are less cautious in their contracting practices. Although the majority of the exporters prefer transactions in writing, for over 40% of the textiles exporters it is still one of the four 'common practices' to suffice with oral agreements in international sales. In addition, 30% of the export firms defined oral agreements, which are not coupled by written documents, as the most common practice in international sales [34] (Figure 15.3). This again confirms the importance of personal relations and confidence in international trade.

Table 15.7 Using oral agreements and firm size

Firm size (no. of employees)	Count Row Pct	not	1st	2nd	3rd	4th	Row Total
		------common practice------					
0 – 50		10 66.7	4 26.7	1 6.7			15 28.3
51 – 500		15 50.0	11 36.7	1 3.3	2 6.7	1 3.3	30 56.6
501 – 1000		2 50.0			2 50.0		4 7.5
1001 – 3000		4 100.0					4 7.5
Column Total		31 58.5	15 28.3	2 3.8	4 7.5	1 1.9	53 100.0

Number of Missing Observations: 4.

In any case, oral agreements are not used by the largest firms where, possibly, the sales manager does not have the discretionary power to conclude an oral agreement on the telephone, and they are not favoured by the smallest firms, where the risk of non-payment may have more serious effects on cash flow (Table 15.7).

---

34 However, it must be added that the export sales may be supported with a settlement method which substitutes, to some extent, for a contract in writing, *i.e.* documentary collections or Ls/C. See *infra* 'Collection methods' in this Chapter.

Table 15.8 Using contracts in writing and firm size

Firm size (no. of employees) Count Row Pct	Contract in writing for important matters — common practice	not common practice	Row Total
0 – 50	5 33.3	10 66.7	15 28.3
51 – 500	15 50.0	15 50.0	30 56.6
501 – 1000	3 75.0	1 25.0	4 7.5
1001 – 3000	2 50.0	2 50.0	4 7.5
Column Total	25 47.2	28 52.8	53 100.0

Number of Missing Observations: 4.

Table 15.9 Putting all transactions into writing and firm size

Firm size (no. of employees) Count Row Pct	All transactions in writing — common practice	not common practice	Row Total
0 – 50	9 60.0	6 40.0	15 28.3
51 – 500	11 36.7	19 63.3	30 56.6
501 – 1000	2 50.0	2 50.0	4 7.5
1001 – 3000	3 75.0	1 25.0	4 7.5
Column Total	25 47.2	28 52.8	53 100.0

Number of Missing Observations: 4.

Similarly, where the transactions are done in writing, the largest firms tend to favour the 'all transactions in writing' choice and the standard contract terms, whereas the smallest are more likely to prefer making written contracts for important matters only (Tables 15.8, 15.9 and 15.10).

Table 15.10 Using standard contracts and firm size

Count Row Pct Firm size (no. of employees)	Standard contracts common practice	Standard contracts not common practice	Row Total
0 – 50	2 13.3	13 86.7	15 28.3
51 – 500	3 10.0	27 90.0	30 56.6
501 – 1000	4 100.0		4 7.5
1001 – 3000	2 50.0	2 50.0	4 7.5
Column Total	11 20.8	42 79.2	53 100.0

Number of Missing Observations: 4.

Table 15.11 Contracting practices and success rate

Count Row Pct **Most common contracting practice**	\multicolumn{7}{c}{Success rate}	
	80%	85%	90%	95%	98%	99%	100%	Row Total
oral agreements only	1 6.3	1 6.3		4 25.0	2 12.5	1 6.3	7 43.8	16 32.7
contract in writing			1 9.1	2 18.2		4 36.4	4 36.4	11 22.4
all transactions in writing			1 5.9	2 11.8	1 5.9	5 29.4	8 47.1	17 34.7
standard contract terms							5 100.0	5 10.2
Column Total	1 2.0	1 2.0	2 4.1	8 16.3	3 6.1	10 20.4	24 49.0	49 100.0

Number of Missing Observations: 8.

The firms which have safer contracting practices have a higher success rate in collecting their receivables arising from exports (Table 15.11).

E. SECURITIES AGAINST THE RISK OF NON-PAYMENT

The term 'security' is used here in a broad sense: it covers the securities which may be required from the customer abroad, *e.g.* a bank guarantee or avalisation of a bill by a bank, as well as the safety methods which are organised by the exporter himself, such as having the receivables insured through export credit insurance.

The answers to the questionnaire show that the textile exporters do not favour requiring security from the importers against the risk of non-payment. One-third of the firms never require their customers to provide security in the form of a bank or corporate guarantee or avalisation of a bill by the same. An additional one-third require security only from those firms which they do business with for the first time, until they establish regular business relations.[35] The reason for this may be the efficiency of the

---

[35] The values have been corrected according to the actual distribution of firms according to firm size.

288 *Making Foreign People Pay*

collection methods used in international trade, which are safe enough without an additional security.

Although the larger export firms must be in a better position to impose conditions on their customers, interestingly, there is an inverse relationship between firm size and obtaining securities. The larger firms, possibly partly because they have safer business contacts based on confidence [36] and partly because of the fact that they use letters of credit [37] more often, require an additional security less frequently (Table 15.12). The less-experienced exporters require securities twice as often as the experienced exporters. That is, 10 out of 15 less-experienced exporters ask their customers for securities, while only 5 out of 10 experienced exporters do the same. Indeed, there appears to be no relation between obtaining securities from the customer and the success rate or frequency of disputes.[38]

Table 15.12 Obtaining securities and firm size

Count Row Pct Firm size (no. of employees)	Security required from the importer against the risk of non-payment			Row Total
	always	never	for new customers only	
0 – 50	7 50.0	3 21.4	4 28.6	14 31.1
51 – 500	2 8.0	11 44.0	12 48.0	25 55.6
501 – 1000	1 50.0	1 50.0		2 4.4
1001 – 3000	1 25.0	3 75.0		4 8.9
Column Total	11 24.4	18 40.0	16 35.6	45 100.0

Number of Missing Observations: 12.

---

36 See *supra* 'Relations with the customers' in this Chapter.
37 See *infra* 'Collection methods' in this Chapter.
38 The exporters who have reliable customers and who believe they do not need contractual securities are right about their opinion. The firms which never obtain security are even slightly more successful and have disputes less often.

A Survey of the Collection and Security Methods used by Exporters 289

If the security methods which are organised by the exporter himself are added to the securities which are required from the importer, the number of exporters who refrain from obtaining any form of security figures at 10 to 20%.[39] These figures are still interestingly high and indicate that many export firms believe that the costs of security methods are often not commensurate with the actual risk of non-payment in international sales.

The most favoured security required from customers is having a bill of exchange honoured / avalised by a bank. This method is especially practical because, in cases where letters of credit or documentary bills (D/A, documents against acceptance) are used, it can be incorporated into the collection method itself. On the other hand, export credit insurance appears as the most preferred method for insuring oneself against the risk of non-payment. This is followed by factoring, which was introduced in Turkey in the 1980s (Figure 15.4).

Figure 15.4

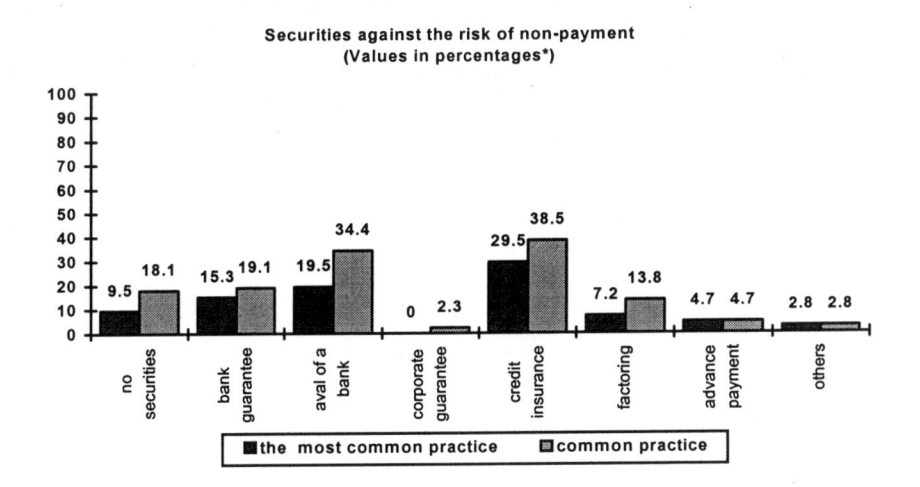

Securities against the risk of non-payment
(Values in percentages*)

	the most common practice	common practice
no securities	9.5	18.1
bank guarantee	15.3	19.1
aval of a bank	19.5	34.4
corporate guarantee	0	2.3
credit insurance	29.5	38.5
factoring	7.2	13.8
advance payment	4.7	4.7
others	2.8	2.8

Valid cases: 50. Missing cases: 7.
(*) Values have been corrected regarding the actual distribution of firms according to firm size.

---

39 Six firms state that 'obtaining no securities' is the most common practice. Three firms state that it is the second common practice, and two firms state that it is the fourth common practice not to obtain securities in any form.

F. COLLECTION METHODS

The collection methods 'cash in advance' and 'cash against goods' (open account) are based on confidence in the business partner. In the former case the payment is made in advance and in the latter the goods are shipped to the buyer, without the counter performance having been secured. After having learned of the importance of relations depending on personal confidence, it is not surprising to find that these collection methods are commonly used by the textile exporters. One-third of the textile exporters define advance payments and/or open accounts as the most common practices for their firm (Figure 15.5).

Obviously, 'cash against goods' is advantageous for the importer, whereas 'advance payments' are advantageous to the exporter. Likewise, the documentary collections are more favourable to the importer who makes the payment against the shipping documents, *i.e.* after the goods have been shipped. Whereas with letters of credit, which are more favourable to the exporter, the payments will be placed, albeit conditionally, at the exporter's disposal before the goods have been shipped.[40] The answers to the Questionnaire indicate that the collection methods which are favourable to the exporter, *i.e.* cash in advance and L/C, are used by the textiles exporters less often than the methods which are favourable to the importer, *i.e.* cash against goods and documentary collections (Figure 15.5).

---

[40] That is, although each of the two methods ensure that no performance will be made without the counter performance having been effected, in case of non-performance by one of the parties, the costs of transporting the goods and/or the transaction costs remain - depending on which of the two collection methods has been used – either on the exporter (*i.e.* in case of documentary collections) or on the importer (*i.e.* in case of L/C).

Figure 15.5

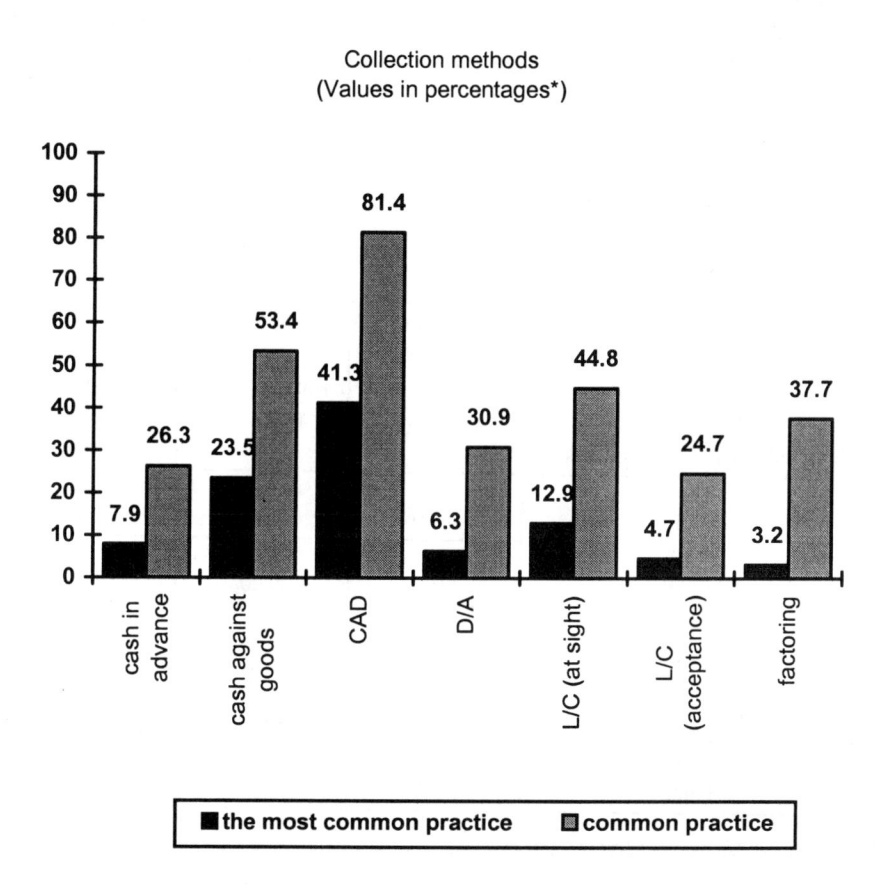

Collection methods
(Values in percentages*)

Method	the most common practice	common practice
cash in advance	7.9	26.3
cash against goods	23.5	53.4
CAD	41.3	81.4
D/A	6.3	30.9
L/C (at sight)	12.9	44.8
L/C (acceptance)	4.7	24.7
factoring	3.2	37.7

Valid cases: 51. Missing cases: 6.
(*) Values have been corrected regarding the actual distribution of firms according to firm size.

'Cash against documents' (CAD) provides the least security for the exporter. It is also the least successful collection method: more than 40% of the export firms which use CAD are among the 'less successful' firms, with a success rate lower than 96%. This is twice the rate of less successful firms in the average for all exporters (Figure 15.6).

The comparison with the firm sizes shows that cash against goods, which is the most advantageous settlement method for the importer, is preferred, especially by the smaller firms. That is, half of the smaller firms use cash against goods as one of the two most preferred methods, whereas only one out of eight larger firms named cash against goods as the second most common practice. The larger firms are likely to use letters of credit more frequently (Tables 15.13 and 15.14), and the smallest firms tend to use the documents against acceptance less often (Table 15.15). As a result, although the methods in the debtor's favour are used more frequently, the larger firms trade to some extent more safely than the smaller ones.

Table 15.13 Using on sight letters of credit and firm size

Count Row Pct	Letters of credit (on sight)		
Firm size (no. of employees)	common practice	not common practice	Row Total
0 – 50	6 40.0	9 60.0	15 29.4
51 – 500	14 50.0	14 50.0	28 54.9
501 – 1000	4 100.0		4 7.8
1001 – 3000	2 50.0	2 50.0	4 7.8
Column Total	26 51.0	25 49.0	51 100.0

Number of Missing Observations: 6.

Table 15.14 Using acceptance letters of credit and firm size

Count Row Pct Firm size (no. of employees)	Letters of credit (acceptance credit) common practice	not common practice	Row Total
0 – 50	1 6.7	14 93.3	15 29.4
51 – 500	12 42.9	16 57.1	28 54.9
501 – 1000	2 50.0	2 50.0	4 7.8
1001 – 3000	2 50.0	2 50.0	4 7.8
Column Total	17 33.3	34 66.7	51 100.0

Number of Missing Observations: 6.

Table 15.15 Using documents against acceptance and firm size

Count Row Pct Firm size (no. of employees)	Documents against acceptance common practice	not common practice	Row Total
0 – 50	3 20.0	12 80.0	15 29.4
51 – 500	12 42.9	16 57.1	28 54.9
501 – 1000	2 50.0	2 50.0	4 7.8
1001 – 3000	2 50.0	2 50.0	4 7.8
Column Total	19 37.3	32 62.7	51 100.0

Number of Missing Observations: 6.

294 *Making Foreign People Pay*

The less-experienced exporters favour working on a cash instead of on a credit basis. They use 'cash in advance', 'cash against documents' and letters of credit on sight more often than do the experienced firms. That is, 9 out of 18 less-experienced firms export goods on a cash in advance basis, while only 2 out of 11 experienced firms do. Similar figures apply for cash against documents and letters of credit to be paid on sight. Exports on credit terms, *i.e.* letters of credit with acceptance credit, documentary bills and 'cash against goods' are accepted more often by the experienced exporters (Table 15.16). Indeed, the less-experienced exporters who depend less frequently on old, established customers [41] are more cautious in their business relations than are experienced exporters. This is evident also from the comparison drawn with the experienced exporters concerning their customs about using credit information services and contractual securities.[42]

Table 15.16 Payment methods and export experience

	\multicolumn{3}{c}{Payment methods based on cash}	\multicolumn{3}{c}{Payment methods based on credits}		
	Payment in advance	Cash against documents	Letters of credit (on sight)	Open account	Documents against acceptance	Letters of credit (on acceptance)
less-experienced (total 18)	9 = 50%	16 = 88%	13 = 72%	11 = 61%	8 = 44%	7 = 39%
experienced (total 11)	2 = 18%	9 = 81%	5 = 45%	6 = 54%	6 = 54%	5 = 45%

Number of Missing Observations: 28.

G. SUCCESS RATES IN COLLECTION OF EXPORT DEBTS

More than half of the textile exporters answering the questionnaire report a success rate of 100% (Figure 15.6).

---

41 See 'Relations with customers' in this Chapter.
42 See 'Credit information' and 'Securities against the risk of non-payment' in this Chapter.

Figure 15.6

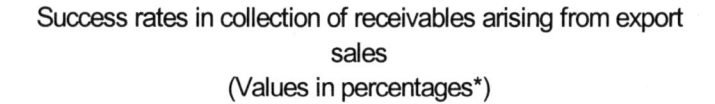

Success rates in collection of receivables arising from export sales
(Values in percentages*)

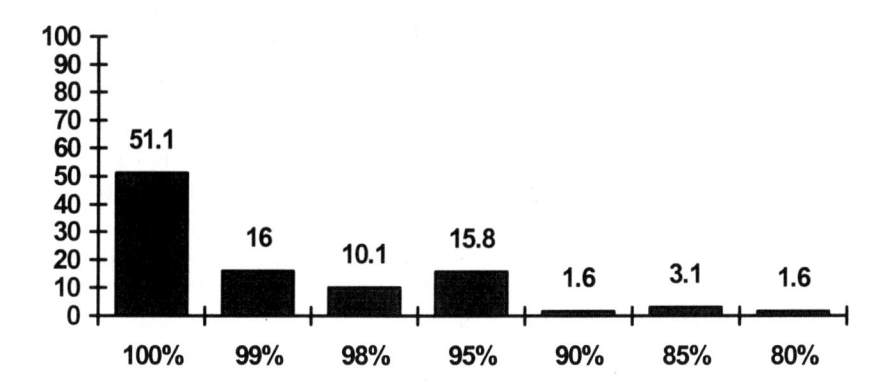

%	100%	99%	98%	95%	90%	85%	80%
	51.1	16	10.1	15.8	1.6	3.1	1.6

Valid cases: 53. Missing cases: 4.
(*) Values have been corrected regarding the actual distribution of firms according to firm size.

Those firms which have bad debts are the small and medium-sized firms. The larger ones are likely to have no unpaid accounts at all (Table 15.17).

This is not necessarily an optimal result, for it is possible that Turkish textile exporters are overly cautious. A business must be able to take risks, which often means it must have a reasonable number of uncollected accounts due from particular 'high-risk customers' which have been compensated, however, by the sales made to others in the same group.[43]

---

[43] See Edwards, 'Risk Management', p. 106: 'the high-risk customers are still in business; they need to purchase goods and services; there are sales and profit to be had from them before they go under'.

Table 15.17 Success rate and firm size

Firm size (no. of employees)	Count Row Pct	85%	90%	95%	98%	99%	100%	Row Total
0 – 50		1 7.7		2 15.4	1 7.7		9 69.2	13 27.1
51 – 500			1 3.6	6 21.4	2 7.1	10 35.7	9 32.1	28 58.3
501 – 1000							3 100.0	3 6.3
1001 – 3000							4 100.0	4 8.3
Column Total		1 2.1	1 2.1	8 16.7	3 6.3	10 20.8	25 52.1	48 100.0

Number of Missing Observations: 9.

The export-oriented firms have more unpaid accounts than the less export-oriented firms. One-third of the firms with a strong export orientation have unpaid accounts amounting to 5% of their receivables arising from export sales, whereas in the latter group only around 10% of the firms have more than 5% bad debts. The less export-oriented firms are likely to refrain from risky export business since they maintain a certain number of domestic customers in their portfolio, to whom they can offer the production in excess of the demand coming from safe foreign customers.

H. DISPUTES RESULTING IN NON-PAYMENT

Interestingly, however, two-thirds of the firms (*i.e.* 35 out of 52) *do* experience disputes resulting in non-payment or late payment of their receivables: it is bad debts, not overdue accounts, which are rare. In this respect, firm size does not play a role. Larger firms experience disputes as often as the smaller firms.

The most frequent reasons for disputes resulting in non-payment are the bank transactions; that is, the question of who must pay the costs of the transaction [44] and a delay in bank services such as late transfer of the

---

[44] Exporter 55.

monies [45] or late delivery of transport documents.[46] This is followed by disputes relating to the quality of goods and especially the importer's demand for a discount for goods which are allegedly of worse quality than that agreed upon in the contract of sale.[47] The third important reason for disputes is delivery of goods before payment has been made (Figure 15.7).

Figure 15.7

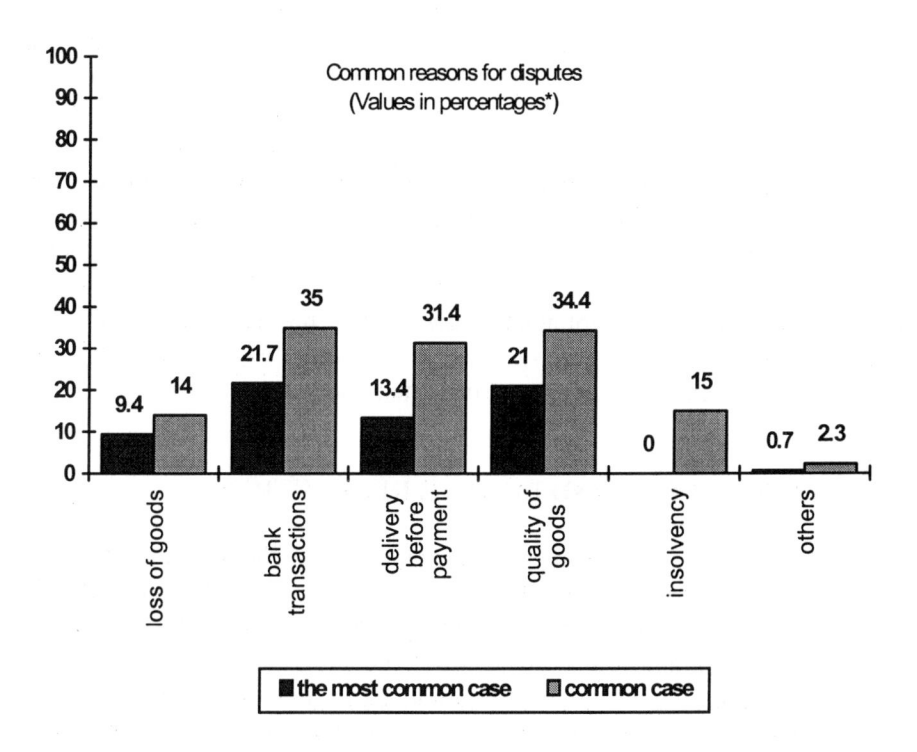

Common reasons for disputes
(Values in percentages*)

Category	the most common case	common case
loss of goods	9.4	14
bank transactions	21.7	35
delivery before payment	13.4	31.4
quality of goods	21	34.4
insolvency	0	15
others	0.7	2.3

Valid cases: 36. Missing cases: 21.
(*) Values have been corrected regarding the actual distribution of firms according to firm size.

---

45 Exporters numbered 5, 12 and 55.
46 Exporters numbered 5, 46 and 55.
47 Exporters numbered 6, 27, 35 and 44. Exporter 6 states that the demands for a discount (which are called 'reclamation' among the textile firms) occur mostly irrespective of the quality of goods, that is to say, where the goods cannot be successfully sold by the customer in the foreign country.

298 Making Foreign People Pay

The disputes resulting from delivery before payment arise especially in case of documentary collections. It was stated above that cash against documents is the least successful collection method.[48] It is also the collection method which most often gives rise to disputes. More than half of the firms which export on a CAD basis undergo disputes resulting from the delivery of goods before payment, followed by the default of the importer. Indeed, a quarter mention this as the most frequent reason for disputes in export sales. It is surprising that the exported goods are quite often delivered to the buyer without the documents representing the title on the goods having been produced by the latter. Seven export firms [49] answer the open question 14 with an account of a story where the goods are collected by the importer from the carrier or from the warehouse without having paid the price of the goods. This happens sometimes as a result of the good relations of the buyer with the warehouseman or the bank taking part in the documentary operation. Particularly, it is reported by exporters 8, 9, 16 and 33 that a bill of lading which has been drawn on the bank (*i.e.* which is valid only after it has been negotiated by the bank to the importer against payment of the price of the goods) is sometimes accepted by the warehouseman or the carrier even if it has not been negotiated by the bank.

I. DEBT RECOVERY AND DISPUTE RESOLUTION

In case of disputes or overdue accounts, the overwhelming majority of exporters prefer to solve the problem via negotiation. It is interesting that, for two-thirds of the export firms, litigation is not a workable course of action which may be applied against the debtors in default.

Where recourse to litigation *is* regarded as necessary, the exporters prefer to hire a foreign lawyer and sue their debtors in the relevant foreign country. There are hardly any differences between the larger firms and the smaller firms in these respects (Figure 15.8).

---

48 See 'Collection methods' in this Chapter.
49 *I.e.* the Exporters numbered 1, 8, 9, 10, 16, 33 and 44.

A Survey of the Collection and Security Methods used by Exporters 299

Figure 15.8

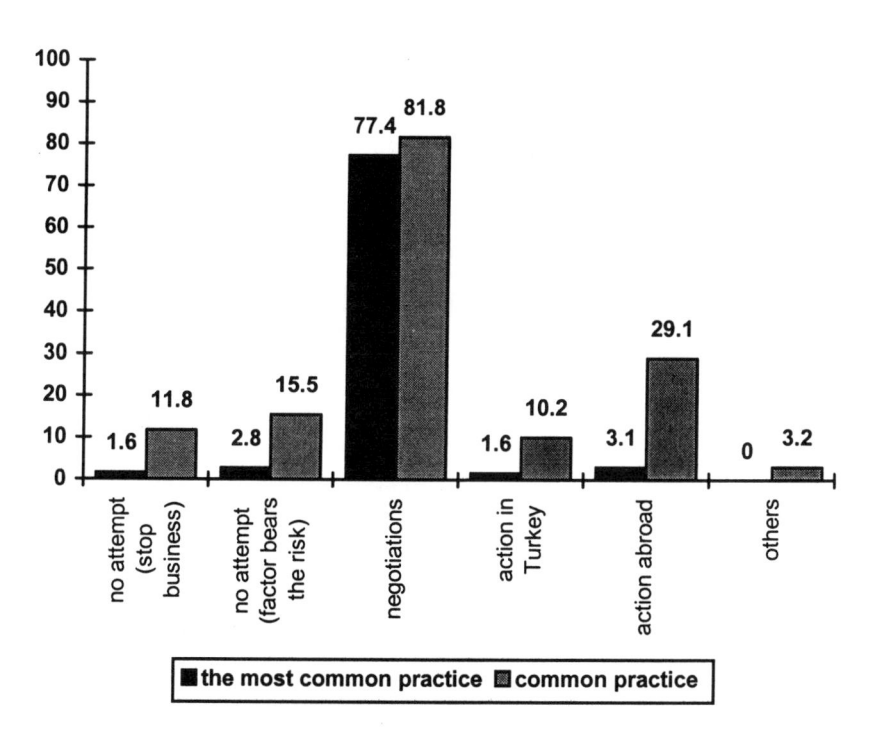

Debt collection / dispute resolution practices
(Values in percentages*)

Practice	the most common practice	common practice
no attempt (stop business)	1.6	11.8
no attempt (factor bears the risk)	2.8	15.5
negotiations	77.4	81.8
action in Turkey	1.6	10.2
action abroad	3.1	29.1
others	0	3.2

Valid cases: 46. Missing cases: 11.
(*) Values have been corrected regarding the actual distribution of firms according to firm size.

16 Conclusions for Part III

It is common knowledge in the sociology of law that only a small proportion of social conflicts, including conflicts of economic nature, find their way to the courts and eventually to enforcement proceedings.[1] It is conceivable that, in the case of cross-border trade, the difficulties created by the 'conflict of laws' resulting from the involvement of different national legal systems in the legal relationship limit mobilisation of the law to an even greater extent. Accordingly, at the beginning of the survey it was expected to find that the judicial methods of debt recovery were used relatively infrequently by the export firms in Istanbul as compared to the actual number of disputed and/or unpaid debts. The results concerning the use of litigation by exporters are thus not surprising, but interesting in their clarity: two thirds of the export firms do not regard litigation as even a *possible* course of action to be considered in case of non-payment by the customer.

It is more interesting to see that, in the great majority of cases, default in payment is followed by direct negotiations between the parties. The language differences do not prevent even the smaller firms from initiating direct negotiations with the customer and, again in the great majority of the cases, these negotiations prove to be successful. The overdue accounts do not remain unpaid. Although two thirds of the textile exporters do run into disputes which may lead to non-payment of the debt, more than half of them have a success rate of 100% in collecting their export receivables.

The success of exporters in collecting their receivables abroad cannot be explained alone by the successful negotiating on overdue accounts. The internationally standardised collection and security methods for avoiding

---

1   See *e.g.* William L. F. Felstiner, Richard L. Abel and Austin Sarat, 'The Emergence and Transformation of Disputes: Naming, Blaming, Claiming . . .', *Law and Society Review* 15, no. 3 – 4 (1980–81), pp. 631–54; Erhard Blankenburg, 'Mobilisierung von Recht', *Zeitschrift für Rechtssoziologie* 1, no. 1 (1980), pp. 33–64.

the risk of non-payment, *i.e.* the methods of 'international credit management', are also used successfully by the export firms.

A common feature of all the credit management methods used by export firms is the importance given to customer relations on the personal level. The personal relations depending on mutual confidence and the firm's prestige play an important role throughout the export business. For example, one-half of the export firms state that they have 'old, established customers' and 'they seldom do business with new customers'. The majority of the exporters use their personal contacts (other textile exporters, their commercial agents and customers abroad) as the most favoured source of credit information. More than a quarter of the export firms define oral agreements which are not coupled to written documents as the most common contracting practice in international sales. The number of exporters who refrain from obtaining any form of security from the importer figures at 10 to 20%. Most exporters use open accounts as a common practice, and so on. Even one of the two most important types of dispute resulting in non-payment, *i.e.* 'the delivery of goods before payment', is a side effect of the good personal relations between the bank or the warehouseman at the port of arrival of the goods and the importer. Indeed, the success of negotiations in resolving disputes may also be explained by the role of the relations at the personal level, where the personal contacts and a good reputation must be maintained for future business deals.[2]

Although there are various differences concerning debt collection, dispute resolution and credit management practices between different groups

---

2 For the sake of fairness, it should be added that personal relationships play a more important role in Turkey than some other parts of the world, *e.g.* Western European countries. According to the results of a recent survey including the records of interviews conducted with 56 foreign firms in Istanbul, this observation is shared by many European businessmen who do business in Turkey. See Müjde Oktay, *Turkish Business Life via the Eyes of Foreign Businessmen* (Istanbul: Istanbul Chamber of Industry, 1996). A Dutch businessman notes that 'if you compare it to Europe, human relations are very important here. A Turkish customer will never deny a claim you have on him. He will honour his word. He is deeply ashamed if he cannot fulfil his commitments'. A British businessman states 'in Turkey, the work ethic is quite different . . . . They don't like documentation, nor do they like rules. They do things spontaneously. . . . What is surprising is that it is unusual to find a customer who would not pay his bills in Turkey'. According to a French manager, 'in Turkey, the verbal part of business is greater than the written part'. A German manager states that 'in Turkish business life, you cannot rely on written contracts. Most business is done by phone'. Having a written contract or even a cheque is no guarantee: "Here a cheque doesn't necessarily mean money, whereas in Germany it does." *Ibid.*, pp. 33, 35, 41, 43, 45, 53.

of exporters which have been made here according to firm size, export orientation and experience in exporting, the dominant importance of personal relations remains valid for all these groups.[3]

The results of the survey illustrate that legal security in international commercial transactions is provided to a large extent by internationally standardised collection and security methods for avoiding the risk of non-payment (*i.e.* by and large, *lex mercatoria* [4]), together with the personal relations between the business people depending on mutual confidence. The role of nationally-established law and the national courts is of marginal importance.

---

3 *I.e.* the differences between the groups in various aspects do not change the general tendency. The differences between various groups in this respect are as follows: (1) The larger firms gain new customers more often through their previous contacts and reputation. They are more likely to use credit information 'where necessary', instead of as a business routine. They less often require contractual securities from the customer. But they use oral agreements less often, and they prefer safer collection methods. (2) The (strongly) export-oriented firms are to some extent less successful in debt collection. (3) The experienced exporters more often have old, established customers. They export more often on a credit basis and use credit information and securities less often. In this respect, even the differences between 'the firms depending on personal relations / old customers' and 'the firms working with agents' are of marginal importance; see *supra* 'the relations with customers' (*i.e.* the firms depending on personal relations / old customers use open accounts more often and they are more likely to prefer negotiations for dispute resolution).

4 See Bernardo M. Cremades and Steven L. Plehn, 'The new lex mercatoria and the harmonisation of the laws of international transactions', *Boston University International Law Journal* 2 (1984), pp. 317–48, at pp. 323 et seq. ('the non-national approach: new lex mercatoria').

CONCLUSION

Globalisation of Private Law Enforcement

Throughout this text, conclusions have been drawn about different aspects of cross-border debt collection.[1] As promised at the beginning,[2] this concluding chapter will attempt to place the research results into context, with reference to current discussions on globalisation of law.

A. THRESHOLDS FOR THEMATISATION OF LAW AND CROSS-BORDER INTERACTIONS

The German sociologist Niklas Luhmann provides a useful framework for interpreting what we observed in the example of cross-border debt collection. Luhmann argues that transformation of a conflict into a legal dispute (what he calls 'thematisation of law' [3]) occurs subject to a number of factors. Defining a conflict in terms of a legal dispute will usually break the communication process on the *de facto* level between the actors to an interaction.[4] Thus, such 'thematisation of law' occurs only if the interaction

---

[1] *Supra* Chapter 8: Conclusions for Part I; Chapter 7: Results of the Comparison between German, English and Turkish Debt Recovery Law; Chapter 13: Conclusions for Part II, and Chapter 16: Conclusions for Part III.
[2] See *supra* Introduction.
[3] Niklas Luhmann, 'Communication about law in interaction systems', in Karin D. Knorr-Cetina and Aaron V. Cicourel (eds), *Advances in Social Theory and Methodology – Toward an integration of micro- and macro-sociologies* (Boston, London and Henley: Routledge & Kegan Paul, 1981), pp. 234–56. For the same article in German language, see Niklas Luhmann, 'Kommunikation über Recht in Interaktionssystem', in Erhard Blankenburg, Ekkehard Klausa, Hubert Rottleuthner and Ralf Rogowski (eds), *Alternative Rechtsformen und Alternativen zum Recht – Jahrbuch für Rechtssoziologie und Rechtstheorie* 6 (Opladen: Westdeutscher, 1980), pp. 99–112.
[4] 'A person is much more closely identified with a legal claim than with a factual claim, which can always be regarded as mistaken and changed if necessary. Starting a legal discussion usually means going beyond a point of no return: one defines oneself

partners are able to cross a so-called 'thematisation threshold' granted by the particulars of the relationship between them as well as by the social environment. According to Luhmann, thematisation thresholds for law is determined by two factors: the degree of predictability of the results of the judicial process,[5] and the prospects of social support for the actor if the outcome of the judicial process turns out unsuccessful for him.[6] '[These] thematisation thresholds work as a kind of filter for the conditions and the circumstances that make raising legal questions probable'.[7] Luhmann further argues that the primitive societies which have not developed an advanced judicial system tend to suppress or avoid legal conflict and, in such primitive societies, the raising of legal issues depends on whether the conflicts can be generalised and whether social support is available from larger groups with a greater capacity for conflict.[8]

In light of the example of cross-border debt collection, it can be said that the 'thematisation thresholds for law' in cross-border interactions are higher than those in domestic interactions. As in primitive societies,[9] the World Society does not have an advanced judicial system supported by an effective enforcement mechanism.[10] This holds true not only for the enforcement of public law (*e.g.* countless examples of the failures of effective law enforcement in war, human rights, taxation of multinational corporations, cross-border environmental pollution, terrorism and drug

---

for the future as prepared to stand up and actively defend one's right.' *Ibid.*, p. 241. However, cf. *infra* and *ibid.*, pp. 251–2 ('de-thematisation of law').

5   'Whoever considers formulating his interests, complaints, expectations or disappointments as legal issues must be able to predict with some degree of certainty how the legal system will dispose of the matter.' *Ibid.*, p. 244.
6   'The more uncertain the future, the more it must be met together.' *Ibid.*, p. 243.
7   *Ibid.*, p. 242. Considering the Implementation Theory, Blankenburg follows Luhmann's theory on thematisation of law for explaining the conflict resolution structure in private law relations. See Blankenburg, 'Die Implementation von recht als Programm', pp. 130–2.
8   *Ibid.*, pp. 240 and 243.
9   Edward Adamson Hoebel, *Das Recht der Naturvölker – Eine vergleichende Untersuchung rechtlicher Abläufe* (Olten: Walter Verlag, 1968), translated by Maria Elisabeth Drude from the English original: *The Law of Primitive Man: A Study in Comparative Dynamics* (Cambridge, Massachusetts: Harvard University Press, 1954), pp. 11–41.
10 See Roger D. Masters, 'World Politics as a Primitive Political System', *World Politics* 16 (1963 – 1964), pp. 595–619, at pp. 597, 608–13.

trafficking [11]), but also for the protection of individual rights in private law.

There is no international judicial system for the resolution of private law conflicts. The rules which apply to cross-border legal interactions are to be found in national provisions as well as international agreements on private international law and the provisions of internationally applicable substantive law created by harmonisation of laws. However, enforcement of these rules for resolution of cross-border disputes is largely implemented by national courts.[12]

Regarding our example of cross-border debt collection, a comparative summary of German, English and Turkish debt recovery laws shows that these national legal systems are comparable to each other.[13] Differences between Common Law and Civil Law systems and different levels of economic development do not have a significant effect on the law and legal practice of these countries. None of the three legal systems contain procedural rules impeding international litigation. As international litigation is regarded as a profitable service industry, foreign parties may even be encouraged.[14] However, statistical data and research conducted in court registries show that access to justice before national courts is indeed limited

---

11 See *e.g.* J. W. E. Sheptycki, 'Law Enforcement, Justice and Democracy in the Transnational Arena: Reflections on the War on Drugs', *International Journal of the Sociology of Law* 24 (1996), pp. 61–75.

12 Enforcement of so-called 'international arbitral awards' is also effected by national courts. Academic literature tends to overstate the role of international commercial arbitration. Statements like 'today there is hardly an international contract without an arbitration clause' (Röhl and Megan, 'Die Rolle des Rechts im Prozeß der Globalisierung', p. 34) are not correct. See *supra* Chapter 5: Role of Lawyers in Cross-Border Debt Collection. Although international statistics on international commercial arbitration are not available, it suffices to say that the two districts courts of Hamburg and Bremen in Germany had the same annual case load of international cases as the ICC International Court of Arbitration, which received 333 cases in 1991 (in 1993, 352 cases), Gessner, 'International Cases in German First Instance Courts', p. 156. The annual number of cases received by other leading international courts of arbitration do not exceed those of the ICC: The American Arbitration Association reported about 300 international cases for 1991. The London Court of International Commercial Arbitration deals with 30 – 40 cases annually. The Chinese International Economic and Trade Arbitration Commission had some 300 pending cases in 1994. Dezalay and Garth, 'Merchants of Law as Moral Entrepreneurs', p. 28.

13 *Supra* Chapter 1: Debt Recovery in Germany; Chapter 2: Debt Recovery in England, and Chapter 3: Debt Recovery in Turkey.

14 *Supra* Chapter 4: Results of the Comparison between German, English and Turkish Debt Recovery Law.

for international cases.[15] This is not a result of legal or procedural rules applied to international cases, but rather due to practical and what may be termed legal-bureaucratic difficulties in cross-border litigation.[16]

Limited access to national courts in cross-border disputes entails a low degree of legal certainty,[17] which in turn raises the thresholds for thematisation of law.[18]

B. SUBSTITUTES FOR THEMATISATION OF LAW

The fact that the thresholds for thematisation of law in cross-border relations are higher than those in domestic relations has a number of consequences which characterise cross-border interactions.

1. Cognitive Mechanisms Versus Normative Order

The anomic structure of cross-border relations due to high thresholds for thematisation of law is compensated for by actors of the global economy through cognitive mechanisms, that is, mechanisms based on collecting information, communication and mutual understanding between the actors.[19] In other words, again with reference to Luhmann's terminology, uncertainty in cross-border interactions is avoided through social expectations formed at a personal level rather than on the programmes (norms) level.[20] The survey on the credit management methods employed by textile

---

15   *Supra* Chapter 6: Recourse to National Courts in Cross-Border Debt Collection.
16   *Supra* Chapter 7: Factors Impeding Access to Justice in Cross-Border Debt Collection.
17   See Volkmar Gessner, 'Globalisation and Legal Certainty', in Gessner and Budak, *Emerging Legal Certainty*.
18   Cf. Luhmann, 'Communication about law in interaction systems', p. 244.
19   For a social theoretical and socio-legal discussion of the cognitive elements of social order as opposed to the normative structures, see Volkmar Gessner, 'Kognitive Elemente sozialer Ordnung', in Monika Frommel and Volkmar Gessner (eds), *Normenerosion* (Baden-Baden: Nomos, 1996), pp. 207–23.
20   For the distinction made between the social expectations based on persons, roles, programmes and value levels, see Niklas Luhmann, *Rechtssoziologie*, 2nd ed. (Opladen: Westdeutscher Verlag, 1983), pp. 81–93. Luhmann's categories on social expectations are applied by Gessner to expectations for legal certainty in international legal interactions. Gessner says 'the more societal processes are differentiated – and globalised – the less they become integrated on the levels of roles and programmes.

exporters in Istanbul provides an example of this. Personal contacts play the most important role in establishing international business relations. Credit information facilities, sometimes referred to as 'credit vetting', are used extensively by exporters. Even the institutions intended to provide security for payments (banks, credit insurance and factoring companies) are used as sources of credit information. Where disputes arise or in the case of (undisputed) overdue accounts, the overwhelming majority of exporters prefer to solve the problem by negotiation. For two thirds of export firms, litigation is not a viable alternative in cross-border debt collection.[21]

'Contracting out' the risk of non-performance is another cognitive mechanism used for uncertainty avoidance in cross-border interactions.[22] Thus, contracts are used as a cognitive mechanism rather than 'documents' which enable resort to normative protection.[23] In this respect, it is interesting to see that 40% of textile exporters in Istanbul conclude oral agreements with their clients rather than contracts in writing.[24]

2. De-thematisation of Law

In cross-border interactions, the actors tend to prefer, instead of resorting to judicial methods of enforcement, what Luhmann calls 'de-thematisation of law'. The term 'de-thematisation of law' refers to the process where, even if a claim has been formulated in terms of a legal demand, the parties choose to end the conflict out of court. De-thematisation of law occurs usually with the help of third parties, as illustrated by mediation and arbitration.[25]

Cognitive mechanisms (negotiations, discourses, flexible contracts, mediation) then prevail over legal certainty'. Gessner, 'Globalisation and Legal Certainty'.

21 *Supra* Chapter 14: Collection and Security Methods Employed in International Trade; Chapter 15: A Survey of the Collection and Security Methods Used by Exporters.

22 See Luhmann, 'Communication about law in interaction systems', pp. 248–50. Cf. *supra* Chapter 14: Collection and Security Methods Employed in International Trade.

23 'It is probably quite rare that with agreement on a contract interaction is thereafter explicitly understood as belonging to the legal system, and its topic fixed accordingly. ... The process aimed at reaching a contract does not require a communication about law. It can be included to prevent certain demands and can help in establishing that an agreement has been reached, but whether turning to law is helpful, or troublesome, or destructive, is something the participants must decide for themselves.' Luhmann, 'Communication about law in interaction systems', pp. 249 and 250.

24 *Supra* Chapter 15: A Survey of the Collection and Security Methods Used by Exporters.

25 Gessner, 'Kognitive Elemente sozialer Ordnung', pp. 221–2; Luhmann, 'Communication about law in interaction systems', pp. 251–2. It must be added that,

312 *Making Foreign People Pay*

One example of such third party assistance for de-thematisation of law is provided by commercial debt collection agencies.

Where they are established, commercial debt collectors are the most important competitors of national courts for enforcement of international as well as domestic claims.[26] Debt collection 'methods' used by commercial debt collectors are of a cognitive character: they only 'communicate' with the debtor by means of letters, telephone calls, personal visits. The debt collector has the triple function of promoting and maintaining communication between the debtor and the creditor. Firstly, he uses what is called the 'third party effect'. This is so called because a third party now in contact with the debtor is unwilling to accept the numerous excuses normally given by the debtor to the original creditor. That is, he is encouraged to negotiate, with the debt collector serving as an intermediary, where negotiation must be taken seriously.[27] Secondly, if out-of-court efforts at collection are unsuccessful and if the creditor decides to 'legal-ise' [28] the dispute, it is the debt collector who will resort to court proceedings. Thus, the business relations between the parties ('the communication system') will be less damaged by the negative effect of thematisation of law. Lastly, with regard to credit information in international business, a bad record with a debt collector is not good for future business prospects. It is no coincidence that many credit reference agencies, domestic or international, also have debt collection departments.[29] These success factors of commercial debt collection are of

---

according to the rules of procedure and substantive law applied by the arbitrators, commercial arbitration can also become a very legally structured, litigation-like form of dispute resolution. See Dezalay and Garth, 'Merchants of Law as Moral Entrepreneurs', pp. 55–8.

26 In 1993, 330 of 550 German debt collection agencies collected a total of DM 6.2 billion. In 1994, just two of the larger debt collection agencies in Germany handled 13,400 cross-border cases. See *supra* Chapter 10: Debt Collection Business of Cross-Border Debts in Germany, and Chapter 9: The Routinisation and Privatisation of Debt Collection. In 1994, an estimated 290.3 million debt cases totalling $ 84.2 billion were placed for collection by US debt collectors. That same year US debt collectors collected more than $15.5 billion of these accounts. (Information collected from the 'Communications Coordinator' of the American Collectors Association.) Cf. *supra* footnote 12 on arbitration.

27 See interviews in Chapter 11: Commercial Cross-Border Debt Collection in England.

28 The term 'legal-ising' is again borrowed from Luhmann, 'Communication about law in interaction systems', pp. 246 and 249.

29 Where social order is dominated by cognitive mechanisms, it is vital for the actors to maintain long-term contacts and a good reputation and not be excluded from the communication systems. Having a bad record with a debt collection/credit reference agency or being expelled from a trade association for credit information may affect a business dramatically. Nothnagel, *Execution durch soziale Interessengruppen*, pp. 10,

particular importance for international commerce, where the threshold for the thematisation of law is higher and where the cognitive elements of the social system are more important than in national societies.[30]

C. COGNITIVE ELEMENTS OF THE NEW WORLD ORDER AND THE ROLE OF THE NATION-STATE

As with public law, the globalisation of the economy has not been followed by a comparative globalisation in private law. The enforcement of private law remains the domain of the nation-state. So-called 'international litigation' is far from satisfactory. As a result, court action is resorted to less frequently by the actors in cross-border interactions than in domestic cases. However, private actors of the global economy have successfully compensated for the normative deficit of the New World Order by using cognitive mechanisms and informal methods of contract enforcement. Modern developments in data processing and communications have contributed to the efficiency of these cognitive mechanisms.[31] As a result, notwithstanding

---

15 and 26; Hoene, *Präventiver Kreditschutz und Zwangsvollstreckung durch Private*, p. 75. See *supra* Chapter 10: Commercial Cross-Border Debt Collection in Germany.

[30] It was no coincidence that Blankenburg's first study on the 'implementation of law as a programme' includes extensive references to Luhmann's theory on thematisation of law. The foregoing conclusions with reference to Luhmann's theory on thematisation of law confirm the accuracy of the approach of the socio-legal Implementation Theory. The reality concerning law enforcement in a given area of law may be considered in its entirety, if and only if the given area of law enforcement is regarded as an area of social interactions ('implementation arena') where the social conflict is processed through diverse legal and non-legal mechanisms in which various implementation actors are involved. In the present study, a research of the various aspects of the whole implementation arena was necessary in order to explore the facts concerning the cross-border debt collection, including a comparative study on the legal mechanisms of debt recovery in a number of selected legal systems (normative programmes), the role of and the mechanisms built by the implementation actors such as national courts, civil execution officers and international lawyers in various countries, the international 'networks' of commercial debt collectors, and the credit managers of export companies, and 'the parties behind the parties' such as credit reference agencies, export credit insurers, *etc.* Cf. *supra* 'Introduction' in this book and Blankenburg, Gawron, Rogowski and Voigt, 'Zur Analyse un Theorie der Implementation von Gerichtsentscheidungen'.

[31] Modern credit information agencies use computer networks. See *supra* Chapter 1: Collection and Security Methods Employed in International Trade, 'Investigating the creditworthiness of the debtor'. For advanced communication techniques in cross-border monetary transfers and avoidance of legal disputes between banks, see Klaus

314   Making Foreign People Pay

the lower levels of legal certainty (or higher thresholds for the thematisation of law) in cross-border interactions, pessimism *vis-à-vis* the actors of the global play or the future of the World Society is unnecessary.[32] Yet this does not mean that the community of nation-states are relieved from all their obligations to provide legal order in the area of cross-border interactions.

1. Legitimacy of Private Law Enforcement

As early as 1899, Nothnagel labelled the 'preventive and repressive effect' of credit information organisations in the area of debt collection a form of 'psychological execution' (*psychologische Exekution*), in contrast and as an alternative to 'personal execution' (*e.g.* imprisonment for debt) and 'real execution' (execution concerning means and assets of the debtor) which are exercised by the State.[33] He referred to various business, professional and labour organisations as well as non-profit clubs as other examples of organisations which exercise psychological execution.[34] These organisations exert a particular form of social control on their own members as well as third parties who have social interactions with the members of the same organisations. A member or a third party who does not honour the legal/moral rules and obligations recognised by the organisation (*e.g.* a member of a trade association who does not obey the rules of fair competition, a debtor who does not pay a member of the same association, or a member of a golf club 'who had been seen driving in the park with a woman of bad character') will be expelled from the organisation or de-

---

Frick, 'Third Cultures versus Regulators: Cross-Border Legal Relations of Banks', in Gessner and Budak, *Emerging Legal Certainty*.

32   According to Luhmann, as opposed to the case for the traditional concept of politically structured national societies (*societas civilis*), the functional primacy of cognitive mechanisms over normative mechanisms is characteristic of the World Society by definition. See Niklas Luhmann, 'Weltgesellschaft', *Archiv für Rechts- und Sozialphilosophie* 57 (1971), pp. 1–35. However, the growing importance of cognitive mechanisms vis-à-vis normative structures of the social order (what is sometimes termed 'norm erosion') is a 'global' fact of the present which is also observed within national societies. Gessner writes that, considering the new communication processes not only at national level between the State and citizens as well as between citizens and businesses, but also at the international level within the World Society, the state of affairs which is defined as norm erosion is considerably less worrying, 'Kognitive Elemente sozialer Ordnung', p. 223.

33   Nothnagel, *Execution durch sociale Interessengruppen*, pp. 1–9 and pp. 36–113.
34   Ibid., pp. 36–224.

prived from further contact (*e.g.* business) with the members of the organisation. In 'psychological execution' not only social norms but also cultural values are exerted, and violation of norms are not sanctioned by the sanction provided for by the norm itself (*e.g.* enforcement of debt by means of execution measures concerning debtors property) but by isolation and exclusion of the individual from the communication system where exchange of information take place. Thus, psychological execution is a form of social control outside the legal system, where cognitive mechanisms are employed instead of legal-ising the conflicts. The term 'psychological' in Nothnagel's terminology is largely interchangeable with the 'cognitive' in Luhmann's writing today.

Although Nothnagel did not study psychological execution with reference to globalisation, he contributes to our discussion in that he called the legitimacy of the cognitive mechanisms he described into question. The legitimacy [35] of the social control exerted by social organisations which involves psychological pressure and stigmatisation is not self-explanatory. Nothnagel asked, with some antiquated legal language, 'may a [private] organisation be permitted to force a third person through psychological pressure, that is against his free will, to give, to do or to guarantee something'.[36] This question is also valid for cross-border activities of commercial debt collection agencies.

As is discussed above,[37] there is no special licensing requirement for debt collection agencies in every country, and the methods employed by some debt collectors often involve harsh treatment of the debtor. Business organisations established by debt collection agencies at domestic as well as international level are also concerned about the black sheep among debt collectors, and are trying to bring a certain discipline to the sector.[38] Extrajudicial methods (or 'psychological execution') exercised by debt collectors

---

35 Nothnagel did not use the term 'legitimacy'.
36 'Ist eine Organisation berechtigt, von dritten Personen durch Anwendung psychologischer Zwangsmittel, also durch Bindung von deren Willen eine Leistung, sei es ein dare, facere oder praestare zu erzwingen?', *ibid.*, p. 16. Nothnagel attempted to answer this question by making a distinction between the protection of legal and mere economic interests of the members of a private organisation, and between those psychological execution measures which have been exerted against the members of the organisation and against the third parties. That is, psychological execution is easier to justify when it is applied against own members of the organisation and for protection of 'legal' rather than 'mere economical' interests. *Ibid.*, pp. 16–7 and pp. 23–5.
37 Chapter 12: Conclusions for Part II.
38 See Chapter 12: Business Organisations of Debt Collection. This is again an example of organisations for psychological execution as described by Nothnagel.

may only be legitimate if the debt collection business is regulated by law. Such regulation must establish the rules applicable to licensing for debt collectors and an effective control concerning their activities. Considering the international activity of debt collection agencies, an international / EU-wide harmonisation of regulations for debt collection is also necessary.[39]

The same is true for credit reference agencies dealing with the cross-border collection, transfer and sale of business information concerning individuals as well as businesses.[40] Other examples of the need for international regulation of structures outside judicial enforcement mechanisms can already be found in the control of the international banking sector, where cognitive mechanisms for conflict resolution leave literally no room for thematisation of law [41] and in international commercial arbitration which is described by Luhmann [42] as one of the cognitive mechanisms for de-thematisation of law.[43]

---

39 See Chapter 13: Conclusions for Part II.
40 See Jans-Peter Lachmann, 'Grenzüberschreitende Informationsverarbeitung', *Anwaltsblatt*, 46. Jahrgang, no. 11 (1996), pp. 545–9.
41 See Frick, 'Third Cultures versus Regulators'.
42 Luhmann, 'Communication about law in interaction systems', p. 251.
43 See for UNCITRAL Model Law on International Commercial Arbitration and new legislation on international commercial arbitration in various countries: Marc Blessing, 'Einleitung zum Zwölften Kapitel', in Heinrich Honsell, Nedim Peter Vogt and Anton K. Schnyder (eds), *Kommentar zum schweizerischen Privatrecht – Internationales Privatrecht* (Basel and Frankfurt am Main: Helbing & Lichtenhahn, 1996), pp. 1285–410, at pp. 1337–45. For a discussion of the legitimacy of international commercial arbitration, see Reza Banakar, 'Reflexive Legitimacy in International Commercial Arbitration', in Gessner and Budak, *Emerging Legal Certainty*. What Banakar calls 'reflexive legitimacy' in this article is different from our traditional concept of legitimacy which is based on the democratic authority of the nation-state and general consent of a national society. Banakar argues that international commercial arbitration provides a cognitive mechanism where not only conflicts are resolved between the given parties, but also generally applicable rules and procedures are developed which will be used in other arbitral procedures between other parties. These generally applicable rules and procedures for the international business community (*lex mercatoria*) are produced and amended through a cognitive process where business people and lawyers from different legal cultures come together in the course of arbitral proceedings. According to Banakar, the legitimacy of international commercial arbitration is to be found in this cognitive mechanism which enables the subjects of the *lex mercatoria* (the international business community) to participate in the relevant law-making process. Although Banakar's theory prompts an interesting discussion on the globalisation of law, this theory is not applicable to our example of cross-border debt collection through commercial agencies. Commercial debt collection is employed for collection of undisputed debts. As is the case for credit information agencies, debt collection services provided by commercial agencies do not entail a communication process where the rules and procedures are reproduced by involve-

2. Protection of the Small People

Considering the role of nation-state in the globalisation of law, the small players in the global game must not be forgotten. These are not small businesses but non-trade small players usually drawn involuntarily into cross-border legal relations (*e.g.* creditors of child support claims, consumer claims for product liability) who are unable to use the cognitive mechanisms and informal enforcement methods of the global game. Nation states, in their role of law maker and law enforcer, and the community of nation states must also concentrate their efforts on developing and maintaining support structures for this latter group. Establishing an effective mechanism for legal aid in international litigation and improving the co-operation between state and charity organisations for cross-border consumer advice and cross-border enforcement of child support claims are among the duties of the community of nation states.[44]

Concerning enforcement of private law in global society, the nation state must redefine its function as supervisor of informal methods of law enforcement (that is, 'legitimising' extra-judicial methods of enforcement), in addition to enforcing the law itself, which has proven to be of marginal importance, except for the case of small people, who need the state's legal protection so that they can get access to justice by surmounting the high thresholds for thematisation of law.

---

ment of the parties to cross-border interactions. Legitimacy for cross-border debt collection business may only be provided by public regulation through the nation-states.

44 See *supra* Chapter 7: Factors Impeding Access to Justice in Cross-Border Debt Collection, 'International legal aid and the lack of consumer advice', and Pierre Guibentiff, 'Cross-Border Legal Issues Arising from International Migrations – The Case of Portugal', Andreas Petzold, 'Obtaining Information on Foreign Legal Systems', Grotheer, 'Cross-Border Maintenance Claims of Children', all under the title 'Small Peoples Claims' in Gessner and Budak, *Emerging Legal Certainty*.

Annexes

ANNEX I

Istanbul Chamber of Industry – Centre for European Law and Politics at the University of Bremen

QUESTIONNAIRE
ON THE COLLECTION AND RISK MANAGEMENT METHODS
USED BY TURKISH EXPORT FIRMS[*]

(Multiple answers are permitted for all questions.)

I. PARTICULARS OF YOUR FIRM

(COMPANY) NAME:
CONTACT PERSON (*e.g.* who has filled in this form):
TELEPHONE NO. OF THE CONTACT PERSON (incl. ext.):

1. What is your field of commercial activity / products?
....
....

2. How many persons do you employ? ....

---

[*] Data which you have provided will remain strictly confidential and will be processed anonymously. Neither the name nor the distinguishing particulars of your firm (size, place of business, *etc.*) will be quoted. However, should you give your written permission, I would be pleased to reproduce your observations and comments referring to yourself and / or your firm. With many thanks for your co-operation.
A. Cem Budak

3. What percentage of your production do you export? (FOB / $): .... %

a) GENERALLY: ....

b) (If data available) ACCORDING TO YEARS:
in the year 1985: ......% in the year 1990: ....% in the year 1991: ......%
in the year 1992: ......% in the year 1993: ....% in the year 1994: ......%

4. To which countries do you export most? (Please give percentages.)

a) .... : c. .... % of my exports.
b) .... : c. .... % of my exports.
c) .... : c. .... % of my exports.

II. QUESTIONS ON THE RESEARCH TOPIC

1. How do you initiate contact with importers from other countries? (Please number the most common practice '1', the next '2', etc.)

- [ ] a) Through the chambers of commerce and industry in Istanbul / in the relevant foreign country.
- [ ] b) Through incoming requests to the relevant trade associations.
- [ ] c) Through a commercial agent in Turkey.
- [ ] d) Through a commercial agent abroad.
- [ ] e) During the trade fairs which I attend in Turkey or abroad.
- [ ] f) Through our personal contacts / our good reputation among the customers.
- [ ] g) Most of our buyers are old, regular customers. We seldom do business with new customers.
- [ ] h) Our company is a subsidiary of a foreign company, and we work exclusively for the parent company.
- [ ] i) Others (please specify):
  ....
  ....

2. Do you research the commercial creditability and solvency of the importer before dealing with him?

☐ a) Always.
☐ b) Never.
☐ c) Where I feel necessary (in which cases?)
....
....
....

3. If your answer to the above question is positive (or 'where I feel necessary'), how do you obtain information about the creditability and solvency of the importer? (Please number the most common practice '1', the next '2', etc.)

☐ a) I obtain information from a commercial credit reference agency.
☐ b) I obtain information from the importer's bank, through my bank.
☐ c) I get information through my personal contacts.
☐ d) Others (please specify):
....
....

4. Do you make agreements with the importers to avoid conflicts which may arise in connection with payment of the price, delivery of the goods, etc. and, where necessary, to contribute to speedy resolution? (Please number the most common practice '1', the next '2', etc.)

☐ a) I make only oral agreements.
☐ b) I make a written contract for some of the matters upon which we agreed.
☐ c) I put all business transactions in writing.
☐ d) I use standard contract forms.
☐ e) Others (please specify):
....
....

5. Do you require security from the importers against the risk of non-payment? (Please see the following question.)

- [ ] a) Always.
- [ ] b) Never.
- [ ] c) We require security only from those firms with which we are doing business for the first time, until we have established regular business relations.

6. Which securities do you require from the importer to avoid the risk of non-payment? (Please number the most common practice '1', the next '2', etc.)

- [ ] a) I require no securities.
- [ ] b) I require a bank guarantee.
- [ ] c) I require the bill of exchange which I have drafted to be honoured / avalised by a bank.
- [ ] d) I require a guarantee / surety from another creditworthy commercial firm.
- [ ] e) I have taken out an export credit insurance policy.
- [ ] f) I have made a forfaiting contract with a bank / credit institution. I require no additional security, because the forfaiter bears the risk of non-payment.
- [ ] g) I work with a factoring company. I require no additional security, because the factoring company bears the risk of non-payment.
- [ ] h) Others (please specify):
  ....
  ....

7. How do you collect the payment for the exported goods? (Please number the most common practice '1', the next '2', etc.)

- [ ] a) Cash in advance.
- [ ] b) Cash against goods.
- [ ] c) Cash against documents.
- [ ] d) Documents against acceptance.
- [ ] e) L / C (sight credit).
- [ ] f) L / C (acceptance credit).
- [ ] g) Factoring.
- [ ] h) Forfaiting.
- [ ] i) Others (please specify):
  ....
  ....

8. What is your success rate in collecting your receivables from the importers?

a) GENERALLY: ....

b) (If data available) ACCORDING TO YEARS:
in the year 1985: ......%   in the year 1990: ......%   in the year 1991: ......%
in the year 1992: ......%   in the year 1993: ......%   in the year 1994: ......%

9. Do you experience disputes with importers, with your insurance company or with your bank which result in non-payment or late or partial payment of the price of the exported goods?

- [ ] a) Yes, often.
- [ ] b) Sometimes.
- [ ] c) Never.

10. If your answer to the above question is yes (or 'sometimes'), what are the reasons for the disputes? (Please number the most common reason '1', the next '2', etc.)

☐ a) Partial or total loss of the goods during transportation.
☐ b) Because of bank transactions (*e.g.* the question of who must pay the costs of the transactions, a delay in bank services such as late delivery of transport documents).
☐ c) Delivery of goods before payment and default of payment of the importer.
☐ d) Importer alleges that the quality of the goods is not satisfactory.
☐ e) The payment difficulties / insolvency of the importer.
☐ f) Others (please specify):
....
....

11. Where a dispute arises between you and the importer or, even in the absence of such disputes, the payment has not been made (fully and on time), which of the following courses of action do you pursue? (Please number the most common practice '1', the next '2', etc.)

☐ a) I do nothing, but I will discontinue business with the respective importer.
☐ b) I try to resolve the problem through negotiations. I do not go to court.
☐ c) The legal staff in our firm commence an action in Turkey.
☐ d) I hire a (Turkish) law firm to commence an action in Turkey.
☐ e) I hire a (foreign) law firm to commence an action abroad.
☐ f) I hire a (foreign) commercial debt collector.
☐ g) I do not react. Because the factoring company / forfaiter bears the risk of non-payment.
☐ h) Others (please specify):
....
....

12. Which of the above courses of action (except 'a' and 'g') is the most successful way of collecting your receivables? What is the rate of success of the course of action which you choose above? (If you can collect the full amount of the claim, please answer '100%'; if half, '50%', etc.)

 – The most successful way of collecting my receivables is ....
 – By using this method, I can collect .... % of my receivables.

13. In general, do you experience difficulties in collecting your receivables from the importers? If your answer is 'yes', would you please comment – including your suggestions for amending the regulations by the government, etc. (You may also use the other side of the page or a separate piece of paper.)

14. Please report a typical case where you experienced difficulties in collecting your receivables from the importers? (You may also use the other side of the page or a separate piece of paper.)

All rights reserved. October 1995

ANNEX II

Ali Cem Budak
Zentrum für Europäische Rechtspolitik
Universitätsallee, GW 1, D-28359 Bremen
Fax: 01049-421-218 3403
01049-421-218 4968

Questionnaire on 'Cross-Border Debt Collection'

in connection with a comparative law doctorate dissertation on the
'Execution of money judgments abroad and cross-border commercial
debt collection in German, English and Turkish law'
(September 1995)

I. Debt collection abroad (Creditor in England – Debtor abroad)[1]

A. Practical importance (frequency and amount of cases and debtors' countries of origin):

- What is the practical importance of the debt collection abroad for your business with respect to the frequency of cases and their amounts? (If data available: the proportion of the annual turnover and the proportion of the total number of cases)

  ....
  ....
  ....
  ....

  1985: ....cases, ...% of all cases, ...% of the annual turnover
  1990: ....cases, ...% of all cases, ...% of the annual turnover
  1994: ....cases, ...% of all cases, ...% of the annual turnover

---

[1] The same questionnaire was also used in Germany, in German language. In the German text, Germany is taken as the place of business of the firm, and the questions were formulated accordingly.

- Which countries are of most practical importance for your debt collection services abroad?
  1. ...., 2. ...., 3. ...., 4. ...., 5. ....

- What is the practical importance of Germany and Turkey? (If data available: the proportion of the annual turnover and the proportion of the total number of cases)

Germany

....
....

1985: ....cases,	.....% of all cases,	.....% of the annual turnover
1990: ....cases,	.....% of all cases,	.....% of the annual turnover
1994: ....cases,	.....% of all cases,	.....% of the annual turnover

Turkey

....
....

1985: ....cases,	.....% of all cases,	.....% of the annual turnover
1990: ....cases,	.....% of all cases,	.....% of the annual turnover
1994: ....cases,	.....% of all cases,	.....% of the annual turnover

B. Distinguishing characteristics of the parties and indebtedness in cross-border debt collection:

- Which lines of business (import and export trade, credit institutions, tourism, insurance, *etc.*) do they come from?
  1. ....
  2. ....
  3. ....
  4. ....
  5. ....

- Is an average debt due from a debtor abroad greater than the same average applicable for debt collection within the jurisdiction? Could you specify the average amount of debts that you collect abroad?
  ....
  ....
  ....
  ....

- Is the percentage of judgment debts higher or lower in cross-border debt collection than that of debt collection within the jurisdiction? (If data available: percentages.)

  ....
  ....
  ....
  ....

  Percentage of judgment debts in:

  a) Debt collection in England and Wales: **b)** Debt collection abroad:
     1985: ....%   1985: ....%
     1990: ....%   1990: ....%
     1994: ....%   1995: ....%

- Are foreign debtors less co-operative? Is the success rate higher or lower?

  ....
  ....
  ....
  ....

- Could you name some special characteristics of parties and 'causes of debt' in cross-border debt collection cases where the debtor resides in Germany or in Turkey?

  ....
  ....
  ....
  ....

C. Debt collection methods used abroad:

- Do you handle cross-border debt collection through your own debt collection agency in England or Wales, or do you cooperate regularly with a corresponding debt collector or sister debt collection agency in the relevant foreign country (especially in Germany and in Turkey)?
  - through my own debt collection agency in England or Wales: ....
  - in co-operation with a sister debt collection agency abroad: ....
  - in co-operation with a corresponding debt collection agency abroad: ....

- Do you have regular co-operation with English and, as the case may be, with the foreign resident (especially Turkish and German) lawyers / law firms?

  in general
  with English lawyers: regularly ..../ occasionally ..../ never ....
  with foreign resident lawyers: regularly ..../ occasionally ..../ never ....
  Because:
  ....

  in Germany
  with English lawyers: regularly ..../ occasionally ..../ never ....
  with German lawyers: regularly ..../ occasionally ..../ never ....
  Because:
  ....

  in Turkey
  with English lawyers: regularly ..../ occasionally ..../ never ....
  with Turkish lawyers: regularly ..../ occasionally ..../ never ....
  Because:
  ....

- Which debt collection methods (telephone / mail / personal visits) do you use? (How) do these methods differ from those used in domestic debt collection?
  ....
  ....
  ....
  ....

- What is your experience of enforcing default judgments against debtors abroad?
  ....
  ....
  ....

D. Debt collection contract:

- Are the debt collection contracts between you and your clients or, as the case may be, the standard contract terms which you use different from those which are used in domestic debt collections? (*e.g.* receiving a simple letter of authority or buying bad debts)

  ....
  ....
  ....

E. Costs:

- What would be your fees and costs for collection of a judgment / non-judgment debt due from a debtor abroad?

  ### a) Judgment debts

  Where the debtor is in Germany / the amount to be collected is: £500   /   £5,000   /   £500,000

  standard fee ....
  success fee (on a contingency basis) ....
  expected external costs ....

  Where the debtor is in Turkey / the amount to be collected is: £500   /   £5,000   /   £500,000

  standard fee ....
  success fee (on a contingency basis) ....
  expected external costs ....

b) Non-judgment debts

**Where the debtor is in Germany /
the amount to be collected is:**   £500   /   £5,000   /   £500,000

standard fee   ....
success fee (on a contingency basis) ....
expected external costs   ....

**Where the debtor is in Turkey /
the amount to be collected is:**   £500   /   £5,000   /   £500,000

standard fee   ....
success fee (on a contingency basis) ....
expected external costs   ....

- Do you use a fixed tariff ?
  ....

F. Difficulties:

- Do you encounter particular difficulties in cross-border debt collection?

	generally	in Germany	in Turkey
– locating the place of residence of the debtor:	....	....	....
– because of differently regulated statutes of limitation:	....	....	....
– because the domestic security rights (*e.g.* floating charges) lose effect abroad:	....	....	....
– because of currency restrictions:	....	....	....
– converting the amount from pounds sterling into the foreign currency:	....	....	....
– others (please specify):	....	....	....

- Are there any other special difficulties encountered in debt collecting in Germany or in Turkey? Please comment.

G. Examples, cases and comments:

- Could you describe a successful / unsuccessful cross-border debt collection case where you have encountered special difficulties or had special observations?
- I would be grateful for any other observations or comments you may have on the subject in general (*e.g.* suggestions for amendments in the laws, *etc.*).

II. Debt collection within the jurisdiction on behalf of the creditors abroad (Debtor in England or Wales – Creditor abroad)

A. Practical importance (frequency and amount of cases and clients' countries of origin):

- What is the practical importance of debt collection on behalf of foreign creditors for your business as to the frequency of cases and their amounts? (If data available: the proportion of the annual turnover and the proportion of the total number of cases.)
  ....
  ....

  1985: ....cases, ...% of the cases, ...% of the annual turnover
  1990: ....cases, ...% of the cases, ...% of the annual turnover
  1994: ....cases, ...% of the cases, ...% of the annual turnover

- Which countries do most of your foreign clients come from?
  1. ....   , 2. ....   , 3. ....   , 4. ....   , 5. ....

- What is the practical importance for your business of your clients from Germany and Turkey? (If data available: the proportion of the annual turnover and the proportion of the total number of cases.)

  from Germany
  ....
  ....

  1985: ....cases, ...% of the cases, ...% of the annual turnover
  1990: ....cases, ...% of the cases, ...% of the annual turnover
  1994: ....cases, ...% of the cases, ...% of the annual turnover

  from Turkey
  ....
  ....

  1985: ....cases, ...% of the cases, ...% of the annual turnover
  1990: ....cases, ...% of the cases, ...% of the annual turnover
  1994: ....cases, ...% of the cases, ...% of the annual turnover

B. Distinguishing characteristics of the parties and indebtedness in debt collection on behalf or foreign clients:

- Which lines of business (import and export trade, credit institutions, tourism, insurance, *etc.*) do they come from?

    1. ....
    2. ....
    3. ....
    4. ....
    5. ....

- Is an average debt to be collected for a foreign client greater than the same average applicable for debt collection within the jurisdiction? Could you specify the average amount of debt that you collect for foreign creditors?

    ....
    ....
    ....

- Is the percentage of judgment debts higher or lower in debt collection for foreign clients than that of debt collection for domestic clients? (If data available: percentages.)

    ....
    ....
    ....

    Percentage of judgment debts in debt collection for

    a) domestic clients: b) foreign clients:

    1985: ....%   1985: ....%
    1990: ....%   1990: ....%
    1994: ....%   1995: ....%

- Are the debtors less co-operative when the creditor is abroad? Is the success rate higher or lower?

    ....
    ....

- Could you name some special characteristics of parties and 'causes of debt' in the debt collection cases where the client resides in Germany or in Turkey?

    ....
    ....

C. Debt collection methods and co-operation with foreign debt collectors:

- Do your clients contact you directly, or do you co-operate regularly with a corresponding debt collector or sister debt collection agency in the relevant foreign country (especially in Germany and in Turkey)?
  - Clients contact our own debt collection agency directly: ....
  - We co-operate with a sister debt collection agency abroad: ....
  - We co-operate with a corresponding debt collection agency abroad: ....

- Do you have regular co-operation with English and, as the case may be, with the foreign resident (especially Turkish and German) lawyers / law firms?

  in general
  with English lawyers: regularly ..../ occasionally ....../ never ....
  with foreign resident lawyers: regularly ..../ occasionally ....../ never ....
  Because:
  ....

  in Germany (for German clients)
  with English lawyers: regularly ..../ occasionally ..../ never ....
  with German lawyers: regularly ..../ occasionally ..../ never ....
  Because:
  ....

  in Turkey (for Turkish clients)
  with English lawyers: regularly ..../ occasionally ..../ never ....
  with Turkish lawyers: regularly ..../ occasionally ..../ never ....
  Because:
  ....

- What is your experience of enforcing foreign default judgments against debtors in England or Wales?
  ....
  ....
  ....
  ....

336 *Making Foreign People Pay*

D. Debt collection contract:

- Are the debt collection contracts between you and your foreign clients or, as the case may be, the standard contract terms which you use different from those which are used for domestic clients? (*e.g.* receiving a simple letter of authority or buying bad debts)
  ....
  ....
  ....
  ....

E. Costs:

- What would be your fees and costs for collection of a foreign judgment / non-judgment debt due from a debtor in England or Wales?

  a) Judgment debts

  **Where the client is from Germany /
  the amount to be collected is:**   £500   /   £5,000   /   £500,000

  standard fee   ....
  success fee (on a contingency basis) ....
  expected external costs   ....

  **Where the client is from Turkey /
  the amount to be collected is:**   £500   /   £5,000   /   £500,000

  standard fee   ....
  success fee (on a contingency basis) ....
  expected external costs   ....

b) non-judgment debts

the amount to be collected is:	£500	/	£5,000	/	£500,000
standard fee	....		....		....
success fee (on a contingency basis)	....		....		....
expected external costs	....		....		....

- Do you use a fixed tariff?
  ....

F. Difficulties:

- Do you encounter particular difficulties in collecting debts for foreign clients?

	generally	for German clients	for Turkish clients
– because of differently-regulated statutes of limitation:	....	....	....
– because foreign security rights (*e.g.* German *Eigentumsvorbehalt*) lose effect in England or Wales:	....	....	....
– because of currency restrictions:	....	....	....
– converting the amount from a foreign currency into pounds sterling:	....	....	....
– others (please specify):	....	....	....

- Are there any other special difficulties encountered in collecting German or Turkish clients' receivables? Please comment.
  ....
  ....
  ....
  ....

G. Examples, cases and comments:

- Could you describe a successful / unsuccessful debt collection case where you have encountered particular difficulties or had special observations in connection with the client being a foreign resident?
- I would be grateful for any other observations and comments you may have on the subject in general (*e.g.* suggestions for amendments in the laws, *etc.*).

III. Some particulars of your firm:

- How many people do you employ?
  ....
- Do you employ an officer especially for cross-border debt collection?
  ....

Data which you have provided will remain strictly confidential and will be processed anonymously.
Neither the name nor the distinguishing particulars of your firm (size, place of business, etc.) will be quoted.
However, should you give your written permission, I would be pleased to reproduce your observations and comments referring to yourself and / or your firm.

With many thanks for your co-operation.

Bibliography

I. LITERATURE

Abel, Richard L. and Philip S. C. Lewis (eds), *Lawyers in Society, Vol. 1: The Common Law World* (Berkeley: University of California Press, 1988), *Vol. 2: The Civil Law World* (Berkeley: University of California Press, 1988), *Vol. 3: Comparative Theories* (Berkeley: University of California Press, 1989).

Access to Justice: Final Report to the Lord Chancellor of the Civil Justice System in England and Wales (London: Her Majesty's Stationery Office, 1996).

Adamson, Hamish, *Free Movement of Lawyers* (London: Butterworths, 1992).

Adler, Michael, 'Alternativen zur Zwangsbeitreibung von Schulden', *Zeitschrift für Rechtssoziologie* 5 (1983), pp. 41–9.

Adler, Michael and Günter Hörmann, 'Schuldbeitreibung und die Gerichte – Bundesrepublik und Großbritannien im Vergleich', in Erhard Blankenburg and Rüdiger Voigt (eds), *Implementation von Gerichtsentscheidungen – Jahrbuch für Rechtssoziologie und Rechtstheorie* 11 (Opladen: Westdeutscher Verlag, 1987), pp. 95–103.

Adler, Michael and Edward Wozniak, *The Origins and Consequences of Default – An Examination of the Impact of Diligence*, Research Report for the Scottish Law Commission No. 5 (Central Research Unit, Scottish Office, 1981).

Akkaya, Cigdem, 'Die Türkei und ihre Migrationspolitik in die EU-Staaten', unpublished text of a lecture held in the Symposium *AusländerIn sein in Österreich und in der EU: Perspektiven im Spannungsfeld politischer Veränderung*, 19 – 20.10.1995, Wien. (This paper can be obtained from Zentrum für Türkeistudien, Overbergstr.27, D-45141 Essen.)

Alberta Law Reform Institute, *Enforcement of Money Judgments*, Volume 1, Report No. 61 (Edmonton: 1991).

Allison, Stephen P., *Debt Recovery* (London: Longman, 1990).

Althenhoff, Rudolf, Hans Busch and Jürgen Chemnitz, *Rechtsberatungsgesetz* (Commentary), 10th ed. (Münster: Aschendorff, 1993).

Arend, Friederich, *Zahlungsverbindlichkeiten in fremder Währung* (Frankfurt am Main, Bern, New York, Paris: Lang, 1989).

Banakar, Reza, 'Reflexive Legitimacy in International Commercial Arbitration', in Volkmar Gessner and Ali Cem Budak, *Emerging Legal Certainty* (Aldershot: Ashgate|Dartmouth, 1998).

Barnard, David and Mark Houghton, *The New Civil Courts in Action* (London, Dublin, Edinburgh: Butterworths, 1993).

Barnet, Richard J. and Ronald E. Müller, *Global Reach – The Power of the Multinational Corporations* (London: Jonathan Cape, 1975).

Bauer, Hellmuth, *Die Zwangsvollstreckung aus inländischen Schuldtiteln im Ausland* (Flensburg: Verlag Kurt Gross, loose-leaf / 1994).

Baum, Lawrence, 'Implementation of Judicial Decisions – An Organizational Analysis', *American Politics Quarterly* 4 (1979), pp. 86–114.

Baumbach, Adolf, Wolfgang Lauterbach, Jan Albers and Peter Hartmann, *Zivilprozeßordnung* (Commentary), 51st ed. (Munich: Beck, 1993).

Baumbach, Adolf, Wolfgang Lauterbach, Jan Albers and Peter Hartmann, *Zivilprozeßordnung* (Commentary), 55th ed. (Munich: Beck, 1997).

Baur, Fritz, Rolf Stürner and Adolf Schönke, *Zwangsvollstreckungs-, Konkurs- und Vergleichsrecht*, 11th ed. (Heidelberg: Müller, 1983).

Beechey, John, 'Litigation', in: Barbara Ford (ed.), *Doing Business in the United Kingdom*, Vol.I (New York: Matthew Bender, loose-leaf / 1993).

Bellers, Jürgen, 'Nationale und internationale Normierungen auf dem Gebiet der grenzüberschreitenden Wirtschaftsbeziehungen', in Klaus Dieter Wolf (ed.), *Internationale Verrechtlichung – Jahresschrift für Rechtspolitologie 1993* (Pfaffenweiler: Centaurus, 1993), pp.127–46.

Benninghaus, Michael M. and Wolfgang Moisek, 'Berufsrecht der Inkassounternehmen', in Walter Seitz (ed.), *Das Inkasso-Handbuch, Recht und Praxis der Inkassounternehmen*, 2nd ed. (Stuttgart: Verlag für Wirtschafts- und Steuerrecht, 1985).

Black, Alastair and Duncan Black, *Enforcement of a Judgment*, 8th ed. (London: Longman, 1992).

Blankenburg, Erhard, 'Mobilisierung von Recht', *Zeitschrift für Rechtssoziologie* 1, no.1 (1980), pp. 33–64.

Blankenburg, Erhard, 'Die Implementation von Recht als Programm', Renate Mayntz (ed.), *Implementation politischer Programme – Empirische Forschungsberichte* (Königstein: Athenäum, 1980), pp. 127–37.

Blankenburg, Erhard, 'Prozeßflucht und Prozeßebbe – Über die Fähigkeit der Gerichte mit Rechtstreitigkeiten fertig zu werden', in Erhard Blankenburg (ed.), *Prozeßflut? – Studien zur Prozeßtätigkeit europäischer Gerichte in historischen Zeitreihen und im Rechtsvergleich* (Cologne: Bundesanzeiger, 1989), pp. 9–21.

Blankenburg, Erhard, 'The Infrastructure for Avoiding Civil Litigation: Comparing Cultures of Legal Behaviour in the Netherlands and West Germany', *Law and Society Review* 28, no.4 (1994), pp. 789–808.

Blankenburg, Erhard (ed.), *Prozeßflut? – Studien zur Prozeßtätigkeit europäischer Gerichte in historischen Zeitreihen und im Rechtsvergleich* (Cologne: Bundesanzeiger, 1989).

Blankenburg, Erhard, Thomas Gawron, Ralf Rogowski and Rüdiger Voigt, 'Zur Analyse un Theorie der Implementation von Gerichtsentscheidungen', *Die Öffentliche Verwaltung* 1986, pp. 274–85.

Blankenburg, Erhard, Walter Gottwald and Dieter Strempel (eds), *Alternativen in der Ziviljustiz – Berichte, Analysen, Perspektiven* (Cologne: Bundesanzeigere, 1982).

Blankenburg, Erhard and Y. Taniguchi, 'Informal Alternatives to and within Formal Procedures', W. Wedekind (ed.), *The Eighth World Conference on Procedural Law – Justice and Efficiency – General Reports and Discussions* (Denever: Kluwer, 1989), pp. 335–60.

Blankenburg, Erhard and Rüdiger Voigt (eds), *Implementation von Gerichtsentscheidungen – Jahrbuch für Rechtssoziologie und Rechtstheorie* 11 (Opladen: Westdeutscher Verlag, 1987).

Blessing, Marc, 'Einleitung zum Zwölften Kapitel', in Heinrich Honsell, Nedim Peter Vogt, Anton K. Schnyder (eds), *Kommentar zum schweizerischen Privatrecht - Internationales Privatrecht* (Basel and Frankfurt am Main: Helbing & Lichtenhahn, 1996), pp. 1285–410.

Boggiani, Antonio, *International Standard Contracts - The Price of Fairness* (Dordrecht, Boston, London: Graham & Trotman / Martinus Nijhoff, 1991).

Bogle, Andrew and John Fuller, *Successful Debt Collecting* (Bristol: Jordans, 1996).

Böhner, Reinhard, 'Forderungseinziehung gegen Unternehmen in der EG', *Schimmelpfeng-Review*, 24 (1979), pp. 69–70.

Bork, Reinhard, '§ 91 IV', in *Stein-Jonas Kommentar zur Zivilprozeßordnung*, Vol. II, 21st ed. (Tübingen: Mohr, 1994).

Boudon, Raymond and Francois Bourricaud, *Soziologische Stichworte* (Opladen: Westdeutscher Verlag, 1992).

Braun, Norman, 'Reduziert das Cannabisverbot den Konsum harter Drogen?', *Zeitschrift für Rechtssoziologie* 18 (1997), pp. 106–23.

Budak, Ali Cem, 'Icra ve Iflas Kanunu'nda Borclu Aleyhine Yapilan Degisiklikler', in Ali Cem Budak (ed.), *Türk, Ingiliz ve ABD Hukukunda Isletmelerin Ödeme Güclügü Sorunlari ve Banka Iliskileri Sempozyumu* (Istanbul: Istanbul Chamber of Industry, 1993).

Bunge, Jürgen, *Zivilprozeß und Zwangsvollstreckung in England* (Berlin: Duncker & Humblot, 1995).

Capell, Jürgen, *Erfolgreich Mahnen - Handbuch für die Mahn- und Inkassopraxis* (Bonn: Rentrop, 1989).

Caplovitz, David, *Consumers in Trouble: A Study of Debtors in Default* (New York - London: Free Press, 1974).

Carver, Jeremy and Christopher Napier, 'United Kingdom', in Charles Platto and William G. Horton (eds), *Enforcement of Foreign Judgments Worldwide*, 2nd ed. (London, Dordrecht, Boston: Graham & Trotman / International Bar Association, 1993), pp. 223–52.

Casson, D. B., *Odgers on High Court Pleading and Practice*, 23rd ed. (London: Sweet & Maxwell / Steven, 1991).

Casson, D. B. and Ian H. Dennis, *Modern Developments in the Law of Civil Procedure* (London: Sweet & Maxwell, 1982).

Cavusgil, S. Tamer, 'Globalization of Markets and Its Impact on Domestic Institutions', *Indiana Journal of Global Legal Studies* 1, no.1 (1993), pp. 83–99.

Celikel, Aysel, *Milletlerarasi Özel Hukuk*, 4th ed. (Beta: Istanbul, 1995).

Cerrahoglu, Fadil, A. F. Basgöz and Peter D. Finlay, 'Turkey', in Philip R. Weems (ed.), *Enforcement of Money Judgments Abroad*, Vol.2 (New York: Matthew Bender, looseleaf / 1994).

Clarke, Brian W., 'The role of credit in world trade', in *Handbook of International Credit Management*, 2nd ed. (Aldershot: Gower, 1995), pp. 3–10.

Clarke, Brian, 'Documentary Letters of Credit', in *Handbook of International Credit Management*, 2nd ed. (Aldershot: Gower, 1995), pp. 222–42.

Clarke, Brian, 'Responsibilities, Expertise and Resource', in *Handbook of International Credit Management*, 2nd ed. (Aldershot: Gower, 1995), pp. 11–5.

Clarke, Brian, 'Sharing the Risk', in *Handbook of International Credit Management*, 2nd ed. (Aldershot: Gower, 1995), pp. 113–7.

Cline, William R., *International Debt: Systematic Risk and Policy Response* (Washington, D.C.: Institute for International Economics, The MIT Press, 1984).

Cohen, Albert K., 'Deviant Behavior', in David L. Sills (ed.), *International Encyclopaedia of the Social Sciences*, Vol. 4 (New York: Crowell Collies and London: Macmillan, 1968), p.148.

Commission of the European Communities, 'Commission memorandum to the Council transmitted on 4 January 1985', *Bulletin of the European Communities, Supplement 2/85*.

Commission of the European Communities, Greenbook on Consumer Access to Justice of 16 November 1993, *COM(93) 576 final*, pp. 77–8.

Cotterrell, Roger, *The Sociology of Law: An Introduction* (London: Butterworths, 1984).

Cremades, M. Bernardo and Steven L. Plehn, 'The new lex mecatoria and the harmonization of the laws of international transactions', *Boston University International Law Journal* 2 (1984), pp. 317–48.

David, Peter, *Zusammenarbeit mit Inkassounternehmen*, 3rd ed. (Munich: Verlag Wirtschaft Recht und Steuern, 1993).

David, René, *The International Unification of Private Law*, International Encyclopedia of Comparative Law, Vol. II, Chapter 5 (Tübingen: Mohr / The Hague - Paris: Mouton / New York: Oceana, 1971).

Dawson, Paul, 'Credit Insurance', in *Handbook of International Credit Management*, 2nd ed. (Aldershot: Gower, 1995), pp. 118–31.

Day, D. M. and Bernardette Griffin, *The Law of International Trade*, 2nd ed. (London, Dublin, Edinburgh: Butterworths, 1993).

Debt Recovery and Insolvency, The Law Reform Commission Report No.36 (Canberra: Australian Government Publishing Service, 1987).

del Busto, Charles, *ICC Guide to Documentary Operations* (Paris: International Chamber of Commerce,1994).

Delamaide, Darrell, *Debt Shock, The Full Story of the World Credit Crisis* (New York: Doubleday & Company, 1984).

Delbrück, Jost, 'Globalization of Law, Politics, and Markets – Implications for Domestic Law – A European Perspective', *Indiana Journal of Global Legal Studies* 1, no.1 (1993), pp. 9–36.

Dezalay, Yves, 'The Big Bang and the Law: The Internationalization and Restructuration of the Legal Field', *Theory, Culture and Society* 9 (1990), pp. 279–93.

Dezalay, Yves and Bryant Garth, 'Merchants of Law as Moral Entrepreneurs: Constructing International Justice from the Competition for Transnational Disputes', *Law and Society Review* 29, no. 1 (1995), pp. 27–64.

Dicey and Morris on Conflict of Laws, Vol.I, 12th ed. (London: Sweet & Maxwell, 1993).

Dietrich, Bernard R., *Inkasso Unternehmungen* (Munich: Hieronymus, 1986).

Dohmann, Barbara and Adrian Briggs, '"Worldwide Mareva" injunctions and the enforcement of foreign judgments in England', in Peter F. Schlosser (ed.), *Materielles Recht und Prozeßrecht und die Auswirkungen der Unterscheidung im Recht der Internationalen Zwangsvollstreckung* (Bielefeld: Gieseking, 1991).

Doig, Barbara, *The Nature and Scale of Diligence*, Scottish Office Central Research Unit Papers, Research Report for the Scottish Law Commission No.1 (Central Research Unit, Scottish Office, 1980).

Doig, Barbara, *Debt Recovery through the Scottish Sheriff Courts*, Scottish Office Central Research Unit Papers, Research Report for the Scottish Law Commission No.3 (Central Research Unit, Scottish Office, 1980).

Doig, Barbara and Ann R. Millar, *Debt Recovery – A Review of Creditors' Practices and Policies*, Scottish Office Central Research Unit Papers, Research Report for the Scottish Law Commission No. 8 (Central Research Unit, Scottish Office, 1981).

Dreitzel, Hans Peter, *Die gesellschaftlichen Leiden und das Leiden an der Gesellschaft*, 3rd ed. (Stuttgart: Enke 1980).

Duncan, Stuart M. and Christopher I. Millar, 'United Kingdom' (national report), in Philip R. Weems (ed.), *Enforcement of Money Judgments Abroad*, Vol.II (New York: Matthew Bender, loose-leaf / 1994).

Durkheim, Emile, *The Division of Labor in Society* (1893) (New York: Free Press and London: Collier Macmillan, 1965), translation by George Simpson.

Edwards, Burt, 'Risk Management', in *Handbook of International Credit Management*, 2nd ed. (Aldershot: Gower, 1995), pp. 98–112.

Edwards, Burt, 'The Range of Risks', in *Handbook of International Credit Management*, 2nd ed. (Aldershot: Gower, 1995), pp. 43–56.

Eggers, Carsten, 'Germany', in Edwin Godfrey (ed.), *Law without Frontiers* (London: Kluwer, 1995), pp. 80–93.

Eksi, Nuray, *Türk Mahkemelerinin Milletlerarasi Yetkisi* (Istanbul: Beta, 1996).

Fafchamps, Marchel, 'The Enforcement of Commercial Contracts in Ghana', *World Development* 24, no.3 (1996), pp. 427–48.

Fage, John and Gary Whitehead, *Supreme Court Practice and Procedure*, 5th ed. (London: Tolley,1992).

Falke, Josef, *Gerichtliche und Außergerichtliche Austragung von Rechtsstreiten – Rechtssoziologische Untersuchungen* (Bremen: University of Bremen, 1984).

Felstiner, William L. F., Richard L. Abel and Austin Sarat, 'The Emergence and Transformation of Disputes: Naming, Blaming, Claiming ...', *Law and Society Review* 15, no. 3–4 (1980–81), pp. 631–54.

Ferid, Murat, *Internationales Privatrecht*, 3rd ed. (Frankfurt am Main: Alfred Metzner, 1986).

Fletcher, Ian F. (ed.), *Cross-Border Insolvency: National and Comparative Studies* (Tübingen: Mohr, 1992).

Flood, John, *The Legal Profession in the United States*, 3rd. ed. (Chigago: American Bar Foundation, 1985).

Ford, Janet, *The Indebted Society – Credit and Default in 1980s* (London – New York: Routledge, 1988).

Frick, Klaus, 'Third Cultures versus Regulators: Cross-Border Legal Relations of Banks', in Volkmar Gessner and Ali Cem Budak, *Emerging Legal Certainty* (Aldershot: Ashgate|Dartmouth, 1998).

Friederichs, Jürgen, *Methoden empirischer Sozialforschung*, 10th ed. (Opladen: Westdeutscher Verlag, 1982).

Friedman, Lawrence M., 'Lawyers in Cross-Cultural Perspective', in Richard L. Abel and Philip S. C. Lewis (eds), *Lawyers in Society, Vol. 3: Comparative Theories* (Berkeley: University of California Press, 1989), pp. 1–26.

Furniss, Helen and Kurt Obermeier, 'United Kingdom' (national report), in Garrigues, Shinobu K. (ed.), *Guide to International Collections* (Minneapolis: American Collectors Association, loose-leaf / 1995).

Galanter, Marc, 'Why the "Haves" Come Out Ahead: Speculations on the Limits of Legal Change', *Law and Society Review* 9 (1974 / 75), pp. 95–160.

Garrigues, Shinobu K. (ed.), *Guide to International Collections* (Minneapolis: Debt Collectors Association, loose-leaf / 1995).

Garrigues, Shinobu K., 'Collecting Beyond Our Borders', *Collector* (July 1995), pp. 12–20.
Gatenby, John K., *Gatenby's Recovery of Money*, 8th ed. (London: Longman, 1993).
Geimar, Reinhold, *Internationales Zivilprozeßrecht*, 2nd ed. (Cologne: Schmidt, 1993).
Gessner, Volkmar, *Recht und Konflikt – Eine soziologische Untersuchung privatrechtlicher Konflikte in Mexiko* (Tübingen: Mohr, 1976).
Gessner, Volkmar, *Methoden und Probleme vergleichender Rechtssoziologie*, Centre for European Law and Politics 'Discussion Paper 2/83' (Bremen: Zentrum für europäische Rechtspolitik, 1983).
Gessner, Volkmar, 'Consumers in the Single Market – A Legal Sociological Approach', in Hanno von Freyhold, Volkmar Gessner, Enzo L. Vial and Helmut Wagner (eds), *Cost of Judicial Barriers for Consumers in the Single Market*, A report for the European Commission, Directorate General XXIV (Brussels: European Commission, October /November 1995), pp. 5–14.
Gessner, Volkmar, 'Institutional Framework of Cross-Border Interaction', in Volkmar Gessner (ed.), *Foreign Courts - Civil Litigation in Foreign Legal Cultures* (Aldershot: Dartmouth, 1996), pp.15–42.
Gessner, Volkmar, 'International Cases in German First Instance Courts', in Volkmar Gessner (ed.), *Foreign Courts – Civil Litigation in Foreign Legal Cultures* (Aldershot: Dartmouth, 1996), pp. 149–207.
Gessner, Volkmar, 'Introduction', in Volkmar Gessner (ed.), *Foreign Courts - Civil Litigation in Foreign Legal Cultures* (Aldershot: Dartmouth 1996).
Gessner, Volkmar, 'Kognitive Elemente sozialer Ordnung', in: Monika Frommel and Volkmar Gessner (eds), *Normenerosion* (Baden-Baden: Nomos, 1996), pp. 207–23.
Gessner, Volkmar, 'Globalisation and Legal Certainity', in Volkmar Gessner and Ali Cem Budak (eds), *Emerging Legal Certainty* (Aldershot: Ashgate|Dartmouth, 1998).
Gessner, Volkmar and Ali Cem Budak (eds), *Emerging Legal Certainty – Empirical Studies on Globalisation of Law* (Aldershot: Ashgate|Dartmouth, 1998).
Gessner, Volkmar and Angelika Schade, 'Conflicts of Culture in Cross-border Legal Relations: The Conception of a Research Topic in Sociology of Law', *Theory, Culture and Society* 7 (1990), pp. 253–77.
Gielen, Baudouin, 'Gerichtsvollzieher in Europa', *Deutsche Gerichtsvollzieher-Zeitung*, 107. Jahrgang, no.1 (1992), pp. 6–8.
Godfrey, Edwin and Anne Damerell, 'England and Wales', in Edwin Godfrey (ed.), *Law without Frontiers* (London: Kluwer, 1995).
Goode, R. M., *Consumer Credit Law* (London: Butterworths, 1989).
Gottwald, Peter, 'Die internationale Zwangsvollstreckung', *Praxis des internationalen Privat- und Verfahrensrechts*, 11. Jahrgang, no.5 (1991), pp. 285–7.
Gottwald, Walther, 'Die Zivilrechts(alltags)praxis – ein Findelkind der Implementationsforschung?', in Raiser and Voigt, *Durchsetzung und Wirkung von Rechtsentscheidungen* (Baden-Baden: Nomos, 1989), pp. 67–85.
Gottwald, Walther, *Streitbeilegung ohne Urteil* (Tübingen: Mohr, 1981).
Graf von Bernstorff, Christoph, 'Grundzüge des Zivilprozeß-, Zwangsvollstreckungs-, Konkurs- und Vergleichsrechts in England', in Christoph Graf von Bernstorff and H. Reinecker (eds), *Zivilgerichtsbarkeit, Zwangsvollstreckung und Konkurs in europäischen Ländern – Teil I: England, Frankreich und Schweiz* (Stuttgart: Deutscher Sparkassenverlag, 1983).
Graf von Bernstorff, Christoph, 'Die Eintreibung von Forderungen durch ausländische Gläubiger in England', *Recht der internationalen Wirtschaft*, 31. Jahrgang, no.5 (1985), pp. 367–73.

Graf von Bernstorff, Christoph, *Vertragsgestaltung im Auslandsgeschäft*, 2nd ed. (Frankfurt am Main: Firtz Knapp, 1991).

Graf von Westphalen, Friedrich, 'Rechtsprobleme des Factoring und des Forfait von Exportforderungen', *Recht der internationalen Wirtschaft*, 23. Jahrgang, no.2 (1977), pp. 80–6.

Greenslade, R. (ed.), *Civil Court Practice* (London, Dublin, Edinburgh: Butterworths, 1994).

Gregory, Janet and Janet Monk, *Survey of Defenders in Debt Actions in Scotland*, Research Report for the Scottish Law Commission No.6 (London: Her Majesty's Stationery Office, 1981).

Grotheer, Kirstin, 'Cross-border Maintenance Claims of Children', in Volkmar Gessner and Ali Cem Budak (eds), *Emerging Legal Certainty* (Aldershot: Ashgate|Dartmouth, 1998).

Grunet, Jens, 'Interlocutory Remedies in England and Germany: A Comparative Perspective', *Civil Justice Quarterly* 15 (1996), pp. 19–43.

Grunsky, Wolfgang, 'Vor § 249', in *Münchener Kommentar zum Bürgerlichen Gesetzbuch* (Commentary), Vol. II, 3rd ed. (Munich: C. H. Beck, 1993).

Guibentiff, Pierre, 'Cross-Border Legal Issues Arising from International Migrations – The Case of Portugal', in Volkmar Gessner and Ali Cem Budak, *Emerging Legal Certainty* (Aldershot: Ashgate|Dartmouth, 1998).

Gümrükcü, Harun, 'EU-Türkei-Beziehungen im Spannungsfeld zwischen Assoziation und Vollmitgliedschaft', in Hagen Lichtenberg, Gudrun Linne and Harun Gümrükcü (eds), *Gastarbeiter – Einwanderer – Bürger?* (Baden - Baden: Nomos, 1996), pp. 27–60.

Gürkan, Ülker, *Hukuk Sosyolojisine Giris*, 2nd ed. (Ankara: Siyasal Kitabevi, 1994).

Guy, Richard and Hugh Mercer, *Commercial Debt in Europe – Recovery and Remedies* (London: Longman, 1991).

Halperin, Jean-Louis, 'The Judicial and Legal Professions in Contemporary History: Forms of Organization in various European Countries', in Volkmar Gessner, Armin Hoeland and Csaba Varga (eds), *European Legal Cultures* (Aldershot: Dartmouth, 1996).

Halsbury's Laws of England, Vol.17, 4th ed. (London: Butterworths, 1976).

Hauck, Hans-Werner and W. Beat Haenni, 'Export Finance Techniques in Europe', in *Handbook of International Credit Management*, 2nd ed. (Aldershot: Gower, 1995), pp. 303–15.

Hedström, Hakan, *Die internationale Verschuldungskrise* (Heidelberg: HVA, 1985).

Heinrich, Dieter, Note on the Judgment of the Court of Appeal, 'OLG Nürnberg' dated 20.9.1983, *Praxis des internationalen Privat- und Verfahrensrechts*, 4. Jahrgang (1984), pp. 162–3.

Hellwig, Hans-Jürgen, 'Formen der Gestaltung der Zusammenarbeit mit dem ausländischen Anwalt', *Anwaltsblatt*, 46. Jahrgang, no.3 (1996), pp. 124–9.

Henry, Stuart, *Private Justice – Towards Integrated Theorising in the Sociology of Law* (London, Boston, Melbourne and Henley: Routledge & Kegan Paul, 1983).

Henssler, Martin, 'Der europäische Rechtsanwalt', *Anwaltsblatt*, 46. Jahrgang, no.7 (1996), pp. 353–65.

Hirsch, Ernest, E., *Rezeption als sozialer Prozess – Erläutert am Beispiel der Türkei* (Berlin: Duncker & Humblot, 1981).

Hoebel, Edward Adamson, *Das Recht der Naturvölker – Eine vergleichende Untersuchung rechtlicher Abläufe* (Olten: Walter Verlag, 1968), translated by Maria Elisabeth Drude.[English original: *The Law of Primitive Man: A Study in Comparative Dynamics* (Cambridge, Massachusetts: Harvard University Press, 1954).]

Hoene, Eberhard, *Präventiver Kreditschutz und Zwangsvollstreckung durch Private* (Berlin: Duncker & Humblot, 1971).

Holch, Georg, 'Mahnverfahren zwischen Schuldnerschutz und Entlastungsfunktion', *Zeitschrift für Rechtspolitik* 14, no.12 (1981), pp. 281–5.

Holzscheck, Knut, Günter Hörmann and Jürgen Daviter, *Praxis des Konsumentenkredits – Eine empirische Untersuchung zur Rechtssoziologie und Ökonomie des Konsumentenkredits* (Cologne: Bundesanzeiger, 1982).

Hörmann, Günter, 'Gerichtliche Schuldbeitreibung und ihre Umwelt – Zur Entwicklung der gerichtlichen und außergerichtlichen Durchsetzung von Geldforderungen in der Bundesrepublic Deutschland', in Erhard Blankenburg and Rüdiger Voigt (eds), *Implementation von Gerichtsentscheidungen – Jahrbuch für Rechtssoziologie und Rechtstheorie* 11 (Opladen: Westdeutscher Verlag, 1987), pp. 72–94.

Hörmann, Günter, *Verbraucher und Schulden* (Baden - Baden: Nomos, 1987).

Hörmann, Günter and Knut Holzscheck, 'Schuldbeitreibung im Konsumentenkredit – Ergebnisse einer empirischen Studie', *Zeitschrift für Rechtssoziologie* 5 (1983), pp. 26–40.

Hoyle, Mark, 'Legal and Regulatory Issues', in *Handbook of International Credit Management* (Aldershot: Gower, 1995), pp. 363–70.

Huleatt-James, Mark and Nicholas Gould, *International Commercial Arbitration* (London: Lovel White Durrant, 1996).

Inkeles, Alex, 'The Emerging Social Structure of the World', *World Politics* 27 (October 1974 – July 1975), pp. 467–95.

Insolvency Law and Practice, Report of the Review Committee (London: Her Majesty's Stationery Office, 1982).

International Debt and the Developing Countries – A World Bank Symposium (Washington D.C.; The World Bank, 1986).

Izveren, Adil, *Hukuk Sosyolojisi* (Ankara: Dokuz Eylül Üniversitesi Hukuk Fakültesi, 1993).

Jäckle, Wolfgang, *Die Erstattungsfähigkeit der Kosten eines Inkassobüros* (Berlin: Duncker & Humblot, 1978).

Jauernig, Othmar, *Zwangsvollstreckungs- und Insolvenzrecht*, 20th ed. (Munich: Beck, 1996).

Jayme, Erik and Rainer Hausmann (eds), *Internationales Privat- und Verfahrensrecht* (Textausgabe), 8th ed. (Munich: Beck 1996).

Johnson, Allan G., *The Blackwell Dictionary of Sociology* (Cambridge, Massachusetts: Basil Blackwell, 1995).

Jürgen, Schmid, *Elektronische Datenverarbeitung im Mahnverfahren* (Munich: V.Florentz, 1991).

Kagan, Robert A., 'The routinization of debt collection: An essay on social change and conflicts in the courts', *Law and Society Review* 18 (1984), pp. 323–71.

Kaplan, B. and K. M. Clermont, *Ordinary Proceedings in First Instance, International Encyclopaedia of Comparative Law*, Vol. XVI, Ch.6 (Tübingen: Mohr / The Hague: Mouton / New York: Oceana Publications, 1984).

Karlen, Delmar and Ilhan Arsel, *Civil Litigation in Turkey* (Ankara: 1957).

Kefalas, Asterios G., *Global Business Strategy – A systems approach* (Cincinnati, Ohio: South-Western Publishing, 1990).

Kegel, Gerhard, *Internationales Privatrecht*, 7th ed. (Munich: Beck, 1995).

Keith, J. A., W. B. Podevin and Claire Sandbrook, *The Execution of Sheriffs' Warrants* (Chichester, West Sussex: Barry Law Publishers, 1996).

Kettel, Brian and George Magnus, *The International Debt Game* (London: Graham & Trotman, 1986).

Kizil, Ahmet and Macide Sogur, *Ihracat-Ithalat Islemleri ve Muhasebe Uygulamasi* (Istanbul: Der, 1995).

Koch, Harald, 'Durchsetzung einer "world-wide Mareva order" in Deutschland', in Peter F. Schlosser (ed.), *Materielles Recht und Prozeßrecht und die Auswirkungen der Unterscheidung im Recht der Internationalen Zwangsvollstreckung* (Bielefeld: Gieseking, 1991).

Kojm, Christopher A. (ed.), *The Problem of International Debt* (New York: The H. W. Wilson Company, 1984).

Kotzorek, Andreas, *Private Gerichte als Alternative zur staatlichen Zivilgerichtsbarkeit – Eine ökonomische Analyse* (Tübingen: Mohr, 1987).

Krauskopf, Lutz, 'Das britische Vollstreckungsrecht', *Blätter für Schuldbetreibung und Konkurs*, 42. Jahrgang, no. 4 (1978), pp. 97–109.

Kropholler, Jan, *Internationales Privatrecht*, 2nd ed. (Tübingen: Mohr, 1994).

Kropholler, Jan, *Europäisches Zivilprozeßrecht*, 5th ed. (Heidelberg: Verlag Recht und Wirtschaft, 1996).

Krüger, Hilmar, 'Das türkische IPR-Gesetz von 1982', *Praxis des internationalen Privat- und Verfahrensrechts*, 2. Jahrgang (1982), pp. 252–9.

Kühn, Wolfgang, 'Deutsche Anwälte international in der Abstiegszone', *Anwaltsblatt*, 38. Jahrgang, no.3 (1988), pp.129–32.

Kulcsár, Kálmán, 'Politics and Legal Policy', in Peter Koller, Csaba Varga and Ota Weinberger (eds), *Theoretische Grundlagen der Rechtspolitik – Ungarisch-Österreichishes Symposium der internationalen Vereinigung für Rechts- und Sozialphilosophie 1990* (Stuttgart: Franz Steiner, 1992), pp. 17–27.

Kuru, Baki, 'Das schweizerische Schuldbetreibungs- und Konkursgesetz in der Türkei', *Zeitschrift für Schweizerisches Recht* 83 (1964), pp. 331–50.

Kuru, Baki, 'Die neue Revision des türkischen Schuldbetreibungs-und Konkursgesetzes', *Blätter für Schuldbetreibung und Konkurs*, 31. Jahrgang, no.2 (1967), pp. 33–45.

Kuru, Baki, 'Wechselbetreibung im türkischen Recht', in Max Kummer and Hans Ulrich Walder (eds), *Festschrift zum 70. Geburtstag von Max Guldener* (Zürich: Schulthess, 1973), pp.177–88.

Kuru, Baki, *Zivilgerichtsbarkeit, Zwangsvollstreckung und Konkurs in europäischen Ländern – Teil II: Griechenland, Italien, Jugoslawien, Portugal, Spanien und Türkei* (Stuttgart: Deutscher Sparkassenverlag, 1983), pp. 359–459.

Kuru, Baki, *Icra ve Iflas Hukuku*, Vol.1 (Istanbul: Evrim, 1988).

Kuru, Baki, *Icra ve Iflas Hukuku*, Vol.2 (Istanbul: Evrim, 1990).

Kuru, Baki, *Hukuk Muhakemeleri Usulü*, Vol.4, 5th ed. (Istanbul: Alfa, 1991).

Kuru, Baki, *Icra ve Iflas Hukuku*, Vol.3, 3rd ed. (Ankara: Seckin, 1993).

Kuru, Baki and Tugrul Ansay, 'Civil Procedure', in Tugrul Ansay and Don Wallace (eds), *Introduction to Turkish Law*, 4th ed. (The Hague: Kluwer, 1996), pp. 179 – 208.

Lachmann, Jens-Peter and Ivo Geis, 'Grenzüberschreitende Informationsverarbeitung', *Anwaltsblatt*, 46. Jahrgang, no.11 (1996), pp.545–9.

Lambert, Robert, 'Operating through Subsidiaries and Affiliates', in *Handbook of International Credit Management*, 2nd ed. (Aldershot: Gower, 1995), pp. 29–39.

Lardinois, Jacques, 'Documentary Collections', in *Handbook of International Credit Management*, 2nd ed. (Aldershot: Gower, 1995), pp. 196–221.

Legal Aid Board (ed.), *Legal Aid – 1994 Handbook* (London: Sweet & Maxwell, 1994).

Luhmann, Niklas, 'Weltgesellschaft', *Archiv für Rechts- und Sozialphilosophie* 57 (1971), pp. 1–35.

Luhmann, Niklas, 'Kommunikation über Recht in Interaktionssystem', in Erhard Blankenburg, Ekkehard Klausa, Hubert Rottleuthner and Ralf Rogowski (eds), *Alternative Rechtsformen und Alternativen zum Recht – Jahrbuch für Rechtssoziologie und Rechtstheorie* 6 (Opladen: Westdeutscher, 1980), pp. 99–112.

Luhmann, Niklas, 'Communication about law in interaction systems', in Karin D. Knorr-Cetina and Aaron V. Cicourel (eds), *Advances in Social Theory and Methodology – Toward an integration of micro- and macro-sociologies* (Boston, London and Henley: Routledge & Kegan Paul, 1981), pp. 234–56.

Luhmann, Niklas, *Rechtssoziologie*, 2nd ed. (Opladen: Westdeutscher Verlag, 1983).

Luther, Gerhard, 'Kollusions- und Fremdrechtsanwendung in der Gerichtspraxis', *Rabels Zeitschrift für ausländisches und internationales Privatrecht* 37 (1973), pp. 660–681 (contains a summary in English).

Martiny, Dieter, 'Rechtsvergleichung und vergleichende Rechtssoziologie', *Zeitschrift für Rechtssoziologie* 1, no. 1 (1980), pp. 65–84.

Martiny, Dieter, Jan Peter Waehler and Martin K. Wolff, *Handbuch des internationalen Zivilverfahrensrechts*, Vol. 3/2, Max - Plancks - Institut für Ausländisches und Internationales Privatrecht (Tübingen: Mohr, 1984).

Martiny, Dieter, 'Anerkennung ausländischer Entscheidungen nach autonomem Recht', *Handbuch des Internationalen Zivilverfahrensrechts*, Vol. 3/1, Max - Planck - Institut für Ausländisches und Internationales Privatrecht (Tübingen: Mohr, 1984).

Masters, Roger D., 'World Politics as a Primitive Political System', *World Politics* 16 (1963 – 1964), pp. 595–619.

Mayntz, Renate, 'Die Implementation politischer Programme – Thoeretische Überlegungen zu einem neuen Forschungsgebiet', *Die Verwaltung* 10 (1977), pp. 51–66.

Mayntz, Renate, 'Einleitung – Die Entwicklung des analytischen Paradigms der Implementationsforschung', Renate Mayntz (ed.), *Implementation politischer Programme – Empirische Forschungsberichte* (Königstein: Athenäum, 1980), pp. 1–19.

McClean, David, *International Judicial Assistance* (Oxford: Clarendon, 1992).

McGrew, Antony, 'Conceptualizing Global Politics', in Antony McGrew and Paul G. Lewis et al., *Global Politics* (Cambridge: Polity Press, 1992), pp. 1–28.

Medicus, Dieter and Karsten Schmidt, '§§ 243 – 254', in *J. von Staudingers Kommentar zum Bürgerlichen Gesetzbuch mit Einführungsgesetz und Nebengesetzen, Zweites Buch*, 12th ed. (Berlin: J. Schweitzer, 1983).

Menne, Heinz, *Das Mahnverfahren* (Neuwied: Luchterhand, 1979).

Morse, Geoffrey, Enid A. Marshall, Richard Morris and Letitia Crabb, *Charlesworth & Morse Company Law*, 5th ed. (London: Sweet & Maxwell, 1995).

Müller, Holger and Götz-Sebastian Hök, *Deutsche Vollstreckungstitel im Ausland – Anerkennung, Vollstreckbarerklärung, Vollstreckung und Verfahrensführung in den einzelnen Ländern* (Neuwied-Frankfurt: Verlag Kurt Gross, loose-leaf / 1988).

Müller, Holger and Götz-Sebastian Hök, *Einzug von Auslandsforderungen*, 3rd ed. (Göttingen: WiRe, 1989).

N.N., *Aktuelle Beiträge über das Inkasso im In- und Ausland*, 2nd ed. (Frankfurt: Schimmelpfeng, 1977).

N.N., *Eigentumvorbehalt in 35 Ländern* (Paris: International Chamber of Commerce, 1993).

N.N., 'Türkei', in *Handbuch der internationalen Zwangsvollstreckung*, Vol.2. (Kissing: Recht und Praxis, loose-leaf / 1994).

N.N., *ICC Rules for Collections – A Commentary* (Paris: International Chamber of Commerce, 1995).

N.N., *Cross Border Debt Recovery: A manual for exporters and importers* (London: Lawyers International Inkasso, 1996).

Nagel, Heinrich, *Internationales Zivilprozeßrecht*, 3rd ed. (Münster: Aschendorf, 1991).

Nelmes, Don, 'Agency Representation', in *Handbook of International Credit Management*, 2nd ed. (Aldershot: Gower, 1995), pp. 16–28.

Nerad, Hasan, 'International Litigation and Arbitration in Turkey', in Volkmar Gessner and Ali Cem Budak (eds), *Emerging Legal Certainty* (Aldershot: Ashgate|Dartmouth, 1998).

Neyer, Jürgen, *Spiel ohne Grenzen – Weltwirtschaftliche Strukturveränderungen und das Ende des sozial kompetenten Staates* (Marburg: Tectum, 1996).

Nomer, Ergin, *Devletler Hususi Hukuku*, 8th ed. (Beta: Istanbul 1996).

Nothnagel, Walther, *Execution durch sociale Interessengruppen* (Wien: Alfred Hödler, 1899).

O'Hare, John and Robert N. Hill, *Civil Litigation*, 7th ed. (London: FT Law & Tax, 1996).

Ohle, Carsten D., 'Das deutsche Inkassogewerbe in Vergangenheit, Gegenwart und Zukunft', in Walter Seitz (ed.), *Das Inkasso-Handbuch, Recht und Praxis der Inkassounternehmen*, 2nd ed. (Stuttgart: Verlag für Wirtschafts- und Steuerrecht, 1985), pp. 1–43.

Oktay, Müjde, *Turkish Business Life via the Eyes of Foreign Businessmen* (Istanbul: Istanbul Chamber of Industry, 1996).

Öktem, Niyazi, *Hukuk Felsefesi ve Hukuk Sosyolojisi*, 2nd. ed. (Istanbul: Istanbul Üniversitesi Hukuk Fakültesi, 1985).

Olgiati, Vittorio, 'Towards a New "Universalis Mercatorum": The Political Economy of the Chamber of Commerce in Milan', in Volkmar Gessner and Ali Cem Budak (eds), *Emerging Legal Certainty* (Aldershot: Ashgate|Dartmouth, 1998).

Osborn's Concise Law Dictionary, 7th ed. (London: Sweet & Maxwell, 1983).

Osborn's Concise Law Dictionary, 8th ed. by Leslie Rutherford and Sheila Bone (London: Sweet & Maxwell, 1993).

Özbilgen, Tarik, *Elestirisel Hukuk Sosyolojisi* (Istanbul: Istanbul Üniversitesi Hukuk Fakültesi, 1976).

Palandt, Otto et al., *Palandt Bürgerliches Gesetzbuch* (Commentary), 56th ed. (Munich: Beck, 1997).

Pasero, Ursula, *Familien Konflikte in Migration* (Wiesbaden: Deutscher Universitätsverlag, 1990), pp. 40–3.

Pekcanitez, Hakan, *Medeni Usul ve Icra-Iflâs Hukukunda Yabanci Para Alacaklarinin Tahsili* (Izmir: Dokuz Eylül Üniversitesi Hukuk Fakültesi, 1994).

Peterson, Alan, 'Financial Legal Services: A Comparative Perspective', in D. L. Carey Miller and Paul R. Beaumont (eds), *The Option of Litigating in Europe* (London, United Kingdom National Committee of Comparative Law, 1993), pp. 149–53.

Petzold, Andreas, 'Obtaining Information on Foreign Legal Systems', Volkmar Gessner and Ali Cem Budak (eds), *Emerging Legal Certainty* (Aldershot: Ashgate|Dartmouth, 1998).

Picton Howell, Zoe, 'Prozessieren in England and Wales: "Discovery"', *Recht der Internationalen Wirtschaft*, 42. Jahrgang, no.12 (1996), pp. 1011–3.

Pieterse, Jan Nederveen, 'Globalization and Hybridisation', *International Sociology* 9, no.2 (1994), pp. 161–8.

Piggert, Horst, 'Das Auslandsinkasso', *Teilzahlungswirtschaft*, 15. Jahrgang, no.1 (1968), pp. 15–6.

Pitts, Paul, 'Customer Risk Assesment', in *Handbook of International Credit Management*, 2nd ed. (Aldershot: Gower, 1995), pp. 74–97.

Posner, Richard A., *Economic Analysis of Law*, 4th ed. (Boston - Toronto - London: Little, Brown and Company, 1992).

Prütting, Hanns, 'Auf dem Weg zu einer europäischen Zivilprozeßordnung – Dargestellt am Beispiel des Mahnverfahrens', in Hanns Prütting (ed.), *Festschrift für Gottfried Baumgärtel zum 70. Geburtstag* (Cologne: Carl Heymanns Verlag, 1990), pp. 457–69.

Prütting, Hanns, *Die Entwicklung eines europäischen Zivilprozeßrechts*, Vorträge, Reden und Berichte aus dem Europa-Institut – Sektion Rechtswissenschaft, Nr. 271 (Saarbrücken: Europainstitut der Universtät des Saarlandes, 1992).

Raabe, Horst, 'Die japanische Zivilprozeßordnung und die Zwangsvollstreckung in Japan', *Deutsche Gerichtsvollzieher-Zeitung*, 102. Jahrgang, no.1 (1987), pp. 5–7.

Raiser, Thomas, 'Wirksamkeit und Wirkung von Zivilrechtsnormen', Raiser and Voigt, *Durchsetzung und Wirkung von Rechtsentscheidungen* (Baden-Baden: Nomos, 1989), pp. 46–65.

Raiser, Thomas and Rüdiger Voigt (eds), Durchsetzung und Wirkung von Rechtsentscheidungen – Die Bedeutung der Implementations- und Wirkungsforschung für die Rechtswissentschaft (Baden-Baden: Nomos, 1989).

Rasehorn, Theo, 'Der Gerichtsvollzieher als "Basis-Implementeur"', in Erhard Blankenburg and Rüdiger Voigt (eds), *Implementation von Gerichtsentscheidungen – Jahrbuch für Rechtssoziologie und Rechtstheorie* 11 (Opladen: Westdeutscher Verlag, 1987), pp. 104–9.

Recommendation No. R (84) 5 of the Council of Ministers of 28.2.1984 (Strasbourg: Council of Europe, 1984).

Rennen, Günter and Gabriele Calibe, *Rechtsberatungsgesetz mit Ausführungsverordnungen* (Commentary), 2nd ed. (Munich: C. H. Beck, 1992).

Report of the Committee on the Enforcement of Judgment Debts, London: Her Majesty's Stationery Office, 1969 (reprint 1977).

Report on Debt Collection, The Law Reform Commission, Report No. LRC 27-1988 (Dublin: The Law Reform Commission, 1988).

Richardson, James (ed.), *Debt Recovery in Europe* (London: Blackstone, 1993).

Robertson, Roland and Laurie Taylor, *Deviance, Crime and Socio-Legal Control* (London: M. Robertson, 1973).

Rock, Paul, 'Observations on Debt Collection', *British Journal of Sociology* 19 (1968), pp. 176–90.

Rock, Paul, *Making People Pay* (London: Routledge & Kegan Paul, 1973).

Rogowski, Ralf, 'Implementation von zivilgerichtlich legitimierten Geldforderungen', in Erhard Blankenburg and Rüdiger Voigt (eds), *Implementation von Gerichtsentscheidungen – Jahrbuch für Rechtssoziologie und Rechtstheorie* 11 (Opladen: Westdeutscher Verlag, 1987), pp. 43–8.

Röhl, Klaus F., 'Schuldbeitreibung als Kontrolle abweichenden Verhaltens', *Zeischrift für Rechtssoziologie* 5 (1983), pp. 1–49.

Röhl, Klaus F., *Rechtssoziologie – Ein Lehrbuch* (Cologne: Carl Heymanns, 1987).

Röhl, Klaus F. and Stefan Magen, 'Die Rolle des Rechts im Prozeß der Globalisierung', *Zeitschrift für Rechtssoziologie* 17, no. 1 (1996), pp. 1–57.

Rosenberg, Leo, Hans Friedhelm Gaul and Eberhard Schilken, *Zwangsvollstreckungsrecht*, 10th ed. (Munich: Beck, 1987).

Roth, Herbert, 'Die Vorschläge de Kommission für ein europäisches Zivilprozeßgesetzbuch – Das Erkenntnsisverfahren', *Zeitschrift für Zivilprozeß* 109, no.3 (1996), pp. 271–313, pp. 271–7.

Rozenberg, Joshua, *The Search for Justice – An Anatomy of the Law* (London: Hodder & Stoughton, 1987).

Schack, Haimo, 'Internationale Zwangsvollstreckung in Geldforderungen', *Der Deutsche Rechtspfleger*, 88. Jahrgang (1980), p. 175–8.

Schack, Haimo, *Internationales Zivilverfahrensrecht*, 2nd ed. (Munich: Beck, 1996).

Schäfer, Hans-Bernd and Claus Ott, *Lehrbuch der ökonomiscen Analyse der Zivilrechts*, 2nd ed. (Berlin: Springer, 1995).

Schäfer, Wilhelm, *Wirtschaftswörterbuch*, Vol.2, 3rd. ed. (Munich: Verlag Franz Vahlen, 1991).

Schär, Kurt F., 'Die wirtschaftliche Funktionsweise des Factoring', in Ernst A. Kramer (ed.), *Neue Vertragsformen der Wirtschaft: Leasing, Factoring, Franchising*, 2nd ed. (Bern and Stuttgart: Paul Haupt, 1992), pp. 275–8.

Schilken, Eberhard, 'Die Vorschläge de Kommission für ein europäisches Zivilprozeßgesetzbuch – einstweiliger und summarischer Rechtsschutz und Vollstreckung', *Zeitschrift für Zivilprozeß* 109, no.3 (1996), pp. 315–36.

Schmitthoff, Clive M., *Schmitthoff's Export Trade – The Law and Practice of International Trade*, 9th ed. (London: Stevens, 1990).

Schneider, H. J. (ed.), *Kriminalität und abweichendes Verhaltens*, Vol.2. (Weinheim - Basel: Beltz, 1983).

Schnorr, Thomas, 'Einzelanwälte und kleine Anwaltsfirmen im internationalen Rechtsverkehr – Eine empirische Untersuchung', *Anwaltsblatt*, 44. Jahrgang, no.3 (1994), pp. 98–104.

Schütze, Rolf, 'Die Anerkennung und Vollstreckung deutscher Zivilurteile in West-Europa', *Deutsches Autorecht*, 52. Jahrgang, no. 4 (1983), pp. 110–115.

Scottish Law Commission, *First Memorandum on Diligence* (Edinburgh: Scottish Law Commission, 1980).

Seitz, Walter (ed.), *Das Inkasso-Handbuch – Recht und Praxis der Inkassounternehmen*, 2nd ed. (Stuttgart: Verlag für Wirtschafts- und Steuerrecht, 1985).

Seitz, Walter, 'Materiellrechtliche und prozessuale Probleme des Inkassorechts', in Walter Seitz (ed.), *Das Inkasso-Handbuch, Recht und Praxis der Inkassounternehmen*, 2nd ed. (Stuttgart: Verlag für Wirtschafts- und Steuerrecht, 1985).

Shapiro, Martin, 'Incremental Decision Making', in S. Sidney Ulmer (ed.), *Courts, Law and Judicial Processes* (New York: The Free Press, 1981), pp. 313–23.

Shapiro, Martin, 'The Globalization Of Law', *Indiana Journal of Global Legal Studies* 1, no.1 (1993), pp. 37–64.

Shaw, Martin, 'Bonds and Guarantees', in *Handbook of International Credit Management*, 2nd ed. (Aldershot: Gower, 1995), pp. 151–63.

Sheptycki, J. W. E., 'Law Enforcement, Justice and Democracy in the Transnational Arena: Reflections on the War on Drugs', *International Journal of the Sociology of Law* 24 (1996), pp. 61–75.

Siehr, Kurt, 'Special courts for conflicts cases: A German experiment', *American Journal of Comparative Law* 25 (1977), pp. 663–80.

Sinclair, Gray, 'Terms and Conditions for International Trade', in *Handbook of International Credit Management*, 2nd ed. (Aldershot: Gower, 1995), pp. 133–50.

Sonderkötter, F., 'Anerkennung deutscher Urteile in Großbritannien', *Recht der internationalen Wirtschaft*, 21. Jahrgang (1975), p. 370 et seq.

Stahrenberg, Cora, *Effektivität des externen Inkassos – Ein Beitrag zur Ausgliederung betrieblicher Funktionen* (Berlin: Duncker & Humblot, 1995).

Stammel, Christine, 'Back to Courtroom? – Developments in the London Reinsurance Market', in Volkmar Gessner and Ali Cem Budak, *Emerging Legal Certainty* (Aldershot: Ashgate|Dartmouth, 1998).

Starr, June, 'Turkish Village Disputing Behavior', in Laura Nader and Harry F.Todd Jr. (eds), *The Disputing Process – Law in Ten Societies* (New York: Columbia University Press, 1978), pp.122–51.

Starr, June and Jonathan Pool, 'The Impact of a Legal Revolution in Rural Turkey', *Law and Society Review* 8, no.3 (1974) pp. 533–60.

Steinbach, Elmar and Rolf Koniffka (eds), Strukturen des amtsgerichtlichen Zivilprozesses, München, 1982.

Stöber, Kurt, *Aktuelle Fragen zur Praxis der Zwangsvollstreckung und des Mahnverfahrens*, 2nd ed. (Cologne:Kommunikationsforum, 1983).

Stöber, Kurt, *Forderungspfändung*, 10th ed. (Bielefeld: Gieseking, 1993).

Stoller, Christoper W., *Transnational Mobility of Lawyers and English Law Firms* (Not published. A report prepared for the Joint Meeting of the Law and Society Association and Research Committee on the Sociology of Law of the International Sociological Association held on 10 – 13 July 1996).

Stone, Peter, *The Conflict of Laws* (London: Longman, 1995).

Storme, Marcel, 'Rechtsvereinheitlichung in Europa – Ein Plädoyer für ein einheitliches europäisches Prozeßrecht', *Rabels Zeitschrift für ausländisches und internationales Privatrecht* 56 (1992), pp. 290–9.

Stubbs, Richard and Geoffrey R. D. Underhill, *Political Economy and the Changing Global Order* (London: Macmillan, 1994).

Stürner, Rolf, 'Das grenzübergreifende Vollstreckungsverfahren in der Europäischen Union', in Walter Gerhardt, Uwe Diederichsen, Bruno Rimmelspacher and Jürgen Costede (eds), *Festschrift für Wolfram Henckel zum 70. Geburtstag am 21. April 1995* (Berlin and New York: Gruyter, 1995), pp. 863–75.

Stürner, Rolf, Note on OLG Düsseldorf, Order dated 10.1.1996, *Zeitschrift für Zivilprozeß* 109, no.2 (1996).

Szilágyi, Péter, 'Zur theoretischen Grundlegung der Rechtspolitik de Gesetzgebung', in Peter Koller, Csaba Varga and Ota Weinberger (eds), *Theoretische Grundlagen der Rechtspolitik – Ungarisch-Österreichishes Symposium der internationalen Vereinigung für Rects- und Sozialphilosophie 1990* (Stuttgart: Franz Steiner, 1992), pp. 104–10.

Tayeb, Monir H., *The Global Business Environment – An Introduction* (London: SAGE, 1992).

Tekinay, Selâhattin Sulhi, Sermet Akman, Haluk Burcuoglu and Atilla Altop, *Tekinay Borclar Hukuku*, 7th ed. (Istanbul: Filiz, 1993).

The International Symposium on Civil Justice in the Era of Globalization, Collected Reports (Tokyo: Japanese Association of the Law of Civil Procedure, 1993).

The Supreme Court Practice 1995 (London: Sweet & Maxwell, 1994).

Thode, Reinhold, '§ 268', in *Münchener Kommentar zum Bürgerlichen Gesetzbuch* (Commentary), Vol. II, 3rd ed. (Munich: C. H. Beck, 1994).

Thomas, Heinz and Hans Putzo, *Zivilprozeßordnung* (Commentary), 17th ed. (Munich: Beck, 1991).

Thomas, Heinz and Hans Putzo, *Zivilprozeßordnung* (Commentary), 19th ed. (Munich: Beck, 1995).

Tilch, H. (ed.), *Deutsches Rechts-Lexikon*, Vol. 1 and Vol. 2, 2nd ed. (Munich: Beck, 1992).

Timmermann, Franz Hubert, 'Die Zwangsvollstreckung im Ausland ist schwierig', *Teilzahlungswirtschaft*, 17. Jahrgang, no. 2 (1970), p. 20.

Tomanbay, Mehmet, *Dis Ticaret Rejimi ve Ihracatin Finansmani* (Ankara: Hatipoglu, 1995), pp. 177–207.

Tomasic, Roman, *The Sociology of Law* (London, Beverly Hills and New Delhi: SAGE, 1985).
Triebel, Volker, Stephen Hodgson, Wolfgang Kellenter and Georg Müller, *Englisches Handels- und Wirtschaftsrecht*, 2nd ed. (Heidelberg: Verlag Recht und Wirtschaft, 1995).
Trubek, David M., Yves Dezalay, Ruth Buchanan and John R. Davis, 'Global Restructuring and the Law: Studies of the Internationalization of Legal Fields and the Creation of Transnational Areas', *Case Western Reserve Law Review* 44, no.2 (1994), pp. 407-98.
Üstündag, Saim, *Icra ve Iflas Kanunu'nun Dünü ve Bugünü* (Istanbul: Evrim, 1990).
Üstündag, Saim, *Medeni Yargilama Hukuku*, 5th ed. (Istanbul: Filiz, 1992).
Üstündag, Saim, *Icra Hukukunun Esaslari*, 6th ed. (Istanbul: Alfa, 1995).
Uyar, Talih, 'Yabanci Para Alacaginin Tahsili', *Istanbul Barosu Dergisi* 68, no.7-8-9 (1993), pp. 572-82.
Uyar, Talih, *Gerekceli - Notlu Ictihatli Icra ve Iflas Kanunu*, Vol. 1 (Ankara: Feryal, 1996).
Van Loon, Francis and Stephane Delrue, 'L'huissier de justice et l'exécution des jugements par voie de contrainte', *Droit et Société*, 30/31 (1995), pp. 413-23.
Voigt, Rüdiger (ed.), *Recht als Instrument der Politik* (Opladen: Westdeutscher Verlag, 1986).
Voigt, Rüdiger, 'Durchsetzung und Wirkung von Rechtsentscheidungen – Forschungsansätze und Forschungsstrategien', in Raiser and Voigt, *Durchsetzung und Wirkung von Rechtsentscheidungen* (Baden-Baden: Nomos, 1989), pp. 11-29.
Voigt, Rüdiger, *Politik und Recht – Beiträge zur Rechtspolitologie* (Bochum: Universitätsverlag Dr. N. Brockmeyer, 1993).
von Freyhold, Hanno and Enzo L. Vial, 'Report on the Cost of Judicial Proceedings in the European Union', in Hanno von Freyhold, Volkmar Gessner, Enzo L. Vial and Helmut Wagner (eds), *Cost of Judicial Barriers for Consumers in the Single Market*, A report for the European Commission, Directorate General XXIV (Brussels: European Commission, October /November 1995), pp. 15-127.
Waehler, Jan Peter, 'Anerkennung ausländischer Entscheidungen nach bilateralen Staatsverträgen', in *Handbuch des internationalen Zivilverfahrensrechts*, Vol. 3/2, Max - Planck - Institut für Ausländisches und Internationales Privatrecht (Tübingen: Mohr, 1984), pp. 213-306.
Wagner, Rolf, 'Verfahrensrechtliche Probleme im Auslandsmahnverfahren', *Recht der internationalen Wirtschaft*, 41. Jahrgang (1995), pp. 89-97.
Walker, Gordon R. and Mark A. Fox, 'Globalization: An Analytical Framework', *Indiana Journal of Global Legal Studies* 3, no.2 (1996), 27 pages in Internet, <http://www.law.indiana.edu/glsj/glsj/html>.
Walker, Ronald and Richard Ward, *Walker & Walker's English Legal System*, 7th ed. (London, Dublin, Edinburgh: Butterworths 1994).
Wasilewski, Rainer, *Streitverhütung durch Rechtsanwälte – Empirische Untersuchung von Umfang, Struktur und Bedingungen außergerichtlicher Beilegung zivilrechtlicher Streitigkeiten durch Rechtsanwälte* (Cologne: Bundesanzeiger / Deutscher Anwaltsverlag, 1990).
Weber, Max, *Wirtschaft und Gesellschaft – Grundriss der verstehenden Soziologie*, 5th ed. (Tübingen: Mohr, 1976).
Welter, Reinhard, *Zwangsvollstreckung und Arrest in Forderungen – insbesondere Kontenpfändung – in Fällen mit Auslandsberührung* (Frankfurt am Main: Wertpapier - Mitteilungen, 1988).

Wenckstern, Manfred, 'Die englische Floating Charge im deutschen internationalen Privatrecht', *Rabels Zeitschrift für ausländisches und internationales Privatrecht* 56 (1992), pp. 624–95.
Wettmann, Reinhart W. and Knut Jungjohann, *Inanspruchnahme anwaltlicher Leistungen – Zugangsschwellen, Beratungsbedarf und Anwaltsimage*, Federal Ministry of Justice and German Law Society (Cologne and Essen: Bundesanzeiger, Deutscher Anwaltsverlag 1989).
Whaley, Douglas J., *Problems and Materials on Consumer Law* (Boston, Toronto, London: Little, Brown and Company, 1991).
Windolp, Albert, 'Das Auslandsinkasso in den Ländern der EWG und EFTA', *Teilzahlungswirtschaft*, 16. Jahrgang, no. 2 (1969), pp. 56–60.
Windolp, Albert, 'Das Inkasso im Ausland', *Schimmelpfeng-Review* 18 (1976), pp. 38–40.
Windolp, Albert, 'Das Inkasso nach deutschem und ausländischem Recht', in *Aktuelle Beiträge über das Inkasso im In- und Ausland*, 2nd ed. (Frankfurt: Schimmelpfeng, 1977), pp. 45–85.
Winters, Karl-Peter, *Der Rechtsanwaltsmarkt – Chancen, Risiken und zukünftige Entwicklung* (Cologne: Otto Schmidt, 1990).
Wolf, Manfred, 'Abbau prozessualer Schranken im europäischen Binnenmarkt', in Wolfgang Grunsky, Rolf Stürner, Gerhard Walter and Manfred Wolf (eds), *Wege zu einem europäischen Zivilprozeßrecht – Tübinger Symposium zum 80. Geburtstag von Fritz Baur* (Tübingen: Mohr, 1992).
Wolff, Martin K., 'Vollstreckbarerklärung', in *Handbuch des internationalen Zivilverfahrensrechts*, Vol. 3/2, Max - Planck - Institut für Ausländisches und Internationales Privatrecht (Tübingen: Mohr, 1984), pp. 307–557.
Wollschläger, Christian, 'Die Arbeit der europäischen Zivilgerichte im historischen und internationalen Vergleich – Zeitreihen der europäischen Zivilprozeßstatistik seit dem 19. Jahrhundert', in: Erhard Blankenburg (ed.), *Prozeßflut? – Studien zur Prozeßtätigkeit europäischer Gerichte in historischen Zeitreihen und im Rechtsvergleich* (Cologne: Bundesanzeiger, 1989), pp. 21–114.

II. STATISTICAL SOURCES AND OTHER SOURCES OF INFORMATION

Broius, Gerhard, *SPSS/PC+ Basics and Graphics – Einführung und praktische Beispiele* (Hamburg: McGraw Hill, 1988).
Devlet Istatistik Enstitüsü, *Adli Istatistikler* (Ankara: Devlet Istatistik Enstitüsü, published annually).
European Consumer Guide to the Single Market (Luxembourg: Office for Official Publications of the European Communities, 1995).
General Directorate of Foreign Investment, *Investing in Turkey* (Ankara: Under-Secretariat of Treasury and Foreign Trade, 1993).
Handelskammer Hamburg, *Bericht 1989* (Hamburg: Handelskammer Hamburg, 1989).
International Financial Law Review 1000 – A Guide to the World's International Law Firms (Euromoney Publications: 1995).
International Monetary Fund, *International Financial Statistics* (Washington, D.C.: IMF, December 1995).

Lord Chancellor's Department, Judicial Statistics - England and Wales (London: Her Majesty's Stationery Office, July 1995).

Martindale-Hubbel Law Directory 1995, 32nd ed. (Summit N. J.: Martindale-Hubbel, 1995).

N.N., 'Übersicht über die Geschäftstätigkeit und den Personalbestand der Gerichtsvollzieher im Jahre 1993', Deutsche Gerichtsvollzieher-Zeitung, 109. Jahrgang, no.9 (1994), p.143.

Nerad, Hasan, Selma Baktir, Esin Taylan and Sevilay Eroglu, Izmir Asliye Ticaret Mahkemelerinde Görülen Davalar ve Hasimsiz Isler Konusunda Arastirma Raporu, Dokuz Eylül Üniversitesi Iktisadi ve Idari Bilimler Fakültesi, 1995 (not published).

Statistisches Bundesamt, Rechtspflege, Fachserie 10, Reihe 2: Gerichte und Staatsanwaltschaften. (Published annually in Wiesbaden, by Verlag Kohlhammer. Renamed in 1990, before 1990 'Zivilgerichte und Strafgerichte'.)

Statistisches Bundesamt, Statistisches Jahrbuch 1996 für das Ausland (Stuttgart: Metzler-Poeschel, 1996).

Statistisches Landesamt Bremen, Statistisches Jahrbuch 1992 (Bremen: Statistisches Landesamt Bremen, 1992).

The Law Society, Trends in The Solicitors' Profession – Annual Statistical Report 1995 (London: Law Society, 1995).

The Professional Directory of Lawyers of the World, 77th ed. (Sacramento, California: Forster-Long, 1995).

Zahlen zur wirtschaftlichen Entwicklung der Bundesrepublik Deutschland 1995, Institut der Deutschen Wirtschaft (Cologne: Deutscher Instituts-Verlag, 1994).

III. DAILY AND BUSINESS PRESS REPORTS

Döhler, Günter, 'Außergerichtliches Mahn- und Inkassowesen – Arbeitsteilung mit den Unternehmen', *Die Welt*, 21.12.1981.

Güthlein, Karin, 'Rote Zahlen ziehen "Schwarze Schatten" an', *Süddeutsche Zeitung*, 11.11.1994.

N.N., 'Der richtige Umgang mit Schuldnern – Herunter mit dem Außenständen!', *Handwerk Magazin*, April 1995.

N.N., 'Schwarze Schatten sind sittenwidrig', *Rhein-Neckar-Zeitung*, 18.3.1995.

N.N., 'Das kostet Recht', *Die Welt*, 29.12.1992.

N.N., 'Die Inkasso-Branche profitiert von Rezession', *Frankfurter Allgemeine Zeitung*, 6.10.1992.

N.N., 'Europäische Inkasso-Branche schließt sich zusammen: Gleiche Richtlinien vom Nordkap bis Sizilien gefordert', *Bilanzbuchhalter*, no.10 (1993), p. 238.

N.N., 'Geldeintreiber greifen oft zu rüden Methoden', *Mitteldeutsche Zeitung*, 13.7.1995.

N.N., 'Inkasso begrüßt Urteil gegen "schwarze Schatten"', *Ludwigsburger Kreiszeitung*, 22.3.1995.

N.N., 'Inkasso-Organisationen der Ärzte', *Frankfurter Allgemeine Zeitung*, 16.7.1993.

N.N., 'Inkassobüros verlangen Phantasiepreise, für die es keine Rechtsgrundlage gibt', *Welt am Sonntag*, 22.01.1995; *Bauern Zeitung – Landwirtschaftliches Wochenblatt*, 28.10.1994.

N.N., 'Kammer-Inkassostelle zog Millionenbeträge ein', *Norddeutsche Neueste Nachrichten*, 8.6.1995.

N.N., 'Manche verschicken Horrorbriefe', *Mitteldeutsche Zeitung*, 23.9.1993.

N.N., 'Mehr Insolvenzen, hohe Forderungsausfälle und geringe Zahlungsmoral', *Frankfurter Allgemeine Zeitung*, 11.11.1994.

N.N., 'Mit oder ohne Gerichtsvollzieher – das ist die Frage', *Wirtschaft und Markt*, January 1995.

N.N., 'Offene Forderungen – Was kann ich selbst tun?', *Wirtschaft in Südwest Sachsen*, May 1995.

N.N., 'Ombudsman vermittelt bei Streitfällen in der Inkasso-Branche', *Leibziger Wirtschaft*, May 1995.

N.N., 'Rechtsanwalt treibt ein', *Fellbacher Zeitung*, 11.01.1995.

N.N., 'Todesangst vor dem Schuldeneintreiber', *Bild am Sonntag*, 15.1.1995.

N.N., 'Inkasso-Dienst gegen Zahlungssünder', *Flensburger Tageblatt*, 15.9.1994.

N.N. [A press release made by the Consumer Centre in Hesse providing consumer tips against debt collectors.], *Bergsträser Anzeiger*, 20-21.8.1994; *Welt am Sonntag*, 14.8.1994; *Funk-Uhr*, September 1994.

N.N. [Annual press conference of Federal Association of German Debt Collection Agencies], *Aachener Nachrichten*, 5.5.1995; *Badisches Tagesblatt*, 5.5.1995; *Bonner Rundschau*, 5.5.1995; *Handelsblatt*, 5.5.1995; *Süddeutsche Zeitung*, 5.5.1995; *Die Welt*, 5.5.1995.

Rudolf, Rainer Chr., 'Wie liest man eine Handelsauskunft richtig?', *Internationale Wirtschaft*, 13.2.1986.

Woo, Junda, 'US International Firms may be Bargains', *The Wall Street Journal*, 20.10.1992.

Zeyer, Fred, 'Datenschützer fordern mehr Informationen von der Schufa', *Frankfurter Allgemeine Zeitung*, 6.3.1985.

Index

—A—

anomie, 176
arbitration, 12, 312

—B—

Brussels Convention on Jurisdiction and the Enforcement of Judgments in Civil and Commercial Matters (1968), 108
business information agencies, 188

—C—

cautio judicatum solvi, 169. *See also* international litigation
City Lawyers, 118
cognitive mechanisms, 310, 313
collection methods, 262, 290
commercial debt, 5
commercial debt collection
  England, 211
    boutique type agencies, 215, 234
    costs, 214
    medium sized agencies, 215, 226
    regulations, 212, 252
    services provided by, 213
    superleague agencies, 215
    superleague firms, 216
  Germany, 187
    characteristics of parties and their receivables, 201
    costs, 195, 208
    debt collection contract, 194
    difficulties, 207
    international cases, 199
    international cooperation, 205
    methods, 204
    regulations, 189, 252
    services provided by, 191
  need for regulation, 251, 253
  Turkey, 253
comparative sociology of law, 8
consumer credit, 5
consumer debts, 5
consumer protection, 6, 170
contract guarantees, 265
Convention on the Carriage of Goods by Sea, 265
credit information, 281
credit insurance, 223, 266, 287
credit reference agencies, 259, 316
cross-border debt collection, 3

—D—

debt collection, 7
  extra-judicial methods of, 7
  judicial methods of, 7
  privatisation of, 183
  routinisation of, 179
debt collection agencies. *See* debt collectors
debt collectors, 164, 312, 315
  business ethic, 244
  costs, 241

efficiency, 240, 251
Germany, 184
professional organisations, 241
   American Collectors Association, 248
   European Collectors Association, 248
   Federation of European National Collection Associations, 247
   Institute of Credit Management, 246
   Institute of Licensed Debt Practitioners, 245
   the Credit Services Association, 245
   the Federal Association of German Debt Collection Agencies, 244
public image, 241, 243
third party effect, 238, 240
debt recovery, 7
creditor's control over the enforcement procedure, 104
efficiency of procedures, 110
England, 43
   administration orders, 68
   attachment of earnings, 65
   basic rules and principles, 48
   civil execution officers, 45
   committal, 69
   costs, 73
   equitable execution, 67
   foreign judgments, 53, 69
   garnishee procedure, 62
   judgment summons, 68
   leave of the court, 50
   preliminary remedies, 71
   protection of the debtor, 70
   stay of execution, 51
   summary procedures, 57
   writ of *fieri facias*, 59
execution officers and courts, 102
foreign judgments, 140. *See also* England, Germany, Turkey
Germany, 21
   attachment, 32
   basic rules and principles, 23
   charging orders, 61
   civil execution officers, 22
   costs, 42
   execution against immovable property, 34
   foreign judgments, 26, 38, 96
   garnishee procedure, 36
   preliminary remedies, 41
   protection of the debtor, 40
   summary procedures, 29, 180, 181
Germany, England and Turkey compared, 101
preliminary remedies, 109
Turkey, 75
   attachment, 89
   attachment of earnings, 95
   basic rules and principles, 78
   civil execution officers, 76
   costs, 100
   foreign judgments, 81
   garnishee procedure, 92
   preliminary remedies, 99
   protection of the debtor, 98
   summary procedures, 86
default judgments, 179
de-thematisation of law, 311
documentary operations, 262

—E—

enforcement of foreign judgments, 140
   cases in English courts, 144
   cases in German courts, 141
   cases in Turkish courts, 142
   reciprocity, 140
enforcement of law, 8
European Agreement on Transmission of Applications for Legal Aid (1977), 172
European summary procedure for debt collection, 106
European Union, 11, 114, 253
export trade finance houses, 264
exporters, 267

—F—

factoring, 184, 263
Federal Association of German Debt Collection Agencies, 197
foreign judgments, 26. *See also* debt recovery

forfaiting, 184, 263

—G—

globalisation, 14
globalisation of law, 17, 317

—H—

Hague Convention on the Service Abroad of Judicial and Extra-judicial Documents (1965), 165
harmonisation of laws, 107, 316
High Court of Justice, 144
  Commercial Court Division, 156

—I—

Implementation Theory, 8
  theory of implementation of judicial decisions, 9
Incoterms, 265
Inkassobüros, 188. *See also* debt collectors
Insolvency Law, 12
insolvency practitioners, 226
International Chamber of Commerce in Paris, 264
international credit management, 257, 258
  contracts, 286
  credit information, 259, 283
    banks, 261
    personal contacts, 261
  customer relations, 275
  debt recovery, 298
  dispute resolution, 298
  disputes resulting in non-payment, 296
  efficiency, 294
  out-sourcing, 263
  role of firm size, 272
  role of personal contacts, 302
  security methods, 265, 287
international law firms, 115
international lawyering, 117
international litigation, 12
  factors impeding access to justice, 159
  bias against foreigners, 161
  costs, 164
  differences between legal systems, 159
  legal aid, 170
  legal-bureaucratic difficulties, 163
  security for costs, 169
  service of documents, 164
  taking evidence, 168
  tracing the debtor, 163
  translation of documents, 167
international cases in Germany, 152
international commercial cases in England, 155
international commercial cases in Turkey, 148
legal-bureaucratic difficulties, 310
involuntary creditors, 155, 258

—J—

judgments on consent, 179
judicial comity, 161

—L—

lawyers, 113
  City Lawyers, 120
  debt collectors, 125, 130
  High Street Solicitors, 119
  Investment Lawyers, 123
  traditional lawyers, 127
legal certainty, 310
legal rationalisation, 182
legal-bureaucratic difficulties, 163
Legitimacy, 314, 315
lex mercatoria, 303
liberalisation of the legal market, 114
limitation periods, 160

—N—

nation states, 317
Niklas Luhmann, 307

—P—

Paul Rock, 3
payment methods. *See* collection methods
primitive societies, 308
private detectives, 164, 188
private international law, 159
programme
 normative programme, 9
 political programme, 9
psychological execution, 314
public debt, 16

—S—

security for costs, 169
settlement methods. *See* collection methods
social control, 6, 186, 314
sociology of debt, 3

standard contract terms, 264

—T—

thematisation of law, 307
third party effect, 312
tort cases, 258
transfer of foreign currencies out of the country, 161

—U—

unification of laws, 159
United Nations Economic Commission for Europe, 257, 265

—W—

Walther Nothnagel, 314
World Society, 308